THE DEER AND THE DRAGON

THE DEER AND THE DRAGON

SOUTHEAST ASIA AND CHINA
IN THE 21ST CENTURY

Edited by Donald K. Emmerson

Stanford | Walter H. Shorenstein
Asia-Pacific Research Center
Freeman Spogli Institute

The Walter H. Shorenstein Asia-Pacific Research Center
Freeman Spogli Institute for International Studies
Stanford University
Encina Hall
Stanford, CA 94305-6055
http://aparc.fsi.stanford.edu

The Deer and the Dragon
may be ordered from:
Brookings Institution Press
https://www.brookings.edu/bipress/
books@brookings.edu

Walter H. Shorenstein Asia-Pacific Research Center, 2020.

Library of Congress Control Number: 2020934260

First printing, 2020

ISBN 978-1-931368-53-7

Contents

Tables and Figures

Tables

Figures

Abbreviations

A2/AD	anti-access/area denial
ABS	Asian Barometer Survey
AC-FTA	ASEAN-China Free Trade Agreement
ACFTA	ASEAN-China Free Trade Area
ADB	Asian Development Bank
AEC	ASEAN Economic Community
AFCA	Asian Financial Cooperation Association
AFTA	ASEAN Free Trade Agreement
AIF	ASEAN Infrastructure Fund
AIIB	Asian Infrastructure Investment Bank
APT	ASEAN Plus Three
ARF	ASEAN Regional Forum
ASEAN	Association of Southeast Asian Nations
BRI	Belt and Road Initiative
BSPP	Burma Socialist Programme Party
CCC	Cambodia Chamber of Commerce
CCCC	Chinese Chamber of Commerce in Cambodia
CCCL	China Chamber of Commerce in Laos
CCG	China Coast Guard
CICA	Conference on Interaction and Confidence Building Measures in Asia
COC	code of conduct
CPB	Communist Party of Burma

CPC	Communist Party of China
CPP	Cambodian People's Party
CPTPP	Comprehensive and Progressive Agreement for Trans-Pacific Partnership
DAC	Development Assistance Committee
DOC	Declaration on the Conduct of Parties in the South China Sea
EAS	East Asia Summit
EEZ	exclusive economic zone
EU	European Union
FDI	foreign direct investment
FTA	free trade agreement
GCC	Guangdong Chamber of Commerce
GDP	gross domestic product
GMS	Greater Mekong Subregion
ICJ	International Court of Justice
INGO	international non-government organizations
KMT	Kuomintang
LDC	least developed country
LMC	Lancang-Mekong Cooperation
LPRP	Lao People's Revolutionary Party
MCA	Malaysian Chinese Association
MCI	Media Chinese International
MDT	Mutual Defense Treaty
MOU	memorandum of understanding
MPAC	Master Plan on ASEAN Connectivity
MRC	Mekong River Commission
MSR	21st Century Maritime Silk Road
MSSI	Malacca Strait Security Initiative
NGO	non-governmental organization
NLD	National League for Democracy
NSC	National Security Commission
NSEC	North South Economic Corridor
NSEDP	National Socio-Economic Development Plan
NTS	non-traditional security
OBOR	One Belt, One Road

OC	overseas Chinese
OCAO	Overseas Chinese Affairs Office
OECD	Organisation for Economic Co-operation and Development
PAP	People's Action Party
PLA	People's Liberation Army
PPP	purchasing power parity
PRC	People's Republic of China
RCEP	Regional Comprehensive Economic Partnership
SAF	Singapore Armed Forces
SAM	surface-to-air missiles
SBY	Susilo Bambang Yudhoyono
SCS	South China Sea
SDNT	Single Draft Negotiating Text
SI	sensitivity interdependence
SLORC	State Law and Order Restoration Council
SOE	state-owned enterprise
SPDC	State Peace and Development Council
SREB	Silk Road Economic Belt
TPP	Trans-Pacific Partnership
UDG	Union Development Group
UNCLOS	UN Convention on the Law of the Sea
UNDP	UN Development Programme
UNOSSC	United Nations Office for South-South Cooperation
VI	vulnerability interdependence
WCEC	World Chinese Entrepreneurs Convention
XUM	Xiamen University Malaysia

About the Authors

ANNE BOOTH is professor emerita, SOAS University of London, having served there as professor of economics with reference to Asia from 1991 to 2014. Prior to that, she was a research fellow in the Australian National University's Research School of Pacific Studies (1979–91) and a lecturer in the University of Singapore's Department of Economics (1976–79). Recent publications include *Living Standards in Southeast Asia: Changes over the Long Twentieth Century, 1900–2015* (2019); *Fiscal Capacity and the Colonial State in Asia and Africa, c. 1850–1960*, co-edited with Ewout Frankema (2019); "Measuring Poverty and Income Distribution in Southeast Asia," *Asian-Pacific Economic Literature* (2019); "Southeast Asian Agricultural Growth: 1930–2010," in *Agricultural Development in the World Periphery: A Global Economic History Approach*, edited by Vicente Pinilla and Henry Willebald (2018); and *Economic Change in Modern Indonesia: Colonial and Post-colonial Comparisons* (2016). Her PhD and BA (Honours) are respectively from the Australian National University and the Victoria University of Wellington.

YUN-HAN CHU is distinguished research fellow in the Institute of Political Science at Academia Sinica and professor of political science at National Taiwan University. He was a visiting associate professor at Columbia University in 1990–91. He specializes in the politics of Greater China, East Asian political economy, international political economy, and democratization. He co-chairs the Executive Council of Global Barometer Surveys, the world's largest social science survey research network, and has served as coordinator of the Asian Barometer Survey, a regional network of opinion research on democracy, governance, and development covering more than 18 Asian countries. He is the author, co-author, editor, or co-editor of 17 books. Recent publications in English include the *Handbook of Democratization in East Asia* (2017) and *Democracy in East Asia: A New Century* (2013). In 2016 he was chosen to be a fellow of the World Academy of Science, having been elected in 2012 to the Academia Sinica, Taiwan's highest scholarly honor.

JOHN D. CIORCIARI is associate professor at the Gerald R. Ford School of Public Policy at the University of Michigan, where he directs the International Policy Center and the Weiser Diplomacy Center. He is also a senior legal advisor to the Documentation Center of Cambodia, an independent NGO dedicated to memory and justice. He has been an Andrew Carnegie Fellow, a Richard Holbrooke Fellow at the Asia Society, a National Fellow at the Hoover Institution, and a fellow at the Shorenstein Asia-Pacific Research Center in Stanford University. His research focuses on international law and politics in the Global South with an emphasis on Southeast Asia. His writings include, as co-author, *Hybrid Justice: The Extraordinary Chambers in the Courts of Cambodia* (2014), and as author, *The Limits of Alignment: Southeast Asia and the Great Powers since 1975* (2010). He holds a DPhil and MPhil in International Relations (University of Oxford), a JD (Harvard Law School), and an AB (Harvard College).

SHANNON CUI is the author of *China's Role and Interests in the Greater Mekong Subregion* (2018). The book is a revised version of the dissertation for which she was awarded a doctorate in political science, with an emphasis on international relations, by the University of Rostock in 2017. She has a master's degree in economics and business administration with a focus on international economic policy, earned at the University of Wuppertal in 2012. Prior to her graduate-level education, she received a bachelor's degree in international economics and trade at Yunnan Normal University in Kunming, China. It was there that she became interested in the Greater Mekong Subregion (GMS). In her book, she argues that tensions due to the asymmetry between small states and a large neighbor can be alleviated by "differentiated cooperation" involving one or more subunits of the larger state. The concept is exemplified in the GMS, which includes five ASEAN states and two provinces of the People's Republic of China, one of them Yunnan.

JÖRN DOSCH is professor/chair of international politics and development cooperation and vice-dean of the Faculty of Economics and Social Sciences at the University of Rostock, Germany. Previous positions include professor of international relations at Monash University (Malaysia Campus) and head of the Department of East Asian Studies at the University of

Leeds. In 2016 he was the inaugural visiting professor at the Saw Swee Hock Southeast Asia Centre at the London School of Economics and Political Science. His research specialties are Asia-Pacific politics and international relations. Recent publications include *The New Global Politics of the Asia Pacific*, with Michael K. Connors and Rémy Davison (2018); and *Malaysia Post-Mahathir: A Decade of Change?*, co-edited with James Chin (2016). Dosch's Habilitation (a German post-doctoral/professorial degree), PhD, and MA are from the Johannes Gutenberg University Mainz.

DONALD K. EMMERSON heads the Southeast Asia Program in the Shorenstein Asia-Pacific Research Center at Stanford University, where he is also a faculty affiliate of the Abbasi Program in Islamic Studies and the Center on Democracy, Development and the Rule of Law. In 2017–19 his writings appeared in *ASEAN @ 50, Southeast Asia @ Risk* (as co-editor/ author), *Asia Policy, Asia Times, Contemporary Southeast Asia, The Diplomat, IPP Review, The Jakarta Post, Journal of Democracy, PacNet, RSIS Commentary, The South China Sea Disputes* (edited by Yang Razali Kassim), *TRaNS: Trans-Regional and -National Studies of Southeast Asia*, and *YaleGlobal*. Earlier books and articles dealt with Southeast Asia–related topics including ASEAN, security, democracy, Indonesia, Islamism, fisheries, and fieldwork. Before coming to Stanford in 1999, he taught political science at the University of Wisconsin-Madison and was a visiting scholar at the Institute for Advanced Study (Princeton) and elsewhere. His degrees are from Yale University (PhD) and Princeton University (BA).

THOMAS FINGAR is a Shorenstein Asia-Pacific Research Center fellow in the Freeman Spogli Institute for International Studies at Stanford University. He taught at Stanford for a decade before spending 23 years in Washington, DC, where he served in positions such as deputy director of National Intelligence for Analysis, chairman of the National Intelligence Council, assistant secretary of state for Intelligence and Research, and director of the Office of Analysis for East Asia and the Pacific. His principal research interests are China's foreign policy and US foreign and national security policy. Recent publications include *Fateful Decisions: Choices That Will Shape China's Future*, co-edited with Jean Oi (2020); *Uneasy Partnerships: China's Engagement with Japan, the Koreas, and Russia in the Era of Reform*, editor (2017); and *The New Great Game: China and South and Central Asia in the Era of Reform*, editor (2016). He earned his PhD and MA in political science at Stanford and his BA in government and history from Cornell.

MIN-HUA HUANG is professor in the Department of Political Science and director of the Hu Fu Center for East Asia Democratic Studies in the

College of Social Sciences at National Taiwan University (NTU). Before joining NTU, he worked at Shanghai Jiaotong University, Texas A&M University, and National Chengchi University. He was also a visiting fellow at the Brookings Institution's Center for East Asia Policy Studies (2014–15). Recent writings include "The Malaise of Globalization in East Asia: Income Inequality, Perceived State Capacity, and Anti-Establishment Attitudes" with Mark Weatherall and Taehee Whang, *Korean Journal of International Studies* (2018); "The Internet, Social Capital, and Civic Engagement in Asia" with Taehee Whang and Lei Xuchuan, *Social Indicators Research* (2017); and "The Sway of Geopolitics, Economic Interdependence and Cultural Identity: Why Are Some Asians more Favorable toward China's Rise than Others?" with Yun-han Chu, *Journal of Contemporary China* (2015). His degrees are from the University of Michigan (PhD), the National Sun Yat-Sen University (MA), and NTU (BA).

MINGJIANG LI is associate professor at the S. Rajaratnam School of International Studies in Nanyang Technological University (Singapore), where he is also coordinator of the China Programme. He has authored, edited, or co-edited 13 books. Among them are *China's Economic Statecraft: Co-optation, Cooperation, and Coercion* (2017); *China and Transboundary Water Politics in Asia*, co-edited with Hongzhou Zhang (2017); and *New Dynamics in US-China Relations: Contending for the Asia Pacific* (2014). Recent articles include "China's Economic Power in Asia: The Belt and Road Initiative and the Local Guangxi Government's Role," *Asian Perspective* (Spring 2019); "A Process-based Framework to Examine China's Approach to Transboundary Water Management" with Hongzhou Zhang, *International Journal of Water Resources Development* (2018); "China's Revisionist Aspirations in Southeast Asia and the Curse of the South China Sea Disputes," *China: An International Journal* (2017); and "A China in Transition: The Rhetoric and Substance of Chinese Foreign Policy under Xi Jinping" with Angela Poh, *Asian Security* (2017). His PhD in political science is from Boston University.

JIE LU is professor of political science at Renmin University of China in Beijing. Previously he taught at American University in Washington, DC. He was also a visiting research fellow at the East Asian Institute in Singapore. His research has focused on local governance, institutional change, public opinion, and political participation in Greater China and East Asia. Writings include "Revisiting the Eastonian Framework on Political Support: Assessing Different Measures of Regime Support in Mainland China," *Comparative Politics* (2019); "Revisiting Political Wariness in China's Public Opinion

Surveys: Experimental Evidence on Responses to Politically Sensitive Questions" with Xuchuan Lei, *Journal of Contemporary China* (2017); and a book, *Varieties of Governance in China: Migration and Institutional Change in Chinese Villages* (2014). Before earning his PhD in political science at Duke University, he received an MA in international relations and a BA in environmental engineering from Tsinghua University.

DANIEL C. O'NEILL is associate professor of political science in the School of International Studies at the University of the Pacific. His book, *Dividing ASEAN and Conquering the South China Sea: China's Financial Power Projection* (2018), analyzes the impact of political institutions in Southeast Asian states on China's efforts to expand its regional influence. Other publications include "China Just Asserted its Hold over the South China Sea. Will ASEAN Nations Push Back?," *Washington Post* (2018); "Cambodia in 2016: A Tightening Authoritarian Grip," *Asian Survey* (2016); "Cambodia in 2015: From Cooperation to Conflict," *Asian Survey* (2016); and "Playing Risk: Chinese Foreign Direct Investment in Cambodia," *Contemporary Southeast Asia* (2014). Before receiving his PhD and MA in political science at Washington University in St. Louis, he taught English in Taiwan. He moved to Taiwan following a 20-year career writing and performing songs in Austin, Texas, during which time he earned his BA in economics from the University of Texas.

KEARRIN SIMS is lecturer in Development Studies at James Cook University (JCU), where he is also convenor of JCU's Master of Global Development program and a research fellow at JCU's Cairns Institute, in addition to chairing JCU's Sustainable Development Working Group. Prior to coming to JCU, he lectured at the University of Newcastle and Western Sydney University. His writings include "Teaching Development Studies in Times of Change," *Asia Pacific Viewpoint* (2018); "Casino Enclaves, Development, and Poverty Alleviation in Laos," *Pacific Affairs* (2017); and "Culture, Community-oriented Learning and the Post-2015 Development Agenda: A View from Laos," *Third World Quarterly* (2015). As a critical development scholar, he is particularly interested in the development transformations taking place in mainland Southeast Asia. He earned his PhD at the Institute for Culture and Society in Western Sydney University and his BA (Honours) at the University of Sydney.

DAVID I. STEINBERG is distinguished professor of Asian Studies emeritus at Georgetown University, whose Asian Studies Program he directed from 1997 to 2007. He was also president of the Mansfield Center for Pacific Affairs. US government positions have included membership in the Senior Foreign

Service and service in the Agency for International Development (USAID) as director for technical assistance for Asia and the Middle East and director for Philippines, Thailand, and Burma affairs. Before joining USAID, he represented the Asia Foundation in South Korea, Burma, Hong Kong, and Washington, DC. He is the author of 15 books and monographs, more than 150 articles, and hundreds of op-eds. His books include *Myanmar: The Dynamics of an Evolving Polity*, editor (2015); *Burma/Myanmar: What Everyone Needs to Know* (2nd edition 2013); and *Modern China-Myanmar Relations: Dilemmas of Mutual Dependence*, with Fan Hongwei (2012). He was educated at the School of Oriental and African Studies, University of London, in Burmese and Southeast Asian studies; holds a Harvard University MA and a Dartmouth College BA; and also studied at Lingnan University (China).

YOHANES SULAIMAN is senior lecturer in the Department of International Relations at the Universitas Jenderal Achmad Yani (Cimahi, Indonesia) and visiting lecturer at the Indonesian Army Staff and Command School. Recent publications include "Whither Indonesia's Indo-Pacific Strategy," *Institut français des relations internationales* (2019); *Indonesia Inc.: Peta Jalan Menuju Poros Maritime Dunia*, with Untung Suropati and Ian Montratama (2018); "Why We Must Learn to Live with a Nuclear North Korea," *GlobalAsia* (2017); and "Indonesia's Strategic Culture: The Legacy of Independence," in *Strategic Asia 2016–17: Understanding Strategic Culture in the Asia-Pacific* (2016), edited by Ashley J. Tellis, Alison Szalwinski, and Michael Wills. His interests include Indonesian strategic culture and diplomatic history; East Asian security and politics; and civil-military relations. He has a PhD and MA in political science from Ohio State University and BA from the University of Wisconsin–Madison.

SEE SENG TAN is president/CEO-elect of International Students Inc. (ISI), a US-based nonprofit organization, and Professor of International Relations at the S. Rajaratnam School of International Studies (RSIS) in Nanyang Technological University (Singapore). His many books include *The Responsibility to Provide in Southeast Asia: Towards an Ethical Explanation* (2019); *The Legal Authority of ASEAN as a Security Institution*, with Hitoshi Nasu et al. (2019); *Multilateral Asian Security Architecture: Non-ASEAN Stakeholders* (2015); *United States Engagement in the Asia Pacific: Perspectives from Asia*, co-edited with Yoichiro Sato (2015); *The Making of the Asia Pacific: Knowledge Brokers and the Politics of Representation* (2012); and *Bandung Revisited: The Legacy of the 1955 Asian-African Conference for International Order*, co-edited with Amitav Acharya (2008).

He earned his PhD at Arizona State University and his MA and BA Honours degrees at the University of Manitoba.

GEOFF WADE is a Canberra-based historian, author, and translator, formerly with the Institute of Southeast Asian Studies in Singapore (2009–13), the National University of Singapore's Asia Research Institute (2002–09), and the University of Hong Kong's Centre of Asian Studies (1996–2002). His publications include *China and Southeast Asia: Historical Interactions*, co-edited with James K. Chin (2019); *Asian Expansions: the Historical Experiences of Polity Expansion in Asia*, editor (2015); *Anthony Reid and the Study of the Southeast Asian* Past, co-edited with Li Tana (2012); *Southeast Asia in the Fifteenth Century: The China Factor*, co-edited with Sun Laichen (2010); "Early Muslim Expansion in South-East Asia, Eighth to Fifteenth Centuries," in *The New Cambridge History of Islam*, edited by David O. Morgan and Anthony Reid (2010); and *Southeast Asia in the Ming Shi-lu: An Open Access Resource*, compilator and editor (2005). His doctorate in history and his undergraduate degree are respectively from the University of Hong Kong and Australian National University.

Introduction and Acknowledgments

This book explores and interprets what has happened and may happen in the physical and conceptual spaces where Southeast Asia and China interact and overlap. The region and its giant neighbor are both complex, let alone the intricacy of what goes on between them. A bird's-eye view of all that activity requires more than one bird. A single analyst, however steeped in expertise and broadened by learning, would struggle to do justice to the heterogeneity of Southeast Asia — multiple states with different histories, cultures, languages, economies, and polities behaving differently for different reasons. The focal point provided by the extra-regional state — China — reduces that diversity, but only to a degree. Whether Southeast Asian diplomats work with Beijing or hedge against it, they tend to keep other entities in mind. These include the United States and Japan, among other outsiders, and the Association of Southeast Asian Nations (ASEAN), to which 10 of the region's states belong. In this challenging light, the multi-authored character of this book makes a virtue of necessity. As for the region's only non-ASEAN state, Timor-Leste, its economically and strategically peripheral role in Sino-ASEAN relations explains the lack of attention it receives.

Some editors impose order in advance. This one did not. Some books offer description at the expense of analysis. This one does not. Contributors were not given questions to answer. Within their zones of expertise, they were encouraged to choose their own topics and develop arguments about them under the broad rubric of Southeast Asia–China relations. The results are intentionally centrifugal, but not random. The authors' chapters were easy to subsume post facto under eight distinct if overlapping themes:

xxii INTRODUCTION AND ACKNOWLEDGEMENTS

overview, *contexts*, *perceptions*, *extensions*, *strategies*, *disparities*, *distances*, and *retrospection*.

Overarching all of these headings and chapters is the broad subject of the book: the nature, dynamics, and implications of inequality between China and the countries of Southeast Asia. The book begins and ends with metaphors relevant to this topic. The first chapter opens with a tale of brain over brawn — mousedeer over dragon — drawn from Southeast Asian folklore that, in effect, questions the fatalist view that size and power must always prevail in Sino–Southeast Asian relations. The final chapter questions Beijing's use of the Burmese term *paukphaw* to liken China-Myanmar relations to friendly familial ties between siblings. As normative responses to empirical asymmetry, these loaded metaphors differently evoke the inequalities of size and power that directly or indirectly influence the patterns of interaction between China and its southern neighbors. Introductory notes on the chapters follow, theme by theme.

Overview

Donald K. Emmerson argues that although asymmetries of size and power favor China in its relations with individual Southeast Asian states, those structural disproportions do not necessarily oblige the latter to do what the former wants. As a multilateral actor, ASEAN is no match for Beijing, weakened as the grouping is by its commitment to consensus, the diversity of its members, and the success of China's proxy-veto diplomacy, especially regarding the South China Sea. Beijing's campaign to build a regional sphere of influence and sideline ASEAN has left its members to deal with China more or less on their own. But they can, and some do, engage in creative diplomacy in search of strategic autonomy, including partnering with outsiders. Beijing alone will not decide the outcome. The future of Southeast Asia in relation to China will be shaped as well by what Southeast Asians, separately or with others, do or fail to do.

Contexts

In his review of the historical context within which China's foreign policies toward Southeast Asia have evolved, **Thomas Fingar** concludes that Beijing has wanted and still wants to ensure that its influence in the region exceeds that of any other major outside power. Seen in that light, the brief border war with Vietnam that China initiated in 1979 may have been meant in part to warn Vietnam's Russian backer against aligning with Hanoi to the detriment of China's regional interest. A decade later, the Cold War's end and the USSR's disintegration created chances for China to engage the region economically and thereby overcome Southeast Asian distrust. By 2009, that goal had been substantially achieved. But relations with the region soon soured for various reasons, not least among them a rising Chinese fear of domestic instability and its expression in a more nationalistic comportment abroad.

Anne Booth's data-rich chapter reviews the economic context of Southeast Asia–China relations, notably trade and investment, from the 1990s through 2018. The notion that China has benefited at the region's expense cannot be sustained. Both sides have gained from their interaction. The diversity of the ASEAN states' economic partners is a major reason why. Also notably diverse are the ASEAN member economies themselves and their experiences with China. Following the activation of the ASEAN-China Free Trade Agreement, for example, although the region's trade deficit with China grew, the trajectories of individual ASEAN economies continued to vary. Looking ahead, the regionalization of ASEAN's trade within an East Asian frame opens one of several choices for economic diplomacy by ASEAN and its member states. But those decisions will likely be influenced at least as much by political considerations as by economic ones.

Perceptions

Relative to China's influence in Southeast Asia, American influence has declined. In drawing this conclusion, **Yun-Han Chu, Min-hua Huang,** and **Jie Lu** take into account the regional hyperactivity of China under Xi Jinping and the uncertainty of American foreign policy under Donald Trump. Reservoirs of Southeast Asian goodwill toward the United States have not dried up, as shown by survey evidence that Southeast Asians consider America's influence, unlike China's, to be largely benign. Beijing's autocratic model is controversial. Yet in surveys of opinion in ASEAN countries as late as 2016, when asked to pick China or the United States as more influential in Asia, only in the Philippines did a majority choose the United States. Majorities in Myanmar, Singapore, and Vietnam picked China. Over time, Chinese primacy may seem less and less avoidable, like it or not. America may not be eclipsed, but the momentum could be China's to lose.

Mingjiang Li asks whether Southeast Asia qualifies as China's "strategic backyard." He is careful to distinguish the empirical reality from the normative judgment connoted by the term and to recognize the differences in how the term is construed in Southeast Asia and what it tends to mean in China. Beijing, without using the term, does think of the region as its strategic backyard in principle. Insofar as that vision implies Chinese control over its neighbors, however, it has not been realized in practice, at least not yet.

China hopes for stable and amicable relations with Southeast Asian states that will benefit its economic growth and extend its political influence in the context of a multipolar world. Neighborly relations have not been frozen, let alone broken. But especially since 2010, suspicions have risen on both sides, some Chinese initiatives have backfired, and a shortage of empathy toward its neighbors has further hampered China's welcome in the region.

Extensions

Donald K. Emmerson assesses China's approach to and behavior in the South China Sea. He identifies several different tactics used by China in advancing its campaign for maritime control. Differing Southeast Asian responses to Chinese pressure are also reviewed. The decades-long search for a code of conduct is described as an "institutionalized mirage" due to ASEAN's continuing commitment to negotiating one, despite intra-ASEAN dissension abetted by Beijing and the elusiveness of agreement with China over the text. The Philippines and Vietnam receive particular attention given the size of their claims and their contrasting responses to Beijing's diplomatic and kinetic moves. The chapter ends by suggesting that one, two, or more Southeast Asian governments consider drafting a brief statement that no single country should control the South China Sea, an avowal that could then be opened for signing by China, America, and any other state.

Geoff Wade reviews how Beijing has attempted to instrumentalize the "overseas Chinese" (OC) in Southeast Asia in support of China's economic and political objectives. He traces the practice from the early 20th century, when Sun Yat-sen tried to rally the OC against the Qing empire, to present-day efforts by China's Overseas Chinese Affairs Office and related agencies to co-opt OC individuals, firms, and organizations on the mainland's behalf. Some Chinese-language OC media have been bought or otherwise guided to slant their content in China's favor. OC social, business, and educational associations are encouraged to identify with their "motherland." In their most intrusive form, these extensions of influence may involve efforts to dilute the identities that OCs possess by virtue of being citizens of countries other than the People's Republic of China (PRC). Beijing is not bent on creating a subversive ethnic presence abroad. But the need for interpretive caution should not disallow further scholarly research on PRC-diaspora relations.

Strategies

Despite pressures from Beijing, Singapore retains strategic autonomy from China. However, as **See Seng Tan** also notes, frictions remain. Singaporeans were angered when an industrial park based on the city-state's expertise and support was established in Suzhou, China, only to face competition from a rival entity sponsored by local officials there. Singaporeans have also resented the seemingly boorish ways of newcomers from mainland China. Yet such annoyances have not been destabilizing, and by diversifying its trade and investment linkages, Singapore has limited its economic vulnerability to China. Nor did the threat of Chinese displeasure stop Singapore from approving an international court's disallowance of China's "nine-dash line" around the South China Sea. Singapore works in various ways with China and America alike. Pressure from Beijing does not augur Singaporean acquiescence in Chinese control.

Indonesia's status as the largest Southeast Asian country has not motivated its leaders to think and act strategically regarding China and its ascendance in the region, argues **Yohanes Sulaiman**. Jakarta has been loath to offend Beijing. Indonesian leaders have instead wanted their country to have "a thousand friends and no enemies." That is not a foreign policy. It is wishful thinking. Rather than adapt defense policy to an external security environment where China is increasingly prominent, military leaders have paid more attention to bureaucratic priorities, such as redressing the mismatch in the armed forces between too many officers and too few positions for them to fill. Indonesia's president is more interested in economic goals—better infrastructure, less poverty. But those priorities need not preclude developing a credible deterrent to China's expansion in the South China Sea or playing a more active and constructive foreign-policy role in ASEAN.

Disparities

Daniel O'Neill locates Cambodia-China relations at the intersection of two disparities — one between the two countries, the other inside Cambodia. The patronage bestowed by the stronger power on the weaker one strengthens strongman Hun Sen and his wealthy, corrupt, and abusive ruling group in the weakest — poorest — state in Southeast Asia at the expense of its disempowered people. Illustrating the argument are the cases of three Cambodian tycoons who have profitably brokered Sino-Cambodian deals. Also noted are the roles of the police and the military. Loyal to Hun Sen, they have guarded the local facilities of companies from China involved with Cambodian tycoons in corrupt land concessions and evictions. Beijing's ways of rewarding such favors have included a $3 million surveillance system for Phnom Penh, supplied free of charge in 2014–15. When Xi Jinping praises China's elite-based "win-win" cooperation with Cambodia, he ignores the losses it inflicts on the lives of the people who live there.

Practitioners of "high-modernist" development in Laos are state-driven, top-down, technocratic, and unwilling to learn from local knowledge and practice. What most concerns **Kearrin Sims** is the disparity between the high-modernist priorities of PRC-sponsored development in Laos and the actual needs of poor Laotians. High modernism, born in the industrializing West, is not a Chinese monopoly. But Beijing is applying its precepts in concert with Vientiane to detrimental effect. China-built rail and highway corridors bypass villagers who lack the land, capital, and local roads to produce and market goods. Hydropower exports from the dams that China builds fill coffers to which the poor lack access. Nor does China-funded urban construction help the largely rural poor, whose precarity is worsened by China-backed rubber plantations that erode soil, threaten watersheds, and replace communal land. By catering to the Laotian state, such projects also fortify its authoritarian rule.

Distances

John Ciorcari reviews the ways in which Cambodia, Laos, Myanmar, Thailand, and Vietnam have been rendered vulnerable to Chinese influence not only by their proximity to China, but also by their physical and geopolitical distance from the United States. As they reflect and influence policy decisions, these distances are fluid. The consequences depend on the degrees and kinds of agency that the five states exercise. As a source of local reassurance or concern, however, the American role warrants particular attention. From the Vietnam War within the Cold War through President Obama's "rebalance" to the "Trump factor," US policy toward mainland Southeast Asia has been a mixture of intermittent commitment, criticisms over human rights, and indifference by default. In future, pending major re-engagement, the autonomy of the northern tier may come to be threatened less by domineering Chinese behavior than by American distraction and lack of interest.

The Belt and Road Initiative spans lengthy distances and multiple states. It is accordingly hard to think of the scheme as informed by a distinctively Chinese policy model. But there is a "Mekong mode" of naturally requisite and benign Chinese primacy that China has used to rationalize its leadership in providing infrastructure in the Southeast Asian countries through which the Mekong River runs. As **Jörn Dosch** and **Shannon Cui** also observe, however, the "natural" — necessary and inevitable — character of Chinese tutelage is contested. Sino-Southeast Asian connectivity via the

Belt and Road Initiative could evolve, along respectively realist, liberal, or constructivist lines, toward asymmetrical dominance, trade-based comity, or norm-sharing identity. But compared with Chinese hegemony, a less exclusively or coercively Sinified scenario is at least as probable, if not more so: that most or all of the ASEAN states will continue to cooperate with all major outside powers.

Retrospection

David Steinberg has the last word in the book. His critique of China-relevant misunderstandings of Myanmar covers, in addition to *paukphaw* propaganda: the legitimating myth of Burma/Myanmar as a nation-state; overblown Cold War fears of Chinese conspiracy; the false promise of federalism; excessive American, Chinese, and Burmese faith in foreign aid and sanctions as leverage toward desired outcomes; liberal democracy as a near-to-medium-term mirage; Washington's and Beijing's overestimation of the importance of China's rise in shaping Myanmar's behavior; the self-assurance that made Beijing so surprised by the suspension of the Myitsone Dam project; and the omission of an insider view of the state as a less than unitary actor. The last point, acknowledged in several other chapters, implicates the external-policy focus of the book, including the convenient metonymy of "Washington" and "Beijing" in this paragraph.

The chapters that follow were written before the coronavirus disease called COVID-19 spread from Wuhan, China, to the world. An edited volume takes long enough to process and publish without further delaying its birth to accommodate late-breaking and still-unfolding events. Suffice it instead to suggest that readers of this book, as they consider its contents, may wish to ask themselves to what extent and in what ways COVID-19 and its ramifications could affect the arguments that the authors make.

To evoke those arguments in the order in which they are summarized above: How will the pandemic influence China's foreign policy and Sino-Southeast Asian relations? Will the contagion weaken or strengthen the diversity of the region's economic partners that has limited its overdependence on China? Will the Chinese origin of the disease and Beijing's response to it make Xi Jinping's authoritarian model more or less attractive in Southeast Asian eyes? In that light, will Beijing lose or gain leverage over its neighborhood? Will COVID-19's impact on China dilute or fortify Beijing's ability to control the South China Sea? As the virus spreads, will it be easier or harder for China to mobilize support among the "overseas Chinese" in Southeast Asia? Will the answers to these questions cause Singapore to reaffirm or rethink its strategic autonomy from China? Will the answers incentivize Indonesia to augment its inward-looking, development-first foreign policy with an outward strategy to lead ASEAN and offset China? Or not?

If the pandemic and its collateral effects severely damage the lives and livelihoods of the poorest and most vulnerable in Cambodia and Laos, will China reconsider the ways in which its policies have worsened corruption, autocracy, and inequality inside those countries? If Beijing offers major medical help to the ASEAN states located closest to China, while Washington does little by comparison, will China's nearest neighbors grow more sanguine about China and more repelled by American indifference? Will China's expensive and expansive Belt and Road Initiative survive the likely future virus-driven blow to the Chinese economy and the possible discrediting of China-sponsored connectivity by the pandemic's spread to other countries? And finally, projecting forward the final chapter's review of misunderstandings regarding Myanmar and China, readers may wish to imagine the possible contents of a book about Southeast Asia, China, and COVID-19 that someone may someday edit or write that would not only answer the above questions but explore as well the new myths and illusions to which that set of three-way interactions will have given rise.

Edited volumes are debt-intensive. This one's editor is deeply indebted to his 15 co-authors around the world: Anne Booth, Daniel O'Neill, David Steinberg, Geoff Wade, Jie Lu, John Ciorciari, Jörn Dosch, Kearrin Sims, Mingjiang Li, Min-hua Huang, Shannon Cui, See Seng Tan, Thomas Fingar, Yohanes Sulaiman, and Yun-han Chu. They wrote insightfully, corresponded productively, waited patiently, and tolerated the editor's efforts to ensure cross-chapter consistency of style.

Equally meriting gratitude for its unstinting support is Stanford University's Shorenstein Asia-Pacific Research Center (APARC). Its director, Gi-Wook Shin, backed the book from inception through gestation to publication. Publications manager George Krompacky expertly shepherded the volume through the copyediting and printing process and commented constructively on substance. Administrative aspects were ably handled by Shorenstein APARC's Southeast Asia Program Coordinator Lisa Lee. The project was born in stimulating conversations with APARC fellow and chapter-author Tom Fingar.

Others to whom thanks are due for helping the volume take shape and bear fruit, whether they knew it or not, include: the late Aileen Baviera, Alex Vuving, Ann Marie Murphy, Bilahari Kausikan, Carl Thayer, Catharin Dalpino, Cheng-Chwee Kuik, Chris Sharman, Danielle Tan, David Medeiros, David (Mike) Lampton, Deepak Nair, Dino Djalal,

Don Keyser, Don Weatherbee, Ellen Frost, Evan Laksmana, Evelyn Goh, Frank Fukuyama, Geoffrey Gunn, Gilberto Teodoro, Greg Poling, Havas Oegroseno, Ian Chong, Ian Storey, Jay Batongbacal, Jean-Marc Blanchard, Joseph Liow, Karl Eikenberry, Kavi Chongkittavorn, Ketian Zhang, Ketut Irawan, Larry Diamond, Lowell Dittmer, Mark Valencia, Mike McDevitt, Mike Montesano, Munir Majid, Nayan Chanda, Paul Schuler, Prashanth Parameswaran, Ralf Emmers, Ralph Cossa, Renato Cruz De Castro, Richard Heydarian, Rizal Sukma, Scott Rozelle, Shawn Crispin, Shen Dingli, Termsak Chermpalanupap, Thanh Hai Do, and Thitinan Pongsudhirak. Apologies to the inadvertently omitted.

Thanking people without first asking their permission to be thanked risks being mislabeled as presumptuous co-optation or, worse, debt-trap diplomacy. Let it therefore be known that responsibility for each chapter's content belongs solely to its autonomous author. The sheer number of individuals named above does at least make more convincing their innocence as to any shortcomings the volume may have. For how could the same book be blamed on so many different people?

Hoping you enjoy the read,

Donald K. Emmerson
Stanford University

THE DEER AND THE DRAGON

CHAPTER 1

The Deer and the Dragon
ASYMMETRY VERSUS AUTONOMY

Donald K. Emmerson, *Stanford University, United States*

A book does not normally begin by doubting its looks — its visual self. This one does. The title and the animals on this volume's front cover raise questions of representation, comparison, and attribution that are intended to occur and re-occur to its readers while turning its pages.

Asymmetry, Diversity, Ingenuity

The *Cervidae* family of hoofed mammals — deer — includes well-known creatures memorialized in the Anglophone West. Among them are Walt Disney's Bambi, the antlered sleigh-pullers of Santa Claus, and the Golden Hind of Sir Francis Drake. They are not the deer in this book. The metaphorically animalized Southeast Asian states discussed herein are mousedeer (or mouse deer) — chevrotains of the genus *Tragulus*. They are the miniature figures standing atop and flanking the book's title on its cover.

Art and fact easily collide. The mousedeer pictured represent all the countries of Southeast Asia — Brunei, Cambodia, Indonesia, Laos, Malaysia, Myanmar (Burma), the Philippines, Singapore, Thailand, Timor-Leste, and Vietnam. For convenience and simplicity, they are identical in shape and color — and equally small. Distortions result. Were the artwork truthful demographically, compared with Brunei's mousedeer icon, the one for Indonesia would be 615 times larger. Some mouse.

As of 2018, an estimated 435 thousand people lived in Brunei compared with 267 million in Indonesia, respectively the least and most populous of Southeast Asia's countries. Of the 11, only one — the Philippines — had more than 100 million people. Only three — Vietnam,

Thailand, and Myanmar — had more than 50 million. A majority fell below 50 million — Malaysia, Cambodia, Laos, Singapore, Timor-Leste, and Brunei — and of these six, each of the smaller four had under 20 million.[1] In contrast, measured by population, Indonesia is unquestionably large, fourth largest in the world in fact.

Southeast Asian states are differentiated along many other lines as well — their physical locations, shapes, and sizes; their histories, societies, cultures, economies, and politics; their geologies, ecologies, ethnicities, religions, and languages. With due regard to the ways in which parts of the People's Republic of China (PRC) differ from each other and aspects of being Chinese also vary, Southeast Asia the region is more diverse than China the country.[2]

The dragon on the cover of this book is a traditional symbol of Chinese imperial divinity and power updated to stand for China itself — and appropriately far larger than the mousedeer pictured above it. In 2018, China's 1.4 billion people more than doubled Southeast Asia's 657 million. China's population is 3,264 times larger than Brunei's. The 267 million people who live in Indonesia amount to less than a fifth of the people who live in China.[3] Economically, the PRC overshadows the entire region. In 2018, China's estimated USD $13.41 trillion gross domestic product (GDP) more than quadrupled the $2.95 trillion figure for all of Southeast Asia's economies combined.[4] But the interactions of Southeast Asian states with China cannot be explained by invoking the actors' relative magnitudes alone. By that monocausal logic, the mousedeer have no choice but to obey the dragon. This book's authors argue otherwise, albeit in different contexts, to different extents, and in different ways.

This chapter acknowledges China's efforts to thwart the strategic autonomy of the Association of Southeast Asian Nations (ASEAN) by using the diversity of its members to forestall the growth of a regional consensus against Beijing. By selectively mixing co-optation with coercion, China has tried to induce particular ASEAN members to censor themselves, especially regarding Beijing's widely disputed claim to most of the South China Sea and its building and arming of land features there. China has also tried to frustrate the collective ability of the association to disagree openly with Beijing.

The "ASEAN Way" of consensus has benefited the institution's longevity by avoiding divisively win-lose votes. From time to time, China's clients inside the grouping have turned that institutional asset into a regional liability by voicing objections to policy positions opposed by Beijing. By casting what are effectively proxy vetoes on Beijing's behalf, ASEAN's China-favoring members have undercut the strategic autonomy of the grouping as measured by its ability to stand up to the PRC. The region's diversity has thus abetted China's drive for influence over its neighbors. Yet that same diversity is also a liability for China. It enlarges the chance, other things being equal, that some Southeast Asian states will, on their own, continue to pursue and try to retain strategic autonomy from China as a matter of their respective national interests, even if ASEAN is hampered in doing so in the collective interest of the region.

In this chapter, these and related ideas are explored in the context of relevant policies and patterns of structure and agency. Such topics include bilateral and multilateral activity and design; meanings of regional centrality and co-optation; China's geo-economic diplomacy; patterns of elite regional opinion; and strategic autonomy's prospects with particular reference to Singapore, Cambodia, the Philippines, and Vietnam in relation to China under Xi Jinping and America under Donald Trump. The challenge of asymmetry captured in the mousedeer-dragon metaphor recurs throughout.[5]

In coining and popularizing another metaphor, a "Thucydides trap" waiting to spring shut on China and the United States, Graham Allison adapted and imported into the 21st century a 5th-century-BCE historian's warning about what could happen when a gap in power between two rivals closes. Allison worried that the growing strength of a rising China could sufficiently alarm a no longer omnipotent America to render war between them unavoidable.[6] Viewed from Southeast Asia, a narrowing of that disparity in strength could ignite a dangerously volatile mix of American apprehension and Chinese ambition. If not contained, the mix could explode and collaterally damage the ASEAN region. That is the lesson of the Thucydides trap for Southeast Asians. Conversely, from their standpoint, closing the gap in clout between Beijing and Washington could be desirable if and when the resulting balance of power is stable enough to check the inclination of either giant to dominate the region.

A fatalistic view would stress the mousedeer's impotence and vulnerability by portraying them as bystanders reduced to watching fearfully while, over their heads, China and America compete for control of Southeast Asia and its people. In that discouraging picture, whether Sino-American disparity shrinks or grows is irrelevant for Southeast Asians, who will remain vulnerable to subordination and exploitation by powerful states. Thucydides, in what could be called his "Melian dictum," phrased that bleak viewpoint as a general rule: "The strong do what they can and the weak suffer what they must."[7] Athens and Sparta, respectively rising and leading powers, did fight the Peloponnesian War. Athens did invade the small island of Melos after which the "Melian dictum" is named. But as guides to Southeast Asia's relations with China today, the structurally determined narratives of doom associated with these ancient events — unavoidable conflagration and subjugation — are helpful less for what they contend than for what they overlook.

Structure matters. But agency is not a property of the strong alone. Weaker powers can be proactive, too, however limited and contingent their agency may be. A trope widely encountered in Southeast Asia during the Cold War imagined two elephants — the United States and the USSR — either fighting or making love, but in either case trampling the inevitably hapless Southeast Asian grass. The binary determinism of that metaphor ludicrously denied to Southeast Asians any willful autonomy at all. At the dawn of this century's third decade, Chinese president Xi Jinping's expansionary and revisionist "China Dream" has begun to collide with Donald Trump's transactional and revisionist commitment to putting "America First." The outcomes of that contest in Southeast Asia will depend more than trivially on what the "grass" does or does not do.

Just because China looms over Southeast Asia on maps, it does not follow that its neighbors can only "suffer what they must." Mousedeer stories are constructive in this context not because they are realistic, but because they conjure an anti-structuralist alternate universe in which the clever weak somehow manage to outwit the bullying strong — and thereby, if only in fantasy, prove the Melian dictum wrong. Mousedeer heroism, however fanciful, is an indigenous cultural reminder to an analyst not to infer impotence and subservience from inequality, and instead to think, realistically but also creatively, outside the boxes that Thucydidean entrapment and Melian destiny represent. The trick, and in a way the task of this book, is to acknowledge and explore the agency of Southeast Asians without recourse to deterministic underestimation on the one hand or to wishful exaggeration on the other.

In both reality and myth, mousedeer are authentically Southeast Asian in character. Most of them live in the remaining forests of Indonesia, Malaysia, and the southern Philippines, and they have been found as well in forested areas in mainland Southeast Asia as far north as Laos and Vietnam. Due to their small size, body shape, and physical agility, they can move quickly through undergrowth, where their fur coloring serves as camouflage. These features help to explain why, in parts of the region, mousedeer have been anthropomorphically recast in folklore as clever tricksters skilled at outsmarting enemies far larger and fiercer than they. In Malay-Indonesian folklore, for instance, the mousedeer Sang Kancil is featured in tales of how the smart though weak can defeat the strong but dumb.[8]

In one such tale, "Mouse Deer Defeats Greedy Dragon,"[9] simplified here for reasons of space, the diminutive hero outwits a voracious and marauding dragon by duping him into thinking that the sky is falling and will crush them both if nothing is done. Mouse Deer has a rope and is tying one end of it around one of his hooves. Big Dragon, curious, asks why. Mouse Deer explains that he will tie the other end around the crossbar in a nearby well and then jump in. The rope will break his descent, and he will be safely inside the well when the sky crashes down. Big Dragon, envious, forces Mouse Deer to surrender the rope and makes him use it to tie the dragon's own foot to the crossbar. When the dragon is sitting on the well's edge waiting for the sky to fall, Mouse Deer pushes him in. Dangling upside down inside the well, with the sky still in its usual place, Big Dragon realizes that he has been tricked. The birds whose catches of fish Big Dragon had been stealing and eating are delighted. "Mouse Deer," they cheer, "you are the smartest animal in the whole world!"

China's Neighbors and the Melian Dictum

In the Mouse Deer story, ingenuity overthrows asymmetry and repeals the Melian dictum, but only thanks to the sheer stupidity — credulity — of Big Dragon. The useful moral of the tale is not that the weak can count on the gullibility of the strong. They cannot. It is that influence is not a function of size alone, that the weak have options, and that creativity counts. As far as options go, the mousedeer genre itself is insufficiently creative. By catering to the myth of a single hero who acts and prevails unilaterally, mousedeer stories ignore the strength-in-numbers option: recruiting other weak actors in a coalition better able collectively to counterbalance a strong opponent.

Mousedeer analogies also ignore the reality that the ASEAN economies have benefited from cooperating with China. If and when, through trade or investment, China helps meet the region's desire for economic development while helping itself as well, assuming both sides proportionally enjoy net gains in welfare, the results may indeed warrant Beijing's favorite accolade — "win-win."[10] It is on matters of security that China's relations with its southern neighbors have tended to be zero-sum, especially regarding the South China Sea and Beijing's expansive claim to that maritime space located in the heart of Southeast Asia.

In Southeast Asia, no Chinese behavior illustrates the Melian binary of strength over weakness more clearly than Beijing's unilateral, adamant, and expansive assertion of full sovereignty over or proprietary rights in virtually all of the waters and land features in the South China Sea. China's claim overlaps to differing extents the also differently overlapping claims made by four ASEAN members—Brunei, Malaysia, the Philippines, and Vietnam—and Taiwan, which has traditionally supported the Chinese position. China claims the right to fish in certain Indonesian waters as well. An allocation of sovereignty decided bilaterally by and between any two of these seven states could violate overlapping claims made by some of the others, who would, understandably, reject a usurping or infringing settlement reached in their absence. The complexity of the situation makes obvious the need for inclusively multilateral negotiation.

Despite this multilateralist logic of cooperation, Chinese diplomacy has been tenaciously bilateralist on matters of sovereignty and sovereign rights. China has insisted on maximizing its preponderance in such negotiations by dealing only with one rival claimant at a time. Beijing even told Southeast Asian states not to talk about the South China Sea among themselves prior to meeting as a group with China. Before the 48th ASEAN Foreign Ministers Meeting was held in Kuala Lumpur in August 2015, Chinese vice foreign minister Liu Zhenmin warned the Southeast Asian foreign ministers not to discuss the South China Sea in China's absence.[11] This pressure to self-censor directly threatened the strategic autonomy that every member of ASEAN, and ASEAN itself, is entitled to enjoy. Beijing's presumptuous admonition also implicitly acknowledged that, if the Southeast Asians did freely caucus among themselves, they might develop a unified position and thereby weaken China's win-lose Melian advantage in structural power.

In Hanoi in July 2010, at a meeting of the ASEAN Regional Forum, America's then secretary of state Hillary Clinton suggested that the conflicts over sovereignty in the South China Sea be addressed in multilateral discussions. She recommended "a collaborative diplomatic process by all claimants" to resolve the disputes.[12] Of the 27 countries attending the forum, 12 spoke in favor of such an approach, including all four self-acknowledged Southeast Asian claimants—Brunei, Malaysia, the Philippines, and Vietnam.

China's foreign minister Yang Jiechi was furious. He neither denounced multilateralism nor quoted the Melian dictum. But the structural determinism in what he did say was clear: "China is a big country and other countries are small countries—and that's just a fact."[13] He made his intimidating reminder more pointedly bilateral by staring at the foreign minister of one small country, Singapore, while delivering it. Yang was later promoted to state councilor and, in 2017, to the Politburo of China's Communist Party.

In 2016, almost as if to reply to Yang's put-down in Hanoi six years before, Singapore's ministry of defense countered the Melian dictum in a front-page piece on the city-state's ability to deter a full spectrum of 21st-century threats. The article did not cast Singapore in a heroic mousedeer role. But it did recap the strategies associated with animal metaphors for Singapore that had evolved since the 1960s when the city-state's founder and first ruler Lee Kuan Yew argued that "in a world where the big fish eat small fish and the small fish eat shrimps, Singapore must become a poisonous shrimp."[14] Lee's Singapore would, in other words, arm itself and fight back, even in defeat, as if to say: You can eat us, and we will suffer what we must, but if you do, you too will die.

Over time, as Singapore's economy and military grew stronger, it had less reason to settle for posthumous revenge. In the 1980s, the killer shrimp as a symbol of deterrence gave way in official doctrine to a porcupine who would not only punish an enemy but survive the experience. Since 2004, in the eyes of some analysts, the porcupine has been replaced by an orca — "agile, intelligent, quick and capable of killing more ferocious sharks with its razor sharp teeth when provoked."[15]

If porcupines are larger than shrimp, orcas — killer dolphins — are larger still. They can and do kill sharks. Even in a high-tech, cyber-vulnerable, 21st-century world, smarts alone are not a sufficient or reliable substitute for superiority in size and power. Scale still matters. Singapore's metaphorical evolution from poisonous shrimp to ruthless orca — from suicide to survival with even a chance of success — may be comforting. Singapore's realistic leaders know, however, that faith in purely kinetic solo success — Singapore, all by itself, surviving and defeating the dragon — is beyond naïve. It is lunacy. But the Melian dictum is wrong. The strong are not immune to constraint and suffering. The weak, too, can possess and exercise agency. For the ASEAN states, asymmetry is not slavery, and the alternative to lunacy is not resignation. Yang Jiechi's reminder that China's clout over Southeast Asia is "just a fact" has not stopped the region's mousedeer from spending on defense.

How much or how little time and thought do defense planners in each ASEAN capital devote to the probabilities of military conflict with China? What rankings and reasons might such officials have assigned to the likelihood of clashing with China compared, for example, to the chance of fighting a fellow member of ASEAN? The invisibility of such provocative calculations due to secrecy does not mean they do not exist.

Consider Cambodia. No ASEAN state appears to have spent more on its defense as a share of GDP in 2017 and 2018.[16] Yet relations between Phnom Penh and Beijing have been uniquely close. In that light, Cambodia's history of conflict with Thailand or Vietnam might explain Cambodian strongman

Hun Sen's stepped-up military spending better than fear of China would. It may not be coincidental, for instance, that Cambodian allocations for defense began rising in the wake of sometimes fatal clashes on the country's border with Thailand in 2008–11.[17] But military spending can serve other purposes — job creation, pay raises, procurement corruption, or military modernization — all with no current or could-be domestic or foreign enemy necessarily in mind.

If defense spending motives and targets are often opaque, so does uncertainty hamper the estimation of a spending country's relative military strength. Two recent and contrasting portrayals of the military endowments of ASEAN states illustrate the point by juxtaposing quantity versus quality, size versus skill. The size of a country appears to be the most influential variable in the data-analytics firm Global Firepower's 2018 ranking of the ASEAN countries from strongest to weakest in military terms.[18] Vast and populous Indonesia tops that list as militarily the most powerful ASEAN member, while tiny Singapore ranks third from the weakest, Laos.

The Lowy Institute's measure of "military capability" is different. It includes, alongside quantitative components, qualitative factors such as experience, organization, intelligence, and readiness to deploy forces rapidly and for a sustained period in a hypothetical confrontation on either land or sea. Proficiency is thus taken into account. Accordingly, Lowy's listing of ASEAN states puts Singapore in first place, above second-place Vietnam and third-place Indonesia. Still more striking is Singapore's top-rung location on Lowy's ladder of ASEAN countries differentiated by "overall power." That multidimensional variable contextualizes "military ability" by adding to it an array of less directly kinetic measures — "defense networks," "resilience," "economic resources," "economic relationships," "diplomatic influence," "cultural influence," and even "future trends." In this understanding of "overall power," Singapore's lead over Indonesia is not only retained; it widens a bit.[19]

These distinctions do not alter China's first- or second-place berth on a listing of all the world's countries by military capacity — just above America (Firepower) or, more plausibly, still just below it (Lowy). The most credibly muscular ASEAN states on Lowy's list do nevertheless pose a hypothetical risk for contingency planners in Beijing. If Singapore, Vietnam, and Indonesia were someday to agree to coordinate their defense policies and capacities in the event of an external threat to their well-being, without mentioning China or any other potential assailant, Beijing would at least be reminded of what a local war could cost. For such a defense agreement to occur, however,

Southeast Asia's "power threesome" would have to set aside the economic, political, and policy differences that continue to keep them apart.

The good news is that, as of 2019, the short-term probability of war between China and an ASEAN state was surely zero or near-zero, and the medium-term chance not significantly higher. The logic of asymmetry combined with a natural preference for peace explains why no ASEAN member, let alone ASEAN itself, is about to start a physical conflict with China. Nor is China eager to make outright enemies of its neighbors, asymmetry's temptations notwithstanding.

How much could an ASEAN country protect itself by relying on a partner as powerful as the United States? Would the Trump administration or one of its successors-to-come defend a single ASEAN country against China if doing so almost assuredly meant full-spectrum Sino-American war? Projecting current conditions, no, although Washington might well consider options short of war. The nature and status of the existing Philippine-American alliance may serve to illustrate the risks and ambiguities involved in relying on outsiders.

Alliance as Deterrence

The 1951 Mutual Defense Treaty (MDT) between the Philippines and the United States would be activated if either party were attacked by a third party, conceivably China, "in the Pacific" or "in the Pacific Area." But such an event would merely oblige Washington and Manila to "consult together" and respond to unspecified "common dangers" in keeping with the two countries' respective "constitutional processes." The American process could even require an authorizing vote in the Senate before war-making action could be taken.[20] The Southeast Asia Collective Defense Treaty that the Philippines and Thailand signed with the United States and five non–Southeast Asian countries in 1954 is technically still in effect. But its wording similarly dilutes the duty of one signer to defend another from attack.[21]

The rise of China has also fostered fears in Manila that, if Beijing did attack, a geographic ambiguity in the MDT's text could serve as a loophole through which Washington could escape its responsibility under the treaty. If the attack took place in the South China Sea, would its waters qualify as part of "the Pacific" or "the Pacific Area"?

In Manila in February 2019, on behalf of the Trump administration, US secretary of state Mike Pompeo answered that question: "As the South China Sea is part of the Pacific, any armed attack on Philippine forces, aircraft,

or public vessels in the South China Sea will trigger mutual defense obligations under Article 4 of our mutual defense treaty."[22] The sea's waters were
thus unequivocally placed within the scope of the MDT. Less noticed was
Pompeo's implied exclusion of private vessels from the category of objects
whose experience of being attacked would activate the treaty. The omission
could be considered an incentive to China to continue its long-standing
practice of harassing the operations of Philippine fishermen in the South
China Sea. Beijing used that tactic again mere weeks after Pompeo spoke.[23]

On paper, the mutual defense treaty is a two-way deal. By its reciprocal
terms, the Philippines should come to the defense of the United States if
the latter is attacked anywhere in the vast "Pacific Area" in which Pompeo
included the South China Sea. Just as some Americans have feared entrapment by Manila in a Sino-Philippine clash, so have Philippine voices been
raised against the risk of enlistment in a Sino-American war.

Just four days after Pompeo's reassurance, Philippine defense secretary
Delfin Lorenzana said his concern was not the need for American reassurance but the risk of "being involved in a war that we do not seek and
do not want."[24] Lorenzana is by no means a Sinophile inclined to bend to
the will of Beijing. He knows that kinetic involvement would not be auto-
matic, but would depend upon procedural decisions that the treaty requires.
Conceivably, the treaty's reciprocal obligations could be revised to operate
in only one direction — making the United States defend the Philippines but
not the reverse. In Washington, however, even under a less "America First"
president than Trump, that idea would likely be dead on arrival. Illustrating
the division of opinion in Manila, Philippine foreign affairs secretary Teodor
Locsin Jr. saw no need to review the MDT, contending instead that "in vagueness lies the best deterrence."[25]

The Philippine case shows that a treaty can give rise to nearly as much
uncertainty as it was meant to replace, especially in a country where disagreements are allowed. Dependent deterrence, reliant on outside help, may
not be dependable. Worth noting in that light is the record of independent,
China-facing deterrence in a Southeast Asian country that has forsworn
alliances: Vietnam.

Of the Southeast Asian states, Vietnam is the one most likely to cause
China to think twice before attacking it. No ASEAN country has a national
identity more animated by historical antagonism toward the PRC and its
imperial antecedents. In the National Museum of Vietnamese History in
Hanoi, large wall maps anachronistically frame invasions of "Vietnam" by
"China" that took place long before the nation-state was even invented.

Since the 3rd century BCE, by one calculation, 21 conflicts of varying intensities and lengths have pitted "Vietnamese" against "Chinese" forces.[26]

This legacy of hostility was renewed in the South China Sea in 1974 when PRC troops seized the Paracel Islands from what was then the Republic of [South] Vietnam, killing an estimated 75 Vietnamese soldiers in the process. Vietnam was reunified as a socialist republic in 1975. Three years later, Vietnam invaded and occupied Cambodia, ousting and replacing Pol Pot's murderous Beijing-backed Khmer Rouge regime. In 1979, China invaded Vietnam to teach it a "lesson" for what it had done to China's ally. The ensuing brief but bloody war took the lives of an estimated "tens of thousands" of Vietnamese and Chinese soldiers.[27] A month later, China's troops withdrew.

China claimed to have successfully delivered its "lesson" to Vietnam. A scholarly consensus, however, supports the argument that in this instance the mousedeer's skill and tenacity surprised, embarrassed, and seriously wounded the dragon, despite the clear numerical superiority of China's forces — 200,000 men, 1,500 artillery pieces, and 400 tanks. Cognizant of the prowess that Vietnam's air defense system had acquired by experience under American attack during the Vietnam War, China kept its planes on the ground.[28] The 1979 war confirmed the Lowy Institute's attention to quality, including experience, alongside quantity in its measure of military capacity. Not coincidentally, following China's withdrawal, the People's Liberation Army (PLA) underwent modernizing reforms, as if it had not only delivered a "lesson" but learned one as well.[29]

A sustainable peace did not follow the 1979 war. Intermittently from then until the normalization of Hanoi-Beijing relations in 1991, the two countries clashed not only along Vietnam's land border with China but also at sea. In 1988 they fought in the South China Sea for control of land features in the Spratly Islands. In March of that year, dozens of reportedly unarmed Vietnamese sailors standing in the water with a Vietnamese flag on Johnson South Reef were mowed down by gunfire from a PLA Navy frigate.[30] China seized the reef and other land features in the Spratlys and has occupied them ever since. Repeatedly over the subsequent three decades and counting, China has harassed Vietnamese ships and fishermen in the South China Sea, including inside Vietnam's exclusive economic zone.[31]

Understandable in this context was the nearly 700 percent jump in the value of arms imported by Vietnam in 2011–16 compared with 2006–11. The increase boosted the country into eighth place worldwide by that measure. Hanoi's acquisitions were made with the water-and-air setting of the South China Sea clearly in mind. The purchases, completed or planned, favored submarines, ships, aircraft, and drones over weapons usable only on land. An analyst who noted these data in 2017 suggested that Vietnam could now pursue its own equivalent of an anti-access/area denial (A2/AD) strategy, alluding to an ability that observers normally reserve for China alone.[32]

Merely buying weapons ensures neither their scrupulous maintenance nor their adroit use. But among ASEAN states, Vietnam's unique and long evident will and wherewithal to resist aggression, a capacity rendered all the more deadly by modern materiel, could at least frustrate a hypothetical Chinese attack for a limited time. And even in the medium to longer term, China would be hard put to transmute victory into pacification and domination. The long reliance of the Philippines on its alliance with the United States, in contrast, reduced Manila's incentive to develop a credible military deterrent of its own. In part for that reason, the Armed Forces of the Philippines are notoriously weak.[33] That weakness in turn helps explain Philippine president Rodrigo Duterte's evident reluctance to stand up to China.[34]

Unlike Manila, Hanoi formally renounces alliances and alignments. As a matter of doctrine, Vietnam anchors its foreign policy in a triple abstention: "no military alliances, no aligning with one country against another, and no foreign military bases on Vietnamese soil."[35] These "three noes" would appear to rule out soliciting and leveraging third-party support against Beijing. But they have not foreclosed creative mousedeer diplomacy in Hanoi. Vietnam's ongoing military-related cooperation with Moscow and Washington is a case in point. Purchases of Russian materiel, including Kilo-class submarines, have bolstered Hanoi's strategic autonomy in kinetic terms, while the warming of Sino-Russian relations has attenuated though not removed Chinese suspicion that Hanoi and Moscow are conspiring to thwart Beijing. Improved relations between Hanoi and Washington have also tended to support the strategic autonomy of Vietnam.

Although it may seem like no more than playing with words, Hanoi has also used creative labeling to tailor what its "three noes" are intended to mean for its interactions with a given country. "No military alliances" has not prevented Vietnam from maintaining a nuanced hierarchy of "partnerships" whose adjectives supposedly indicate how close its relations with a given country actually are. On that listing in 2019, the top—most adulatory—level of recognition was reserved for any country that had earned a "comprehensive strategic cooperative" partnership with Vietnam. China sat there all by itself, presumably enjoying its tripled accolade.

Vietnam's partnership with America, in contrast, merited only a single adjective: "comprehensive." All of the other major powers' relations with Vietnam were at least "strategic." Did Hanoi privately assuage Washington that a "comprehensive" partnership necessarily included a strategic aspect? Did Hanoi assure Beijing that Vietnamese-American relations were not "strategic" because that would imply a nascent alliance to be leveraged against China in violation of the three noes? Speculation aside, the eighth iteration of America's joint Naval Engagement Activity with Vietnam did take place off Cam Ranh Bay in 2018.[36] That training exercise included rehearsing the handling of unplanned maritime encounters, a proficiency of use to Vietnam as it faces Chinese harassment in the South China Sea. In sum, a mousedeer's ingenuity may lie partly in the difference between what it says and what it quietly continues to do.

Formally and uniquely in Southeast Asia, the Philippines and Thailand are still designated by treaty as American allies. But that status has long ceased to predict the foreign-policy behavior of either state. In the 21st century, the more contingent, multipolar, and therefore uncertain international relations become, the more obsolete will the fixed and permanent commitments implied by alliances appear to be.

The ASEAN Way and Beijing's Way

Resignation and passivity among Southeast Asians are natural responses to the massive asymmetries in economic and military power that favor China over its ASEAN neighbors and allow Beijing to assert itself forcefully on land and sea. These imbalances and pressures, made more pointed by doubts about the reliability of outside help, are naturally conducive to fatalist pessimism in the region. Apart from romantic optimism, which is vanishingly scarce, there are three obvious alternatives to versions and degrees of deference toward and dependence on China: go-it-alone deterrence, constrained by what a single country can afford; external reliance on outsiders to counterbalance; and regional coalition-building designed to incubate a united front of Southeast Asian states determined to negotiate with China from a unified position of collective strength. National deterrence and extra-regional alliance having been covered above, albeit within constraints of space, the third option — intra-regional cohesion — is reviewed next.

The sole conceivable candidate for a region-wide experiment along regional lines is ASEAN, whose 10 countries together, in effect, account for nearly all of Southeast Asia.[37] In tandem with the manifold differences among its members, however, ASEAN's own makeup and procedures have rendered the grouping incapable of forging a common front against Chinese regional expansion.

ASEAN is an intergovernmental organization of sovereign states. It is not a transnational agency endowed with executive power. Its states have not delegated to their organization the authority to represent them in world affairs. Gathered in a summit, the 10 can make decisions on behalf of ASEAN as an organization, but those decisions do not enforceably overrule the members' own policies. Member-state sovereignty is protected by the principle of non-interference, while the principle of consensus — the ASEAN Way — preserves the ability of a single member to block whatever it dislikes, whether the objection is authentic or attributable to pressure by an outside power such as China. A case in point is China's success in co-opting Cambodia into service as a proxy whose veto, if wielded, can block any ASEAN statement on the South China Sea that Beijing dislikes.

Iconic in this regard was the shambolic ending of the 45th meeting of ASEAN foreign ministers in Phnom Penh in July 2012. In February and again in June, Phnom Penh and Beijing had signed agreements providing for nearly $750 million in Chinese loans to Cambodia. In July, at China's behest, Cambodia blocked any specific reference to the South China Sea disputes in the foreign ministers' communiqué at the end of their meeting. Chinese officials may even have gone so far as to telephone guidance to that effect to the Cambodian delegation during the discussion.[38] Beijing did not and does not want ASEAN to have an independent position on the matter of maritime sovereignty that might express or imply criticism of China's sweeping claim.

Accordingly, despite a decades-long record of 44 completed meetings and agreed-upon communiqués behind them, the ASEAN foreign ministers failed to issue any statement at all. Less than two months later, in September, Cambodia's state secretary for finance announced that, in addition to more than $500 million in Chinese loan agreements then signed or planned, China's foreign minister had just promised an outright "gift" worth $24 million that Cambodia would be free to use on any priority project.[39] Phnom Penh and Beijing were thus able to link and ostensibly satisfy two different interests — Cambodia's in economic development, China's in regional primacy — in a way that overrode and thwarted a third interest: the collective interest of Southeast Asians in uniting to defend their region's strategic autonomy from outside interference. How much of China's material largesse wound up supporting avarice rather than welfare in a country long ranked as the most corrupt in Southeast Asia is a separate question.[40]

The institutionalized power of a single member state to veto a draft ASEAN resolution critical of China makes it easier for Beijing to export self-censorship to Southeast Asia. But Chinese bribery is not the only culprit. Diverse views among member states independently impede agreement on sensitive matters, including whether and how much to resist Beijing. More often than not, ASEAN's members have tolerated Beijing's efforts to twist arms and buy silence. The partly fear-based case for maintaining a façade of comity with China and of agreement among themselves rationalizes the Southeast Asian states' forbearance. The longer ASEAN's members continue to furnish Beijing with diplomatic cover to divide and manipulate them, the harder it will be to distinguish the self-censoring ASEAN Way from the censorship-mongering "Way of Beijing."

In addition to cultivating proxy roadblocks inside ASEAN, China has sought to weaken the grouping through what could be called "preemptive co-optation" — presumptively claiming a consensus that does not exist. PRC foreign minister Wang Yi's itinerary through Brunei, Cambodia, and Laos in April 2016 illustrated the gambit and its risks. At each stop he reaffirmed Chinese economic support for the hosting government. At the end of the trip, in Laos, he announced that all three ASEAN countries had joined China in agreement — a "consensus" — supporting the Chinese position that the South China Sea was none of ASEAN's business, although he worded the alleged agreement's content more diplomatically than that.[41]

Asked about this allegedly four-way concurrence, ASEAN's secretary-general Le Luong Minh said that ASEAN was unaware of any such agreement. He had "heard nothing" from Laos or from Brunei as to "what was agreed or what [had] happened" during Wang's visits. Even more notable was a Cambodian government spokesman's on-the-record disavowal: "There has been no agreement or discussions, just a visit by a Chinese foreign minister."[42] Nor did the statements made by the Laotian and Bruneian foreign ministries following their meetings with Wang mention the South China Sea or any agreement with China related to it.[43] In this instance at least, preemptive co-optation failed to yield the acquiescence that Beijing desired.

As if to further negate Wang's announcement, Le added that "an ASEAN country cannot negotiate with China on disputes that involve other ASEAN countries," as the South China Sea disputes certainly did and still do.[44] That comment was less effective than it might have seemed, however, for Wang had not claimed that he and his hosts had negotiated the disputes themselves. A bolder riposte would have urged China to stop excluding ASEAN from any dispute-settling role. But that would have meant bypassing the ASEAN Way of consensus, risking Chinese wrath, and likely incurring demurrals by Cambodia and other ASEAN members, whether China-friendly or China-cowed. Le could not argue that China and the ASEAN claimant states should put the maps of their sovereignties on the same table for multilateral negotiation. That would have exceeded his mandate to administer but not lead the association.

Their demurrals notwithstanding, none of Wang's three hosts gave Beijing cause for outright alarm. None criticized China's maritime claim. And in withholding public support for China's desire to ban ASEAN from playing any role in resolving the disputes over sovereignty in the South China Sea, their intent was likely less to challenge Beijing than to avoid appearing, in the eyes of their co-members in ASEAN, complicit in China's effort to incapacitate the association. Nor has the option known as "ASEAN Minus X" gained traction — the idea that the four ASEAN claimant states should settle their own differences first, the better to deal as a united group with Beijing's divide-and-defeat effort to control the maritime core — the heartwater — of Southeast Asia. China is willing to meet with ASEAN's members as a group to discuss rules of behavior in the South China Sea, but not to negotiate allocations of sovereignty, let alone question China's claim.

Two months after Wang Yi's tour, a new brouhaha arose to replay the debacle that had closed the ASEAN foreign ministers' meeting in Phnom Penh four years before. In June 2016 in Yuxi, China, an ASEAN-China Special Foreign Ministers Meeting derailed, embarrassing ASEAN once more. Wang Yi hosted the event and co-chaired it with his Singaporean counterpart. Censorship with Chinese characteristics again fed the fiasco. Basically, Wang Yi tried to bully the ASEAN states into accepting an utterly anodyne draft joint statement with China, prepared by China, whose 10 points spared China even an implicit whiff of dissatisfaction with its behavior in the South China Sea.

The Southeast Asians were not persuaded. They had a statement of their own. It "expressed serious concern over recent and ongoing developments" that had "eroded trust and confidence" and "increased tensions" that could "undermine peace, security and stability in the South China Sea." It stressed "the importance of non-militarisation and self-restraint." It singled out "land reclamation" as a possibly tension-raising activity. It called such happenings "an important issue in relations between ASEAN and China." The implied criticisms of Beijing were hard to deny.

Wang Yi not only rejected the statement. He successfully pressured his ASEAN counterparts to bury it.[45] Cambodia and especially Laos, ASEAN's chair at the time, played key proxy spoiler roles. As if the intra-ASEAN rancor stoked by Wang were not embarrassing enough, the China-censored draft that some ASEAN members had resisted was released as a "media statement," only to be retracted soon after. As for the meeting in Yuxi, it broke up — no consensus, no statement, nothing.[46]

In one sense, ASEAN's initial courage notwithstanding, China won that round. To Beijing's demanding ears, silence by manipulated stalemate was better than even a veiled remark that might have been thought to question China's assertive comportment at sea. But the dragon also lost in that it failed to cajole or intimidate its mousedeer guests into public and unanimous agreement with its position. ASEAN also won and lost. China's effort to censor and rubber-stamp the outcome failed. But whereas the ASEAN foreign ministers had said in their draft that they could not "ignore what is happening in the South China Sea," Chinese intimidation obliged them, at least officially and textually on this occasion, to ignore exactly what Chinese intimidation was making happen in those waters.

In July 2016, a month after the fiasco in Yuxi, an international arbitral court declared China's position and conduct in the South China Sea to be at variance with international maritime law. But the judges' rebuke of Beijing did not precipitate the vocal and sustained global approval that would have been needed to institutionalize their ruling. Nor did US president Barack Obama's administration campaign on the ruling's behalf, even as China vilified the court and refused to implement its decision. The ASEAN states, meanwhile, knew from Beijing's anger that it would punish them if they championed what the judges had done.

In the wake of the ruling, intra-ASEAN divisions again played into China's hands. Benigno Aquino III was then president of the Philippines, a claimant state. His administration had brought the original "suit" against Beijing on Manila's behalf. By the time the court issued its ruling, however, his elected successor, Rodrigo Duterte, had replaced him. Duterte chose not to take yes for an answer. Ignoring the judgment's net benefit to the Philippines, Duterte virtually reversed course, letting his new leverage lie fallow and cultivating Chinese investments instead — commitments that Beijing was more than willing to pledge, though less willing to fund.[47] Fortunately for Duterte, the Philippine economy continued to grow at one of the region's most rapid rates.

The lesson of these embarrassments is that ASEAN is losing its centrality. But in what sense? ASEAN has never been central to the daily living or thinking of the 650 million people who live in its member countries; that was never the grouping's intent. For the more than five decades since its birth in 1967, its self-imposed lack of domestic centrality and corresponding reverence for member sovereignty have helped ASEAN survive. In view of the extreme diversity of its region, had its leaders fostered a more intrusive version of centrality, directly involving the association in possibly controversial issues of domestic consequence for its member states, local pushbacks could have splintered the group. By making ASEAN less centralized, less impactful, and less contentious, the association's founders made it more likely to last. Concomitantly underfunded and understaffed, the ASEAN secretariat in Jakarta has kept its profile low.[48]

In a tolerably stretched comparison with Europe, given the empowerment and bureaucratization of the European Union (EU), one could say that, in Southeast Asia, the lack of a Brussels prevented a Brexit. But at what price in terms of ASEAN's coherence, purpose, and ability to respond to China? While Xi Jinping works to "rejuvenate" his country, far less attention is paid in Southeast Asia to renovating ASEAN to improve its capacity to defend and strengthen the strategic autonomy of its region.

Centrality and Connectivity

ASEAN has long prided itself on its "centrality" in regional affairs. But centrality is an ambiguous term. It can refer to ASEAN's location, to its importance, or to both, and they are not the same. ASEAN can look at a map and liken itself to the interoceanic hyphen at the heart of the "Indo-Pacific." That aspiration was evident in 2019 when the grouping proposed the adoption of "ASEAN Centrality as the underlying principle for promoting cooperation" across the entire "Indo-Pacific region."[49] But how realistic is that dramatically enlarged desire? The behavioral centrality of ASEAN — its operational importance — will signally depend on whether the grouping is supported, disregarded, or undermined by powerful outsiders, notably China and the United States.

Many Southeast Asian analysts define and defend ASEAN's centrality in geopolitical terms: the neutral but helpful bridging role of the hyphen in a "Sino-American" cold war that may already be underway. Southeast Asian leaders are understandably reluctant to align their countries with either China or the United States, as if both were equally worthy of circumspection if not suspicion. But Chinese and American policies challenge the strategic autonomy of Southeast Asia to different extents and in different ways. Opinions differ as to the scope of the PRC's ambitions, but there can be little doubt that the rejuvenation of China proposed and pursued by Xi Jinping is intended to return the Middle Kingdom to more than passive importance. If that assertive campaign is successful — a large if — it could reduce if not replace the diplomatic centrality that ASEAN has managed to acquire and retain since the end of the Cold War. America, by comparison, is too distant, too preoccupied on other fronts, and arguably too chastened by previous foreign misadventures to aspire to control the South China Sea, let alone Southeast Asia.

Notwithstanding the modesty of ASEAN's centrality as a reliable host of international meetings rather than a major shaper of their outcomes, the association deserves full credit for its innovations. During propitious regional and global conditions in the 1990s, ASEAN's diplomatic creativity blossomed. Knowing that ASEAN was not designed to be a supranational body with its own foreign policy, the group's leaders developed its comparative advantage as a catalyst and convener of interstate discourse and activity. No longer constrained by the Cold War, ASEAN innovated a dense Venn diagram of "ASEAN Plus" initiatives that all had ASEAN in common. A raft of acronyms ensued. The ASEAN Regional Forum (ARF), ASEAN Plus Three (APT), the East Asia Summit (EAS), the ASEAN Free Trade Agreement (AFTA), and the Southeast Asian Nuclear-Weapon-Free Zone Treaty (SEANWFZ) all date from the '90s. Earlier initiatives were augmented. ASEAN's Dialogue Partners (ASEAN Plus One), for instance, grew in number from six to ten.

ASEAN deserves full credit for birthing and incubating these regional arrangements and hosting the related events. But the diplomatic centrality of the association depended in no small measure on the absence of a proactive counter-center. The continued willingness of China's leaders to follow the advice proffered in the 1980s by their predecessor Deng Xiaoping — keep a low profile and focus on domestic economic reform — allowed ASEAN's centrality to proceed unrivaled by Beijing.

Xi Jinping broke that mold. As general secretary of the Communist Party of China since 2012, China's president since 2013, and chair of multiple commissions and shadowy "leading small groups," Beijing's new strongman dramatically raised his country's profile abroad. In October 2013 in Indonesia, he announced his 21st Century Maritime Silk Road (MSR) initiative, the southern counterpart of a Silk Road Economic Belt (SREB) that he had unveiled the month before in Kazakhstan. Basically, these pathways of physical infrastructure and diverse parallel projects were meant to connect China westward to Europe — MSR mainly by water via the South China Sea, the Indian Ocean, and the Mediterranean Sea, SREB mostly by land across Eurasia. Incorporating both of these schemes is Xi's massive and wide-ranging Belt and Road Initiative (BRI), as it came to be called.

The BRI is essentially bilateral in nature. China is the hub from which spokes of connectivity in construction, trade, investment, and finance are meant to radiate to and through dozens of recipient countries. In that design, the proactive and impactful centrality of China could not be more evident. ASEAN's plural composition and lack of sovereign authority prevents it from playing such a role. An ASEAN region perforated by the fanned-out infrastructure of a vast bilateralist BRI is thus at risk of becoming a collection of pathways and projects disproportionally serving the operational reach and centrality of China.

As if to hedge against that future, in 2016, three years after the MSR through Southeast Asia was announced, ASEAN's leaders launched a Master Plan on ASEAN Connectivity (MPAC) 2025. Aimed mainly at linking the ASEAN economies more closely and smoothly together, the plan was ambitiously tasked to achieve "a seamlessly and comprehensively connected and integrated ASEAN [region] that will deliver tangible benefits to ASEAN citizens" by its targeted year.[50] But ASEAN is not a country, "ASEAN citizens" do not exist, and its Master Plan lacks a master — an executive agency such as a government equipped with the sovereign power and ability to implement the plan, or at least push it forward.

Abstractly compared and other things held equal, bilateralism is more efficient than multilateralism — fewer actors — whereas multilateralism is more legitimate than bilateralism — more participation. Concerns in Southeast Asia that China's BRI could outperform and undermine ASEAN's MPAC 2025 illustrate the difference.[51] ASEAN's scheme was born from disappointment over the performance of ASEAN's first multilateral MPAC, begun in 2010. But the revised version — MPAC 2025 — still suffers from inefficiency due to the need to coordinate policies and take decisions involving all 10 member states; national borders continue to impede momentum toward "seamless" regional integration.

Meanwhile the legitimacy of the BRI has suffered in Southeast Asian eyes from evidence that its empowered Chinese hub is more interested in using the ASEAN states-as-spokes in its own interest than in generating "tangible benefits" for Southeast Asians.

Criticisms of the BRI have been articulated in all of the ASEAN states that have hosted its projects. Complaints have targeted high project costs, above-market rates on loans, and unrepayable debts whose conversion into equity could give China controlling stakes in host-country facilities and resources. China's practice of supplying Chinese labor to build BRI infrastructure has denied jobs to locals in need of paid work. The clearing of land for project use has displaced poor families with no recourse, scant compensation, and little or no regard for the environmental damage done. In host countries near China's borders, despite the need for electricity in project areas, the energy generated by BRI ventures has been disproportionally earmarked for China's own use. Dam projects on the Mekong River and its tributaries are constricting the supply of water for planting and fishing by Southeast Asians farther downstream.[52]

Beijing is not single-mindedly trying to impoverish the ASEAN states. China's party-state is not a smoothly operating machine free of friction between its moving parts. Corruption and competition among Chinese actors and agencies and among their counterparts in Southeast Asia share blame for what has gone wrong with the BRI. Unfortunately, apportioning that responsibility is obstructed by the sheer opacity of the BRI. In the accurate words of one analyst writing in 2019, "Despite its grand scale there is still no reliable list of BRI projects, no disclosure of the lending standards China follows, nor even the amount China has invested."[53] Reinforcing this lack of transparency in China are incentives for reciprocal secrecy in hosting countries, especially those under venal and autocratic rule.

Further obscurity follows from Beijing's penchant for ambiguity. Consider the equivocations embedded in Wang Yi's 2017 acknowledgment that China "has no intention of designating clear geographic boundaries" for the BRI; that it somehow represents "international cooperation in its essence"; and that it "is not a member's club, but a circle of friends with extensive participation."[54] A *China Daily* story in April 2019 praised Xi Jinping for working "to connect China with 152 countries through the Belt and Road Initiative," but left unsaid how many are actually connected to the PRC, in what ways, and to what extents.[55] The BRI does nevertheless have a strategic purpose: to elevate and invigorate the behavioral centrality — the operational importance — of China to Asia and the world, and not only in economic terms. Xi Jinping himself has acknowledged the initiative's political ambition by describing the BRI as "an important pathway to improve global development patterns *and global governance* [italics added]."[56]

The BRI's country-by-country, hub-and-spokes pattern locates Beijing indispensably at the center of its "circle of friends" and ensures that it will never be outnumbered at the negotiating table. Analysts can therefore be forgiven for speculating that, if the BRI is a prototype, it augurs a Sinocentric model of interstate relations and project management based on separated spokes, asymmetric influence, and deference to Beijing. Nor do the official "eight requirements" that BRI-participating states and organizations must meet encourage confidence that China is willing to accommodate a variety of partners and ideas. The very first condition is that the participants "effectively promote unity of thought." BRI participants are also required to "effectively promote public opinion," including "strengthen[ing]" unidentified "theories," and to propagate the also unspecified "spirit of the Silk

Road," apparently while evincing China-guided "unity of thought" as to what those "theories" and that "spirit" are.[57]

Lofty rhetoric and grounded reality are not the same. The BRI is necessarily decentralized in actual practice by its sheer complexity — the global spread of its projects and the multiplicity of entities and actors they involve both in project-hosting countries far from Beijing and inside China itself. But complexity does not ensure a level playing field for host and guest alike. The operational meaning of the abstract and seemingly benign concept of coordination warrants brief illustration in the case of Thailand.

Countries that sign up for the BRI are required to promote "concerted coordination."[58] When Beijing began negotiating a BRI project with Bangkok involving high-speed rail, Thai officials were angered when their Chinese counterparts treated the term as a euphemism for greater Chinese control, including extraterritorial rights to commercial use of the land on either side of the planned tracks.[59] Excessive too, in Thai eyes, were the proposed rate of interest on Chinese loans, China's desired ownership role, and the likely costs of construction, further complicated by issues involving labor recruitment and the environment. Bangkok also bridled at Beijing's unaccommodating demeanor. Affronts included project maps written, against explicit Thai wishes, in untranslated Chinese.[60] Eventually the Thai side rejected Chinese funding and sought to replace it from domestic sources. When those proved insufficient, Bangkok reopened the bidding to foreign lenders without privileging Chinese banks.

The future centrality of ASEAN will depend on more than what happens to the BRI. For the foreseeable future, ASEAN will not disappear, in part because it is not powerful enough to be controversial. But it is at least conceivable that, in the years and decades to come, China's infrastructural penetration of Southeast Asia will tie the region to China in roads and railroads, ports and dams, resource extraction and energy generation, not to mention digital protocols and could-be surveillance algorithms in cyberspace. In that unlikely but imaginable event, ASEAN's sun will be outshone.

Anxiety, Destiny, Autonomy

In Southeast Asia, diverse conditions and variables will shape the success or failure of the BRI and the irrelevance or centrality of ASEAN. Not least among those influencing factors will be the opinions of Southeast Asians themselves, especially in elite circles equipped with knowledge of and access to the making of foreign policy in their respective countries. In

November-December 2019, the Singapore-based ASEAN Studies Centre at the ISEAS-Yusof Ishak Institute surveyed such opinions in purposive samples drawn in all 10 ASEAN-member countries. Of the 1,308 respondents who took part, 40 percent were officials in the public sector and 36 percent were analysts in universities or think tanks. The rest (and their percentage shares) were in business (11), in the media (7), or in non-governmental organizations (7).[61]

At the 2nd Belt and Road Forum in Beijing in April 2019, Xi Jinping did not acknowledge the mounting criticisms of the BRI — that its activities inflicted burdensome debt, were closed to inspection, fostered environmental damage, and were tainted by corruption. But he likely had such charges in mind when he pledged to make the BRI "open, green and clean."[62] Six months later, the ISEAS survey asked its respondents to evaluate his promise of reform: "Are you convinced that this approach will lead to a fairer deal for your country as a recipient of BRI loans?" Nearly two-thirds (64 percent) of those who replied had "little or no confidence" that it would. Only in Brunei did a majority have "some or full confidence" that "a fairer deal" would be forthcoming.

ISEAS had administered a similar survey throughout the ASEAN region a year earlier, in November-December 2018. Both surveys included a question about trust in China and one about China's rise. Those findings too were unkind to Beijing. On the matter of trust, confidence in China to "do the right thing" for "global peace, security, prosperity and governance" was low in 2018 and even lower a year later. Among those who answered the trust question, the proportion who were "confident" or "very confident" that China would "do the right thing" shrank from 20 percent (2018) to 16 percent (2019). Those who expressed such confidence in the United States actually grew from 27 to 30 percent — notwithstanding Trump's idiosyncratic presidency and the tit-for-tat spat that broke out between American and ASEAN leaders during the ASEAN summitry in Bangkok in November 2019,[63] a mere week before the second survey began. That said, those expressions of assurance were dwarfed by the increasing majority with "no or little confidence" in China (from 52 to 60 percent) and the stable majority with no or little confidence in the United States (from 51 to 50 percent).[64]

In the 2019 ISEAS survey, respondents were shown five statements and asked to choose the one that "most accurately reflects your view of China's re-emergence as a major power with respect to Southeast Asia." Compared with the scarcity of confidence that China would "do the right thing" in world affairs, the views of China's rise were even less likely to please Beijing. Or so it would seem. A miniscule 1.5 percent of the respondents chose the answer most obviously favorable to China, namely, that "China is a benign and benevolent power." In contrast, a 38 percent plurality agreed that "China is a revisionist power and intends to turn Southeast Asia into its sphere of influence." Almost as many — 35 percent — affirmed that "China is gradually taking over the US'[s] role as a regional leader." Only 19 percent thought it was "too early to determine China's strategic intentions at this moment." And even fewer — 7 percent — agreed that "China is a status quo power and will continue to support the existing regional order."[65]

What does it mean that nearly three-quarters — 73 percent — of the Southeast Asian respondents saw China as a "revisionist" power bent on turning their region into its "sphere of influence" (38 percent) or as "gradually" replacing America as "a regional leader" (35 percent)? Some of those who chose either of these answers may have wanted such a shift to occur. Given the survey's other results, however, respondents were more likely anxious at the prospect of Southeast Asia's induction into a Sinosphere led from Beijing. Would Xi Jinping's China rather be feared than loved? If so, seen from Beijing, the survey's results could be good news.

Apart from love or fear, a third motivation behind the answers is also possible: fatalism — that China's primacy is Southeast Asia's destiny, like it or not. If China's presence in Southeast Asia continues to expand — bolstered perhaps by the indifference or unreliability of the United States — the more inescapable China's eventual dominance in "its" neighborhood may appear to be. The PRC's comparative advantage in the ASEAN region plausibly rests more on Southeast Asians' awareness of China's superior economic and military clout than on empathy with or attraction to China itself. Signs of that clout in addition to Chinese money, products, and markets would include Beijing's growing coercive power, its acts of intimidation in the South China Sea, and its relative success in pressuring Southeast Asians to censor themselves regarding China's behavior and "core interests."[66]

Unable or unwilling to convert regional fear into love, China may find it easier and more effective to rely on cognition over emotion: to speak and act in ways that will convince Southeast Asian influentials of the sheer inescapability of Chinese sway over the region. Deference to Beijing would no longer require the deferent to censor themselves; they would sincerely and pragmatically defer, wanting to be on the side of history.

Notable among Southeast Asians who think along these lines is Kishore Mahbubani, a Singaporean analyst known for celebrating China, castigating "the West," and advising his small country to accommodate if not actually kowtow to its giant neighbor to the north. Mahbubani called the Melian dictum "an eternal rule of geopolitics." "Small states," he wrote, "must always behave like small states" — fated as they are to cater to big ones. In relations between unequals, might really does make right. For fear of annoying Beijing, Singapore should not criticize China's expansionist ambition in the South China Sea, not even in politely vague and allusive terms. Another prominent Singaporean analyst, Bilahari Kausikan, disagreed. Singapore had not survived and prospered "by being anybody's tame poodle." Its citizens were not so "stupid" as to ignore meaningful "asymmetries of size and power." But that knowledge did not oblige them to "grovel or accept subordination" as normal. "No one respects a running dog," Kausikan added. "What kind of people does Kishore think we are?"[67]

Relevant in this context is Xi Jinping's repeated characterization of China and its Southeast Asian neighbors as a single "community of common destiny."[68] The phrase may appear to contradict the Melian dictum by replacing the inequality that is supposed to make small states suffer with the empathy implied by a "community" of states with a shared future. But reciprocal empathy based on egalitarian fraternity is not an obvious or inevitable "common destiny" that China and the ASEAN countries share. More plausibly, their destiny flows from their inescapable physical proximity and their incongruity in size and power, just as Foreign Minister Yang reminded his Singaporean counterpart in Hanoi in 2010. Viewed from Beijing, it is those starkly unequal conditions that could help to convince China's neighbors that their future as small states living in China's shadow requires their "inevitable" deference to Beijing — as the Melian dictum would expect and Mahbubani would advise.

In December 2018, the astute doyenne of foreign-policy studies in Indonesia, Dewi Fortuna Anwar, restated a growing worry in Southeast Asia: "that ASEAN and its 10 member states may be forced to choose between China and the US."[69] She wondered whether Southeast Asians could withstand Chinese and American pressures to pick one or the other side in strategic feuding increasingly reminiscent of the Cold War. She worried that the region could become again a theater for proxy conflicts between powerful outsiders.

Resisting partisan alignment with either China or the United States and avoiding collateral damage from the rivalry between them, Dewi wrote, would require of ASEAN and its constituent states one thing above all: strategic autonomy. She noted that ASEAN and its individual members were highly diverse, relatively weak, and located in a part of the world notably susceptible to Sino-American competition. The strategic autonomy of these Southeast Asian actors, she argued, was not a luxury — something they could decide they could not afford. It was a necessity if they expected to survive.

Inadvertently reprising the metaphor for asymmetry featured in this book, Dewi ended her piece with the hope that "ASEAN can take inspiration from the familiar Southeast Asian fable of the wily 'Kancil' or mousedeer that often outwits much bigger animals, the moral of the story being that those who are weaker must be more cunning and clever" than those who are strong.[70]

How collectively "cunning and clever" has ASEAN been? The evidence is discouraging. Southeast Asia's diversity, China's intervention, and the veto-empowering ASEAN Way have prevented the grouping's 10 members from leveraging their regional association into a united front that could have enabled them to deal more effectively with Beijing's pressures and demands. ASEAN's disunity has been plain to see. The four member states with self-described claims to parts of the South China Sea, for example, have done almost nothing to resolve their overlapping territorial avowals. A resolution of their disagreements might not only have strengthened the four states' bargaining position vis-à-vis China. It might even have generated momentum toward an ASEAN-wide definition and defense of the strategic autonomy of Southeast Asia as a whole.

In 2011–15, Australian maritime analyst Carl Thayer wrote a series of papers for ASEAN's consideration. In them he proposed, creatively and in helpful detail, the drafting and signing of an ASEAN Treaty of Amity and Cooperation in Southeast Asia's Maritime Domain.[71] Such a compact would have strengthened the strategic autonomy of Southeast Asia. To the extent that Southeast Asian officials were even aware of his idea, however, they ignored it. So did the region's policy scholars. Emailed in 2015 and again in 2019 about the fate of his idea, Thayer replied both times that it was "dead in the water."[72]

Absent effective collective action, it has been up to each individual ASEAN country to develop its own ways of trying to strengthen its China-facing autonomy by and for itself. In their efforts to avoid exclusive alignment with either China or the United States, ASEAN's members have hedged against both. Often, the hedger chooses to cooperate first with one of the two and then with the other, but does so in limited ways meant to deny the chosen power a full embrace while assuring the unchosen one that it is not being rejected.

The intended message conveyed alternately to China and the United States in this sequence is: "Do not expect me to work only with you. At times, I may work with your rival as well, and I reserve the right to do so."

Strategic autonomy in this sense is not a rejection of alignment. It is an allocation of limited gestures that help to preserve the possibility of alignment, at least inside the mind of each big power hoping to be aligned with. A move meant to assuage Beijing while cautioning Washington is accompanied or followed by a move to assuage Washington while cautioning Beijing. Such moves reference strategic autonomy without announcing it. And the autonomy they imply is not of the region; it is national in nature.

Structure, Agency, Prospect

In different ways, the Thucydides trap, the Melian dictum, the Belt and Road Initiative, and Yang's infamous "just a fact" remark all showcase the causal power of structure. So do the China-favoring imbalances of size and strength in Sino-Southeast Asian relations. Underestimated in this emphasis on structural frameworks and connectivity by design is the role of agency, including the structure-altering agency of empowered individuals, most notably Xi Jinping and Donald Trump.

Unbothered by the term limits faced by Trump, Xi has begun the cultivation of a long-run sphere of Chinese influence in Asia—a durably enlarged version of Chinese primacy reliant, as needed, on structures and linkages of China's own making, including the operational legacies of the BRI. But Xi's campaign to achieve "the great rejuvenation of the Chinese nation" does not require a Chinese assault on the liberal-capitalist-democratic international order fostered by American agency after World War II. Xi's China has more to gain from continuing to work selectively within the current version of that established system while developing supplementary and prospectively alternative arrangements—would-be institutions that could be called upon to amplify the agency of Beijing.[73]

What is striking about this proto-structural strategy is how limited its achievements have proven to be. In 2014 in Shanghai, for example, Xi keynoted that year's Conference on Interaction and Confidence Building Measures in Asia (CICA). During and after the meeting, he criticized alliance-based security concepts as Cold War relics that Asian countries should "completely abandon" in favor of a "new regional security cooperation architecture" to be led by CICA so that Asian problems can "be solved by Asians themselves."[74] What sounded like a structure-upending move, however, proved to be little more than rhetorical in nature. The conference failed to take up Xi's call. CICA was too Central Asian in leadership and location;

its members were too many and too divided; and its focus on counterterrorism sidelined broader issues of Asian security.

Neither has the Hainan-based Boao Forum for Asia or the Beijing Xiangshan Forum successfully implemented Xi's Asia-for-Asians line. As for the Belt and Road Forum, held biennially in Beijing, those who attended in 2019 were reported to have come from "more than 150 countries"[75] — hardly a constituency for putting Asia first. China has been either unable or uneager to develop a Sinocentric set of Asianist alternatives to the multilateral platforms for regional security discourse that ASEAN continues to host. The unattractive aspects of Beijing's agency continue to hamper its ability to innovate and sustain a multilateral Sino-Southeast Asian "community of common destiny" structured to magnify China's influence.

The BRI is global in scope. If it succeeds, its infrastructural legacy of corridors, ports, and intersections could be used to propagate and institutionalize rules and models made in China, thereby amplifying the agency of Beijing. But that same connectivity could alienate host countries along the BRI's corridors for fear of what accelerated intimacy with China could bring, including the dangers of infection from viruses such as the one that arose in Wuhan in December 2019.

In the contest between agency and structure in American foreign policy under Trump, structure never had a chance. His presidential role in world affairs will likely be remembered for having displayed the obsessed agency unleashed by his own personality — narcissistic, vindictive, paranoid, mendacious, and willfully uninformed — locked in battle with less-than-properly sycophantic allies and with multilateral institutions whose plural nature necessarily denies him sole possession of the spotlight.

The good news for Southeast Asians as of 2019 was that Trump's propensity for chaos had not weakened their ability to exercise strategic autonomy vis-à-vis China. On the contrary, American steps toward counterbalancing China were undertaken more vigorously during Trump's tenure than they were during Obama's. Security cooperation between the United States and Southeast Asian partners helped to diversify the latter's foreign-policy options beyond simply deferring to China to protect themselves from being bullied by it.

More than 120 million votes were cast in the 2016 US presidential election. To widespread surprise, Trump won by a mere 107,000 votes in only three of the country's 50 states.[76] The unpredicted trumped the expected. Although Xi Jinping need not fear an election, changing conditions and "black swan" contingencies will alter China's future, too.[77] The decline in China's rate of economic growth could accelerate. China's bubble of debt could burst. Another virus in China could spiral out of control. Domestic discontent could stoke nationalist anger. Abroad, Xi's signature project, the BRI, could wind up costing China too much in red ink, failed projects, and lost goodwill. Party leaders could blame Xi for such failings and perhaps even challenge him, to further destabilizing effect.

China's deficit in soft power and its corresponding surplus in repellent power were amply evident in 2019. Along China's rim, thousands of young self-labeled Hong Kongers, by demonstrating for human rights and against Beijing, demonstrated the extent of Beijing's failure to appropriate their identity despite decades of legal and economic affiliation with the mainland. Among Taiwan's residents, China's importance to the island's economy could not slow the growth of a robustly local identity. Beijing's high-tech repression of Muslims in Xinjiang naturally stifled pro-China sentiment among their co-religionists elsewhere in the world. Chinese intimidation in the South China Sea, as in Xinjiang, suggested that Beijing would rather be feared than loved. However diverse these instances and consequences of agency were, they all implicated, first, Beijing's desire to convert imbalances of power into structures of control, and second, the difficulty and collateral damage that Xi's China faces in trying to bring that conversion about.

This is not to say that Xi's expansionist agenda cannot succeed. It could. It could even set the stage for the lasting hegemony of the PRC in Southeast Asia, or for the absorption of Laos and Cambodia into a "greater China," leaving a cluster of ASEAN's more maritime members to steer what is left of the group. Inside China, conceivably, a series of shocks, shortcomings, and protests could persuade Xi or a successor to engage in serious reform at home, enhance Chinese soft power abroad, and facilitate a stable trans-Pacific peace.

Conceivable, too, is a hot war between China and America that would originate in Southeast Asia and render fully kinetic the already worsening economic and diplomatic animosity between the two powers. Such a calamity is extremely unlikely, however, and especially so as a matter of unprovoked and premeditated official agency on Beijing's or Washington's part. An unwanted war could flare up from a match struck in the South China Sea. Sino-American naval jostling in those waters, however, has become almost routine. A full-spectrum effort to blockade the Malacca Strait could trigger a war, but the plausibility of an American or a Chinese motivation to take that precipitating step requires assumptions too strenuous to be plausible. More lethal risks lie in Northeast Asia or, beyond geography, in cyberspace.

This chapter has both featured and undermined the structural asymmetry that distinguishes China from Southeast Asia. Southeast Asia's diversity contributes to the region's political disunion by inhibiting strategic consensus and opening chances for China to divide and disable ASEAN. But that same variety helps to limit the effectiveness of a one-size-fits-all "Beijing way" of dealing with its neighbors.

The obsolescence of alliances and the shift to calibrated partnerships has benefited the strategic autonomy of individual ASEAN states by giving them options that were less available in the either-or context of the Cold War. Those national autonomies serve to remind Beijing not to rely too heavily on its success in neutering ASEAN as a strategic actor capable of standing up to China — an achievement already enabled by the group's intergovernmental rather than supranational design operating in tandem with the lowest-common-denominator ASEAN Way. At the same time, Southeast Asians who define and defend the centrality of ASEAN as a mere convener of meetings unintentionally frustrate the substantive centrality and creativity of Southeast Asian policymakers, not least by discouraging the formation of like-minded mini-coalitions inside ASEAN that could more effectively face China's overweening ambitions in the South China Sea. In this unpromising context, lacking the regional shield that ASEAN cannot provide, it makes sense for Vietnam and other member states to look for extra-regional partners while improving their national capacities for physical deterrence, notwithstanding China's size and strength.

If there is a single conclusion to be drawn from this chapter, it is this: The future of Southeast Asia will greatly and probably decisively depend on what its individual states themselves either do or fail to do. This expectation turns full circle back to the moral of the mousedeer story with which the chapter began. Not back to the romantic fantasy of go-it-alone heroism whereby a little chevrotain thwarts a big but stupid dragon using nothing more than a piece of rope and an obvious ploy. Back, instead, to the more useful understanding that strategic autonomy necessarily begins at home. Outsiders can help or hurt. But nothing can substitute for the creativity of Southeast Asian states in individual and joint pursuit of their own and their region's security.

Notes

1 "Countries in South-Eastern Asia," in "South-Eastern Asia
Population," Worldometer, accessed 13 October 2018, http://www
.worldometers.info/world-population/south-eastern-asia-population.

2 Without homogenizing let alone essentializing the different empirical
referents of "Han" ethnicity, suffice to note that an estimated 92 percent
of China's population are covered by that term. "Chinese Ethnic
Groups," Travel China Guide, https://www.travelchinaguide.com/intro
/nationality, based on the Fifth National Population Census (2000).

3 "Population of China (2018 and Historical)" and "South-Eastern Asia
Population (2018 and Historical)," Worldometer, accessed 13 October
2018, http://www.worldometers.info/world-population/south-eastern
-asia-population and http://www.worldometers.info/world-population/
china-population.

4 Sourced from the data portal *Statista*, https://www.statista.com
/statistics/263770/gross-domestic-product-gdp-of-china and https://
www.statista.com/statistics/796245/gdp-of-the-asean-countries on 2
February 2020.

5 This is not to suggest that Sino-Southeast Asian relations are
necessarily zero-sum. Brantly Womack has usefully argued, for example,
in his *China among Unequals: Asymmetric Foreign Relationships in
Asia* (Singapore: World Scientific, 2010), 3–4, that asymmetric relations
between a small state and a large one need not be unstable or hostile
if the former is willing to defer to the latter to gain the assurances that
the latter is willing and able to provide in return. He has also argued
that whereas asymmetric relations tend to be less subject to control
by the smaller country, the larger country tends to be less attentive
to their details. In principle, that relative lack of attention may allow
the smaller state a limited degree of freedom it might not otherwise
have. Of particular interest with reference to the mousedeer-dragon
analogy featured here, however, is his estimation that the smaller state,
compared with the larger one, "will be more agile and less trusting of
the overall climate of the relationship." For more, see his *Asymmetry
and International Relationships* (New York: Cambridge University
Press, 2016).

6 Graham Allison, *Destined for War: Can America and China Escape the
Thucydides Trap?* (New York: Houghton Mifflin, 2017).

7 For more, see Donald K. Emmerson, "ASEAN between China and America: Is It Time to Try Horsing the Cow?," *TRaNS: Trans -Regional and -National Studies of Southeast Asia* 5, no. 1 (January 2017): esp. 7–8 and, on Thucydides and Allison, 20–21, 23.

8 In other Southeast Asian cultures, other animals play the trickster role. In Laotian folklore, for example, a rabbit and a monkey respectively outwit an elephant and a crocodile. See Regina Beach, "11 Fascinating Lao Folk Tales and Legends," *Culture Trip*, 7 November 2018, https://theculturetrip.com/asia/laos/articles/11-fascinating-lao-myths-and -legends.

9 "Pelanduk Mengalahkan Naga Yang Rakus" [Mouse deer defeats greedy dragon], Sekumpulan Cerita's Blog, 4 June 2010, https://sekumpulancerita.wordpress.com/2010/06/04/pelanduk-mengalahkan -naga-yang-rakus.

10 China uses the term "win-win" loosely and often. It appeared, for example, four times and "all-win" once in a single paragraph of Xi Jinping's keynote speech at the Boao Forum for Asia on China's Hainan Island on 29 March 2015, as seen on China.org.cn, http://www.china .org.cn/business/2015-03/29/content_35185720.htm. (On the implications of a genuine "win-win" for China's soft power in the region, see Evelyn Goh, "The Modes of China's Influence: Cases from Southeast Asia," *Asian Survey* 54, no. 5 [2014], https://as.ucpress.edu/content/54/5/825.) Nor does official Chinese secrecy regarding the PRC's aid to other countries facilitate the calculation of proportional gains in welfare.

11 "China Wants No Talk of South China Sea at Tuesday's Asean Meeting in Kuala Lumpur," *South China Morning Post*, 3 August 2015, https://www.scmp.com/news/china/diplomacy-defence/article/1846145 /china-wants-no-talk-south-china-sea-tuesdays-asean. Knowledgeable ASEAN diplomats told this chapter's author of being warned not even to gather informally in an unscheduled meeting with one another to discuss and determine a unified position that would only later be conveyed to Beijing.

12 As she explained in her "Press Availability," U.S. Department of State, Hanoi, 23 July 2010, https://2009-2017.state.gov/secretary/20092013 clinton/rm/2010/07/145095.htm.

13 John Pomfret, "U.S. Takes a Tougher Tone with China," *Washington Post*, 30 July 2010, http://www.washingtonpost.com/wp-dyn/content /article/2010/07/29/AR2010072906416.html. Also see Donald K.

Emmerson, "Singapore and Goliath?," *Journal of Democracy* 290, no. 2 (April 2018): 76–82.

14 Requoted by Major Bernard Tay, "Is the SAF's Defence Posture Still Relevant as the Nature of Warfare Continues to Evolve?," *Pointer, Journal of the Singapore Armed Forces* 42, no. 2 (2016): 33, n. 4, https:// www.mindef.gov.sg/oms/safti/pointer/documents/pdf/Vol42No2_3%20 SAF%27s%20Defence.pdf.

15 Tay, "Is the SAF's Defence Posture," 25, including n. 8 on 33.

16 "Southeast Asia: Defence Spending as % GDP, 1993–2018," in Tim Huxley, "Why Asia's 'Arms Race' Is Not Quite What It Seems," World Economic Forum, 12 September 2018, https://www.weforum.org/agenda /2018/09/asias-arms-race-and-why-it-doesnt-matter. Although this source omits Laos for lack of recent data, in 2013 its military spending was thought to be a mere one-fifth of 1 percent of its GDP; "Laos — Military Expenditure (% of GDP)," Trading Economics, accessed 3 March 2019, https://tradingeconomics.com/laos/military-expenditure-percent-of-gdp -wb-data.html.

17 See, e.g., Prashanth Parameswaran, "Cambodia Boosts Defense Budget for 2016," *The Diplomat*, 3 December 2015, https://thediplomat .com/2015/12/cambodia-boosts-defense-budget-for-2016.

18 "Southeast Asian Powers Ranked by Military Strength," Global-Firepower, accessed 3 March 2019, https://www.globalfirepower.com /countries-listing-southeast-asia.asp. Brunei is omitted, and beyond their apparent emphasis on quantity, the proprietary methods used to generate the ranking are unclear.

19 See "Military Capability," "Overall Power," and "Methodology," in "Asia Power Index 2018," Lowy Institute, Sydney, accessed 3 March 2019, https://power.lowyinstitute.org.

20 *Mutual Defense Treaty Between the United States and the Republic of the Philippines; August 30, 1951*, Lillian Goldman Law Library, Yale Law School, New Haven, CT, https://avalon.law.yale.edu/20th_century/phil001 .asp, Articles III-V.

21 *Southeast Asia Collective Defense Treaty (Manila Pact); September 8, 1954*, Lillian Goldman Law Library, Yale Law School, https://avalon .law.yale.edu/20th_century/usmu003.asp, Article IV. The body that would have implemented the treaty was dissolved in 1977.

22 See John Reed, "Pompeo Assures Philippines of Mutual Defence in South China Sea," *Financial Times*, 1 March 2019, https://www.ft.com/content/d7bee564-3bf8-11e9-b72b-2c7f526ca5d0.

23 See, e.g., Niharika Mandhana, "China's Fishing Militia Swarms Philippine Island, Seeking Edge in Sea Dispute," *Wall Street Journal*, 4 April 2019, https://www.wsj.com/articles/chinas-fishing-militia-swarms-philippine-island-seeking-edge-in-sea-dispute-11554391301.

24 Lara Tan, "Lorenzana Warns of 'Chaos during Crisis' with So-called Vague US-PH Defense Treaty," CNN Philippines, 5 March 2019, https://cnnphilippines.com/cnn-website/search/2019/3/5/US-Philippines-mutual-defense-treaty.html.

25 Patricia Lourdes Viray, "Lorenzana Contradicts Locsin on US-Philippines Treaty Review," *Philstar Global*, https://www.philstar.com/headlines/2019/03/05/1898877/lorenzana-contradicts-locsin-us-philippines-treaty-review.

26 "List of Wars Involving Vietnam," Wikipedia, https://en.wikipedia.org/wiki/List_of_wars_involving_Vietnam. The "Chinese" opponents of "Vietnam" in these engagements included, chronologically, the Qin and Han Empires, the Wu, the Liang, the Sui, the Great Tang, the Great Han, the Great Song, the Mongol Empire, the Great Yuan, the Great Ming, and the PRC.

27 Nguyen Minh Quang, "The Bitter Legacy of the 1979 China-Vietnam War," *The Diplomat*, 23 February 2017, https://thediplomat.com/2017/02/the-bitter-legacy-of-the-1979-china-vietnam-war/.

28 Peter Tsouras, "War of the Dragons: The Sino-Vietnamese War, 1979," *Military History Magazine*, 11 April 2016, https://www.historynet.com/war-of-the-dragons-the-sino-vietnamese-war-1979.htm. That Tsouras should have elevated Vietnam to dragon status alongside China adds metaphorical cachet to a country that has earned that appellation from other analysts as well, in keeping with the prominence of dragons in both Vietnamese and Chinese culture and folklore.

29 See, e.g., King C. Chen, "China's War against Vietnam, 1979: A Military Analysis," *Journal of East Asian Affairs* 3, no. 1 (Spring/Summer 1983): 233–63; and Markus B. Liegi, *China's Use of Military Force in Foreign Affairs: The Dragon Strikes* (New York: Routledge, 2017), 214.

30 Chinese footage of the massacre was included (4:57–6:19) in a pro-Hanoi film created with the help of "some Vietnamese students in Germany" in May 2009. Ten years later the video had garnered more than

1.6 million views on YouTube. See "Evidence[s] of China's Crime: The Spratly Islands Massacre," accessed 5 March 2019, https://www.youtube.com/watch?v=Uy2ZrFphSmc; and Greg Torode, "Spratly Islands Dispute Defines China-Vietnam Relations 25 Years after Naval Clash," *South China Morning Post*, 17 March 2013, https://www.scmp.com/news/asia/article/1192472/spratly-islands-dispute-defines-china-vietnam-relations-25-years-after.

31 For example: Nguyen Phuong Linh and Michael Martina, "South China Sea Tensions Rise as Vietnam Says China Rammed Ships," Reuters, 6 May 2014, https://www.reuters.com/article/us-china-seas-fishermen/south-china-sea-tensions-rise-as-vietnam-says-china-rammed-ships-idUSBREA4603C20140507.

32 Felix Heiduk, "An Arms Race in Southeast Asia? Changing Arms Dynamics, Regional Security and the Role of European Arms Exports," SWP Research Paper 10, German Institute for International and Security Affairs, Berlin, August 2017, 5, 20, https://www.swp-berlin.org/en/publication/an-arms-race-in-southeast-asia.

33 Edu Pinay, "Philippines Capability to Stop Ship Intrusions 'Very Weak,'" *Philippine Star*, 28 August 2019, https://www.philstar.com/headlines/2019/08/28/1947073/philippines-capability-stop-ship-intrusions-very-weak-dnd.

34 Jim Gomez, "Duterte: Can't Stop China in Disputed Seas, Won't Risk Clash," AP News, 22 July 2019, https://apnews.com/841e38011f084772be1bb74199f9235e.

35 Derek Grossman and Dung Huynh, "Vietnam's Defense Policy of 'No' Quietly Saves Room for 'Yes,'" *The Diplomat*, 19 January 2019, https://thediplomat.com/2019/01/vietnams-defense-policy-of-no-quietly-saves-room-for-yes.

36 Peter Rathmell, "Navy to Train with Vietnam amid Rising Tensions with China," *Navy Times*, 6 July 2017, https://www.navytimes.com/news/your-navy/2017/07/06/navy-to-train-with-vietnam-amid-rising-tensions-with-china.

37 The cautionary "in effect" references Timor-Leste. Respectively small and tiny in physical and economic size, it enjoys little to no regional influence as it hopes and waits to become ASEAN's 11th member. See Truston Jianheng Yu, "2019: The Year of Timor Leste in ASEAN?" *Jakarta Post*, 13 December 2018, http://bit.ly/2LkwPFd.

38 Rann Reuy, "Cambodia Takes $430m China Loan," *Phnom Penh Post*, 14 June 2012, https://www.phnompenhpost.com/business/cambodia -takes-430m-china-loan; and Alex Willemyns, "Cambodia Blocks Asean Statement on South China Sea," *Cambodia Daily*, 25 July 2016, https:// www.cambodiadaily.com/news/cambodia-blocks-asean-statement-on -south-china-sea-115834.

39 Reuters, "China Gives Cambodia Aid and Thanks for ASEAN Help," 4 September 2012, http://reut.rs/O86FFo. A Southeast Asian analyst familiar with the proceedings told this author in November 2012 that Chinese diplomats had been phoning guidance to the Cambodians while the meeting was taking place.

40 See Peter Tan Keo, "Corruption in Cambodia?," *The Diplomat*, 10 December 2013, https://thediplomat.com/2013/12/corruption-in-cambod ia; and Euan Black, "Cambodia Still Most Corrupt Country in Southeast Asia, Says Transparency International," *Southeast Asia Globe*, 26 January 2017, https://southeastasiaglobe.com/cambodia-still-corrupt-country -southeast-asia-says-transparency-international.

41 Bhubhindar Singh, Shawn Ho, and Henrick Z. Tsjeng, "China's Bogus South China Sea 'Consensus,'" *National Interest*, 14 June 2016, https:// nationalinterest.org/feature/chinas-bogus-south-china-sea-consensus -16589.

42 Jack Davies, "Gov't Plays Down ASEAN Split over South China Sea," *Phnom Penh Post*, 26 April 2016, https://www.phnompenhpost.com /national/govt-plays-down-asean-split-over-south-china-sea.

43 Singh, Ho, and Tsjeng, "China's Bogus South China Sea 'Consensus.'"

44 Tang Siew Mun, "Hang Together or Hang Separately?," *Straits Times*, 12 May 2016, http://str.sg/4o5U.

45 See "Media Statement by the Asean Foreign Ministers after the Special Asean-China Foreign Ministers' Meeting in Kunming, Yunnan Province, China, 14 June 2016." The retracted statement was still accessible as of 29 March 2019 at https://asean.org/storage/2012/05/MEDIA-STATEMENT -BY-THE-ASEAN-FOREIGN-MINISTERS-AFTER-THE-SPECIAL -ASEAN-CHINA-FOREIGN-MINISTERS%E2%80%99-MEETING -IN-KUNMING-YUNNAN-PROVINCE-CHINA-14-JUNE-2016.pdf.

46 For more, see Prasanth Parameswaran, "What Really Happened at the ASEAN-China Special Kunming Meeting," *The Diplomat*, 21 June 2016, https://thediplomat.com/2016/06/what-really-happened-at-the-asean -china-special-kunming-meeting; and Rozanna Latiff, "Southeast Asian

Countries Retract Statement Expressing Concerns on South China Sea," Reuters, 15 June 2016, http://reut.rs/21lLEYG.

47 Richard Heydarian, "Under Duterte, Philippines Enjoying An Investment Boom, But Don't Thank China," *Forbes*, 25 March 2018, https://www.forbes.com/sites/richardheydarian/2018/03/25/under-duterte -philippines-enjoying-an-investment-boom-but-dont-thank-china.

48 With an estimated annual budget of merely $20 million and only 300 staff in 2016, the ASEAN secretariat is expected to organize more than a thousand meetings every year. Nor does the funding and staffing appear to have increased significantly in response to higher workloads; the roughly 300 figure for staff, e.g., remained constant in 2014–18. By comparison, in 2018, the secretariats of the European Union had some $220 billion to spend annually and roughly 43,000 employees. "'No Reforms' for ASEAN Anytime Soon," *Jakarta Post*, 25 November 2017, https://www.thejakartapost.com/seasia/2017/11/25/no-reforms-for-asean -anytime-soon.html; and "EU Administration — Staff, Languages and Location," European Union, https://europa.eu/european-union/about-eu /figures/administration_en. Deepak Nair deserves thanks for his input regarding the size of ASEAN's staff.

49 "ASEAN Outlook on the Indo-Pacific," 23 June 2019, https://asean .org/storage/2019/06/ASEAN-Outlook-on-the-Indo-Pacific_FINAL_2206 2019.pdf.

50 *Master Plan on ASEAN Connectivity 2025* (Jakarta: ASEAN Secretariat, August 2016), 39, https://asean.org/storage/2016/09/Master -Plan-on-ASEAN-Connectivity-20251.pdf.

51 Joycee A. Teodoro, "ASEAN's Connectivity Challenge," *The Diplomat*, 27 June 2015, https://thediplomat.com/2015/06/aseans-conn ectivity-challenge.

52 See, for example, Diana J. Mendoza, "The Belt and Road Initiative and ASEAN: Cooperation or Opportunism?," *BusinessWorld*, 12 November 2018, https://www.bworldonline.com/the-belt-and-road- initiative-and-aseancooperation-or-opportunism; and Bertil Lintner, "China Winning New Cold War on the Mekong," *Asia Times*, 24 June 2019, https://www.asiatimes.com/2019/06/article/china-winning-new- cold-war-on-the-mekong.

53 James Crabtree, "China Needs to Make BRI More Transparent and Predictable," *Financial Times*, 25 April 2019, https://www.ft.com/con tent/3c5d6d14-66ac-11e9-b809-6f0d2f5705f6.

54 Wang is quoted in Wu Gang, "SOEs Lead Infrastructure Push in 1,700 'Belt and Road' Projects," *Caixin Global* (Beijing), 10 May 2017, https://www.caixinglobal.com/2017-05-10/soes-lead-infrastructure-push-in-1700-belt-and-road-projects-101088332.html.

55 Syed Ali Nawaz Gilani, "Europe Needs to Unite with China's Belt & Road Initiative," *China Daily*, 9 April 2019, https://www.chinadaily.com.cn/a/201904/09/WS5cac5f99a3104842260b53b0.html. *China Daily* is published by the Publicity Department of the Communist Party of China. According to the official "Belt and Road Portal," as of July 2019, two months later, only 136 countries had concluded "cooperation agreements" with the PRC.

56 Xinhua, "Xi Gives New Impetus to Belt and Road Initiative," *China Daily*, 28 August 2018, https://www.chinadaily.com.cn/a/201808/28/WS5b84994fa310add14f388114.html. See also "BRI: A Boon to the World," *China Today* 67, no. 10 (October 2018): 19.

57 "'Eight Requirements' in 'The Belt and Road,'" Guidance under the Office of the Leading Group for the Belt and Road Initiative Hosted by the State Information Center, *Belt and Road Portal*, accessed 20 January 2020, https://eng.yidaiyilu.gov.cn/ztindex.htm.

58 "Concerted coordination" is the third of the "Eight Requirements."

59 Interview with a knowledgeable analyst, San Diego, CA, 26 January 2016.

60 Yukako Ono, "China's High-speed Railway Ambitions Hit Snags," *NIKKEI Asian Review*, 21 December 2017, https://asia.nikkei.com/Politics/China-s-high-speed-railway-ambitions-hit-snags.

61 S. M. Tang et al., *The State of Southeast Asia: 2020 Survey Report* (Singapore: ISEAS-Yusof Ishak, January 2020), 1, 5, https://www.iseas.edu.sg/images/pdf/TheStateofSEASurveyReport_2020.pdf. Percentage shares by country of residence were: Brunei (7), Cambodia (2), Indonesia (11), Laos (2), Malaysia (13), Philippines (11), Singapore (17), Thailand (7), and Vietnam (12). In relations to the sizes of their populations, Indonesia and Singapore were, respectively, under- and over-represented.

62 Xi Jinping, "Working Together to Deliver a Brighter Future for Belt and Road Cooperation," keynote speech, Second Belt and Road Forum for International Cooperation, Beijing, PRC Ministry of Foreign Affairs, 26 April 2019, https://www.fmprc.gov.cn/mfa_eng/zxxx_662805/t1658424.shtml; and Chun Han Wong and James T. Areddy, "China's Xi Vows New Direction for 'Belt and Road' After Criticism," *Wall Street Journal*,

26 April 2019, https://www.wsj.com/articles/chinas-xi-vows-new-direct
ion-for-belt-and-road-after-criticism-11556249652.

63 Natnicha Chuwiruch and Philip Heijmans, "Asean Leaders Snub U.S.
Summit After Trump Skips Bangkok Meeting," Bloomberg, 4 November
2019, https://www.bloomberg.com/news/articles/2019-11-04/asean
-leaders-snub-u-s-summit-after-trump-skips-bangkok-meeting.

64 Tang et al., *State of Southeast Asia*, 43 and 50. In this source, "2019"
and "2020" are years of publication. The surveys were conducted,
respectively, in 2018 and 2019.

65 Tang et al., *State of Southeast Asia*, 35.

66 Jinghao Zhou, "China's Core Interests and Dilemma in Foreign Policy
Practice," *Pacific Focus* 34, no. 1 (April 2019): 31–54, https://onlinelibrary
.wiley.com/doi/full/10.1111/pafo.12131.

67 Kishore Mahbubani, "Qatar: Big Lessons from a Small Country,"
Straits Times, 1 July 2017, http://str.sg/4aqG; and Belmont Lay,
"Ambassador-at-large Bilahari Kausikan Rebuts LKY School of Public
Policy Dean Kishore Mahbubani," Mothership, 2 July 2017, https://
mothership.sg/2017/07/ambassador-at-large-bilahari-kausikan-rebuts-lky
-school-of-public-policy-dean-kishore-mahbubani. For more, including
the context, see Emmerson, "Singapore and Goliath?"

68 Nadège Rolland, "Eurasian Integration 'a la Chinese': Deciphering
Beijing's Vision for the Region as a 'Community of Common Destiny,'"
Asan Forum, 5 June 2017, http://www.theasanforum.org/eurasian-integ
ration-a-la-chinese-deciphering-beijings-vision-for-the-region-as-a
-community-of-common-destiny.

69 Dewi Fortuna Anwar, "ASEAN Amidst the US-China Rivalry,"
ASEANFocus 6 (2018), 6–7, https://www.iseas.edu.sg/images/pdf/ASEAN
Focus_December2018_Final.pdf.

70 Ibid.

71 See Carlyle A. Thayer, "ASEAN and the South China Sea: A Dual
Track Approach?," High-Level International Workshop on Managing
the South China Sea Conflict from an ASEAN Perspective, Center
for Southeast Asian Studies, Jakarta, Indonesia, 26 June 2015, 15–16,
including the references in n. 26, https://www.scribd.com/document
/269815799/Thayer-ASEAN-and-the-South-China-Sea-A-Dual-Track
-Approach (registration required).

72 Personal communications, 3 November 2015 and 15 June 2019.

73 Nadège Rolland, *China's Vision for a New World Order*, Special Report #83, National Bureau of Asian Research, Seattle, Washington, January 2020, 40–41, 44–47, https://www.nbr.org/wp-content/uploads /pdfs/publications/sr83_chinasvision_jan2020.pdf.

74 Shannon Tiezzi, "At CICA, Xi Calls for New Regional Security Architecture," *The Diplomat*, 22 May 2014, https://thediplomat.com /2014/05/at-cica-xi-calls-for-new-regional-security-architecture.

75 State media estimates cited by Ben Westcott and Nanlin Fang, "China's Billion-dollar Belt and Road Party: Who's in and Who's out," CNN, 26 April 2019, https://www.cnn.com/2019/04/26/asia/belt-and -road-summit-beijing-intl/index.html.

76 Tim Meko, Denise Lu, and Lazaro Gamio, "How Trump Won the Presidency with Razor-thin Margins in Swing States," *Washington Post*, 11 November 2016, https://www.washingtonpost.com/graphics/politics /2016-election/swing-state-margins.

77 John Jullens, "China: The Mother of All Black Swans," *Strategy+Business*, 11 July 2013, https://sb.stratbz.to/2w0z90r.

CHAPTER 2

China's Changing Priorities in Southeast Asia
SECURITY AND DEVELOPMENT IN HISTORICAL CONTEXT

Thomas Fingar, *Stanford University, United States*

Official descriptions of China's policies toward other countries typically cite abstract principles and typologies as the basis for understanding Beijing's priorities and policies. In 2017, for example, a Chinese white paper on Asia-Pacific cooperation referenced the "Five Principles of Peaceful Coexistence," aimed at "mutually beneficial" outcomes, and distinguished unspecified "major" from "small and medium-sized" countries.[1] In earlier statements, the "first," "second," and "third worlds" stood respectively for major powers, neighboring states, and developing countries.[2] Such generalities are superficially clear, but they are not very helpful for comprehending, explaining, or predicting China's interactions with the countries of Southeast Asia or anywhere else. China, like all other countries, may sometimes speak or act in ways inconsistent with its declared principles. At a regional security forum in Hanoi in 2010, for example, then foreign minister Yang Jiechi pointedly told his Southeast Asian counterparts: "China is a big country, other countries are small countries, and that's just a fact."[3]

Contrary to the uniformity implied by these generalizations, a comparative analysis of China's interactions with other countries over recent decades reveals both the diversity of ways in which China has interacted with them and the consistent patterns underlying that behavior. Explanations of that behavior can then be sought in the answers to three empirical questions: how a country relates to China's security, what the country can contribute to China's drive to develop its economy, and what the country in question wants from China.[4]

Security and Development: Priority Concerns

Security and development have long been priority Chinese concerns. They were key considerations in Mao Zedong's decision to align with the Soviet Union within weeks of proclaiming the establishment of the People's Republic of China (PRC) in 1949. Ideological affinity and prior history doubtless influenced Mao's decision to "lean" to the Soviet side in a then emerging bipolar world.[5] More important, however, were his judgments that the United States and "the imperialists" posed a threat to China's security that had to be counterbalanced, and that Stalin would help China develop its economy.

Stalin's vision of "multiple autarky" for nations in the "socialist camp" was fully consistent with Mao's aspirations to transform China into a rich and powerful nation. Mao nevertheless broke with Moscow in the late 1950s and launched a series of ill-conceived and unsuccessful attempts to accelerate China's modernization through politically induced change.[6] Mao's search for a uniquely Chinese path to modernity had left China weaker and less developed than the countries it feared and wished to overtake. To make up for lost time and reduce China's vulnerability, Deng Xiaoping and other veteran party leaders abandoned experimentation in favor of the approach to development that had enabled Japan and Taiwan to modernize more quickly than the PRC.[7]

In order to risk — or justify — the shift from Mao's extremely "self-reliant" strategy of development, Deng and his colleagues reassessed and redefined China's security situation and developed new methods for managing threats from abroad. They abandoned Mao's judgment that war with China's adversaries was both inevitable and imminent. They replaced it with Deng's assertion that war was still inevitable but, thanks to changes in the international system and imagined successes during the Maoist era, no longer imminent. This gave China a window of opportunity to pursue rapid modernization with the goal of making China stronger and more independent, the better to deter or defeat aggression against it.

The interconnected goals — security and development — became the most important determinants of Chinese policy toward specific countries in the post-Mao era. The starting points for determining whether and how to engage a particular country appear to have been twofold: an assessment of the extent to which a country endangered or strengthened China's security, combined with an assessment of that country's ability to contribute to China's quest for development. Countries at the top of Beijing's list of foreign-policy concerns were of two kinds: those seen as posing the greatest direct threat to China (or as most able and likely to counterbalance a serious threat from elsewhere), and those most able and potentially willing to assist China's drive for rapid development (by providing what China needed most in the successive stages of its development). Lower priorities were reserved for countries that posed lesser dangers and were less able to contribute to China's development.

This framework is neither static nor merely historical. Actual and perceived threats continue to change over time, as do China's developmental needs and the actual and perceived potentials of other countries to meet those needs. As these variables change, specific Chinese goals and policies vis-à-vis other countries change as well. A similar dynamic shapes the ways that other countries perceive China's actions, intentions, and potential threats to, or opportunities for, the attainment of these countries' own policy objectives. The results are a vector: the outcome of interaction between Chinese and other-country moves and responses. The focus of this chapter is on China's perceptions of Southeast Asia and its goals and actions regarding the region; other chapters take up the reverse side of the equation.

FIGURE 2.1 China's perceptions of security threats and development contributions by world region as of 1979

Perceived regional contribution to China's development	Perceived regional threat to China's security: **High**	Perceived regional threat to China's security: **Low**
High	North America (US) Northeast Asia (Japan)	Europe
Low	Eurasia (USSR)	Africa (sub-Saharan) Latin America Middle East South and Central Asia Southeast Asia

SOURCE: Author.

NOTE: In this and the following figures, the ranking of regions is alphabetical and does not indicate intensity. These are snapshots at one point in time; relative positions can shift over time.

Figure 2.1 offers a global context for China's relations with Southeast Asia by comparing this author's judgments as to how that region and others were viewed by China in 1979 along this chapter's organizing dimensions—security and development. The diagram is a snapshot approximation of how Beijing appears to have assessed the relative importance of different parts of the world in that twice-pivotal year. Twice-pivotal because it was then—three decades after the PRC's birth, three years after Mao's death—that two turning points occurred. In January 1979, diplomatic relations were finally established between China and the United States. In February, China invaded Vietnam, triggering a brief but bloody war along their shared land border.

Placement of the regions in Figure 2.1 is subjective and based mainly on the observed sequence and manner in which Beijing sought to engage countries in different regions. By crossing security and development, the matrix assumes that these were Beijing's priority concerns: to address what it saw as the greatest regional threats to its security and the greatest regional potentials for speeding its development. Chinese animosity toward Vietnam was of course high. But China's leaders believed they had taught Vietnam a proper "lesson" for having overthrown China's Khmer Rouge ally in Phnom Penh, and there was little to fear from the Americans following their earlier defeat in Vietnam. Nor had Washington risen to its former enemy's defense. Further reassurance could be drawn from the normalization of Sino-American relations. That said, in Beijing's eyes, the United States still posed a potential threat far greater than any that Southeast Asia could muster.

Figure 2.1 argues accordingly that in 1979 Southeast Asia was seen by Beijing as posing a relatively low level of threat to China, while also relatively unable or unlikely to do much to alleviate threats to China coming from elsewhere in the world. The diagram also represents a perception by Beijing that the region had little to offer by way of the training, technology, capital, and markets that China needed to jump-start its quest for modernization. Perception aside, the ways in which China has actually interacted with Southeast Asia—before 1979 and during the phases of China's subsequent rise—are examined below.

Setting the Stage:
China's Relations with Southeast Asia before 1979

For hundreds of years, geography was the most important factor shaping China's perceptions, concerns, and interactions with the peoples and states of Southeast Asia. Proximity facilitated interaction and made it difficult for mainland Southeast Asians to avoid being influenced if not dominated by their much larger neighbor to the north. The extent of such dominion waxed and waned, primarily as a function of how effectively successive Chinese dynasties managed domestic challenges and how much attention they could devote to "vassal" kingdoms beyond the border of China proper. China's version of history maintains that the vassal states accepted and even desired Chinese dominance because of their respect and admiration for their neighbor's superior culture. Southeast Asian historians differ. In reality, China's influence was greatest when China was strong and least when China was weak.[8]

The extent of China's influence was also a function of India's relative power and, beginning in the late 18th century, the extent to which Western powers were able to insert themselves into the region. Chinese tend to emphasize the expansionist and aggressive designs of the European states and downplay the desire of Southeast Asians for partners able to counterbalance China, and to downplay as well the importance of China's own internal problems. History rendered in this way taught two lessons that continue to shape Chinese views of the region. The first is the long-standing belief that *mainland Southeast Asia — more recently, the adjacent waters as well — belongs within China's natural and rightful sphere of influence.*[9] The second is that *the region is critical to China's own security*, and that when outside powers insinuated themselves into the region, they weakened and constrained China and contributed to the breakdown of domestic order in the Middle Kingdom.[10] Taken together, these two lessons cause China to view with displeasure and concern involvement in the region by major outside powers, and to view interaction with such powers involving Southeast Asia as a zero-sum struggle to defend China's influence and decrease its vulnerability.[11]

History and proximity are relevant to China's engagement with the region after 1979 in another important way, namely, the presence and status of Chinese-diasporic populations throughout the region. Generally, these communities had not been well integrated into the larger society. They retained imagined if not real ties to their homeland. They were found mainly in urban areas, where they engaged in trade and mercantile activities, and they often acquired more wealth than the native populations among whom they lived. Such diasporic groups played a role in the competition between Beijing and Taipei for influence and diplomatic recognition, in China's efforts to subvert indigenous governments, and in the forging of economic ties with China in the post-1979 era of its reform and opening.[12]

The salience of security concerns and the lessons of history gave rise to or were reflected in a series of quite different Chinese policies toward Southeast Asia during the period from 1949 to 1979. The first phase of PRC policy toward the region was the product of China's desire to exclude other powers from the region, not including the Soviet Union with which Beijing was aligned through the 1950s. Opposed to French efforts to retain control of Indochina, China recognized the Democratic Republic of Vietnam soon after it was formed in 1950. Determined to limit the influence of the former colonial powers and dissuade the newly independent states of the region from joining the "imperialist camp," Beijing established diplomatic ties with Burma (Myanmar) and Indonesia despite their imputed "bourgeois" character. Another factor was China's desire to bolster its legitimacy — and security — by persuading countries to switch recognition from the Republic of China to the PRC.[13]

Beijing's efforts to persuade Southeast Asian nations not to join the "imperialist camp" acquired more urgency after Thailand and the Philippines joined the Southeast Asia Treaty Organization in 1954. "Nonalignment" and the "solidarity" of newly independent and developing countries were concepts originated by India and Indonesia but quickly embraced by China, in part because nonalignment held the promise of preventing states in the region (and elsewhere) from forging relations with major powers that could jeopardize China's security. Determined to prevent the United States from intervening and insinuating itself further into the region, at the 1954 Geneva Conference China pressed for an immediate ceasefire in Indochina, the neutralization of Laos and Cambodia, and the temporary partitioning of Vietnam. Beijing wanted to end fighting between the northern and southern parts of Vietnam in order to deprive the United States of an excuse to intervene in ways that would threaten China's security.[14]

In the 1960s Mao's decision to break with the Soviet Union and Washington's increasing involvement in Vietnam changed China's view of its own security, including its policies toward Southeast Asia. The ideological rift with Moscow transformed China-USSR relations in the region from partnership to rivalry. Seen from Beijing, Moscow's engagement with states in the region was intended to surround and constrain the PRC.[15] The Soviet Union was viewed as intruding into China's rightful sphere of influence. Countering Soviet influence in the region became a priority objective of Chinese foreign policy.

One of the ways Beijing sought to counter and contain Soviet influence was by competing for the loyalty of communist parties across Southeast Asia. This competition took many forms. They ranged from the provision of economic and military assistance to the Democratic Republic of Vietnam, then the only communist-party-led state in the region, to rhetorical and material support for communist-led or affiliated insurgencies in Cambodia, Laos, Indonesia, Malaysia, and elsewhere. The Chinese maintained that such support for insurgencies did not violate the five principles of peaceful coexistence among governments because it was undertaken through party-to-party relations. Beijing's casuistry reassured few in the region.

The ethnic-Chinese diaspora in Southeast Asia afforded Beijing another way to gain and exercise influence in its competition with Moscow. Chinese immigrants had long been discriminated against, and most communist groups were established in urban areas where many Chinese lived. Exerting influence through local communist parties and local Chinese communities became a way to counter Moscow's superior ability to provide material support to the national governments being challenged by the leftist insurgencies that China backed. Beijing's efforts cleverly capitalized on this way of offsetting the asymmetry with Moscow. But except in the case of Cambodia, Beijing's approach proved largely counterproductive, with long-term negative consequences for its relations with the region.

Increased US support for the Republic of Vietnam (South Vietnam), enabled by the terms agreed to by the major powers in Geneva, more directly threatened China's own security, not the outcome desired by Beijing when it pressed Ho Chi Minh to accept the agreement's terms. Helping North Vietnam defeat the United States acquired high priority in Chinese foreign policy as a way of diminishing the American threat to China while rivaling Soviet support to Hanoi in order to counter Moscow's influence as well. Perhaps the best indicator of how important these goals were to Beijing is the amount of assistance provided to Vietnam during a period in which the Cultural Revolution convulsed China and the country's own economy was in shambles.[16]

This brief summary of the evolution of PRC views of and policies toward Southeast Asia before 1979 ignores many important details and differences among countries in the region, but it highlights patterns and priorities useful for analyzing what happened after the beginning of reform and opening in December 1978. Worth noting in that context are these features of the pre-1979 period: 1) *the extent to which Chinese policies were shaped by security concerns and the range of options for countering and mitigating threats seen to come primarily from external powers (the United States and, later, the Soviet Union); 2) the limited extent of China's interactions with Southeast Asian governments (except Vietnam and Cambodia); 3) the ultimately negative and counterproductive effects of Beijing's pursuit of its objectives by working through communist insurgents and the Chinese diaspora;* and 4) *the low salience and limited scope of economic considerations involving Southeast Asia.*[17] These were not the only factors shaping Chinese (and Southeast Asian) perceptions in 1979, but they certainly were among the most important.

From 1979 to 1990: More Continuity than Change

Figure 2.1 depicts the author's estimate of threats to China's security and the contributions to its development, real or potential, that Beijing associated with different world regions in 1979. In Beijing's eyes, Southeast Asia was less important on one or both of these dimensions than were other regions (including the US-in-North-America, Japan-in-Northeast-Asia, and the USSR-in-Eurasia). Beijing gave greater urgency to countering threats and obtaining high-priority development inputs — capital, technology, training, and markets — originating elsewhere in the world. Southeast Asia was not unimportant. But at the start of the reform-and-opening phase, it was less important to Beijing than were other regions, or than it would become later during China's rise.

Supporting this judgment is the sequence in which Beijing expanded and deepened its engagement with particular regions. No region was ever neglected completely, and the scope of China's engagement with multiple regions and countries accelerated simultaneously over time. But for the first decade after 1979, the broad pattern of Chinese interactions centered on the United States, Western Europe, and Japan. Southeast Asia and South Korea began to receive noticeably greater attention only in the 1990s. Only later did China's engagement with South and Central Asia, the Middle East, sub-Saharan Africa, and Latin America pick up speed.[18]

Generalizations at the regional level are useful. But Chinese decision-makers certainly did not adopt a one-size-fits-all approach in their dealings with the countries of Southeast Asia or any other region. Within Southeast Asia, for example, at the start of the period examined here, Beijing cared more about the security threat from Vietnam than it did about Singapore or Indonesia, and Chinese leaders knew, for instance, that Singapore potentially could contribute more to China's modernization than could Laos or Cambodia. The author's assessment of the relative positions of the states in the region on the threat-help matrix as of 1979 is depicted in Figure 2.2.

At the beginning of 1979, China was still adjusting to the end of the Vietnam War and how it might impact China's security. The United States had withdrawn all troops from Vietnam, but Hanoi had aligned with Moscow, ousted China's Khmer Rouge allies from Cambodia, and gained more influence in Laos than Beijing enjoyed. The United States remained allied with Thailand and the Philippines. But the perceived threat from Washington and its allies was lower and more long term than that posed by Moscow and its allies in mainland Southeast Asia. China's rivalry with the Soviet Union during the 1960s and '70s had helped to improve Beijing's relations with Washington, culminating in the establishment of diplomatic ties on 1 January 1979. But the methods China had used to counter Soviet influence in Indochina had failed.

Beijing's policy regarding Southeast Asia in early 1979 reflected other calculations as well. One was a judgment that the region had little to contribute to the first phase of China's quest for development because it lacked the technology and investment capital that China needed, and its markets were too small to kick-start export-led growth. This meant that China need not make a special effort to improve relations and build engagements with countries and companies in the region. It also meant that if China wished to take actions to improve its security that might affect Southeast Asians, it could do so without jeopardizing their contributions to its development.

FIGURE 2.2 China's perceptions of security threats and development contributions by Southeast Asian country as of 1979

SOURCE: Author.

That said, Chinese leaders knew that actions to boost Chinese security in Southeast Asia could trigger adverse reactions elsewhere, reactions
that could hamper China's ability to obtain the technology, training, and
other developmental inputs only available to it from the United States and
other developed countries. In weighing this risk, Beijing appears to have
placed faith in its ability to work the US-USSR-PRC strategic triangle to its own
advantage. The logic ran thus: If Beijing again used force against Hanoi,
as it had in January, Washington would quietly or openly endorse the further punishment of its recent enemy, while Moscow would likely not allow
such an attack to trigger a Soviet reply in kind. China also seems to have
calculated that punishing Vietnam would not antagonize other countries
in the region (except Cambodia and Laos). Beijing may have reasoned as
well that those other countries would worry more about threats to themselves coming from Vietnam than from a more distant and still poor and
backward China. In this way, China's leaders appear to have reconciled the
tension between its stoking threats to its security and risking assistance for
its development. On 17 February 1979, China launched a border war against
Vietnam. Vietnamese forces fought hard, the incursion was blunted, and a
month later the conflict was over.

Beijing's long-term security objective in Southeast Asia was then — and
still is — to ensure that its own regional influence exceeds that of any other
major power. By invading Vietnam, China meant to teach a lesson to the
region's other countries as well: that they, too, must respect China's interests. Beijing's decision to start the war may have been motivated not only
by Hanoi's removal of Pol Pot's murderous regime in Phnom Penh, but
equally by Hanoi's alignment with Moscow against the interests and desires
of Beijing.

The low salience of economic matters in China's view of Southeast Asia
in 1979 has been noted. Countries in the region could not contribute much
to China's modernization at that early stage. Beijing did nevertheless try
to enlist Southeast Asian skills, networks, and financial resources. It did
so by appealing directly and indirectly to the ethnic Chinese, rather than
seeking cooperation and assistance from regional governments. Beijing made
patriotic calls for the diaspora to aid the motherland and offered prospects
of economic gain and of possibly thereby gaining the respect that indig-
enous-ethnic-majority politicians might have withheld. Entrepreneurial
know-how and Chinese-language skills thus helped to jump-start China's
progress.[19]

That said, there were few incentives for China to seek closer ties with
individual countries in the region, or vice versa. Interaction was limited and

largely consistent with patterns of the past. Changes and adaptations did occur, however. Vietnam emerged as the strongest country on the Southeast Asian mainland. Thailand and other states grew less confident about the American commitment to a region where Washington had just lost a long and costly conflict. Bangkok hedged its bets by turning to Beijing for arms and political support to counterbalance Vietnam. China was happy to provide arms because doing so would weaken Thailand's alliance ties with the United States and foster links with Thailand's politically powerful military commanders.[20] The initiative came from Thailand and was motivated by concern about Vietnam, but it paved the way for deeper Chinese engagement with the Thai military, companies, and government.

China's relations with other states in the region remained relatively unchanged during the 1980s. Vietnam, Cambodia, and Laos relied heavily on assistance from and ties with the Soviet Union. This constrained their interactions with China because Moscow's relations with Beijing remained fraught and China had made Moscow's support for Vietnam's occupation of Cambodia one of the "three obstacles" that Beijing insisted must be removed before PRC-USSR relations could improve.[21] Anti-communist sentiment, the legacy of China's support for communist insurgencies, and the absence of sufficient economic incentives to strengthen relations with the PRC limited Indonesian, Singaporean, Malaysian, and Philippine interest in improving relations with China. Nor did Beijing try very hard to expand bilateral ties. China's relations with Myanmar improved somewhat, but Beijing was no more successful than other countries in influencing that military regime until the following decade.

None of China's relations with countries in the region were completely stagnant during this period. Modest increases in leadership visits and trade flows did occur. But the situation at the end of the 1980s remained basically what it had been at the decade's beginning.[22] That was about to change, however, largely as a result of developments in the arenas explored below. China did not cause or shape many of these changes, but separately and together they altered how China saw Southeast Asia and what it could do and did there.

From 1990 to 2009: New Opportunities, New Approaches

The first and largest arena was the international system itself. The collapse of the Soviet Union in 1991 transformed that environment and dramatically impacted China's security situation. In Southeast Asia, the demise of the

USSR led quickly to the termination of Moscow's relationships with Vietnam, Cambodia, and Laos — ties that Beijing had regarded as designed, at least in part, to threaten China's security and impede restoration of its rightful and historic role as the dominant power in the region. More importantly, from Beijing's perspective, it degraded China's anti-Soviet value to the United States and made it prudent for China to be more attentive to American international concerns.[23] In Vietnam, Laos, and Cambodia, the loss of Soviet funding and protection also changed how these states viewed China.

A second and more incremental set of developments that changed the possibility spaces of China and the countries of Southeast Asia was the accelerated spread of globalization made possible by advances in information technology and low-cost transportation. Beijing's reform policies and abundant supply of low-cost labor had begun to make it a major participant in and beneficiary of globalized production.[24] Integration into the globalized economy did not happen overnight. It would take a decade for many Chinese investments made early in the reform era to come on line, prove their value, and link to facilities in Southeast Asia. By the end of the 1980s, many steps in manufacturing and assembly had migrated to the region from Japan, South Korea, and Taiwan. Ethnic-Chinese businesses in particular were engaged in this process, some of which moved portions of their operations to China for economic and patriotic reasons.

Developments inside China were a third arena. The cumulative effects of accelerating Chinese growth opened economic possibilities for Southeast Asians. Opportunities for the region were also created by the 1989 crackdown in Beijing known as the "Tiananmen incident." In the latter case, Western sanctions leveled against China indirectly benefited Southeast Asia, as Beijing sought to compensate for the rebuff by expanding economic and political contacts with less censorious developing countries.

A fourth set of factors affecting China's perceptions and possibilities involved domestic changes in other countries, including in Southeast Asia. Examples included the 1986 "Edsa" or "People Power Revolution" in the Philippines; democratic transitions in South Korea and Taiwan that began in 1986–87; the 1988 uprising and crackdown in Myanmar; the apparently greater stability of democratic politics in Thailand; the beginning of Vietnam's policy of "Doi Moi" (renovation) in 1986; and steady economic growth in Malaysia and Indonesia fueled by Japanese investment and growing Southeast Asian participation in globalized production. Taken together, these developments created new opportunities for China and new incentives for countries in the region to become more active internationally.

The fifth and final arena encompassed US policy behavior in the immediate aftermath of the Cold War. Southeast Asia did benefit from American support for global and regional institutions. Yet the United States did not rush back into the region to fill the "vacuum" created by the USSR's demise. Indeed, some Southeast Asians feared that Washington would cede economic primacy to Japan and become bogged down elsewhere in the world to the point of neglecting their own countries.[25] Alongside opportunity, uncertainty about US intentions and comments also colored the foreign-policy outlooks and actions of Southeast Asian states.

Taken together, the developments summarized above enabled Beijing to view the situation in Southeast Asia in the 1990s as less threatening to China's interests than it had been before. Security remained Beijing's highest priority, but the region was now viewed as less dangerous and easier to manage. Thailand and the Philippines were still allied with the United States, but Beijing's relations with Thailand had grown closer thanks to arms sales and the beginnings of economic collaboration. Encouragingly from China's standpoint, the Philippines had made clear that it wanted the United States to depart when its military basing agreements expired in 1991–92. The more favorable security situation enabled China to be less defensive and demanding in its dealings with states in Southeast Asia. China was less apt to worry that non-aligned countries would join security arrangements hostile to China's interests. Feeling safer, China could act as a better neighbor than before. As security concerns decreased, economic opportunities grew. Demand rose in China for resources from abroad — oil, gas, timber, metals, and agricultural products.

In tandem with these trends, Beijing launched a vigorous campaign to change China's image in the region. Disparagingly described by some as a "charm offensive," the campaign began in the early 1990s. Aid packages, infrastructure projects, and trade deals accompanied trip diplomacy and the incantation of hoary principles of non-interference and mutual respect. It worked. China managed to overcome substantial distrust and dislike engendered by its past support for communist insurgents and its perceived efforts to use the Chinese diaspora to advance China's interests at the host nations' expense. Given the depth of suspicion and antipathy that had to be overcome, this was no mean achievement.[26]

By the end of this period, China had become a main trading partner of many countries in the region, and the major benefactor of some of them. It did so, in part, by befriending leaders and regimes shunned by others. It developed particularly close relations with the two least savory regimes in Southeast Asia: Myanmar and Cambodia. The developed democracies had distanced themselves from Myanmar following suppression of the "8888 Uprising" that began there on 8 August 1988. Western sanctions were levied on the military regime. Beijing stepped in, providing arms and aid to what had become a pariah state, winning major access and influence. A similar story unfolded in Cambodia. Its authoritarian leader, Hun Sen, was ostracized by much of the international community for staging a "coup" in 1997 against co-prime minister Norodom Ranariddh and the non-communist parties then in the government. China reversed its former animosity toward Hun Sen, whom Hanoi had installed in power after overthrowing the pro-China Khmer Rouge regime. While Beijing cultivated Phnom Penh's allegiance with economic aid and political support, Sino-Cambodian relations warmed.

FIGURE 2.3 China's perceptions of security threats and development contributions by Southeast Asian country as of 2009

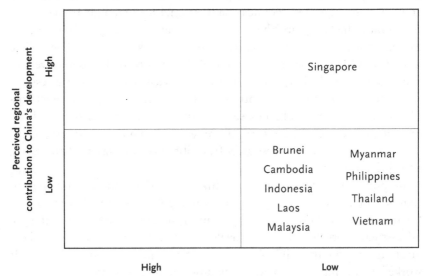

SOURCE: Author.

By 2009, Chinese politicians, diplomats, and businesspeople had considerably improved their country's image in Southeast Asia. High-level visits by Chinese leaders, bilateral trade, investment flows into the region from China (and lesser amounts in the other direction), Chinese aid, Chinese tourists, and other signs of engagement were on an upward trajectory throughout the region. In this context, China's rise was generally well received there because China acted like a good neighbor, boosting local prosperity, and because of the contrast between Chinese attentiveness and a seeming American lack of interest in the region. China's image also gained from the impression among many Southeast Asian leaders that their neighbor had been more sensitive to their concerns than the United States had been during the Asian Financial Crisis of 1997–98. But if China and its regional partners were pleased with the warmth of their relations, things began to cool as the decade drew to a close.

Since 2009: Aberration or the New Normal?

For nearly two decades, China's approaches to and interactions with Southeast Asia had been notably successful, especially so given the disparities of size and power, and the historical legacy of more imperious Chinese attitudes and actions during the first several decades of the People's Republic. Economically, all countries in the region were becoming increasingly dependent on China. But tying their own prosperity—and to some extent the legitimacy of their governments—to a rising China had given rise to more confidence than concern.[27] China's rhetoric and, increasingly, its actions supported the proposals and preferences expressed by the Association of Southeast Asian Nations (ASEAN). Beijing's declarations of peaceful intent seemed to assuage local worries about the magnitude and pace of China's military buildup. From China's perspective, the region was becoming an increasingly important source of inputs needed for development, a more important market for Chinese exports, and more and more dependent on the People's Republic. Politically, economically, and in terms of security, developments in the region appeared favorable to Beijing and to the incorporation of the region into a Chinese sphere of influence.

By 2009, China had become the preeminent power in Southeast Asia. The Soviets were gone. The Americans were far away and preoccupied in the Middle East. Japan's economy remained stagnant. India eschewed "anti-China" alignment with countries in Southeast Asia. China's southern flank was more secure than it had been for two centuries, and Southeast Asian countries—tiny Singapore excepted—were sufficiently comfortable living with China that they did not seek an external counterbalance to its preeminence. Given this situation, one would have expected both China and its partners in Southeast Asia to continue cultivating ties and avoiding actions that might harm arrangements that seemed to be working for all.

It did not happen. Instead, starting in 2010, countries in the region implicitly rebuked China in their display of eagerness for a more visible

US presence and more vocal American support for the peaceful resolution of territorial disputes, freedom of navigation, and respect for maritime norms.[28] Beijing's approach to many countries and issues also changed in 2010, for reasons that remain unclear.

These changes in behavior were widely construed to mean that China was becoming less cooperative, more assertive, and more nationalistic.[29] The hardening of Beijing's approach to other countries was not limited to Southeast Asia. One thinks of Beijing's apparent decision to halt rare-earth mineral exports to Japan after a Chinese fishing boat rammed Japanese coast guard vessels near the Senkaku/Diaoyutai islands in September 2010, or Chinese threats to European nations following the announcement that jailed dissident Liu Xiaobo would receive the 2010 Nobel Peace Prize. But the harder line was more striking in Southeast Asia because it contrasted so starkly with the behaviors that had worked so well for China during the preceding 20 years.

Chinese accounts invariably blame others for initiating actions to which China had no choice but to respond.[30] Some, even most, of these claims may be accurate. But they beg the question as to why Beijing chose to respond as harshly as it did and, more importantly, why it chose to act and react in ways that were likely to — and did — not only jeopardize China's security and political goals in Southeast Asia, but risk adversely affecting China's development as well.

Chinese may believe, as they claim, that the increase in tension between China and its neighbors was caused by American efforts to sow distrust of China in the region — part of a US plan to contain China.[31] The assertion is implausible. It was Beijing's assertion of its "indisputable" claim to nearly all of the South China Sea that prompted Southeast Asians to resent and fear China and grow more eager to ensure America's commitment to the region.

Beijing's behavior is not easily explained. Did China expect the region's economic dependence to preclude opposition to its wishes? Did it believe its own rhetoric about US decline and consider Washington unwilling or unable to sustain a protective presence in Southeast Asia? Clearly these imputations of compliance were wrong. Yet there is still little evidence that Beijing is attempting a course correction designed to reduce tensions and refurbish its image. A more plausible accounting may be found in the heightened salience and impact of the domestic component of China's security calculus.

By the second decade of this century, China's leaders appeared, with reason, to be more concerned about dangers to internal stability and the legitimacy of Communist Party rule than about perceived or imagined threats from abroad.[32] One indicator of increased concern about internal stability was the establishment of a National Security Commission (NSC), announced at the Third Plenum of the 18th Party Congress in November 2013. Another is the fact that, since 2011, the budgets approved by the National People's Congress have allocated more money for internal security than for national defense. The NSC's creation, too, appears to have been meant mainly to address domestic threats.[33]

Beijing had — and has — good reason for concern. Unrest in Xinjiang and other interior regions is increasing. Local demonstrations protesting corruption, environmental degradation, and other manifestations of poor governance exceed 100,000 per year. Economic growth is slowing, and with it the ability to provide jobs and better living conditions. Urbanization and social media have made it far easier for information to circulate and for people to mobilize than was true 25 years ago, when rising expectations and political discontent triggered the events that led to Tiananmen.

For more than three decades, regime legitimacy has rested largely on economic performance and the Communist Party's embrace and promotion of Chinese nationalism. With the economic pillar becoming shakier, the party is relying more heavily on nationalism and the staunch defense of China's sovereignty, territorial integrity, and "core interests." This is not just a matter of choice. China's leaders must attend to public demands to take resolute and uncompromising positions on issues related to sovereignty. To appear irresolute could open the door to protests denouncing the actions or intentions of other countries, implicitly perhaps criticizing the party as well. Beijing fears such demonstrations because they could easily morph into opposition to corruption, unsafe food and water, or any of a multitude of other government and party shortcomings.

An inverse correlation likely exists between the leadership's concern about domestic stability and its ability to compromise on foreign-policy issues. The more the leaders worry about internal security, the less room they have to bargain on matters of sovereignty.

Applying the security-and-development framework used in this chapter, one can say that Beijing is willing to anger Southeast Asians, possibly jeopardizing Southeast Asia's contribution to China's development, for two reasons. First, although China's leaders know that the region is more important for their country's economic growth than it was in the past, they do not believe that Southeast Asia's contribution is critical enough to modify Chinese behavior in the security realm. Second, China is also sanguine regarding Southeast Asia because, in Beijing's view, the region has grown so dependent economically on China that its states are unlikely to endanger their own economies and the associated performance legitimacy they enjoy by disrupting economic ties with their giant neighbor. China's leaders would prefer not to incur risks in this regard. But doing what they consider necessary to meet domestic threats supersedes in their eyes any benefit to be gained by adopting a less adamantly nationalist stand on the South China Sea.

Summary and Projection

This chapter, compared with others in this volume, has purposely focused more closely on Chinese foreign policy and paid less attention to Southeast Asian outlooks and actions. It should be clear nevertheless that China's interactions with each of the countries in the region since 1979 have spanned a wide range of issues and opportunities. No country has been a passive target of Chinese initiatives; engagement is a two-way street. What happened in the situations examined here — and in others undiscussed for lack of space — was shaped by initiatives and responses from both actors in any given dyad between China and a Southeast Asian state, and sometimes by interaction with a third party such as the United States or another state in the region. Overarching the diversity of China's country-specific engagements, the historical trajectory of China's many interactions with the region as a whole was — and is — a vector representing the outcome of numerous steps and stratagems pursued by players with multiple objectives and different degrees of skill and leverage. But the changes in that overall pattern were neither random nor the sum of merely ad hoc developments.

What China did or, more accurately, what it attempted to do vis-à-vis the region and specific countries at specific points in time, can be explained — and could have been predicted, at least in general terms — by viewing the Southeast Asian country in question through the two Chinese lenses recommended herein: first, Beijing's security concerns and calculations; and second, its assessment of what that country could contribute to China's economic development.

This chapter has argued that during the first phase of China's reform and opening, its leaders saw in Southeast Asia neither a high-priority security concern nor an especially productive current or potential contributor to Chinese economic growth. To the extent that the region commanded foreign policy attention, it was mainly because Beijing was concerned about Moscow's relationship with Vietnam, viewing it as an effort to prevent China from gaining influence in the region.

In the early 1990s, Beijing's security outlook changed, thanks largely, but not exclusively, to developments occurring outside China and Southeast Asia, not least among them the Soviet implosion. The perceived threat to China's security diminished as China's economic interest in the region grew. Beijing implemented this shift in priorities through substantial and successful efforts to improve and expand its relationships with countries in the region. But in 2009–10, security concerns were again given priority on Beijing's agenda. This time they centered more on threats to internal stability and regime survival than on external adversaries. But to address those concerns, China's leaders chose to play the nationalism card. The adamant manner in which they did so rekindled worry and hedging behavior in Southeast Asia. China and the states in Southeast Asia are responding to this new situation in different ways and to different extents that are explored more fully in the chapters that follow. Adjustments are being made to mitigate security concerns and preserve mutually beneficial economic relations. But the story is not over. As they did in the turbulent wake of the Cold War's ending, exogenous developments could again change perceptions, priorities, and calculations in China and Southeast Asia alike.

Notes

1 "China's Policies on Asia-Pacific Security Cooperation," State Council Information Office, 11 January 2017, http://english.gov.cn/archive/white _paper/2017/01/11/content_281475539078636.htm.

2 See, for example: "China's Diplomacy," *People's Daily Online*, http:// english.people.com.cn/92824/92845/92870/index.html; "China's Foreign Policy," *People's Daily Online*, http://english.peopledaily.com.cn/china /19990914A128.html; and "Chairman Mao's Theory of the Differentiation of the Three Worlds is a Major Contribution to Marxism-Leninism," *Beijing Review*, no. 45, 4 November 1977, 29–33.

3 See John Pomfret, "U.S. Takes a Tougher Tone with China," *Washington Post*, 30 July 2010, http://www.washingtonpost.com /wp-dyn/content/article/2010/07/29/AR2010072906416.html.

4 For more on these ideas, see Thomas Fingar, "China and South/Central Asia in the Era of Reform and Opening," in *The New Great Game: China and South and Central Asia in the Era of Reform*, ed. Thomas Fingar (Stanford, CA: Stanford University Press, 2016).

5 As in, for example, Dieter Heinzig, *The Soviet Union and Communist China, 1945–1950: The Arduous Road to the Alliance* (Armonk, NY: M.E. Sharpe, 2004).

6 See Allen S. Whiting, "The Sino-Soviet Split," in *Cambridge History of China, Volume 14*, eds. Roderick MacFarquhar and John K. Fairbank (Cambridge, UK: Cambridge University Press, 1987), 478–538; and John W. Lewis, "The Social Limits of Politically Induced Change," in *Modernization by Design*, ed. Chandler Morse (Ithaca, NY: Cornell University Press, 1969), 1–33.

7 See Ezra F. Vogel, *Deng Xiaoping and the Transformation of China* (Cambridge, MA: Belknap, 2011), chs. 7–11.

8 For more, see John King Fairbank, ed., *The Chinese World Order: Traditional China's Foreign Relations* (Cambridge, MA: Harvard University Press, 1968).

9 See Fairbank, *The Chinese World Order*; Warren I. Cohen, *East Asia at the Center* (New York, NY: Columbia University Press, 2000); and Aileen S. P. Baviera, "China's Relations with Southeast Asia: Political Security and Economic Interests," PASCN Discussion Paper No. 99-17, Philippine APEC Study Center Network, Philippines, https://pascn.pids.gov.ph/files/ Discussions%20Papers/1999/pascndp9917.pdf.

10 See, for example, Zhang Xiaomin and Xu Chunfeng, "The Late Qing Dynasty Diplomatic Transformation: Analysis from an Ideational Perspective," *Chinese Journal of International Politics* 1, no. 3 (July 2007): 405–55.

11 See Richard Weitz, "Why US Made Hanoi Move," *The Diplomat*, 18 August 2010, http://thediplomat.com/2010/08/why-us-made-hanoi-move/.

12 See Paul J. Bolt, *China and Southeast Asia's Ethnic Chinese* (Westport, CT: Praeger, 2000); and Leo Suryadinata, "'Overseas Chinese' in Southeast Asia and China's Foreign Policy," in *China and Southeast Asia, Vol. VI*, ed. Geoff Wade (London: Routledge, 2009), 117–55.

13 By 1979 all countries in the region had switched recognition to the PRC except Singapore (which did so in 1990) and East Timor (which only gained its independence, as Timor-Leste, in 2002).

14 See, for example, John W. Garver, *Foreign Relations of the People's Republic of China* (Upper Saddle River, NJ: Prentice Hall, 1993), ch. 5.

15 See Nicholas Khoo, *Collateral Damage: Sino-Soviet Rivalry and the Termination of the Sino-Vietnamese Alliance* (New York, NY: Columbia University Press, 2011), ch. 2.

16 See Chen Jian, "China's Involvement in the Vietnam War, 1964-69," *China Quarterly* 142 (June 1995): 356–87.

17 Suryadinata, "'Overseas Chinese'"; and Jay Taylor, *China and Southeast Asia: Peking's Relations with Revolutionary Movements,* 2nd ed. (Westport, CT: Praeger, 1976).

18 This generalized pattern is derived from the author's observations and analysis of China's relations with all regions of the world since 1975, and from research conducted for *The New Great Game: China and South and Central Asia in the Era of Reform* and *Uneasy Partnerships: China's Engagement with Japan, the Koreas, and Russia in the Era of Reform,* ed. Thomas Fingar (Stanford, CA: Stanford University Press, respectively 2016 and 2017).

19 See, for example, Elena Barabantseva, "Trans-nationalizing Chineseness: Overseas Chinese Policies of the PRC's Central Government," *Asien* 96 (July 2005): 7–28, http://jpkc.fudan.edu.cn /picture/article/357/e0/2b/9dbe4b404392944b2ebf1d82d076/9812a964 -abd6-4153-afcb-742c4fed9b3e.pdf.

20 See, for example, Daniel Byman and Roger Cliff, *China's Arms Sales: Motivations and Implications* (Santa Monica, CA: Rand, 1999).

21 See Khoo, *Collateral Damage*.

22 See Ian Storey, *Southeast Asia and the Rise of China: The Search for Security* (London: Routledge, 2011), ch. 1.

23 Ending the conflict in Cambodia was one such issue. See, for example, Gareth Evans, "Cambodia Then and Now: Commemorating the 1991 Peace Agreement," keynote address, University of New South Wales Law School, Sydney, 6 August 2011, http://www.gevans.org/speeches /speech444.html.

24 See Peter Draper, "The Shifting Geography of Global Value Chains: Implications for Developing Countries, Trade Policy, and the G20," *Global Summitry Journal* 1, no. 1 (2013): 1–40; and Dinos Stasinopoluos, "China's Role in Global Value Chains," *NewEurope*, 2 June 2013, http:// www.neurope.eu/article/china-s-role-global-value-chains.

25 See, for example, Diane K. Mauzy and Brian L. Job, "U.S. Policy in Southeast Asia: Limited Re-engagement after Years of Benign Neglect," *Asian Survey* 47, no. 4 (July/August 2007): 622–41.

26 Storey, *Southeast Asia and the Rise of China*, ch. 2.

27 Perceived economic dependence on China rested, in part, on the percentage of Southeast Asian exports that went to the PRC. That is a misleading indicator, however, because many of these regional exports to China are in the form of intermediate goods destined for final assembly in China and onward shipment to the United States, Japan, or Europe. The region continues to depend ultimately on developed-economy markets, not on China's still limited level of final-product demand.

28 See, for example, M. Taylor Fravel, *Policy Report: U.S. Policy Towards the Disputes in the South China Sea Since 1995* (Singapore: S. Rajaratnam School of International Studies, March 2014), http://taylorfravel.com /documents/research/fravel.2014.RSIS.us.policy.scs.pdf; and Michael Yahuda, "China's New Assertiveness in the South China Sea," *Contemporary China* 22, no. 81 (2013): 446–59.

29 See Alastair Iain Johnston, "How New and Assertive Is China's New Assertiveness?," *International Security* 37, no. 4 (Spring 2013): 7–48.

30 See "China Blames Philippines for Latest South China Sea Incident," Reuters, 26 February 2014, http://www.reuters.com/article/2014/02/26 /us-china-philippines-idUSBREA1P0I320140226.

31 See "China Blames U.S. for Stoking Tensions in South China Sea," Reuters, 9 May 2014, http://www.reuters.com/article/2014/05/09/us -china-usa-idUSBREA4804Z20140509.

32 Perceived threats include the suspicion if not conviction that it is only a matter of time before the United States employs military force to thwart China's rise. Imagined threats reflect more extreme paranoia or, more often, dangers contrived for political reasons, such as recent assertions that Japan is returning to its militaristic past.

33 See Roman Pogorelov, "Chinese National Security Committee," *New Eastern Outlook*, 22 June 2014, http://journal-neo.org/2014/06/22/rus -komitet-gosudarstvennoj-bezopasnosti-kitaya/; and Ben Blanchard and John Ruwitch, "China Hikes Defense Budget, to Spend More on Internal Security," Reuters, 5 March 2013, http://www.reuters.com/article /2013/03/05/us-china-parliament-defence-idUSBRE92403620130305.

CHAPTER 3

ASEAN-China Trade and Investment

DIVERSITY VERSUS DEPENDENCE

Anne Booth, *University of London, United Kingdom*

symmetry matters. Extreme differences in size necessarily color assessments of the risks and rewards to Southeast Asia's economies resulting from their interactions with China's far larger economy. But the contrast need not disadvantage the smaller partner. The contrary can be argued: that Southeast Asians gain more than they lose by their proximity to Chinese markets and capital. This chapter relies mainly on years of data on trade and investment between the Association of Southeast Asian Nations (ASEAN) and China to assess whether, in these interactions, the economies of Southeast Asia have been, on balance, more constrained or more enabled.[1]

Following an overview of Southeast Asian economic success in the 1990s, when critiques of China's rise were still uncommon, the chapter situates the ASEAN countries and China within the manufacturing networks that drove the growth of "Factory Asia." Patterns of trade in goods and flows of investment and people between ASEAN and China are discussed next. Attention is then paid to several regional trading arrangements, notably the ASEAN-China Free Trade Agreement. A set of conclusions based on this analysis closes the chapter.

Opportunity or Threat? China's Rise in East Asia

In the eyes of observers in the early 1990s, Southeast Asia was hardly languishing in the shadow of China's booming growth. Successful economies in Southeast Asia were instead praised as role models for the developing world. The World Bank's widely read report on "the East Asian miracle"[2] did not even include China among the eight East Asian economies that had "got their policies right" and had thereby achieved rapid development and equitable distributions of income. Four of those "miracles" — Singapore, Malaysia, Thailand, and Indonesia — were in Southeast Asia. There were doubts at the time about growth prospects in Cambodia, Laos, Myanmar, and Vietnam, but the doubters focused on the need for economic reform inside these countries and did not worry that China's growth might impede Southeast Asia's.

Nor was it China's fault that the 1997–98 financial crisis and ensuing capital outflows badly damaged several Southeast Asian economies, especially Indonesia and Thailand, and slowed their subsequent recovery. Even allowing for these reversals, most of the region remained more prosperous than China. In 2000, the per capita gross domestic products (GDPs) of five of the ASEAN's 10 members equaled or exceeded China's; only the Philippines, Cambodia, Laos, Myanmar, and Vietnam lagged China by that measure. Another deceleration in 2001 was caused not by China but by a decline in world demand for electronics exports that especially affected Malaysia and Singapore. Meanwhile China boomed, and its rapid if decelerating growth continued through 2016. Yet in per capita GDP terms that year, despite having surpassed Indonesia and the Philippines and preserved its lead over Vietnam, Laos, Myanmar, and Cambodia, China still had not caught up with Singapore, Brunei, Malaysia, or Thailand.[3]

When China joined the World Trade Organization at the end of 2001, views of China's impact on the developing world, including Asia, began to change. It was reasonable to expect China's integration into the global economy to pose both opportunities and threats to other countries, including in Southeast Asia. On the opportunity side, one could note and project the beneficial effects of China's expanding appetite for imports of Southeast Asian goods and services.[4] One could also anticipate rising Chinese investment into the ASEAN region, especially to satisfy increasing Chinese demand for raw materials and energy resources. A further opportunity could be seen in China's burgeoning capital goods industries and their ability to offer plant and equipment to Southeast Asians more cheaply than counterpart firms in Japan, Europe, or the United States.

Represented on the threat side, however, were fears that firms in ASEAN would lose out to their Chinese rivals in competing to export labor-intensive manufactures — textiles, garments, footwear, toys, low-end electronics — to the advanced economies in the Organisation for Economic Co-operation and Development (OECD). Such fears were buoyed in November 2000 when then Chinese premier Zhu Rongji first proposed a free trade agreement between China and the ASEAN states. Observers worried that Chinese imports would flood into Southeast Asia, drowning local producers. Manufacturers in Southeast Asia could lose twice, it was thought, in production for both foreign and domestic markets alike, thereby jeopardizing ASEAN's economic growth. John Wong and Sarah Chan, for example, noted "the broad similarity in trade structures and the fundamentally competitive nature of Sino-ASEAN economic relations."[5]

Chinese investment was another source of concern. China was leveraging its abundant endowment of cheap labor by massively building and upgrading its physical infrastructure while also improving its legal and regulatory environments. Worries rose within ASEAN that China would become a magnet for foreign direct investment (FDI), diverting needed capital from Southeast Asia.[6] Not only would new FDI increasingly prefer Chinese over Southeast Asian destinations. Multinational corporations that had already established export bases in Malaysia, Thailand, and Indonesia would be tempted to relocate to China to take advantage of lower production costs, better logistics, and the large domestic market.

In the early years of this century, the evidence seemed to favor the pessimists over the optimists — obstacles over opportunities. Studies using computable general equilibrium (CGE) models among other quantitative methods showed that, in labor-intensive products, China would continue to take market share away from other developing economies, including in Southeast Asia.[7] The abolition of quotas in the global textile and garment trade was expected to help make China a formidable rival among Asian exporters.[8] The reasons cited for China's comparative advantage included low labor costs per unit of output and the economies of scale afforded by the country's large and rapidly growing domestic market, compared with conditions in other developing economies.

China's expanding market did attract exports from Southeast Asia. But even after China entered the WTO, many non-tariff barriers stayed in place, including inefficient Chinese customs administration and weak provincial enforcement of rules and regulations governing imports. And if labor-intensive manufacturing in ASEAN for export was likely to suffer from Chinese competition, agricultural and resource-based exports were set to expand. The rapid growth of ASEAN's trade with China, especially regarding those exports, created benefits for its member economies by enlarging and improving, respectively, the volume and terms of trade.[9]

Having grown by 9.5 percent in 2011, China's economy soon slowed to "only" 7.3 percent growth in 2014.[10] Observers who had focused on the benefits versus the costs to Southeast Asia of China's robust growth were obliged to shift analytic gears and begin estimating the regional effects of the rapidly *cooling* Chinese economy. In light of China's prior breakneck pace, many analysts had assumed that its GDP would continue to expand at an annual rate of 7 to 9 percent, despite evidence of exaggeration in the official statistics for those earlier years.[11] By the latter part of 2015, however, as China's stock market fell and doubts about the data rose, China's deceleration and its detrimental effects grew more evident. In Southeast Asia, as in Africa, those effects stemmed especially from reduced Chinese demand for raw materials such as oil, gas, and coal. China's slowdown also threatened to lower its demand for Southeast Asian components of Chinese manufactured goods. The next section considers those chains of added value.

Losing Out or Linking In? The Challenge of "Factory Asia"

By the early 21st century, flows of value in parts, components, and intermediate goods or accessories had become the most dynamic activity in international trade. By 2009 those flows accounted for more than half of all non-fuel merchandise trade. The specialization of different economies along these value chains has altered the nature of global commerce. In "Factory Asia" the borders of countries are crossed and re-crossed by sequences and networks of production, as billions of parts and components are assembled in plants across Asia and dispatched to markets all over the world. As early as 2001 in Southeast Asia, parts and components accounted for as much as half of total trade in the Philippines, and a smaller but significant share of all trade in Malaysia, Thailand, and Vietnam as well.[12]

In 2010, measured by value added in US dollars, China edged out the United States to become the world's premier manufacturing country. By 2013 China's lead had grown to 23 percent of total global manufacturing value, well ahead of the United States at 17 percent. The sole Southeast Asian country among the top 15 by this measure in 2013 was Indonesia, in 13th place with less than 2 percent.[13] But it would be wrong to infer, from China's evident prowess in making and shipping products, that the exporting economies of ASEAN were on the losing end of retail competition with China for shares in foreign markets for similar goods.

Instead, the rising role of China in this pattern of specialized trade squeezed out the developing economies of Southeast Asia much less than it linked them in. In Asia some of the higher-wage economies did suffer from stagnating or falling exports of textiles, footwear, garments, and the like, as their comparative advantage in those products diminished.[14] But China's rise and the robust growth of the global economy as a whole until 2008 created

opportunities for at least some of the ASEAN economies to integrate themselves into global production networks. In Thailand these opportunities
enabled a rapid growth of plants, many Japanese-owned, producing vehicles, vehicle parts, and computer components. In the Philippines, exports
of electronic products rose rapidly, sped mainly by investment by Japanese
and American multinationals. Indonesia, in contrast, was criticized for "not
participating vigorously" in the production networks that were evolving
across Northeast and Southeast Asia.[15]

Indonesia's supposedly poor performance could not be blamed on China.
Poor logistics and cumbersome customs procedures inside Indonesia were
at fault, as well as inadequate investment in education, which had made it
hard for many firms to find labor with appropriate skills. The labor problem
had been aggravated by legislation, introduced in 2003, that raised minimum wages and made it more difficult and expensive for firms to dismiss
workers. Indonesian exchange-rate policy was also at fault. While exports
of oil, gas, coal, and agricultural products boomed, at least partly due to
growing Chinese demand, the rupiah-to-dollar rate was kept at a level that
left many labor-intensive industries uncompetitive in markets not only in
the OECD countries but elsewhere in Asia as well.

Initially, Indonesia's problem in the years after 2006 was not the poor
performance of its exports in general. It was particularly the adverse impact
of thriving commodity exports on other export-linked parts of the economy — collateral damage familiar from the oil-boom years of the 1970s.
Indeed, in dollar terms, Indonesian exports grew faster than the total for
all ASEAN economies between 2006 and 2014, and faster than the national
rates of export growth in Brunei, Malaysia, the Philippines, and Singapore.[16]
Indonesia's dollar export earnings did steadily fall after 2011. By 2016 they
were lower than they had been in 2010. More important than China as
a cause of that decline, however, were falling prices for some Indonesian
commodities.

On balance, the Indonesian experience showed that export streams
could expand rapidly even in an economy that was not well integrated into
"Factory Asia" networks, whether these were tied to China or not.

How Much Do ASEAN's Members
Depend on Trade with China?

In comparisons of different patterns of trade and whether a given pattern
"helps" or "hurts" a given trader, interdependence is typically preferred

to dependence. Leaving aside the many other conditions and variables that could confirm or undermine such a judgment, a statistical question remains: How extensively and uniformly has Southeast Asian trade in general "depended" on trade with China in particular?

First, the context: In 2016 the estimated total value of merchandise exported from or imported into the ASEAN economies stood at a robust USD $2.2 trillion — down from $2.5 trillion in 2014, but up from $1.9 trillion in 2008.[17]

The 16 percent increase between 2008 and 2016 was achieved despite a dip in 2009 caused not by China but by that year's global recession, and further dips in 2015 and 2016, again the result of global problems. Southeast Asia had already shown its resilience by recovering from the dire economic crisis of 1997–98 — another calamity for which China was not responsible. The growth in ASEAN's total trade until 2015 occurred in the context of globally expanding trade from the late 1990s through 2014 — a favorable environment that benefited from China's increasing participation in world commerce over that period.

The ASEAN economies' dependence on trade with China did increase, both in absolute terms and as a proportion of all ASEAN trade. As shown in Table 3.1, while ASEAN's exports to China as a share of global ASEAN exports rose almost fivefold, from 2.3 percent in 1996 to 11.3 percent in 2015, the comparable figure for ASEAN's imports from China climbed even faster — from 2.6 to 19.5 percent. In addition, ASEAN's global trade became less diversified, as European and Japanese shares in that trade declined, although in absolute terms Southeast Asia's transactions with all three of these countries/regions continued to expand. Meanwhile, between these upward and downward percentage trends, trade between ASEAN's member economies, expressed as a proportion of all ASEAN trade, increased slightly.

These data do suggest a proportional increase in ASEAN's trade dependence on China. Yet intra-ASEAN trade was the more important contributor to the overall growth in total trade that the ASEAN economies enjoyed. Table 3.2 allocates responsibility for the 2002–14 increases in the value of ASEAN's exports and imports. It shows and compares the percentage shares of those increases attributable to internal trade within ASEAN and to external trade between ASEAN and China. With regard to ASEAN's exports, the difference is striking. Merchandise exported by Southeast Asians to one another's countries accounted for nearly twice as much of the increase in the value of total ASEAN exports in 2002–14 as did the region's exports to China — 27 compared with 14 percent. By this measure, ASEAN's export success did not depend unduly on the China market.

TABLE 3.1 ASEAN's exports and imports with its top eight trading partners expressed as shares of all ASEAN exports and imports (%)

	Exports		Imports	
	1996	2015	1996	2015
ASEAN	25.0	25.8	18.3	21.9
China	2.3	11.3	2.6	19.5
Japan	13.3	9.7	20.9	11.4
EU	14.5	10.8	16.4	9.2
South Korea	2.9	3.9	3.8	7.0
India	1.2	3.3	0.8	1.8
Australia	1.9	2.8	2.5	1.7

SOURCE: For 1996, *ASEAN Statistical Yearbook 2001* (Jakarta: ASEAN Secretariat, 2001), 58–63; for 2015, "ASEAN Statistics," ASEAN.org, accessed 31 July 2016, http://asean.org/resource/statistics /asean-statistics.

NOTE: Trade data shown include with ASEAN itself and are shown as a share of *all* ASEAN exports and imports worldwide for the years listed. The ASEAN figure for 1996 does not include later joiners Laos and Myanmar (1997), Cambodia (1999), and Vietnam (July 1995). From 1996 to 2014, the European Union's members grew in number from 12 to 27.

TABLE 3.2 Contribution to the 2002–14 growth in ASEAN exports and imports by country or region (%)

	1996	2015
ASEAN	26.7	22.6
China	14.4	21.3
EU	8.4	8.3
South Korea	4.0	7.2
Japan	8.3	6.2
USA	6.7	5.1
India	3.8	2.8
Australia	3.9	2.0
Other	26.1	24.5
Total	102.3	100.0

SOURCE: For 2002, *ASEAN Statistical Yearbook 2010* (Jakarta: ASEAN Secretariat, December 2010), 89 (Table V.14), http://www.asean.org/storage/images/archive/documents/asean _statistical_2010.pdf; for 2014, "ASEAN Statistics," ASEAN.org, accessed 24 April 2016, http://asean .org/resource/statistics/asean-statistics.

NOTE: The exports column total exceeds 100 percent due to rounding.

The data on imports into ASEAN in Table 3.2 tell a different story. Intra-ASEAN imports and China-to-ASEAN imports contributed similarly to the growth in overall imports into Southeast Asia — 23 and 21 percent, respectively. But ASEAN as a group has run deficits in its trade with China since the early 2000s, and the imbalance has worsened significantly, from $13 billion (2010) to $45 billion (2013), $64 billion (2014), $78 billion (2015), and $81 billion (2016).[18]

TABLE 3.3 Trade between ASEAN countries and China, showing total trade and Southeast Asian balances (US$ billions)

	Trade with China (2013)		Trade with China (2014)	
	Total trade	Country's surplus or deficit	Total trade	Country's surplus or deficit
Vietnam	65.5	−31.7	83.6	−43.8
Singapore	75.9	−15.8	79.7	−18.1
Indonesia	68.4	−5.5	63.5	−14.6
Cambodia	3.8	−3.0	3.8	−2.8
Philippines	38.0	−1.7	44.5	−2.5
Brunei	1.8	−1.6	1.9	−1.6
Laos	2.7	−0.7	3.6	−0.1
Thailand	71.2	5.8	72.6	4.0
Myanmar	10.2	−4.5	25.0	6.2
Malaysia	106.1	14.2	102.0	9.2
Total ASEAN	443.6	−44.5	480.2	−64.1

SOURCE: National Bureau of Statistics of China, *China Statistical Yearbook* 2015 (Beijing: China Statistics Press, 2015), Table 11-6.

NOTE: Trade deficits are indicated by minus signs. Deficits and surpluses from the original Chinese data have been reversed to convey Southeast Asian vantage points. Column totals may not sum to the exact amount due to rounding.

That said, the worsening skew in China's favor bears viewing in a wider context. First, Southeast Asia is not alone in its reliance on imports from China. China continues to run a surplus in its trade, not just with ASEAN, but with the world as a whole, to the chagrin of a number of countries. Second, the ASEAN economies as a group have consistently enjoyed substantial if irregular trading *surpluses* with the world as a whole. In the 10 years from 2007 through 2016, for example, ASEAN's surpluses with the world (including itself) ran from a high of $110 billion (2007) to a low of $24 billion (2013) for a median of $69 billion between 2015 and 2016.[19]

Third, ASEAN's burgeoning deficit in its trade with China applies only to the region as a collective entity. Concealed in that statistic are the variety of trade relations with China experienced by particular Southeast Asian economies. Most notably, China's figures for 2014 displayed in Table 3.3 show that Vietnam alone accounted for by far the largest part of the total share of the $64 billion deficit in ASEAN's trade with China in that year, around 68 percent of the total. In contrast, if these data are accurate, Malaysia, Thailand, and Myanmar actually ran surpluses with China in 2014.

TABLE 3.4 Breakdown by share of ASEAN countries' 2013 trade with China and other countries in ASEAN, and the same countries' total 2014 trade with ASEAN (%)

	2013 exports		2013 imports		Total trade with ASEAN, 2014
	To China	To ASEAN	From China	From ASEAN	
Cambodia	3.0	14.2	32.6	30.7	25.7
Myanmar	26.7	49.2	30.5	35.3	42.0
Vietnam	10.0	13.7	27.9	16.2	13.9
Malaysia	13.4	28.1	16.4	26.7	26.9
Indonesia	12.4	22.3	16.0	29.0	25.6
Laos	14.0	47.6	15.5	75.8	64.9
Thailand	11.9	25.9	15.1	17.8	22.6
Philippines	12.2	16.0	13.1	21.8	19.6
Singapore	11.8	31.4	11.7	20.9	26.2
Brunei	1.4	23.1	11.3	51.0	27.2
Median	12.05	24.5	15.75	27.85	25.95

SOURCES: The breakdown of 2013 imports and exports comes from *ASEAN Community in Figures—Special Edition 2014: A Closer Look at Trade Performance and Dependency, and Investment* (Jakarta: ASEAN Secretariat, 2014), 16–20. Total 2014 trade with ASEAN is from "Intra- and Extra-ASEAN Trade, 2014," ASEAN Statistics, Table 18, accessed 24 June 2018, http://www.asean.org/storage/2015/12/table18_asof21Dec2015.pdf.

NOTE: Percentages reflect the value of trade, not its volume.

Trade data are not always consistent across statistical sources.[20] Discrepancies aside, however, the available data caution against exaggerating how much Southeast Asia depends on trade with China. Regarding exports, the ASEAN figures used in Table 3.4 show that in 2013 only one Southeast Asian country's exports to China amounted to more than about a fourth of its total merchandise shipments to other countries — Myanmar at 27 percent. In that year, China's share of all exports from a given ASEAN country ranged from a trivial 1.4 (Brunei) and 3 (Cambodia) to a modest 10 to 14 (for Vietnam, Singapore, Thailand, the Philippines, Indonesia, Malaysia, and Laos in that order). The data also underscore the importance of particular circumstances, country by country. Brunei's shipments of oil and gas, for instance, go mainly to countries such as Japan and South Korea with which it has long-term contracts, while Cambodia's labor-intensive manufactures tend to fare poorly in competition with equivalent products for sale inside China.[21]

On the import side in Table 3.4, proportional dependence in 2013 was greater on the whole than it was for exports, but not markedly so, and again, the interesting differences are country-specific. The most China-dependent importers in Southeast Asia were Cambodia, Myanmar, and Vietnam. Each of these ASEAN countries absorbed from China alone between 33 and 28 percent of the total value of its imports in that year. Especially unbalanced was Cambodia. A third of its imports came from China, more than for any other ASEAN country, yet China took in return a mere 3 percent of Cambodia's exports. The high proportional reliance of Myanmar and Vietnam on imports coming from China reflected the southward balance of trade across these ASEAN countries' land borders with China, and in Myanmar's case the effect of Western sanctions as well.

Substantial diversity also marks the extents to which the 10 ASEAN economies trade with one another.

In 2014, while Laos was conducting 65 percent of its total trade with ASEAN partners, only 42 percent of Myanmar's total trade was with ASEAN. Vietnam, at only 14 percent, was least focused on trading with its fellow ASEAN-member countries. All of the other ASEAN economies conducted less than 30 percent of their trade with one another in 2014. This evidence, together with the median scores in Table 3.4, is unkind to a regionalist argument that Southeast Asia as a whole depends excessively on trading with China.

Neither does China dominate the flow of FDI into Southeast Asia, as can be seen in Table 3.5. Streams of FDI into the ASEAN region have fallen sharply twice since the 1990s, but neither decline can be blamed on China's success as a competing magnet for foreign capital. These shrinkages owed far more to the onset of the Asian Financial Crisis in 1997 and the global recession that began 10 years later. As for the flow of specifically Chinese investment into the ASEAN region over those years, it never amounted to more than a trickle compared with the inflows from the European Union (EU), Japan, or the United States, or from country-to-country investments inside Southeast Asia. China's share of the FDI that entered Southeast Asia over those years was never large enough for a possible decline in its size to have singled out China as somehow "hurting" the region's economy for lack of interest. Neither did China's share expand to the point of crowding out other sources of FDI and thereby "hurt" Southeast Asia through overdependence. As Table 3.5 shows, China's contribution to the flow of capital into the ASEAN economies from around the world did rise sharply after 2000, but from an extremely low (0.1 percent) base in that year to a modest 7 percent in 2013 — still much smaller in size than the flows from either the EU, Japan, or ASEAN.[22] More relevant for local well-being than the origins of the capital that entered the region in those years was its having more than quintupled in value — observable in the bottom line of Table 3.5.

TABLE 3.5 Global flow of foreign direct investment into ASEAN by originating region or country (%)

	1995	2000	2010	2013
EU	24.6	42.2	18.9	22.0
Japan	27.4	4.4	11.1	18.7
ASEAN	16.5	5.6	15.1	17.4
China	0.5	0.1	4.0	7.1
United States	15.4	31.6	12.2	3.1
Other	15.6	16.1	38.7	31.7
Total	100.0	100.0	100.0	100.0
Total, US$ billions	28.2	21.8	100.4	122.4

SOURCE: *ASEAN Community in Figures—Special Edition 2014*, 86 (Table 6.2).

NOTES: The ASEAN figure for 1995 excludes later joiners Laos and Myanmar (1997), Cambodia (1999), and Vietnam (July 1995). The European Union's 12 member states as of 1 January 1995 grew to 27 as of 1 January 2014 (and to 28 as of mid-2018).

TABLE 3.6 Foreign direct investment flows into and out of Southeast Asia and China (US$ billions)

	Southeast Asia			China		
	Inflows	Outflows	Net	Inflows	Outflows	Net
2009	46.1	41.5	+4.6	95.0	56.5	+38.5
2010	106.2	55.5	+50.7	114.7	68.8	+45.9
2011	93.5	54.9	+38.6	124.0	74.7	+49.3
2012	108.1	50.7	+57.4	121.1	87.8	+33.3
2013	126.1	67.2	+58.9	123.9	101.0	+22.9
2014	132.9	80.1	+52.8	128.5	116.0	+12.5

SOURCE: *World Investment Report 2015: Reforming International Investment Governance* (New York and Geneva: UNCTAD, 2015), A3–A6, Table 1, http://unohrlls.org/custom-content/uploads/2013/09/UNCTAD-World-Investment-Report.pdf.

Arriving FDI has not been spread evenly across Southeast Asia. In 2013, around half of the total inflow into the region from any country went to Singapore, followed by 15 percent to Indonesia and around 10 percent each to Thailand and Malaysia.[23] Indonesia, the largest economy in ASEAN, has also been favored by Chinese FDI, having led the region in cumulative investment received from China from 2005 to 2014. Indeed, worldwide over that decade, the only countries that took in more Chinese FDI were the United States, Australia, Canada, Brazil, Great Britain, Russia, Kazakhstan, and Peru, in that order.[24]

Limited space prevents a country-by-country assessment of the extent to which China's and ASEAN's competition for incoming FDI has been win-win or zero-sum. Nonetheless worth noting is a study that found the influx of all FDI into Malaysia to have been positively correlated with all FDI entering China, suggesting a plus-sum game.[25] Corroborating region-wide evidence that China has not elbowed ASEAN aside in competition for incoming FDI appears in Table 3.6. From 2009 to 2014, global FDI into Southeast Asia rose faster by value than it did into China, actually surpassing China's intake in 2013 and 2014.

Future speeds and amounts will change, of course, but retrospective claims that the ASEAN countries have "lost out" to China lack validity. Also notable in Table 3.6 are the consistently greater amounts of inflows over outflows for both Southeast Asia and China in every year from 2009 to 2014. Noteworthy too are the net annual inflows over outflows of FDI shown in Table 3.6. Inflows exceeded outflows in both Southeast Asia and China in every year from 2009 to 2014. Furthermore, insofar as a region or country can be said to benefit when more FDI arrives than leaves, that benefit has been greater in Southeast Asia than in China in most of those years. From underperforming China in 2009 with a much smaller margin of intake over outgo — $5 billion compared to China's $39 billion — by 2014 Southeast Asia had reversed that difference to $53 billion for the region compared to $39 billion for China.

Has the ASEAN-China FTA Helped or Hurt Southeast Asia?

The impetus to negotiate what would become the ASEAN-China Free Trade Agreement (AC-FTA) came from Beijing. Chinese premier Zhu Rongji proposed the idea in 2000. A decade later its provisions began to enter into force — in 2010 for the six earlier and wealthier members of ASEAN, five years later for Cambodia, Laos, Myanmar, and Vietnam. Chinese officials greeted with enthusiasm the agreement's embodiment in the ASEAN-China Free Trade Area. In the official eyes of Beijing, China and ASEAN were advantaged by physical proximity and economic complementarity. Senior officials in the Asian Development Bank also praised AC-FTA as an important vehicle for trade-led recovery in Southeast Asia. AC-FTA was portrayed as an opportunity for the ASEAN countries to "latch on to China's production network" and sell to Chinese consumers.[26] The reaction in ASEAN was more muted, although the ASEAN secretary-general did say that the free trade area "will benefit both sides and help lift the world economy out of the crisis."[27]

On strictly economic grounds, the official applause at the birth of AC-FTA might seem rather odd. Because the participating countries already belonged to the WTO, they were in theory already committed to non-discriminatory free trade at the global level. Nor did many of the supporters of the agreement bother to spell out the economic benefits that its provisions would bring, either to China or to China's co-joiners in Southeast Asia. The business communities in the participating countries, it was said, had contributed little to AC-FTA's creation — a process driven largely by political considerations.[28] Some Philippine analysts feared that the arrangement would merely legalize the widespread smuggling of Chinese footwear, garments, shoes, and other products to the further detriment of domestic producers.[29] In January 2010, no doubt also worried about AC-FTA's domestic impact on local producers, the Indonesian government tried but failed to get ASEAN to postpone the inauguration of the free trade area until January 2011.

Philippine and Indonesian concerns stemmed in part from a fear of repeating Thailand's experience in 2004, when an "early harvest" trade experiment with China caused problems for Thai farmers. On that occasion, some 200 tariffs on fruits and vegetables between Thailand and China were removed. Thailand was soon flooded with Chinese products. Thai farmers, who had expected to gain access to China, discovered that their agricultural exports were still subject to various tariff and non-tariff barriers on the Chinese side. Tsinghua University economist Hu Angang described China's trade strategy as "half open" — "free trade on the export side and protectionism on the import side."[30]

A door only half-open evoked images of China inundating Southeast Asia with goods ranging from garments and footwear to steel, for sale at bargain prices, while taking in return only those products, mainly unprocessed raw materials, that China needed for its own industrialization. Additionally worrisome to Southeast Asians was the accumulation by Chinese producers of large inventories of unsold manufactures due to slowed world demand following the global recession that had begun in 2008–09 — goods available for below-cost export. Although some of these claims of imminent harm were made by high-cost local producers hoping to protect their inefficiencies from cheaper imports, fears of dumping were real.

Indonesian concerns were summarized in October 2010 by a lecturer at the University of Indonesia, Makmur Keliat. He reported a consensus among Indonesians that their own agricultural products and manufactured goods were "extremely uncompetitive" compared with those arriving from China. Many Indonesians, he argued, saw AC-FTA not as helping ASEAN and China alike but as fostering "cutthroat competition that will have negative impacts on the development of Indonesian economic capabilities in the long term."[31] Others saw Chinese policies as essentially neo-colonial; in trying to satisfy its hunger for raw materials, China was in effect seeking to re-impose an exploitative pattern of trade on Southeast Asia. The durability of these views suggests that they reflect widely held beliefs in Indonesian business, media, and political circles. But how realistic are they?

The answer is: somewhat. The evident growth of Indonesia's merchandise exports since 2002 shows that Indonesia's traded goods are sufficiently competitive in global markets for such expansion to occur. Yet exports have grown from other Southeast Asian economies across a greater range of goods and services from machine components to tourist arrivals. While exports from Indonesia to China have been concentrated in mineral fuels, coal, and vegetable oils, imports from China to Indonesia have featured manufactures and machinery. Far from altering this "colonial" distinction, AC-FTA may have reinforced it, by enlarging Indonesia's trade surplus with China in commodities while boosting Indonesia's trade deficit with China in manufactures.[32]

What does seem clear is that China's prowess as an exporter of manufactured products has forced Indonesia to consider that its own comparative advantage as an exporter may lie less in making and selling labor-intensive, value-added goods than in shipping commodities such as coal, natural gas, rubber, and palm oil.[33] Other ASEAN countries in AC-FTA have managed to increase their exports of more sophisticated manufactures and services. Whether Indonesia will be able to do this in future will rest heavily on its ability to educate a more skilled labor force and improve the extent and quality of its infrastructure.

Discrepancies in the data on trade, already referred to, complicate appraisals of AC-FTA. Figures on trade between Southeast Asia and China released by the ASEAN Secretariat in 2014 showed the region having run deficits in its merchandise trade with China since 1994, three decades in all.[34] China's own figures disagreed. For example: Whereas ASEAN showed its region having run large deficits — Chinese *surpluses* — in 2010 and 2011, amounting respectively to $13 billion and $25 billion, China's data

reversed the difference. They showed Southeast Asia enjoying large surpluses — Chinese *deficits* — in those same years: $17 billion in 2010 and
$23 billion in 2011.[35]

Such huge and sign-reversing differences are hard to explain. Mis-
invoicing may have been part of the problem. The contradiction could also
stem from a political use of trade data by Beijing insofar as Southeast Asian
concerns about China would be assuaged if they thought their balance with
China was positive — that they were exporting more to China than they
were importing from it.

Statistical anomalies aside, however, it is not tenable to argue that China
has managed to use trade or investment to subjugate Southeast Asia as
a region. When examining costs and benefits to ASEAN from its ties with
China, the evidence must be examined contextually, case by case. As shown
in Table 3.4, in 2013, in only two of ASEAN's 10 countries — Cambodia and
Vietnam — did the percentage of all imports from anywhere that arrived
from China exceed the corresponding percentage that came from other
ASEAN countries. Table 3.4 also indicates that on the export side in that year,
every ASEAN economy sent less to China than to its fellow ASEAN members.
Other data show that from 2009, the year before AC-FTA came into operation,
to 2015, China enlarged its share of ASEAN's total trade by less than four
percentage points — from 11.6 to 15.2 percent.[36] As for FDI, in 2013, a mere
7 percent of all Chinese investment worldwide trickled into Southeast Asia
(Table 3.5). It is also worth remembering that, for Southeast Asians, AC-FTA
is not the only trade game in town. The ASEAN economies have trading agreements with Japan, South Korea, India, Australia, and New Zealand as well.
Taken together, these five countries' shares in ASEAN's total trade and total
inward investment outweigh the comparable shares attributable to China.

China has not taken part in planning two other regional economic
arrangements: the ASEAN Economic Community (AEC) and the Trans-
Pacific Partnership (TPP). They and the Regional Comprehensive Economic
Partnership (RCEP) bear brief mention here. Officially established in January
2016, the AEC aims to turn Southeast Asia into a single, integrated base
for production and marketing across all 10 ASEAN-member economies.
Notwithstanding the AEC's inauguration, the process to achieve those
objectives is far from completion. That is not surprising. Six decades of
integration have still not turned the European Union into a single market,
especially not in the service sector, where Southeast Asia lags as well. The
AEC is meant to strengthen Southeast Asia, but even if it succeeds, the future
ups and downs of the ASEAN economies' interactions with China will impli-
cate factors and actors outside the region.

In February 2016, Brunei, Malaysia, Singapore, Vietnam, and eight other countries including the United States, but not China, signed on to the TPP. In January 2017 Donald Trump became the 45th American president. Three days later he fulfilled his campaign promise to withdraw the United States from the TPP. In March 2018 the remaining 11 members decided to maintain the initiative under a new name — the Comprehensive and Progressive Agreement for Trans-Pacific Partnership (CPTPP). Without the United States, the revised accord shrank in scale. But less than a year later, in December 2018, the reduced agreement came into effect, and three more ASEAN states — Indonesia, the Philippines, and Thailand — were reported to be interested in joining.[37] Looking forward, the CPTPP could beneficially lessen its members' reliance on non-member China, but that could antagonize China to the detriment of the region.

A third project in progress, RCEP, has been under negotiation since 2012. A 24th negotiating round was held in New Zealand in October 2018.[38] The pact would, if concluded, span 18 countries including all 10 ASEAN states and China, but not the United States. Some may fear that if an RCEP including China succeeds, and the CPTPP absent China and the United States fails to deliver, Beijing will gain major sway in Southeast Asia. But again, such an outcome would likely result from the interaction of variables and contingencies beyond the mere presence or absence of Beijing or Washington in this or that scheme.

Conclusions

The evidence and reasoning in this chapter sustain conclusions under five headings: mutual gains, multiple partners, country differences, contingent balances, and future choices.

Mutual gains A zero-sum judgment that China's economy has risen at the expense of Southeast Asia's cannot survive contact with the actual record of economic interactions between the two. The benefits of these exchanges and engagements have been distributed unevenly across the region. Certainly, some Southeast Asian makers of labor-intensive exports — textiles, garments, footwear, less complex electronics — have had trouble competing with Chinese products. Although Chinese demand for energy resources and other commodities has fed the growth of Indonesia's economy, for example, that benefit may have reduced the urgency felt by Indonesians to climb the added-value ladder in manufacturing for export. But it is clear that the economies of both Southeast Asia and China have gained from their interactions.

Multiple partners Neither as a trader nor as an investor has China dominated Southeast Asia. The variety of the ASEAN countries' economic partners
has limited the region's dependence on any single outsider, including China.
China's percentage share in ASEAN's total trade has grown rapidly in recent
decades, but only from low single digits to around 15 percent. Viewed from
Southeast Asia, ASEAN-China trade has become tilted in favor of imports.
The region buys more from China than it sells to it. Placed in context,
however, the skew is not alarming. China did account for a fifth of the
growth of all ASEAN imports from 2002 to 2014. But flows of imports from
the EU, Japan, and the United States together made up another fifth of that
growth, in addition to another fifth consisting of imports from and to the
ASEAN countries themselves (Table 3.2). As for the country origins of FDI
arriving in Southeast Asia since 1995, that pattern has become substantially
more diversified over time, with China contributing a mere 7 percent of the
inflow in 2013 (Table 3.5). Looking forward, even if Chinese investment
in the region slows down, the decline should have little impact, given how
negligible that stream of capital already is and the variety of countries from
which ASEAN draws the many other streams.

Country differences In discussions of Southeast Asia's relations with
China, care should be taken not to homogenize the region, as if its 10 members were similar. They are not. Country by country in 2013 and 2014, the
absolute values of total (two-way) trade with China varied from as little
as $2 billion for Brunei to as much as $100 billion for Malaysia (Table
3.3). Expressed as proportional shares of each country's worldwide trade
in 2014, total trade with China ran from a little more than a tenth for
Vietnam to two-thirds for Laos (Table 3.4). Different factors explain these
differences. Western sanctions on Myanmar, for example, redirected the
flow of that country's exports away from the OECD economies and toward
Asia, including China. Those who would generalize region-wide should
keep these particulars in mind.

Contingent balances Trade is dynamic. ASEAN as a whole registered a
trade deficit with China in 2014 that was almost half again greater than
the region's deficit in 2013 (Table 3.3). But a single country, Vietnam, contributed more than two-thirds of that addition to the regional imbalance.
Malaysia and Thailand ran surpluses with China in 2013. In 2014 Myanmar
joined them in that regard. That said, since AC-FTA first came into effect
for the more advanced ASEAN members in 2010, the trade deficit run by the
region as a whole has increased. Whether that negative trend will continue
will reflect a host of contingencies, including the impact of slowing growth
in China.

Future choices Southeast Asia, China, Japan, South Korea, Taiwan, and Hong Kong together shipped or received the bulk — some three-fifths — of the ASEAN region's imports and exports in 2014, up from roughly half of those flows in 1996 (Table 3.2). Policy choices arise: Should ASEAN leverage this East Asian base into priority support for a future East Asian Economic Community? Or should ASEAN encourage more of its members to join geographically broader arrangements such as the CPTPP, hoping thereby to maintain or enlarge the diversity of its partners in trade and investment as insurance against dependence on China or any other one source? Or should ASEAN, as an intergovernmental rather than a supranational body, not even try to shape its members' choices?

Distrust of China and fear of its possible future dominion over Southeast Asia will likely push some ASEAN governments toward a trans-Pacific frame. Leaders in Jakarta among other ASEAN capitals could, on the other hand, lose interest in new regional involvements, turn toward nationalism, and resort to protection. Still others in Southeast Asia may seek even closer ties to Chinese markets, investors, and funds. Arguments regarding the economic considerations reviewed in this chapter will influence these choices, but they will likely respond at least as much to political events and conditions.

Notes

1 In this chapter, unless otherwise specified, "trade" means merchandise or goods trade. This definition includes manufactured goods and their components, agricultural commodities, and materials including ores and fuels, but it excludes services. Trade in services is not covered here for lack of space and adequate data. Trade in services between ASEAN and the rest of the world has grown overall, but it is hard to know how much of that growth can be attributed to flows from Southeast Asia to China or to flows from China to Southeast Asia. Also, "investment" here means foreign direct investment, not portfolio investment. Finally, for convenience, "ASEAN"—the Association of Southeast Asian Nations—is used interchangeably with "Southeast Asia" to reference the organization's 10 member states, where an IMF-estimated 651 million people resided in 2018. An 11th Southeast Asian country, Timor-Leste, with a population of one million, does not belong to ASEAN and is not covered herein. ASEAN the organization has a secretariat in Jakarta, but its authority is intergovernmental not supranational.

2 World Bank, *The East Asian Miracle: Economic Growth and Public Policy* (Oxford, UK: Oxford University Press, 1993).

3 The comparisons reflect per capita GDPs in these countries in US dollars at purchasing power parity (PPP). The figures in 2016 were: Singapore USD $87,855; Brunei $77,404; Malaysia $27,267; Thailand $17,270; China $15,489; Indonesia $11,720; Philippines $7,812; Vietnam $6,424; Laos $6,348; Myanmar $5,429; and Cambodia $3,861. *Key Indicators for Asia and the Pacific 2017* (Manila: Asia Development Bank, 2017), 144 (Table 2.2).

4 As did Elena Ianchovichina, Sethaput Suthiwart-Narueput, and Min Zhao, "Regional Impact of China's Accession to the WTO," in *East Asia Integrates: A Trade Policy Agenda for Shared Growth*, eds. Kathie Krumm and Homi Kharas (Washington, DC: World Bank, 2004), 22.

5 John Wong and Sarah Chan, "China-Asean Free Trade Agreement: Shaping Future Economic Relations," *Asian Survey* 43, no. 3 (May–June 2003): 523.

6 Wong and Chan, "China-Asean Free Trade Agreement," 517.

7 Jose L. Tongzon, "ASEAN-China Free Trade Area: A Bane or Boon for ASEAN Countries?," *The World Economy* 28, no. 2 (2005): 194. Most

of these studies depended on GCE models, and the results were to a considerable extent dictated by the parameters chosen.

8 Barry Eichengreen and Hui Tong, "How China Is Reorganizing the World Economy," *Asian Economic Policy Review* 1 (2006): 79; also Ianchovichina, Suthiwar-Narueput, and Zhao, "Regional Impact," 36.

9 David Roland Holst, "ASEAN and China: Export Rivals or Partners in Regional Growth?," *World Economy* 27, no. 8 (January 2004): 1273; Ian Coxhead, "A New Resource Curse? Impacts of China's Boom on Comparative Advantage and Resource Dependence in Southeast Asia," *World Development* 35, no. 7 (2007): 1110; Yongzheng Yang, "China's Integration into the World Economy: Implications for Developing Countries," *Asian-Pacific Economic Literature* 20, no. 1 (2006): 54.

10 World Bank, "GDP Growth (Annual %)," http://data.worldbank.org /indicator/NY.GDP.MKTP.KD.ZG.

11 Harry X. Wu, "Re-estimating Chinese Growth: How Fast Has China's Economy Really Grown?," Special Briefing Paper, China Center for Economics and Business, The Conference Board, June 2014.

12 See Richard Baldwin, "Managing the Noodle Bowl: The Fragility of East Asian Regionalism," Discussion Paper No. 5561, Centre for Economic Policy Research, London, 2006, http://econpapers.repec.org /paper/cprceprdp/5561.htm; Mona Haddad, "Trade Integration in East Asia: The Role of China and Production Networks," Policy Research Working Paper WPS 4160, World Bank Group, Washington, DC, March 2007, 11, https://doi.org/10.1596/1813-9450-4160.

13 Manufacturers Alliance for Productivity and Innovation (MAPI), "China Solidifies Its Position as the World's Largest Manufacturer," 30 March 2015.

14 Prema-Chandra Athukorala, "The Rise of China and East Asian Export Performance: Is the Crowding-Out Fear Warranted?," *The World Economy* 32, no. 2 (2009): 260; Haddad, "Trade Integration in East Asia," 21.

15 For the Philippines, see Jane T. Haltmaier et al., "The Role of China in Asia: Engine, Conduit or Steamroller?," International Finance Discussion Paper No. 904, Board of Governors of the Federal Reserve System, Washington, DC, 2007, 32–35, https://www.federalreserve.gov /pubs/ifdp/2007/904/ifdp904.pdf; For Indonesia, see Indermit Gill and Homi Kharas, *An East Asian Renaissance: Ideas for Economic Growth* (Washington, DC: World Bank, 2007), 29.

16 *ASEAN Statistical Yearbook 2014* (Jakarta: ASEAN Secretariat, July 2015), 59 (Table V.5).

17 *ASEAN Statistical Yearbook 2016/2017* (Jakarta: ASEAN Secretariat, December 2017), 61 (Tables 5.2 and 5.3).

18 See Table 3.3 in this chapter; and *ASEAN Economic Community Chartbook 2016* and *2017* (Jakarta: ASEAN Secretariat, October 2016 and November 2017), 26 (Table 4.5) and 26 (Table 4.5), respectively.

19 "ASEAN Trade in Goods (in US$)," *ASEANstats*, ASEAN Secretariat, Statistics Division, accessed 21 June 2018, https://data.aseanstats.org /trade.php.

20 Although the Chinese data for 2013 used in Table 3.3 show Malaysia and Thailand running surpluses that year, for example, figures from the World Bank have these countries running deficits. On this anomaly, and on Vietnam's trade deficit with China, see Nargiza Salidjanova and Iacob Koch-Weser, *China's Economic Ties with ASEAN: A Country-by-Country Analysis*, Staff Research Report (Washington, DC: U.S.-China Economic and Security Review Commission, 2015), 28–31, http://www .uscc.gov/sites/default/files/Research/China's%20Economic%20Ties%20 with%20ASEAN.pdf.

21 Salidjanova and Koch-Weser, *China's Economic Ties*, 29–35.

22 Other sources put the figure for 2013 as low as 2.3 percent (Salidjanova and Koch-Weser, *China's Economic Ties*, 6).

23 *ASEAN Community in Figures — Special Edition 2014: A Closer Look at Trade Performance and Dependency, and Investment* (Jakarta: ASEAN Secretariat, 2014), 85 (Figure 6.5), http://www.asean.org/storage /images/ASEAN_RTK_2014/ACIF_Special_Edition_2014.pdf.

24 Derek Scissors, "China's Outward Investment Healthy, Puzzling," AEI Research, American Enterprise Institute, Washington, DC, January 7, 2015, 5 (Table 2), https://www.aei.org/wp-content/uploads/2015/01 /Chinas-outward-investment.pdf. As Scissors's title implies, Chinese outward investment data are hard to interpret. A large percentage of the outbound flow goes to Hong Kong, the Cayman Islands, and the British Virgin Islands, and much of this ends up back in China. Flows of investment from mainland China do go to Southeast Asia via Hong Kong, but it has been argued that in Cambodia and Vietnam, some of this capital, registered as coming from the mainland, is in fact owned by companies in Taiwan, Hong Kong, or Macao. For more, see Nargiza Salidjanova, *Going Out: An Overview of China's Outward Foreign*

Direct Investment, USCC Staff Research Report (Washington, DC: U.S.-China Economic and Security Review Commission, 2011); Julia Kubny and Hinrich Voss, *China's FDI in ASEAN: Trends and Impact on Host Countries* (Bonn: German Development Institute and Leeds University Business School, 2010); and Yun Schuler-Zhou and Margot Schuller, "The Internationalization of Chinese Companies," *China Management Studies* 3, no. 1 (2009): 25–42.

25 Prema-Chandra Athukorala and Swarnim Wagle, "Foreign Direct Investment in Southeast Asia: Is Malaysia Falling Behind?," *ASEAN Economic Bulletin* 28, no. 2 (2011): 126.

26 As quoted in Marwaan Macan-Markar, "ASIA: China-ASEAN Free Trade Area Sparks Cautious Optimism," Inter Press Service, 19 January 2010, http://www.ipsnews.net/2010/01/asia-china-asean-free-trade-area -sparks-cautious-optimism/.

27 Anne Booth, "China's Economic Relations with Indonesia: Threats and Opportunities," *Journal of Current Southeast Asian Affairs* 30, no. 2 (2011): 141–60, https://www.soas.ac.uk/cseas/events/file72193.pdf.

28 John Ravenhill, "The 'New East Asian Regionalism': A Political Domino Effect," *Review of International Political Economy* 17, no. 2 (May 2010): 178–208.

29 Walden Bello, "The China-Asean Free Trade Area: Propaganda and Reality," *Focus on the Global South*, 18 January 2010, http://focusweb .org/node/1564. In the Philippines, according to Amado M. Mendoza Jr. and Richard Javad Heydarian ("The Philippines," in *ASEAN-China Free Trade Area: Challenges, Opportunities and the Road Ahead*, eds. Keith E. Flick and Kalyan M. Kemburi [Singapore: S. Rajaratnam School of International Studies, 2012], 58–66), many "smuggled or hoarded" low-cost Chinese goods were not included as imports in official trade data. If that were true in 2014, the officially stated Philippine trade deficit with China for that year — $1.4 billion — could be too low. The figure is from Philippine Statistics Authority, "Foreign Trade Statistics of the Philippines: 2014," https://psa.gov.ph/content/foreign-trade-statistics -philippines-2014.

30 As quoted by Bello, "China-Asean Free Trade Area."

31 Makmur Keliat, "Hot Issues in Sino-RI [Republic of Indonesia] Relations," *The Jakarta Post*, 27 October 2010, http://www.thejakarta post.com/news/2010/10/27/hot-issues-sinori-relations.html.

32 Stephen V. Marks, "The ASEAN-China Free Trade Agreement: Political Economy in Indonesia," *Bulletin of Indonesian Economic Studies* 51, no. 2 (August 2015): 287–306.

33 Marks, "The ASEAN-China Free Trade Agreement." For more on China-Indonesia, see Booth, "China's Economic Relations."

34 *ASEAN Community in Figures*, 8.

35 Data problems are discussed further in Anne Booth, "Economic Relations between China, India and Southeast Asia: Coping with Threats and Opportunities," in *Trade, Development, and Political Economy in East Asia: Essays in Honour of Hal Hill*, eds. Chandra Athukorala, Arianto A. Patunru, and Budy P. Resosudarmo (Singapore: Institute of Southeast Asian Studies, 2014), 79–81.

36 For 2009 data, see *ASEAN Statistical Yearbook 2014*, 69 (Table V.12); for 2015, see: "ASEAN Trade by Selected Partner Country/Region, 2015," ASEAN Statistics, http://asean.org/storage/2015/12/table19_as-of-10-June -2016.pdf.

37 "CPTPP to Come into Force after Six Countries Ratify It," *Boreneo Post Online*, 14 April 2018, http://www.theborneopost.com/2018/04/04 /cptpp-to-come-into-force-after-six-countries-ratify-it/.

38 Australia, Department of Foreign Affairs and Trade, Regional Comprehensive Economic Partnership, "Twenty-second Round of Negotiations—28 April–8 May 2018, Singapore," 14 May 2018, http:// dfat.gov.au/trade/agreements/negotiations/rcep/news/Pages/twenty -second-round-of-negotiations-28-april-8-may-2018-singapore.aspx.

CHAPTER 4

China Seen from Southeast Asia
PATTERNS OF OPINION

Yun-han Chu, *Academia Sinica, Taiwan*
Min-hua Huang, *National Taiwan University, Taiwan*
Jie Lu, *American University, United States*

As the most populous country and one of the two largest economies in the world, a rising China has challenged American hegemony in virtually every respect.[1] In response, the Obama administration "pivoted" toward Asia. The move showed America's desire to retain its regional dominance, strengthen its East Asian alliances, and upgrade its engagements with the members of the Association of Southeast Asian Nations (ASEAN), all with a view toward managing, restraining, or even containing China's rise. China meanwhile, led since 2013 by President Xi Jinping, moved assertively and ambitiously to ensure a favorable regional and global context for its further ascent. These moves showed China's desire to enhance its international influence and prepare for a possible future showdown with the United States.

Coverage of these developments in academe and the media has focused on how, in Southeast and Northeast Asia, China and the United States have competed militarily, economically, and in diplomacy. By flexing their respective muscles, each power has sought to demonstrate to the other its capability and commitment. Showing off one's "hard power" generates valuable information for counterparts and observers, who accordingly update their assessments and reconsider their strategic choices. Nevertheless, as Joseph Nye has famously argued,[2] one can also deploy "soft power" in the hope of making others more receptive to one's own preferences and goals. China and the United States alike have taken part in soft-power competition in East Asia.

In 2007, then president Hu Jintao told the 17th Congress of the Chinese Communist Party that China needed to enhance "the soft power of its culture."[3] Since then, the Chinese government has invested billions of dollars in the cultivation, improvement, and use of its soft-power resources. In 2014, Hu's successor Xi Jinping reminded his colleagues and cadres that "we should increase China's soft power, give a good Chinese narrative, and better communicate China's messages to the world."[4]

In the resulting charm offensive, China has presented itself as a responsible rising power sincerely hoping to contribute to a new regional and global order — a "harmonious world" expressing "the shared destiny of human beings." On behalf of that vision, China has launched a worldwide public-diplomacy campaign. Hundreds of Confucius Institutes have been opened around the world. China Global Television Network runs 24-hour news channels in major languages. Over time, Beijing has offered tens of thousands of scholarships to attract foreign students to study in China. By 2017, in Southeast Asia alone, China had established 31 Confucius Institutes, 32 Confucius Classrooms, and more than 500 scholarships for ASEAN citizens to attend classes in China.[5]

An obvious purpose of soft-power projection is to render public opinion in the target countries more favorable toward China. Yet few analysts have used systematic survey research to determine how its East Asian neighbors view a rising China. In this chapter, we use the latest two rounds of the Asian Barometer Survey (ABS), through 2016, to develop a picture of what East Asians think of China and its rise.[6] Our analysis begins with an overview of the competitive Sino-American context within which our findings should be seen.

Xi Jinping's China

The days when Beijing preferred a low-key foreign policy are over. Xi Jinping's China is busy, even hyperactive, regionally and around the world. Chinese initiatives to foster economic partnership, regional integration, and multilateral cooperation in East Asia and globally, not to mention Xi's wide-ranging campaign against home-grown corruption, reflect his status as the most powerful Chinese leader since Deng Xiaoping. Formally, Xi shares power with six other members of the Standing Committee of the Central Political Bureau (Politburo) of the Communist Party of China in a long-standing system of collective leadership. The new president has, nevertheless, taken into his own hands decision-making power over all important policy domains. His strong and activist authority reflects his personal confidence in the bigger role that he believes China can and should play in world affairs.

China's more assertive if not aggressive role is also enabled by the resources and instruments that are available to Beijing. Consider the economic leverage at China's disposal due to its prolonged prior economic growth. Already in 2014, according to the International Monetary Fund, China's gross domestic product adjusted for purchasing power parity (PPP) reached USD $17.6 trillion — $200 billion more than the United States' $17.4 trillion figure. In 2015, the rapidly thickening outflow of Chinese foreign direct investment topped $120 billion, and since then China has become a net capital exporter. China's economy remains a major engine for global growth even as its own rate has slowed. In 2016, China contributed an estimated 39 percent of that year's worldwide growth.[7] China is already the top trading partner for most of the countries in Southeast Asia, and Xi Jinping has pushed for more Chinese investment in the region and even more trade as well. Investments from China are transforming the smaller ASEAN members like never before, especially Laos, Cambodia, and Myanmar.[8]

China's new proactivity is evident as well in its increased willingness to project its vision and express its demands on a larger scale than previously. China under Xi has eagerly broadcast far and wide its "Chinese Dream" of national rejuvenation and its claim to global economic leadership of the developing world. Xi's China has also demanded that other countries respect its core interests, especially its territorial integrity, including Chinese sovereignty in the East and South China Seas and over Tibet and Taiwan. Meanwhile Beijing has sought to enlarge its agenda-setting role by proposing a "New Model of Great Power Relations" between China and the United States; by reviving the idea of a Free Trade Area of the Asia-Pacific to be achieved through the Asia-Pacific Economic Cooperation forum; and by driving the 2016 G20 Summit toward its "Hangzhou Consensus," to cite some examples.

Most stunning of all has been the 2013 launching and subsequent juggernaut growth of a project whose scope and buzz would have been unthinkable just a few years earlier: China's plan for "One Belt, One Road," later renamed the Belt and Road Initiative (BRI). The BRI, including its Maritime Silk Road initiative through Southeast Asia, has become the geo-economic and geopolitical hallmark of Xi's global strategy.[9] Related developments have included the 2015 launching of the Asian Infrastructure Investment Bank and the 2017 enlargement of the Shanghai Cooperation Organization to include India and Pakistan. All of these moves illustrate China's ambition to rewrite the rules of economic engagement and the parameters of globalization.

China has also grown visibly less self-restrained about flexing its military muscles. The commissioning of its first aircraft carrier, the *Liaoning*, in 2012 signified Beijing's desire to project hard power far beyond its coastal waters. In addition, China has taken a more confrontational approach toward the disputes over sovereignty in the South and East China Seas. Chinese military exercises in these waters have become more frequent. Massive China Coast Guard ships have been deployed to patrol disputed water space. In the name of providing peaceful public services, land features in the South China Sea (scs) have been enlarged, built upon, and equipped with military infrastructure. The People's Liberation Army Air Force is being upgraded with cutting-edge capabilities, from anti-satellite missiles and stealth bombers to hypersonic glide vehicles. President Xi's China is resolved to counterbalance the United States and compete with it head-on in the hard power realm.

Against this background, relative to China's influence in Southeast Asia, American influence has declined. It is in the context of this reconfiguration of the region's strategic landscape that we turn now to how people in Southeast and Northeast Asia view and compare China and the United States.

China's Influence Perceived and Assessed

The impact of a country's soft-power messaging depends on how it is received. It is conventionally thought that while Asian publics are increasingly aware of China's growing economic and political power, they are not necessarily persuaded by its stated foreign policy objectives, nor necessarily approving of Chinese intentions insofar as these can be known, much less attracted to China's political system. Reliable data on public opinion in multiple Asian countries are needed to verify this received view.

A number of cross-national survey databases already exist, such as those generated by the Pew Global Attitudes Project and the BBC World Service's GlobeScan. Some of Pew's findings in 2017 are featured below. But these efforts have tended to cover only a few Asian countries. From autumn 2014 to spring 2016, the Fourth Wave of the Asian Barometer Survey (ABS-4) was administered in 14 East Asian jurisdictions — 12 members of the UN plus Taiwan and Hong Kong — using jurisdiction-wide probability sampling and face-to-face interviews. (For convenience here, all of these sites are referred to collectively as countries.) The ABS's Third Wave (ABS-3) was administered from winter 2010 to winter 2012 in 13 of these countries; only in Myanmar could the research not be done. (For clarity, data from ABS-4 are identified by the implementation period 2014–16, data from ABS-3 by 2010–12.) Several questions in both waves were related to the rise of China. The answers show how citizens in the region have viewed China in recent years in the context of its growing activity, influence, and stature.

TABLE 4.1 Which has the most influence in Asia now, China or the United States? (%)

	2010–12			2014–16			Point change in "China" response
	China	United States	Other	China	United States	Other	
South Korea	56	31	13	67	25	8	+11
Hong Kong	71	21	8	66	24	10	−5
Taiwan	67	21	12	63	23	14	−4
Japan	61	29	10	61	27	12	0
Mongolia	66	13	21	61	9	30	−5
Vietnam	69	15	16	60	18	22	−9
Myanmar	—	—	—	57	32	11	—
China	56	33	11	56	31	13	0
Singapore	60	28	12	54	29	17	−6
Thailand	42	44	14	49	19	32	+7
Malaysia	36	43	21	42	46	12	+6
Indonesia	23	41	36	37	37	26	+14
Cambodia	26	58	16	28	48	24	+2
Philippines	17	65	18	22	59	19	+5
Median*	58	30	15	57	27	18	−1

SOURCES: Asian Barometer Survey, Third Wave (ABS-3), conducted in 2010–12; and Asian Barometer Survey, Fourth Wave (ABS-4), conducted in 2014–16.

NOTE: *Median excludes respondents in China. Myanmar was not surveyed in 2010–12 but is included in the three medians for 2014–16. Including it in the calculation of the latter medians has no effect on those for "China" or "Other" and changes the median response for "United States" trivially from 26 to 27 percent. Respondents in the "Other" columns chose Japan, India, or another country (other than China or the United States) as having the most influence in Asia.

Both of the Asian Barometer surveys asked, "Which country has the most influence in Asia now?" Respondents could choose "China," "Japan," "India," "United States," or name a different country, including their own. Immediately notable in Table 4.1 is the clustering of Southeast Asian countries toward the bottom of the table where respondents were *least* likely to be impressed by Chinese influence. Leaving aside the views of their own country held by Chinese themselves, respondents in all of the eight Southeast Asian countries surveyed in 2014–16 were *less* likely to credit China's influence than were their counterparts in any of the five Northeast Asian countries covered. Very roughly put, the greater the physical distance from China, the less common the recognition of superior Chinese power. Notable too is the prominence of supposedly "Confucian" cultures toward the top of the table, among the majorities most taken with China's importance, compared with the culturally more diverse and less impressed Southeast Asian societies lower down. Of course merely seeing China as influential, as a matter of cognition, need not imply fear, admiration, or any other value judgment on the part of the beholder.

The country medians in Table 4.1 are revealing. By that measure in 2010–12, excluding China itself and without Myanmar for lack of data, a country-median 58 percent of East Asian respondents saw China as having the most influence in Asia in 2010–12 (ABS-3), as did a comparable 57 percent in 2014–16 (ABS-4). In contrast to that substantial acknowledgment, only 27 percent of those who responded in 2014–16 saw the United States as most influential, down slightly from 30 percent in 2010–12. Overall, in the later period, China was considered most influential over the United States by a convincing margin of two to one.

In Southeast Asia, the distributions of perceived American versus Chinese influence favored China less decisively. In Vietnam and Singapore, larger proportions chose China than chose the United States in 2010–12 and did so again in 2014–16. In Malaysia, Cambodia, and the Philippines, however, the opposite was true on both occasions: more in these countries gave the top spot in influence to the United States, not to China. While Indonesians chose the United States as having more influence than China in the first survey, by 2014–16 the percentage of Indonesians who believed either the United States or China had the most influence was tied at 37 percent.

Most dramatically of all, in Thailand, those who chose the United States shrank 25 points, from 44 to 19 percent, by far the largest drop from ABS-3 to ABS-4 in any country covered. The May 2014 coup in Thailand and ensuing tension in Thai-US relations almost certainly figured in this result, whether as an expression of Thai nationalism, or in recognition of Washington's inability to prevent the takeover in Bangkok, or both. Yet China benefited less from the plunge in perceived American influence than might have been expected. The 25-point US loss accompanied a much smaller 7-point Chinese gain.

Nevertheless, appraisals of US influence set aside, respondents in most — five — of the seven ASEAN states covered in both surveys were pro-portionally *more* inclined to credit China as number one in influence in 2014–16 than respondents in those countries had been several years before. The two exceptions were Vietnam and Singapore, where China-choosing respondents declined proportionally from the first to the second survey. Concomitantly, setting aside views of China, perceptions of the United States as the most influential *fell* proportionally in most — four — of these seven Southeast Asian states, and changed only trivially in the countries where it rose — up 3 percent each in Malaysia and Vietnam, up 1 percent in Singapore.

The plusses and minuses in the rightmost column in Table 4.1 are telling: the chronological gains for China from 2010–12 to 2014–16 were uniquely bunched in Southeast Asia, not in Northeast Asia (South Korea excepted). By this measure, if the Obama administration's pivot toward Southeast Asia was meant to convey America's salience in that region, it failed to convince those who lived there, although that failure could perhaps have been even more severe in the absence of Washington's move.

Esteem and disesteem

Cognition aside, how do East Asians *feel* about the influence of China and the United States? In 2010–12 and again in 2014–16, respondents were asked whether China's influence in Asia does more harm than good or more good than harm. These data are shown in Table 4.2.

The focus of this chapter is on China, not the United States, and the 67 percent median-country favorable assessment of China's influence in Asia for 2014–16 is good news for Beijing. However, as noted by Yun-han Chu and Yu-tzung Chang, the ABS-4 data in fact support a different comparative conclusion: respondents were actually less favorable toward Chinese influence, with most of them seeing US influence as "largely benign," and their views of China's influence sharply divergent.[10]

Appraisals of China's influence in 2014–16 were widely dispersed across East Asia and polarized toward the ends of the spectrum of opinion. As shown in Table 4.2, country percentages commending China were less than a third in Japan (11 percent), Vietnam (20), Myanmar (28), and Mongolia (32); few and evenly divided in the Philippines (41) and Taiwan (55); and two-thirds-or-more positive in Indonesia (67), Cambodia (67), Singapore (71), South Korea (75), Malaysia (75), Hong Kong (78), and Thailand (86). At the most flattering extreme, the image of Chinese influence as, on balance, beneficial for East Asia attracted a near-unanimous 98 percent of respondents inside China — the far end of a range 87 percentage points in length, from extreme-skeptical Japan to ostensibly hyper-patriotic China. From these country-by-country results one may infer that while many East Asians were glad to see China rise, some thought it a threat and viewed its ascent with apprehension.

TABLE 4.2 Favorable views of China's influence (%)

	2010–12	2014–16	Change in points
China	97	98	+1
Thailand	68	86	+18
Hong Kong	82	78	−4
Malaysia	77	75	−2
South Korea	53	75	+22
Singapore	78	71	−7
Cambodia	71	67	−4
Indonesia	64	67	+3
Taiwan	59	55	−4
Philippines	73	41	−32
Mongolia	33	32	−1
Myanmar	—	28	—
Vietnam	56	20	−36
Japan	19	11	−8
Median*	66	67	+1

SOURCES: ABS-3 (2010–12) and ABS-4 (2014–16).

NOTE: *Median excludes respondents from China. "Favorable" summarizes responses that China was doing "much more" or "somewhat more" good than harm.

Also worth noting in Table 4.2 is that, from 2010–12 to 2014–16, only four surveyed countries registered significant changes in the proportions of respondents who found the net effects of Chinese influence in East Asia to be beneficial. Positive appraisals rose sharply in South Korea and Thailand. They fell even more sharply in the Philippines and Vietnam. The 2014 coup in Bangkok and the resulting junta's tilt toward Beijing likely contributed to the 18-point improvement in China's image among Thais, while rising Manila-Beijing and Hanoi-Beijing tensions over the SCS doubtless played roles in the steep losses to China's reputation — a 32-point drop in the Philippines, 36 points down in Vietnam — in what were at that time its two staunchest maritime rivals in Southeast Asia.

Plus-plus opinions

"The pursuit of power among nations must no longer be seen as a zero-sum game," said US president Barack Obama in 2009, with Sino-American relations very much in mind.[11] Foreign-policy analysts have largely ignored his advice. Their inclination to treat China-US relations in either-or terms has, if anything, increased since 2009, due in part to rising tensions in the SCS.

TABLE 4.3 Correlation between favorable views of both Chinese and American influence in Asia, 2014–16

	Correlation
Thailand	+.408**
Malaysia	+.314**
Indonesia	+.308**
Singapore	+.284**
Myanmar	+.125**
Cambodia	+.023
Philippines	+.009
Vietnam	−.017
China	−.102**

SOURCE: ABS-4 (2014–16).

NOTE: **Statistical significance at the 0.05 level (two-tailed). China's coefficient is shown for comparison. The coefficients indicate positive and negative correlations between favorable views of Chinese and American influence expressed by the same respondent. Plus signs indicate a probability that respondents in a given country thought both China and America were doing more good than harm in Asia. Negative signs indicate a probability that respondents approved of China's influence but not America's, or vice-versa.

Yet as Table 4.3 shows, public opinion in Southeast Asia during 2014–16 saw both China and America in relatively positive terms. To those surveyed in Southeast Asia, a belief that China was doing more good than harm did not require a concomitant belief that the United States was doing more harm than good — or the other way around. Many of the respondents were disposed to think reasonably well of both of these big powers, that both were doing at least some good for Asia. By the same token, skepticism toward Beijing implied skepticism toward Washington as well. Among Southeast Asians, the correlation was strongest in Thailand. As Thais warmed toward China, especially following the May 2014 coup in Bangkok and its immediate condemnation by Washington, Thai views of their country's long-standing ties to the United States did not immediately cool. Surveyed in September–October 2014, Thai respondents were inclined to welcome Chinese and American influence alike. At the opposite (bottom) end of the spectrum in Table 4.3 stands China, whose respondents did apparently, to a modest extent, entertain zero-sum views of their own country's behavior in Asia versus that of the United States, seeing Chinese influence as more good than bad, American influence as more bad than good.

In most Asian countries, in the authors' opinion, informed people welcome the strong presence of both powers, knowing that they are not mutually replaceable: if the United States cannot replace China as the locomotive of economic growth, China can hardly replace the United States as the ultimate guarantor of their country's security. In this context, Sino-American competition could be a plus-sum game, and a balanced Asian presence of both powers might serve the region's economic and security interests best. That said, in countries experiencing a popular backlash against globalization, public opinion could turn against China and America alike. People who feel harmed by economic opening, financial instability, and foreign competition may object not only to Chinese economic penetration and expansion. They may also resent America's role as the primary architect of an inegalitarian neoliberal economic order that has fostered inequality while facilitating Chinese gains. The American presidency of Donald Trump may exacerbate these uncertainties, as noted toward the end of this chapter.

The Selective Attractions of Democracy and Development

Space constraints preclude full coverage of the myriad considerations that affect the motivations behind Southeast Asian views of China. One such consideration that the surveys did cover, however, is emulation: the relevance of China and other countries as preferred or rejected models of democracy and development.

Democracy

ABS researchers measured "perceived democratic distance" on a 10-level scale from "completely undemocratic" to "completely democratic." Respondents in all countries except China were asked to assign a level to China and a level to his or her own country. The ratings for China were low (less democratic); the ratings for the United States were high (more democratic); and the own-country ratings were in between. Distances from one's own country to China were then compared with positive appraisals of China's influence in Asia by respondents of that country to see whether greater distances implied less or more positive appraisals.

In the eight Southeast Asian countries surveyed in 2014–16, perceived democratic distance between China and one's own country was *unrelated* to whether respondents viewed China in either positive or negative terms. The authoritarian character of China was by and large acknowledged, but perceived democratic distance from China did *not* predict a less (or more) generous view of its large undemocratic neighbor. Democracy simply did not matter, and that is good news for Xi Jinping. Awareness of his government's repressive rule did not significantly diminish support for Chinese influence in Asia.

The results regarding the United States were very different. Respondents in China were not asked to estimate the democratic distance between their own country and the United States. Across the rest of East Asia, however, the perceived difference between own-country and American levels of democracy correlated strongly with a favorable view of US influence in Asia. Respondents in many East Asian countries credited America with a level of democracy substantially higher than the perceived level at home and also held a positive view of American influence in Asia. In 2014–16, *before* the presidency of Donald Trump, the soft power of American democracy was appreciated, at least relative to the state of democracy in the respondent's own East Asian country, and the greater the gap, the stronger the support for American influence.

Development

Democracy is one thing, development quite another. Even if the authoritarian, one-party-dominant nature of China's *political* system, as perceived by Southeast Asian respondents, did not affect their assessment of Chinese influence in East Asia, one would have expected Southeast Asians to want their countries to emulate China's extraordinary *economic* success. Arguably, that success should have lifted the Chinese model of development into first place in Southeast Asian eyes, compared with competing models represented by the United States and other relatively advanced countries. Accordingly, in 2010–12 and 2014–16, respondents were asked, "Which country should be a model for your country's future development?" In their answers, they could choose either China, India, Japan, Singapore, the United States, their own country, or the model offered by a country not on the list.

The results, shown in Table 4.4, refute the hypothetical relative magnetism of China's development model in Southeast Asia. Not included in the table for space reasons are the findings for Northeast Asia, but they also contradicted the expected appeal of China's development model. In Japan, Mongolia, South Korea, and Taiwan, no model was *less* attractive than China's.[12]

That said, several aspects of the distribution of preferences for development models in Southeast Asia displayed in Table 4.4 are worth noting: the overall unattractiveness of the China model; its steep loss of popularity in Vietnam; the resilience of the American model; the losses of preference for own-country models in Thailand, Vietnam, and Malaysia; and Singapore's enduring pride in its own model.

TABLE 4.4 Which country is preferred as a model for the future development of one's own country? (%)

	Survey year	United States	Own country	Japan	Singapore	China
Reaffirmers						
Philippines	2010	**68**	0	17	6	7
Philippines	2014	**66**	1	17	8	6
Cambodia	2012	**42**	5	22	6	6
Cambodia	2015	**47**	3	12	3	15
Indonesia	2011	26	8	**35**	13	14
Indonesia	2016	17	13	**34**	16	16
Singapore	2010	24	**38**	17	NA	13
Singapore	2015	22	**36**	16	NA	17
Switchers						
Thailand	2010	16	**46**	12	8	16
Thailand	2014	18	8	**27**	13	23
Vietnam	2010	9	**42**	16	10	22
Vietnam	2015	29	6	**38**	19	2
Malaysia	2011	8	**34**	31	11	14
Malaysia	2014	11	17	**31**	17	21
Other						
Myanmar	2015	10	**27**	23	18	1

SOURCES: ABS-3 (2010–12) and ABS-4 (2014–16).

NOTE: "Reaffirmers" are the countries whose respondents' most preferred model did not change from the first to the second survey, unlike the "switchers," whose most preferred model did change. Numbers in bold italics indicate the most preferred model among respondents in that country. NA = not applicable.

Considering only the columns of percentages in Table 4.4 for 2014–16, the relative appeal of the five models on offer runs, in declining order: the United States, Japan, Singapore, one's own country, and China. These results should not be over-interpreted, however. Exactly what "development" denoted and connoted in the minds of the respondents in each country at the time of each survey cannot be known with any precision. To the extent that they were thinking of "development" as a macroeconomic process or achievement, China's laggard position seems anomalous in the light of China's stellar historical record of aggregate material growth. The incongruity is reduced, on the other hand, if respondents understood the concept more in political terms.

Further complicating the picture is how the respondents construed a Chinese or any other model of development. If, for instance, the popularity of the United States as an exemplar expressed the respondents' desire for an American as opposed to a Chinese standard of living, then development was construed as an outcome not a process — an end in itself, never mind the means. That said, for Beijing, the implications of Table 4.4 for soft-power competition between America and China in Southeast Asia are more cautionary than encouraging. As for the sharp 20-point drop in Vietnamese desire for the China model from 2010 to 2015, it is surely no coincidence that Beijing-Hanoi relations over the SCS also worsened in those years.

Leaving Myanmar aside for lack of coverage in the earlier survey, the Southeast Asian countries were almost evenly split between so-called reaffirmers, whose preferred model on the first survey was chosen again on the second, and so-called switchers, whose preference changed.[13] The Southeast Asian countries sampled were far more fickle in this regard than were their Northeast Asian counterparts. The sole "switchers" in the latter group were the Mongolians; they preferred their own Mongolian model in 2010, but favored the US model in 2015, albeit by modest margins on both occasions. The relative volatility of Southeast Asian public opinion since 2010 may imply further changes in the future, depending on contingencies such as domestic leadership changes, the foreign policies of outsiders, and the situation in the SCS. Relevant, too, is the presidency of Donald Trump, as will be shown below.

Of particular interest among the three Southeast Asian switchers — Thailand, Vietnam, and Malaysia — is the own-country preference that they shared in the first survey and their shared preference for Japan in the second. The shift was sharpest in Vietnam, where support for the China model and the US model, respectively, fell 20 points and rose by the same interval from 2010 to 2015. But of these three Southeast Asian switchers, not one switched to the United States.

If these results should sober Beijing, they are no reason for American celebration either. Among Southeast Asian countries in 2014–16, respondents in only two — the Philippines and Cambodia — preferred the US model of development, while Japan's model was the favorite in four — Indonesia, Thailand, Vietnam, and Malaysia. Given the reluctance of Southeast Asians to align markedly, let alone irrevocably, toward either Washington or Beijing, could Tokyo offer an increasingly popular alternative in years to come? That is far from certain, but it is conceivable, to the likely greater chagrin of China's leaders compared to their American rivals. Again, however, to speculate along such clearly geopolitical lines is to risk misconstruing what the term "development" actually meant to such diverse informants in such different places at different times.

Obama, Trump, Xi, and the Redistribution of Confidence

Of the many policy-shaping changes in the political economy of East Asia, three stand out. First: China has replaced Japan as the center of economic gravity in the region. Second: US president Donald Trump has abdicated American economic leadership in the Asia-Pacific, if not also the world. Third: Chinese president Xi Jinping continues to postpone the liberalization of his country's political economy while reinforcing aspects of its authoritarian character.

Barring a change in these three trends, East Asia (including Southeast Asia) will become one of the few regions in the world where an undemocratic regional power — China — dominates the agenda for regional economic cooperation, and perhaps the only world region where relatively democratic countries will be economically integrated with and dependent upon one core country whose political economy is, by comparison, authoritarian and statist. China's distinctively post-socialist but illiberal political system no longer stands in the way of forming closer economic ties with its comparatively democratic neighbors. Given the influence of that Chinese core, one can also expect the overall environment in East Asia to become more hospitable toward relatively autocratic or hybrid regimes, as in Thailand, Cambodia, and Malaysia, and generally more conducive to the spreading and deepening of more or less despotic politics in the larger region.

Notwithstanding this prospect, however, as the ideological cleavage — liberal vs. illiberal — withers away, concentrations of economic power inside countries could jeopardize the prospect of authoritarian integration on Chinese terms. The benefits and risks of entanglement with China's economy are unevenly distributed within nearly every East Asian society. If China aspires to become a more respectable architect of regional integration and champion of free trade, it will have to create a regional environment more conducive to socially inclusive economic growth. Otherwise, inside most of China's trading partners, material inequality, sociocultural resentment, and corresponding political polarization may undermine domestic support for a Sinophile foreign policy. Beijing needs especially to acknowledge the sensitivity of ethnic cleavage in each of the two countries, Indonesia and Malaysia, where an ethnic-Chinese minority and a Muslim majority cohabit on fragile terms.

In spring 2014, the Pew Research Center surveyed public support for the respective presidents of the United States and China at that time, Barack Obama and Xi Jinping, in several East Asian countries, including three in Southeast Asia — the Philippines, Vietnam, and Indonesia. In a second survey done in spring 2017, Pew replaced Obama's name with Donald Trump's (inaugurated in January 2017) and administered the otherwise identical questions to East Asians again.

In these surveys, respondents were asked how much confidence they had that each president would "do the right thing regarding world affairs" — Obama and Xi in 2014, Trump and Xi in 2017, four questions in all. Possible answers included "a lot," "some," "not too much," or "no confidence at all."[14] Table 4.5 combines the first two of these choices to represent "substantial confidence" in a given president.

The results? First, in each of the six countries covered, confidence in President Trump in 2017 was significantly if unevenly below what the level of confidence in President Obama had been in 2014. Steepest were the declines in South Korea and Australia, down 71 and 52 percentage points respectively. Least abrupt were the reductions of confidence in Vietnam, down 13, and the Philippines, down 25. In the latter two countries, respondents appeared more willing to give the White House's new occupant the benefit of the doubt. Vietnamese and Filipino respondents would likely have wondered, for example, whether Trump would or would not continue Obama's opposition to Beijing's actions against Hanoi's and Manila's claims in the SCS.

Second, the decline in presidential support from Obama to Trump was *not* accompanied by a wave of confidence in President Xi sufficiently strong and widespread enough to leave Trump consistently or significantly far behind. Only in three countries in 2017 did Xi garner proportionally greater confidence than was accorded to Trump — in Indonesia, Australia, and South Korea, respectively by 11, 14, and 21 percentage points. Results in the other three cases were the other way around: Trump bested Xi in the Philippines by 16 points, in Japan by 24, and in Vietnam by 40. This lack of an either-or relationship between an American and a Chinese leader, where trusting one entails mistrust for the other, reinforces the inclusive logic implied by the positive correlations in Table 4.3, where to varying degrees Southeast Asian respondents were shown to be capable of holding simultaneously favorable views of American *and* Chinese influence in Asia.

Worth noting at the same time, however, is that both Tables 4.3 and 4.5, despite reporting evidence from different surveys on different questions at different times, show the Philippines and Vietnam as outliers of sorts in Southeast Asia — relatively more either-or in their appreciations of

TABLE 4.5 "Substantial confidence" in US/Chinese presidents (%)

Country	Year	Obama (2014) vs. Trump (2017)	Xi (2014) vs. Xi (2017)	US vs. Chinese president, point change
Philippines	2014	94 (O)	32 (X)	62 more for Obama than Xi
Philippines	2017	69 (T)	53 (X)	16 more for Trump than Xi
Change (+/−)		−25 pts	+21 pts	
Vietnam	2014	71 (O)	31 (X)	40 more for Obama than Xi
Vietnam	2017	58 (T)	18 (X)	40 more for Trump than Xi
Change (+/−)		−13 pts	−13 pts	
Indonesia	2014	64 (O)	36 (X)	28 more for Obama than Xi
Indonesia	2017	23 (T)	34 (X)	11 more for Xi than Trump
Change (+/−)		−41 pts	−2 pts	
Japan	2014	66 (O)	6 (X)	60 more for Obama than Xi
Japan	2017	24 (T)	11 (X)	24 more for Trump than Xi
Change (+/−)		−42 pts	+5 pts	
Australia	2014	81 (O)	81 (X)	The same for Obama and Xi
Australia	2017	29 (T)	43 (X)	14 more for Xi than Trump
Change (+/−)		−52 pts	−38 pts	
South Korea	2014	88 (O)	57 (X)	31 more for Obama than Xi
South Korea	2017	17 (T)	38 (X)	21 more for Xi than Trump
Change (+/−)		−71 pts	−19 pts	

SOURCES: Richard Wike, et al., *Global Publics Back U.S. on Fighting ISIS, but Are Critical of Post-9/11 Torture* and *U.S. Image Suffers as Publics around World Question Trump's Leadership* (Washington, DC: Pew Research Center), respectively June 2015, p. 20, and June 2017, pp. 4 and 82.

NOTE: "Substantial confidence" means respondents answered that they had "a lot" or "some" confidence that the leader in question would "do the right thing regarding world affairs." Lack of confidence cannot be directly inferred from this data as respondents may have had no opinion or preferred not to answer.

American vs. Chinese influence and in their confidence in the two American presidents over Chinese president Xi. Nor does it appear coincidental that Hanoi and Manila have claims to the SCS and have defended them robustly in the face of contrary claims and rival actions by Beijing. That said, Rodrigo Duterte's presidency in the Philippines and his intermittent tilting toward China and against America have likely affected Philippine opinion. To the extent that popular sentiment follows presidential rhetoric, Duterte's criticism of the United States could help explain the drastic decline in the confidence of Filipinos in Trump in 2017 compared with their confidence in

Obama in 2014. Duterte's turn toward China may also have contributed to the correspondingly notable increase in confidence accorded to the Chinese president, even though that gain for Xi was not enough to surpass Philippine confidence in Trump.

Cognitive Primacy, Impaired Democracy, and the Desire for Balance

As the evidence in this chapter has shown, neither in Southeast nor in Northeast Asia have the reservoirs of good will toward the United States, built up over the years, dried up. But President Trump should not take that cushion for granted, as his popularity relative to Obama's has clearly shrunk. Even before Trump's presidency, in the 2014–16 ABS survey, the Philippines was the only country at that time where even a simple majority of those questioned believed that America had the most regional influence. And that was *before* Trump's decision to withdraw the United States from the Trans-Pacific Partnership and thereby to strengthen, inadvertently or not, the impression of American disengagement from the region. Meanwhile, China's various policy initiatives, not least among them its Maritime Silk Road Initiative through Southeast Asia, have fed the conclusion that America is yesterday's power. The hyperactivity of Beijing detailed at the start of this chapter is paying off.

Insofar as Asians continue to identify with democracy as a political model and American-style democracy remains appealing in Asia, Washington will retain its long-standing soft-power advantage in these regards. But the about-face in foreign policy that Trump's presidency seems to represent is eating away at this asset. That said, China's authoritarian model remains controversial, and the United States will not be eclipsed in soft power if it can rescue its presently dysfunctional system and offer an alternative to economic reliance on China.

East Asians are unwilling to cast their lot with one side in the strategic competition between the United States and China. East Asians by and large do not believe they could or should replace American with Chinese influence, or Chinese influence with an American variety. The two versions are not incompatibly attractive in the eyes of East Asians. A balance may indeed best serve their interests. If President Trump does decide to try to contain China, he should not expect much support from Asian countries, Japan plausibly excepted. Southeast Asian countries especially are dependent on China economically. They know that China will always be their neighbor.

None wishes to join an effort to contain China—an impossible project in any event.

The latest Asian Barometer evidence presented in this chapter shows both uniformity and divergence in East Asian views of China. On the one hand, in Table 4.1, majorities in most East Asian countries see China as the single most influential state in Asia—South Korea, Hong Kong, Taiwan, Japan, Mongolia, Vietnam, Myanmar, China itself, and Singapore, in diminishing order. Yet that is not true of public opinion in four of the Southeast Asian countries surveyed. In Thailand, Malaysia, Indonesia, and Cambodia, no could-be or would-be chief influencer is seen as warranting that accolade by a majority of respondents. In the Philippines, a majority still sees the United States playing that role.

Nevertheless, and likely aided by the policies and personality of President Trump, the momentum is China's to lose. In these purely cognitive terms, setting aside the range of East Asian feelings toward China from amity through indifference to enmity, it is the like-it-or-not perception of Chinese primacy that deserves this chapter's final word.

Notes

1 Thomas J. Christensen, *The China Challenge: Shaping the Choices of a Rising Power* (New York, NY: W. W. Norton & Company, 2015).

2 Joseph Nye, *Soft Power: The Means to Success in World Politics* (New York, NY: Public Affairs, 2004).

3 "Hu Jintao Calls for Enhancing 'Soft Power' of Chinese Culture," *Xinhuanet*, 15 October 2007, http://news.xinhuanet.com/english /2007-10/15/content_6883748.htm.

4 Quoted in David Shambaugh, "China's Soft-power Push," *Foreign Affairs*, 16 June 2015, https://www.foreignaffairs.com/articles/china /2015-06-16/china-s-soft-power-push.

5 "Confucius Institute/Classroom," *Hanban*, http://english.hanban.org /node_10971.htm. Thailand hosted the most institutes (15), followed by Indonesia (6), the Philippines (4), Malaysia (2), and Cambodia, Laos, Singapore, and Vietnam (1 each). Brunei and Myanmar had none.

6 The Asian Barometer Survey is an international research network dedicated to studying public opinion and democracy through surveys of public opinion in Asia. The network's regional headquarters in Taipei is co-hosted by the Institute of Political Science, Academia Sinica, and the Center for East Asia Democratic Studies at National Taiwan University. The survey's methodology and other details are accessible at www .asianbarometer.org.

7 Stephen S. Roach, "Global Growth — Still Made in China," *Project Syndicate*, 29 August 2016, https://www.project-syndicate.org/comm entary/china-still-global-growth-engine-by-stephen-s--roach-2016-08.

8 David Roman, "China Is Transforming Southeast Asia Faster than Ever," *Bloomberg*, 6 December 2016, https://www.bloomberg.com/news /articles/2016-12-05/china-transforms-frontier-neighbors-with-cash-for-rails-to-power.

9 Flynt Leverett and Wu Bingbing, "The New Silk Road and China's Evolving Grand Strategy," *The China Journal* 77 (January 2017): 110–32.

10 Yun-han Chu and Yu-tzung Chang, "Battle for Influence: Perceptions in Asia of China and the US," *Global Asia* 12, no. 1 (Spring 2017): 108. Respondents were also asked to evaluate China's influence on their own respective countries. On this score as well, the United States fared better than China, as noted by Chu and Chang, "Battle for Influence," pp. 108–09.

11 "Transcript: President Obama Delivers Remarks at U.S.-China Strategic and Economic Dialogue," *The Washington Post*, 27 July 2009, http://www.washingtonpost.com/wp-dyn/content/article/2009/07/27/AR200907201280.html.

12 Kai-Ping Huang and Bridget Welsh, "Trends in Soft Power in East Asia: Distance, Diversity and Drivers," *Global Asia* 12, no. 1 (Spring 2017): 113 (Figure 1). Asking respondents in China for their preferred model while offering China's own model as a possible answer yielded signs of political desirability bias. That set of answers was therefore dropped.

13 These labels are so-called because, of course, the people who answered ABS-3 were not the same people who answered ABS-4.

14 Respondents could also say they did not know, or refuse to answer. Drawn from the data as presented by Pew, the percentages are aggregated in Table 4.5 as "substantial confidence," i.e., the sum of "a lot of" and "some confidence." Also taken into account are these additional four options: "not too much confidence," "no confidence at all," "do not know," and "declined to answer." Even when combined by Pew, the third and fourth options — no answer — were typically small. In Indonesia in 2017, however, they were large enough to matter: one-fifth of the Indonesian respondents in that year did not know how to answer the confidence-in-Trump question, or were unwilling to do so, and the non-response rate regarding confidence in Xi was even higher — 36 percent.

CHAPTER 5

Southeast Asia through Chinese Eyes
A STRATEGIC BACKYARD?

Mingjiang Li, *Nanyang Technological University, Singapore*

[The South China Sea] is our backyard, we can decide what vegetables and flowers we want to grow [there].
–Senior Colonel Li Jie, People's Liberation Army, 16 September 2015[1]

Backyards are locations. A backyard is subjectively strategic if the household in front regards it as vitally important. The actual status of a strategic backyard depends on the extent to which the household has managed to control that adjacent space. China views Southeast Asia as its strategic backyard. But that vision has not been implemented — at least not yet. This chapter explores the perception and why it has not become practice.

"Strategic" Southeast Asia?

In September 2015 someone going by "Liang5a" posted this comment to a story in *The Diplomat*:

ASEAN [Association of Southeast Asian Nations] was created by the US to encircle and contain China. . . . [I]t is time for ASEAN to be disbanded as a tool of aggression by the West. ASEAN should be replaced by an organization led by China. This can be called a Nanyang Commonwealth. Such a China led organization will then be stable and dynamic. And peace and prosperity will then put an end of the hundreds of years of Western conquest and destruction. Only under the leadership of China does SE Asia have a chance to equal Europe. Without China's help and protection, the West will return to colonize SE Asia again and SE Asia will immediately slip down to the level of Africa.

These statements were soon rebutted by "Richard Chak," a self-described third-generation ethnic Chinese living in an ASEAN country. ASEAN, he wrote, had been created not by the United States but by several Southeast Asian states. Replacing ASEAN with a "Nanyang Commonwealth" was a "ridiculous idea" that "no ASEAN nation will agree to." He warned against making the positions of ethnic Chinese in Southeast Asia "more difficult by suggesting such absurd dangerous ideas." He was proud of his Chinese ancestry and culture, but "we are no Western running dog. I totally disagree with you[r] proposition."[2]

This exchange illustrates in extreme form the disagreement between a few in the household and many in the yard — between the extreme nationalism and ethno-chauvinism of some Chinese views of China's backyard and the broader resistance to such ideas among Southeast Asians, including those of Chinese descent. Viewed in the light of elite-level discourse, however, such a viscerally Sino-expansionist plan to oust ASEAN from "China's backyard" sounds like a quaint vestige of the Maoist days when China was known for exporting ideological slogans, not electronic devices.

During the Cold War, Beijing did regard ASEAN as a mainly anti-China grouping. But that negative view waned in the 1990s, despite lingering suspicion. A newer and more positive perception reflected China's growing awareness of its own share of responsibility for the state of its relations with Southeast Asia. Beijing came to recognize how those relations were constrained by historical memories, issues involving the ethnic Chinese, China's own military power, its competitive economy, and disputes over the South China Sea (SCS).[3] By the late 1990s and early 2000s, Beijing had developed a fairly sophisticated understanding of ASEAN, as the mainstream foreign policy community in China concluded that partnering with Southeast Asian states could further Chinese interests near and far.

Distinguishing the near from the far, analysts have argued that China sees Southeast Asia as its strategic backyard.[4] Yet the "strategic backyard" metaphor has been poorly understood, to the detriment of clarity about China's aspirations in the region.

A better understanding of China's strategic interests in Southeast Asia can be gained by examining Chinese perceptions of both the positive value of the region for China and the negative scenarios there that Beijing wants to avoid. A full review of these two sets of issues is beyond the scope of this chapter. But such a comprehensive assessment would support the conclusion that, in the short to medium term, China's strategic goals in Southeast Asia include several related hopes: that China and the region will maintain stable and friendly relations; that the region's states will display a satisfactory level of trust in China; that the region will become China's dependable economic partner, especially by supplying resources to fuel China's economic growth; that China will enjoy strong political influence in the region; that China will be able to use the region as a springboard toward wider objectives, including growing its soft power and using it to improve China's global image and promote multipolarity in the world; and finally, on the negative-scenario side, that neither ASEAN nor any of its member states will join or support a strategic alignment against China, let alone participate in China's containment, by themselves or at the instigation of a third power such as the United States.

In short, China wants to become the most influential power in Southeast Asia. It is on that basis that we can meaningfully infer from Beijing's outlook on Southeast Asia a subjective construction of the region as China's "strategic backyard." That said, one can differ on the extent to which, in Chinese eyes, that construction licenses Beijing to intervene in Southeast Asia wherever, whenever, and however forcefully it desires.

To be fair, when Chinese leaders, officials, and analysts articulate their intentions for and expectations of Southeast Asia, they do not label it using a Chinese-language equivalent of the term "strategic backyard" that would connote the goals noted above. Probably they fear that saying so could invoke profound suspicions in Southeast Asia regarding China's objectives and likely behavior. But this should not prevent us from using the term to analyze China's policies toward the region.

The Chinese themselves have described Southeast Asia as, for China, a uniquely strategic place. The many Chinese official documents and scholarly papers that make this point tend to do so in similar ways. Often featured are the region's strategic location: its proximity to China, its gateway position between the Pacific and Indian Oceans, and its role as a global hub for maritime trade and transport. Attention may also be drawn to Southeast Asia's attractive markets and natural resources; its historical and ethnic connections to China; its vulnerability to rivalrous outside powers; and efforts by ASEAN to manage regional affairs.[5]

The recurrence of these attributes in Chinese writing dates back at least to the early 1990s. In later years, however, as China found itself in dire need of material resources from many parts of the world to sustain its rapid economic growth, Chinese references to Southeast Asia began to attach particular importance to the region as a source of energy, minerals, timber, agricultural products, and other resources. Because in Southeast Asia such inputs are simultaneously available and nearby, the region was even termed the "priority base" on which China's economy had to rely.[6]

Peacefully Rising in a Harmonious World, or Intervening along a Strategic Frontier?

Historically, the perception of Southeast Asia as a convenient zone of opportunity has been reinforced by the presence of larger or more powerful countries along the rest of China's borders — Japan in the east, Russia to the north and northwest, and India in the southwest. In this discouraging context, Southeast Asia was a propitious exception, the ASEAN states being small-to-medium-sized powers traditionally unable to threaten China to any major degree.

That calculation helps to explain why China's relations with Southeast Asian states were not notably adversarial at the turn of this century or for much of its first decade. ASEAN's members were mainly viewed as current or potential partners for long-term cooperation with China and for stability along its southern periphery. Chinese analysts argued that the rise and expansion of ASEAN supported a stable and multipolar balance of power in the Asia-Pacific region. ASEAN was credited in such accounts with serving Chinese interests by helping to balance and stabilize relations between the United States, China, and Japan.[7] From this optimistic viewpoint, it followed that ASEAN could help moderate the hegemonic ambitions of the United States and other Western powers in Southeast Asia, and that accordingly China should pursue trust, consensus, cooperation, and shared development with the organization's member states.[8]

Illustrating this positive outlook were the linked images of China peacefully rising in a harmonious world. In 2003 China proclaimed its "peaceful rise" in the hope of countering rhetoric about a "China threat" and fostering economic cooperation on behalf of China's development.[9] The ASEAN economies were targeted as partners for such cooperation. The negotiation of an ASEAN-China Free Trade Area, from a preliminary agreement in 2002 until its launching in 2010, was in part meant to win recognition by the Southeast Asian states that China really was rising peacefully. Meanwhile, in 2007, China announced its commitment to bringing about a "harmonious world," and again Southeast Asia was deemed a key site for the implementation of China's idea.[10]

These slogans were not naïve. They were symbols wielded to reduce the possibility of big-power rivalry or hegemony on the nation's Southeast Asian doorstep, a development that would pose a risk to China's security. China's rulers had not forgotten the Opium Wars of the 19th century — the maritime arrivals of foreign invaders along the southern coasts, and the uses of Southeast Asia to launch and provision those invaders' attacks. In the eyes of mainstream Chinese analysts, China's maritime margins had long been treated as danger zones of possible strategic competition, most notably and recently pitting Washington against Beijing. The United States especially was seen as determined to weaken China's influence, to sabotage China-ASEAN relations, and even to contain China outright.[11] The United States has always wanted and tried to manipulate Southeast Asian states into checking China's influence and preventing China from challenging American predominance.[12] Efforts by Washington to intensify its engagement with ASEAN and its member states — expanding security ties, increasing joint military exercises — were omens of encirclement.[13] Promoting good relations with Southeast Asia was in this context an instance of realpolitik.[14]

Realpolitik was explicit in the concept of China's "strategic frontier" (*zhanlüe bianjiang*) circulated in 2004 in a paper by a Peking University professor, Chen Fengjun.[15] Following other analysts, he noted the combination of complexity and risk entailed by geography — the ringing of China by more than 20 adjacent states on land or sea. But his strategic frontier was neither a natural nor a political boundary. He applied the idea instead, in policy terms, to those areas along China's periphery where the country's security could be safeguarded proactively using Chinese power and influence. That frontier, he argued, could and should be expanded in keeping with the extension of China's national interests to events and conditions in many parts of the world, an enlargement driven in turn by China's economic growth and political ascent.

Chen's maximalist formulation pictured China's strategic backyard running from Northeast Asia through Southeast Asia to South Asia and on through Central Asia — a vast U-shaped chain of zones of real or potential concern. Along this mutable "strategic frontier," Southeast Asia stood out because of its location and resources, especially including those of the South China Sea, deemed crucial to meeting China's needs to explore and exploit maritime space.[16]

The activist connotations of Chen's frontier jibed with the idea that China should develop the capacity to play a strong interventionist role, notably in Southeast Asia. An article published in the influential Chinese journal *Strategy and Management* in the late 1990s did indeed contend that, in Southeast Asia, China should possess the capacity and the will to prevent conflicts, resolve crises, and generally maintain regional order.[17] That essay came close to envisioning a Monroe Doctrine with Chinese characteristics. But its recommendation was not taken up by other Chinese analysts and was not even hinted at by Chinese leaders or officials. In actual policy practice, there has been no strong evidence to suggest that Beijing is inclined to do so. The case of Myanmar's relations with China is perhaps a good example. Myanmar's political transformations in the past few years have led to a significant reduction of China's influence in the country and the suspension of some major bilateral cooperation projects, such as the Myitsone Dam. Beijing is upset about Myanmar's engagement with the West and the losses that Chinese companies have had in Myanmar, but has refrained from adopting a heavy-handed approach to compel Myanmar to change its policy toward China.[18] China is concerned that a too-coercive approach would backfire and help push many regional states even closer to the United States and other external powers. Whether or not an interventionist view will grow and become dominant in the future remains to be seen. In the further future, we have reasons to believe that it is certainly possible that such an idea could become a part of China's policy in its neighborhood. Today, more and more Chinese, including officials and analysts, realize that China should get prepared to use its hard power to protect its expanding interests throughout the world, especially Chinese investments and personnel in foreign countries.[19] Neighboring regions may become the first target in the coming decades.

The Dragon's Charm: Engaging ASEAN

Leaving aside the perceptions and prescriptions of Chinese foreign-policy scholars, the comprehensive and ongoing vigor of Chinese diplomacy in Southeast Asia since the early 2000s leaves little doubt as to the importance of the region viewed from Beijing. If "strategic" means "significant" in the sense of meriting special attention, the makers of Chinese foreign policy did then and still do view Southeast Asia as their strategic backyard. In the first years of this century, Chinese leaders might have tried to prevent ASEAN from preempting Beijing's eventual primacy in the region. ASEAN's efforts to create, host, and maintain frameworks of multilateral cooperation in East Asia and the Asia-Pacific area could have been seen in Beijing as threatening eventual Chinese influence. But ASEAN posed no credible threat to China's rise. On the contrary, by opening opportunities and alleviating suspicions, Chinese leaders saw that Sino-ASEAN cooperation could speed China's ascent. Far from shunning East Asian regionalism ASEAN-style, China signed up and joined in.

As noted above, the first reference by a Chinese official to China's "peaceful rise" occurred in 2003. In that same year, China became the first of ASEAN's dialogue partners to accede to the ASEAN Treaty of Amity and

Cooperation in Southeast Asia. Also in 2003, China and the 10 ASEAN states jointly declared the Strategic Partnership for Peace and Prosperity, which specified cooperation in political, social, economic, security, regional, and world affairs. Illustrating such involvements was China's record of participation in the ASEAN Regional Forum and ASEAN Plus Three since those meetings were first convened, respectively, in 1994 and 1997. Sino-ASEAN comity would be extended further in 2005 and 2010 when China joined the ASEAN-initiated East Asia Summit and the ASEAN Defense Ministers Meeting Plus at their respective inaugurations. Beijing's presence in these settings implied acquiescence in the prominence of ASEAN in regional diplomacy including the "ASEAN Way" of valuing consensus while avoiding confrontation.

In these engagements, China has emphasized the non-controversial ways in which it could be seen as a good neighbor to Southeast Asia. In offering to help the ASEAN states grow their economies, educate their societies, and strengthen their "non-traditional" (non-military) security, Beijing has hoped in part to direct Southeast Asian attention away from China's controversial ambitions in the South China Sea and limit the scope and intensity of Southeast Asian objections to China's seeming claim of sovereignty over most of that body of water.

In expanding educational cooperation, for example, China has significantly boosted the allocation of officially funded scholarships to the ASEAN states since 2005. According to the Chinese Ministry of Foreign Affairs, the number of such stipends has grown by 50 percent annually from 2008 to 2013. The 3,337 scholarships to ASEAN countries that China provided in 2010 represented a 329 percent increase over 2005.[20] By 2014, there were close to 120,000 Chinese students studying in ASEAN countries and over 70,000 Southeast Asian students studying in China. As of August 2015, China had helped set up 30 Confucius Institutes and 30 Confucius Classrooms in Southeast Asian countries.[21] In 2012, China and Southeast Asian nations agreed on the Double 100,000 Students Mobility Program — 100,000 Chinese students in ASEAN countries and 100,000 Southeast Asian students in China by 2020. The current trend indicates that this objective could be achieved far before the scheduled deadline. Since 2008, China has organized the annual China-ASEAN Education Cooperation Week. This platform has proven to be useful. From 2008 to 2013, China and ASEAN countries signed as many as 386 agreements on educational cooperation through this platform, involving over 200 universities, research institutes, and private businesses.[22]

China has also joined the ASEAN states in plans to cooperate against non-military threats such as natural disasters and transnational crime. These have included the Joint Declaration on Cooperation in the Field

of Non-Traditional Security Issues (2002) and a memorandum of understanding (MOU) (2004) regarding its implementation. A new MOU (2009)
extended the declaration for another five years (2010–14). Cooperation on
non-military security was also furthered, in 2011, at the Second ASEAN-China
Ministerial Meeting on Combating Transnational Crime. Most analysts
would agree that actual Sino-ASEAN cooperation on regional non-traditional
security (NTS) issues has been short of substance. This is particularly the
case if we examine Beijing's involvement in the maritime areas of Southeast
Asia. But it is also true that the joint activities between China and mainland
Southeast Asian countries in response to NTS challenges have been expanding
quite notably over the past 20 years. A good example is the joint patrols
conducted among China, Myanmar, the Laos, and Thailand in the upper
part of the Lancang-Mekong River.

China's willingness to take up these "softer" topics for cooperation with
Southeast Asian states downplayed but did not preclude diplomacy on the
far "harder" business of resolving or at least managing the intractable disputes over sovereignty in the SCS. In October 2002, China and ASEAN finally
signed an unenforceable Declaration on the Conduct of Parties in the South
China Sea (DOC). Although its optimistic terms would, over time, be widely
ignored, the DOC's existence did contribute in part to the maintenance of
peace and stability in the SCS in the years following its adoption. While
retaining its own claim to sovereignty, Beijing did not renounce the DOC
process. Eventually, in July 2011, China agreed to the Guidelines for the
Implementation of the DOC, an eight-point document. A few months later, in
November, at an ASEAN-China summit in Indonesia, Beijing committed RMB
¥3 billion to the ASEAN-China Maritime Cooperation Fund, which would
finance practical projects in the spirit of the DOC such as maritime research,
human resources training pertaining to maritime affairs, environmental
protection, and search and rescue procedures at sea. In the subsequent years,
Beijing urged other claimant states and even non-claimant ASEAN countries
to utilize the fund in partnership with China. By 2014, a total of 17 projects had been approved and financed by the fund. These projects involved
China-Southeast Asian cooperation in fish-farming technologies, marine
environment monitoring, and networking of major ports. Now Beijing is
keen to use the fund for projects under the 21st Century Maritime Silk Road
initiative.[23] In this same "soft" vein, in 2015, China launched the Year of
ASEAN-China Maritime Cooperation.[24]

The Dragon's Money: Economic Statecraft

Economic policies have figured prominently among China's ways of dealing with Southeast Asia. Over the past decade, Beijing has extended major financial support to the ASEAN economies, especially those on the mainland near to China and thus most obviously in its backyard.

The amounts are impressive. In 2009, China started a USD $10 billion China-ASEAN Fund on Investment Cooperation and added a $15 billion credit, including $1.7 billion in preferential loans, later enlarged to $6.7 billion. The fund was meant to serve more than 50 infrastructure-development projects in Southeast Asia. According to its president, Li Yao, the fund invested in 10 projects in the first round of investment by early 2015, involving nearly $1 billion and all ASEAN countries except Vietnam and Brunei.[25] In 2011 Beijing also lavishly backed the Master Plan on ASEAN Connectivity (MPAC) adopted by the ASEAN states in Hanoi the previous year. In support of MPAC, China committed a $10 billion credit including $4 billion in preferential loans, the rest at commercial rates. Six Chinese banks were to administer the $6 billion in commercial loans to develop Southeast Asian infrastructure, energy, and natural resources.

A yet more notable instance of China practicing economic statecraft in Southeast Asia is the ASEAN-China Free Trade Area (ACFTA). Seen from Beijing, ACFTA was from the beginning a strategic design. Anticipated benefits to China's own economy were important, but they were not decisive.[26] When then premier Zhu Rongji raised the idea in 2000, he told his colleagues that in negotiating freer trade with the ASEAN countries, China should stick to the principle of "giving more and benefiting less, giving first and benefiting later."[27]

When the 1997–98 Asian Financial Crisis struck China's backyard, Beijing gained sympathy in ASEAN capitals by not devaluing the renminbi at the possible expense of competing exports from Southeast Asia. Beijing's initial strategic purpose in pursuing ACFTA was to lock in the trust that China had gained during the crisis and thereby to undercut regional fears of a "China threat." At the same time, although China's leaders hoped that its membership in the World Trade Organization, achieved in 2001, would render the Chinese economy more competitive, they also knew that this could become a cause for concern in Southeast Asia. It was partly to forestall such a worry that Beijing offered to create a free trade area with ASEAN's economies. In 2002, a framework was drawn up and agreement was reached to conclude the negotiations by 2010. ACFTA was announced, on time, at the start of the deadline year.

In China's longer-term view, however, trust was not an end in itself. The confidence in China to be won through "win-win" economic cooperation today could be leveraged for additional benefit tomorrow. The indispensability of China's economy to the economies of Southeast Asia would allow Beijing to convert that advantage into influence on matters of politics and security. Some in China describe this straightforwardly as "using economic means for political purposes" (*yi jing chu zheng*).[28] Others have gone further to argue that China-ASEAN economic integration could eventually help to legitimate a new security system in an Asia-Pacific no longer led by the United States.[29]

If current trends continue, the economies of China and Southeast Asia will become even more intertwined. A burgeoning source of such interlinkage is the inflow of foreign direct investment (FDI) from China. From 2003 to 2010, Chinese FDI in ASEAN countries soared from $120 million to $4.4 billion in value. Although total FDI from China to the rest of the world grew impressively by 288.8 percent on average annually in 2003–10, the comparable figure for Chinese FDI to Southeast Asia was 448.9 percent. The diverse end-uses of Chinese money include financing, mining, manufacturing, wholesale and retail sales, power generation, and the provision of gas and water.[30]

Noteworthy is the increasing share of Chinese FDI into Southeast Asia received by Cambodia, Laos, Myanmar, and Vietnam — the ASEAN economies nearest to China by land and in that sense most immediately part of its backyard. Direct Chinese investment in these four countries accounted for 29.8 percent of China's total FDI in Southeast Asia in 2003. By 2010, that share had risen to 44.5 percent.[31] One might speculate in this context that, if such a trend were to continue, Beijing might become more inclined to consider converting its economic importance into politico-security influence in its "nearest abroad," compared with trying to do so in the more distant, maritime, and proportionally less Chinese-invested parts of Southeast Asia.

The Dragon's Borders: Yunnan and Guangxi

Typically in studies of one state's relations with other states, the featured state is treated wholly or mainly as a unitary actor. Writings on China's international relations are no exception, including this chapter, whose stylistic choices also cater to an image of China as singular, centralized, and purposeful — the metaphor of China as a dragon, the metonymy of Beijing as synonymous with China, and the imputation of personhood to "Beijing" as in "Beijing might become more inclined to consider. . . ."

Clearly these figures of speech are conventional, not literal, in nature. But they beg an empirical question: To what extent and how do the outlooks and policies toward Southeast Asia found in China's provinces differ from those conveyed by the central government?

China's backyard is a helpful metaphor in this context because it brings to mind an adjacent house and, inside it, a household comprising more than one person. The question of plurality can then be refocused: How do the actors who live in the back of the house, nearest to Southeast Asia, relate to the region?

Virtually the entire land border between China and Southeast Asia runs between two Chinese provinces and three ASEAN states. Yunnan abuts Myanmar, Laos, and Vietnam from northwest to southeast. Guangxi adjoins Vietnam further southeast to the end of the land border at the Gulf of Tonkin (Chinese *Beibu*, Vietnamese *Bac Bo*) before turning into a seacoast north of China's island province of Hainan.

Broadly speaking, as sources of policy toward Southeast Asia, Yunnan and Guangxi differ from Beijing mainly in placing a higher priority on the benefits they hope to gain locally from closer economic ties with Southeast Asia. Security is important to provincial leaders. But they are willing to defer to Beijing on that sensitive topic and eager, within national policy contexts, to pursue and enlist cross-border projects on behalf of their own economic growth.

Yunnan

Yunnan and its officials have played key roles in forging and enlarging China's cross-border engagements with Southeast Asia. When the Greater Mekong Subregion (GMS) was created in 1992 with the help of the Asian Development Bank, Yunnan took its place within that river-linked area as its sole provincial member alongside five countries, not only adjacent Myanmar, Laos, and Vietnam but Cambodia and Thailand as well. The scope of the arrangement covered a wide range of sectors including trade, tourism, and investment. Over the ensuing decades some $11 billion in project funding was spent in the participating economies on infrastructure alone.[32]

Prior to the 2002 agreement to negotiate ACFTA, the GMS platform was the most important subregional economic cooperation mechanism in existence between China and Southeast Asia. Within GMS, officials in Yunnan's capital, Kunming, took the lead in proposing railway, highway, and airport projects to improve transport linkages between their province, Laos, and

Vietnam. Provincial officials were instrumental in deepening the Lancang-Mekong River for commercial navigation and they helped to manage the resulting traffic. The building and 2008 opening of a highway from Kunming to Bangkok owed much to their advocacy and involvement. They were also active in cross-border telecommunication projects, and along with other GMS members they pushed for trade facilitation measures years before the 2010 inauguration of ACTFA. More recently, in January 2015, oil began flowing to Kunming through a 24,000-kilometer pipeline from Maday Island off the west coast of Myanmar, paralleling a pipeline for natural gas opened the previous October. Yunnan's provincial authorities were at the forefront of the campaign to build these links.

In proposing and pushing such plans, officials in Kunming were well aware of the economic gains to Yunnan they would bring. For many years, local leaders in Yunnan had hoped and worked to transform their province into a massive transportation nexus (*da tongdao*) connecting the vast western reaches of China to Southeast and South Asia. In 2009, while touring Yunnan, then president-cum-party-chief Hu Jintao had encouraged the province to become the "gateway" between China and its neighbors to the south and west.[33] The provincial government seized the opportunity to make "constructing the gateway" a priority task for Yunnan in foreign affairs, and they continue to advance the idea.

Guangxi

Guangxi is smaller than Yunnan, and unlike that province, it borders neither Myanmar nor Laos, only Vietnam. Those distinctions help explain why Guangxi was a late-comer to China-ASEAN relations. But like their equivalents in Yunnan, officials in Guangxi have tried to promote such ties and use them to the benefit of their own province. Early in the 2000s, Guangxi stepped up its efforts to compete with Yunnan for Beijing's attention and support. An early success was the decision to locate the annual China-ASEAN Expo permanently in Guangxi's capital city, Nanning.

In 2004, Vietnam proposed to build its economic relations with China along "two corridors" and within "one circle." China agreed. The corridors ran on land from Nanning and Kunming, respectively, to cities and provinces in Vietnam. The circle encompasses the Tonkin Gulf bordering Guangxi, China's Guangdong and Hainan provinces bordering the SCS, and another five littoral provinces in Vietnam.

Beginning in 2006, Guangxi tried to expand these shapes into a greatly extended Pan-Beibu Gulf Economic Cooperation Zone that would include not only parts of southwestern and southeastern China but, traced counterclockwise around the scs, Vietnam, Malaysia, Singapore, Indonesia, Brunei, and the Philippines as well.[34] As seen from Nanning, the enlarged zone would incorporate the Mekong subregion inland, a corridor down the mainland from Nanning to Singapore, and a maritime extension across the scs. Guangxi has tried hard to get Beijing and the other relevant central governments to make this vast area an official part of the evolving framework of ASEAN-China cooperation.

As the years have gone by, policymakers in Guangxi have learned just how much the maritime disputes over sovereignty in the scs obstruct economic partnering there. The focus of the Pan-Beibu scheme has therefore shifted to the land, notably the Nanning-Singapore economic corridor. According to senior officials in Beijing, the central government would be willing to provide finance and technology for the corridor's construction, including the renovation of high-speed railways and highways between Nanning and Singapore. Nanning hopes that the corridor will facilitate Sino-ASEAN trade, tourism, and investment including supply chains across land borders and transactions between port cities on the scs. Implicit in these plans is Guangxi's aim to become an indispensable hub of traffic between China's middle and western mainland and nearly all of ASEAN's economies.

The Guangxi government has not been simply waiting for a final decision by top Chinese and ASEAN leaders. Local leaders in Guangxi have been, on their own, pushing for cooperation with ASEAN's economies. Provincial leaders have visited the relevant capitals in Southeast Asia to promote Guangxi's proposals. Guangxi's officials are convinced that the province's land and sea connections with Southeast Asia make it a prime site for China's use in engaging the neighbors. Beijing finally rewarded Guangxi's efforts in 2008 by approving the blueprint for a Beibu Bay Economic Zone. Since then, the province has stepped up its efforts to build port facilities in three coastal cities along the Beibu Gulf — Beihai, Qinzhou, and Huangchenggang.

Steps taken by Guangxi to leverage its location for economic returns have also included setting up trade-focused bonded and manufacturing zones to take advantage of the China-ASEAN Free Trade Area. According to a senior Guangxi government official, Guangxi's trade with ASEAN countries increased from $830 million in 2003 to $29.01 billion in 2015. The ASEAN region has been Guangxi's number one trade partner for the past 15 consecutive years.[35] With further improvements in China-ASEAN connectivity and in Guangxi's manufacturing capacity, other things being equal, China's and ASEAN's economic relations should strengthen as well.

In October 2013, Chinese president Xi Jinping proposed the 21st Century Maritime Silk Road (MSR) initiative during his visit to Indonesia. Under this initiative, the Chinese authorities are keen to engage with ASEAN countries in five areas of connectivity: infrastructure, trade, finance, policy, and culture. A lot of actual policy attention will focus on infrastructure connectivity, trade, and investment cooperation. Some flagship projects with Chinese funding have been agreed upon or are in the pipeline, for instance the Jakarta-Bandung railway, the Kunming-Bangkok railway, the upgrading of Lancang-Mekong subregional cooperation, the upgrading of ACFTA, and the Indochina economic corridor. Local governments in Yunnan, Guangxi, and Guangdong provinces are strongly interested in working with ASEAN countries to carry out the MSR. Guangxi, for instance, is trying to establish a network of major ports in Guangxi and Southeast Asia. The implementation of the MSR is very likely to result in significant growth of China's economic influence in Southeast Asia and further increase the asymmetry in China-ASEAN economic relations that favors Beijing.

The Dragon's Breath: Claiming the South China Sea

Southeast Asians acknowledge the economic importance of China and seek to benefit from linkages with it. China's economic diplomacy is meant to multiply, deepen, and use these material ties. Given the disparity in size between China and its ASEAN neighbors, it is not hard to argue in this context that flows of trade, aid, debt, and investment are binding Southeast Asia ever more closely to China. By this economic logic, the transformation of Southeast Asia into China's backyard is already well underway. Even if that debatable projection turns out to be true, however, the subordination of Southeast Asia to China will remain incomplete unless the backyard becomes the property of the house in security terms as well.

Three major issues have hindered the development of Beijing's security relations with the region: China's military build-up, its tenuous security relations with ASEAN states, and its assertive actions in the SCS. The third issue deserves attention here because nothing is more detrimental to Beijing's standing in Southeast Asia than its maritime behavior. A separate chapter in this book deals more fully with the SCS. The focus here is on Chinese positions and perspectives — the extent to which Southeast Asia is, or is considered by Beijing to be, China's *strategic* backyard.

The most salient aspects of China's view of the SCS have been the scope and the vagueness of its proprietary claim of sovereignty inside the controversially encompassing and much discussed "nine-dash line."

The Ministry of Foreign Affairs in Beijing has repeatedly said that "China has indisputable sovereignty over the islands in the SCS and the adjacent waters, and enjoys sovereign rights and jurisdiction over the relevant waters as well as the seabed and subsoil thereof."[36] This statement, already ambiguous, has been rendered even more so by expansive references to "historical waters" claimed by China in "major parts" of the "sea areas" in question.[37] The Chinese themselves have loosely used unclear terms to describe their country's ostensible sovereignty over "water territory,"[38] "ocean territory,"[39] "maritime territory,"[40] or "territorial seas."[41]

The Chinese public seems to believe that all of the SCS belongs to China. Chinese pupils have read in their history and geography textbooks that the People's Republic of China includes even James Shoal (*Zengmu Ansha*). Claimed by Malaysia, the shoal lies some 1,250 miles from the Chinese mainland, well beyond China's continental shelf, but a mere 50 miles from the Malaysian state of Sarawak in northern Borneo.[42] Such maximalist views are shared by a fairly large segment of Chinese international relations experts who do not specialize in maritime affairs.[43] Their writings and comments, along with the People's Liberation Army Navy's (PLAN) exercises in the SCS, have reinforced the public opinion that projects China's sovereignty across the entire body of water and all of the land features within it.

Some Chinese experts on maritime law have advocated a more limited understanding of China's claim based on the United Nations Convention on the Law of the Sea (UNCLOS), and some among China's foreign-policy analysts have joined them in advocating this narrower, UNCLOS-based view. Their effort to downsize China's claim in accordance with international law has so far failed, however, due largely to opposition from the military and other maritime enforcement agencies. For them, and especially the PLAN, the SCS is China's own sea zone.

The agencies responsible for enforcing Chinese maritime law are inclined to regard the SCS as China's actual or proposed "jurisdictional waters" or "jurisdictional rights." With this entitlement in mind, these units have stepped up their efforts on behalf of Chinese maritime rights and interests, including access to fishing and energy resources. They have become more willing to use force to block or interfere with the comparable efforts by other claimant states in areas of overlap between those countries' exclusive economic zones (EEZs) and the Chinese nine-dash line. Chinese oil companies, in particular the China National Offshore Oil Corporation, have been especially active in energy exploration and extraction. When clashes occur, the Ministry of Foreign Affairs, whatever privately held views its officials might have, is obliged to back the Chinese agencies and their assertions of entitlement.

Chinese decision-makers are seriously constrained by the hard-line position taken in public by their government on the SCS and by patriotic public opinion. Many in Chinese society think that the authorities have not been firm enough in advancing China's claims and opposing those of others. During Beijing's confrontation with Manila over Scarborough Shoal in 2012, the *Global Times* ran an attitude survey in seven Chinese cities. Most of the respondents were unworried by the prospect of a physical conflict. Three-fifths thought such a conflict would not occur or was unlikely, and nearly four-fifths endorsed the use of military force to counter "foreign provocations and encroachments."[44]

The differences inside China regarding the nature of its maritime claim may not have been resolved, but they have been reduced in favor of a more adamant stance. Some Chinese media have sent intimidating messages to the Philippines and Vietnam. China's *Global Times* stated in an editorial:

> Some of China's neighbouring countries have been exploiting China's mild diplomatic stance, making it their golden opportunity to expand their regional interests. . . . But if a situation turns ugly, some military action is necessary. . . . If these countries don't want to change their ways with China, they will need to prepare for the sounds of cannons. We need to be ready for that, as it may be the only way for the disputes in the sea to be resolved.[45]

The Chinese military has been flexing its muscles. The agencies responsible for enforcing maritime law have been given more leeway to implement a heavy-handed approach.

The Ministry of Foreign Affairs has been conflicted. It has resolutely defended China's position and actions while at the same time trying to mend fences with Southeast Asian countries. Within the Chinese political system, however, the ministry is far too weak to control the messaging on a matter as important as China's claim, especially when tensions rise. Unable to decide Chinese policy or shape Chinese discourse on such an important matter, the ministry has preferred to go along with the toughening of Beijing's messaging on the SCS. Yet that more intransigent stance, by triggering fear and opposition in Southeast Asia, frustrates China's desire to establish the region as a cooperative and quiescent backyard in strategic terms. One may even venture to say that as long as China's status in the SCS remains controversial and unresolved, Southeast Asia will not become China's strategic backyard.

Conclusion

Broadly speaking, China's reputation in Southeast Asia has evolved through two phases. Roughly from the turn of the century to 2010, China enjoyed rising influence in Southeast Asia, driven most notably by growing economic ties, especially trade. It was only in 2009 that Beijing formally conveyed its nine-dash line to the United Nations in apparently non-negotiable terms. In 2010, at an ASEAN Regional Forum meeting in Hanoi in the presence of her Chinese and Southeast Asian counterparts, then secretary of state Hillary Clinton clearly stated an American "national interest in freedom of navigation, open access to Asia's maritime commons and respect for international law in the South China Sea."[46] The American strategic "rebalance" to Asia was in part a response to China's heightened profile in Southeast Asia and Washington's desire to forestall any real or imagined Chinese effort to exclude it from the SCS. China's foreign minister was visibly angered by her remarks.

Southeast Asian suspicions of Chinese intentions are more evidence of the current and more confrontational phase of relations between claimants in the SCS and between Washington and Beijing. Yet the successes of Chinese diplomacy are hard to deny. The diversity of Southeast Asian views on the SCS has prevented ASEAN from either endorsing or opposing any government's maritime claims, China's included. But Chinese pressure has served Beijing by reinforcing that incapacity. Cases in point in 2012 included ASEAN's failure to say anything about the Sino-Philippine standoff at Scarborough Shoal, effectively won by China, and ASEAN's failure to issue any final communiqué at the end of its ministerial meeting in Cambodia.

The divisive impact of the SCS disputes on China-ASEAN relations should not be exaggerated. The tensions have not, for example, caused a freezing, let alone a breaking of relations, between China and any of the Southeast Asian claimant states — Brunei, Malaysia, the Philippines, or Vietnam. Yet the region is still far from having become China's strategic backyard in the full sense of subordination that the metaphor implies. China has not become the single most influential power in Southeast Asia. Distrust of China persists. Southeast Asian support for the American rebalance, though mainly tacit or implicit in nature, is a clear indication that China cannot, at least not yet, strategically realign the region.

New challenges for Beijing have emerged even in the economic realm where China has been so proactive. A major expenditure of Chinese resources in Myanmar could not stop its leaders from diversifying their interstate relations. Some ASEAN countries, notably Vietnam, have been cool toward China's effort to enlist its neighbors in plans for subregional integration such as the Pan-Beibu Gulf economic zone. Further evidence of a desire in Southeast Asia to hedge against the prospect of Chinese economic primacy in the region was the participation of four ASEAN states — Brunei, Malaysia, Singapore, and Vietnam — in talks toward an American-backed Trans-Pacific Partnership (TPP) that did not include China. In 2018, after newly inaugurated US president Donald Trump decided to withdraw his country from the TPP, the pact was reconstituted as the Comprehensive and Progressive Agreement for Trans-Pacific Partnership. In 2018, still without China, its 11 remaining members, including Japan, Australia, and the four ASEAN states, signed on to the revised accord, which came into effect that December.

State-owned corporations are responsible for the great majority of Chinese investments in Southeast Asia.[47] Many of these quasi-official firms have not lived up to international standards regarding labor rights and environmental protection. Instances of controversy involving the activities of these companies have included Myanmar's suspension of Chinese investment in the Myitsone Dam project and the popular protest waged against Chinese investment in bauxite mining in Vietnam's central highlands.

The often poor quality of China's investments in Southeast Asia follows in part from China's own economic limitations. Its relative deficiency in technology compared with what more advanced economies offer makes China less attractive as an economic partner, other things being equal. China's appeal is also limited by the virtual absence in the region of Chinese non-governmental organizations, which are discouraged in China itself. Beijing has expressed a strong desire to help Southeast Asian states address non-traditional security problems, yet little has been done due in part to the underdevelopment of civil society inside China. Southeast Asians have come to realize China's difficulty in supplying public goods that are not directly linked to its own economic interest.

There is a problem of empathy as well. When viewing Southeast Asia's relations with China, most of China's foreign-policy analysts seem disinclined to put themselves in the shoes of their southern neighbors. China's elite has a hard time understanding why Southeast Asian countries are apprehensive of China. Chinese influentials tend to dismiss any expression of regional misgivings toward China as nonsense. China's military modernization, which Chinese people regard as a natural component of their national rejuvenation, is a major source of concern to many in Southeast Asia. But instead of trying to understand that concern, many Chinese regard it as a conspiracy against China.

Critical views in China toward ASEAN have grown in recent years. More and more Chinese analysts believe that ASEAN countries have neither appreciated nor reciprocated China's goodwill and generosity. They believe that some ASEAN countries have purposefully invited the United States into regional affairs and supported the American "rebalance" to Asia in order to check China's influence in the region. On the SCS issue in particular, many in China's foreign-policy elite believe that ASEAN's claimant countries have colluded with Washington against China. Often in China, deaf ears have greeted suggestions that regional states have been alienated not by conspiring outsiders but by China's own unilateral assertions in the SCS, and that in this way Beijing has actually helped Washington pivot toward Southeast Asia.

A consensus seems to have emerged in China that it is time for toughness in the defense of threatened Chinese interests. On Beijing's list of policy priorities, the protection of Chinese rights (*wei quan*) has overtaken the assurance of stability in the neighborhood (*zhoubian weiwen*). If this shift in mindset continues, it could diminish the chance that China will limit itself to peaceful means if in future it tries to turn Southeast Asia into its strategic backyard not just subjectively, as a matter of belief, but objectively, as a matter of control.

Notes

1 Quoted by Jeff Smith, "The US-China South China Sea Showdown," *The Diplomat*, 21 October 2015, http://thediplomat.com/2015/10/the-us -china-south-china-sea-s.

2 The exchange took place in the comments section for Shannon Tiezzi, "ASEAN's Economic Future," *The Diplomat*, 25 September 2015, accessed 17 October 2015, http://thediplomat.com/2015/09/aseans -economic-future/.

3 云华[Yun Hua], "中国与东盟的安全" [Security relations between China and ASEAN countries],《东南亚研究》[Southeast Asian studies] 1 (1995): 7–9.

4 See, for instance, Andrew Scobell, "China's Geostrategic Calculus and Southeast Asia — The Dragon's Backyard Laboratory," in *China's Activities in Southeast Asia and the Implications for U.S. Interests: Hearing before the U.S.-China Economic and Security Review Commission*, 111th Cong. 2 (4 February 2010) (Prepared Statement of Dr. Andrew Scobell, Associate Professor, Texas A&M University, College Station, Texas), https://www.uscc.gov/sites/default/files/ transcripts/2.4.10HearingTranscript.pdf; Michael R. Chambers, "The Evolving Relationship between China and Southeast Asia," in *Legacy of Engagement in Southeast Asia*, eds. Ann Marie Murphy and Bridget Welsh (Singapore: Institute of Southeast Asia, 2008), 298.

5 See, for instance, 许宁宁[Xu Ningning], "中国与东盟关系现状、趋势、对策" [The state, trend, and future policy in China's relations with ASEAN],《东南亚纵横》[Around Southeast Asia] 3 (2012): 51–55; 李庆四 [Li Qingsi], "中国与东盟关系：睦邻外交的范例" [China-ASEAN relations: A good example of good-neighborly diplomacy],《国际论坛》 [International forum] 6, no. 2 (2004): 30–34; 李晓伟 [Li Xiaowei], "中国与东南亚合作的地缘战略思考" [Geo-strategic considerations for China-Southeast Asia cooperation],《云南民族大学学报》[Journal of Yunnan Nationalities University] 25, no. 3 (2008): 68–73; 中国现代国际关系研究所东盟课题组 [China Institutes of Contemporary International Relations (CICIR) research team on ASEAN], "中国对东盟政策研究报告" [Research report on China's policy toward ASEAN],《现代国际关系》[Contemporary international relations] 10 (2002): 1–10; 陈峰君 [Chen Fengjun], "加强中国与东盟合作的战略意义" [The strategic implications of strengthening China-ASEAN relations],《国际政治研究》 [Studies of international politics] no. 1 (2004): 24–28, 68.

6 Li, "Geo-strategic Considerations."

7 陆建人 [Lu Jianren], "世纪之交:中国对东盟的外交战略" [China's diplomatic strategy toward ASEAN at the beginning of a new century], 《太平洋学报》[Pacific studies] 1 (1998): 42–47; CICIR Research Team, "Research Report on China's Policy toward ASEAN."

8 Lu, "China's Diplomatic Strategy."

9 The term "peaceful rise" was first proposed by Zheng Bijian, the former vice president of the Central Party School, in a speech at the Bo'ao Forum in November 2003—see "A New Path for China's Peaceful Rise and the Future of Asia" in *China's Peaceful Rise: Speeches of Zheng Bijian 1997–2004*, https://www.brookings.edu/wp-content/uploads/2012/04/20050616bijianlunch.pdf; former Chinese president Hu Jintao used the "peaceful rise" lexicon in December 2003 at a meeting commemorating the 110th birthday of Mao Zedong—see "胡锦涛在纪念毛泽东诞辰110周年座谈会的讲话" [Hu Jintao's remarks at a meeting commemorating Mao Zedong's 110th birthday], 中国共产党新闻网 [Chinese Communist Party news network], accessed 10 April 2016, http://cpc.people.com.cn/GB/69112/70190/70193/14286125.html. Starting in 2004, Chinese leaders and scholars replaced the term with "peaceful development," fearing the word "rise" may fuel suspicions in some countries toward China's growing power.

10 王玉主 [Wang Yuzhu], "中国与东盟: 双边关系中的相互依赖与战略合作" [China and ASEAN: Interdependence and strategic cooperation in their bilateral relations], 《创新》[Innovation] 1 (February 2008): 42–45.

11 Li, "China-ASEAN Relations"; CICIR Research Team, "Research Report on China's Policy toward ASEAN."

12 陈建荣 [Chen Jianrong], "东盟在美国亚太战略中的地位及布什政府的东盟政策" [ASEAN in U.S. Asia-Pacific strategy and the Bush Administration's ASEAN policy], 《东南亚研究》[Southeast Asian studies] 5 (2003): 25–30.

13 魏红霞 [Wei Hongxia], "布什政府对东盟的政策及其对中国的影响" [The Bush administration's ASEAN policy and its implications for China], 《东南亚研究》[Southeast Asian studies] 4 (2006): 56–62.

14 CICIR Research Team, "Research Report on China's Policy toward ASEAN." See also 程永林 [Cheng Yonglin], "中国-东盟战略伙伴关系与我国的地缘安全利益研究" [China-ASEAN strategic partnership and China's geo-security interests], 《广东省社会主义学院学报》[Journal of Guangdong Institute of Socialism] 2 (2004): 66–69.

15 Chen, "Strategic Implications."

16 Chen, "Strategic Implications."

17 马志刚 [Ma Zhigang], "东盟新安全环境与中国对应战略(东盟形势报告节选)" [The new security environment for ASEAN and China's policy response], 《战略与管理》 [Strategy and management] 2 (1999): 43–46.

18 Chenyang Li and James Char, "China-Myanmar Relations since Naypyidaw's Political Transition: How Beijing Can Balance Short-term Interests and Long-term Values," RSIS Working Paper No. 288, S. Rajaratnam School of International Studies, Singapore, March 2015.

19 See, for instance, Foreign Minister Wang Yi's statement at a press conference in March 2016, "王毅谈海外利益保护:探索中国特色的维权之路" [Wang Yi's remarks on protection of overseas interests: Exploring modality for rights-protection with Chinese characteristics], Ministry of Foreign Affairs of the People's Republic of China, 8 March 2016, accessed 12 April 2016, http://www.mfa.gov.cn/web/wjbzhd/t1345905.shtml.

20 "中国—东盟合作:1991–2011" [China-ASEAN cooperation: 1991–2011], Ministry of Foreign Affairs of the People's Republic of China, accessed 10 April 2016, http://www.mfa.gov.cn/chn//gxh/xsb/wjzs/t877316.htm.

21 "中国教育部部长袁贵仁在第八届中国—东盟教育交流周开幕式上的主题演讲"[Keynote Speech by Chinese minister of education Yuan Guiren at the opening ceremony of the 8th China-ASEAN Education Exchange Week], 中国-东盟教育信息网 [China-ASEAN Educational Information Network], accessed 12 April 2016, http://www.caedin.org/article.jsp?id=2088&itemId=67.

22 杨华 [Yang Hua], "中国—东盟文化交流的'黄金十年'" [The golden decade in China-ASEAN cultural exchanges], 《东南亚纵横》 [Around Southeast Asia] 4 (2014): 71–75.

23 康霖,罗亮 [Kang Lin and Luo Liang], "中国—东盟海上合作基金的发展及前景" [The development and prospect of the China-ASEAN maritime cooperation fund], 《国际问题研究》 [International studies] 5 (2014): 27–36.

24 See Prasanth Parameswaran, "China's Plan for ASEAN-China Maritime Cooperation," The Diplomat, 1 April 2015, http://thediplomat.com/2015/04/chinas-plan-for-asean-china-maritime-cooperation/.

25 "专访中国-东盟投资合作基金总裁李耀" [An interview with Li Yao, president of the China-ASEAN investment cooperation fund],《南方都市报》(深圳) [Southern metropolitan daily], 21 January 2015.

26 王玉主 [Wang Yuzhu], "自贸区建设与中国东盟关系 — 一项战略评估" [The construction of the FTA and China-ASEAN relations: A strategic assessment],《南洋问题研究》[Southeast Asian affairs] 1 (2012): 9–20.

27 Wang, "The Construction of the FTA."

28 Wang, "The Construction of the FTA."

29 Cheng, "China-ASEAN Strategic Partnership."

30 唐志武, 王岩 [Tang Zhiwu and Wang Yan], "中国对东盟直接投资问题研究" [A study on China's FDI in ASEAN countries],《税务与经济》[Taxation and economy] 3 (15 May 2012).

31 Tang and Wang, "A Study on China's FDI in ASEAN Countries."

32 Asian Development Bank, "Overview of the Greater Mekong Subregion," accessed 10 August 2016, http://www.adb.org/countries/gms/overview.

33 See 邓久翔, 杨跃萍 [Deng Jiuxiang and Yang Yueping], "中国对外开放战略向西南转移 云南成开放桥头堡" [China's opening up strategy shifts to the southwest / Yunnan becomes an open bridgehead] 中国共产党新闻网 [Chinese Communist Party news network], 4 December 2011, accessed 4 April 2019, http://theory.people.com.cn/GB/16487501.html.

34 For more details about the Pan-Beibu scheme, see Gu Xiaosong and Li Mingjiang, "Beibu Gulf: Emerging Sub-regional Integration between China and ASEAN," RSIS Working Paper No 168, S. Rajaratnam School of International Studies, Singapore, January 2009.

35 "中国与东盟营商环境互联互通效果显现" [The business environment and connectivity between China and ASEAN improve], Sina Finance, accessed 15 August 2016, http://finance.sina.com.cn/roll/2016-08-12/doc-ifxuxhas1770354.shtml.

36 Note verbale dated 7 May 2009 from the Permanent Mission of the People's Republic of China to the United Nations addressed to Secretary-General of the United Nations and to the Commission on the Limits of the Continental Shelf, CML/17/2009, accessed 10 August 2016, http://www.un.org/Depts/los/clcs_new/submissions_files/mysvnm33_09/chn_2009re_mys_vnm_e.pdf.

37 See, for example, Nguyen Hong Thao and Ramses Amer, "A New Legal Arrangement for the South China Sea?," *Ocean Development & International Law* 40 (2009): 333–49.

38 Wang Qian, "China to Dive into Mapping Seabed," *China Daily*, 14 September 2011.

39 Wang Xinjun, "China One Step Closer to Developing Aircraft Carrier," *China Daily*, 1 August 2011.

40 "Refitting Aircraft Carrier Not to Change Naval Strategy," *China Daily*, 27 July 2011.

41 Zhang Zixuan, "Cultural Relics Discovered under Sea," *China Daily*, 17 May 2011.

42 "China's Navy Extends Its Combat Reach to the Indian Ocean," U.S.-China Economic and Security Review Commission Staff Report, 14 March 2014, accessed 12 August 2016, https://www.uscc.gov/sites/default /files/Research/Staff%20Report_China%27s%20Navy%20Extends%20 its%20Combat%20Reach%20to%20the%20Indian%20Ocean.pdf.

43 Based on the author's interviews with more than 80 Chinese scholars since 2009.

44 "南海局势微妙，八成国人支持军事回应南海问题" [South China Sea situation becoming tricky; 80 percent of Chinese support military response to the dispute], 北方网 [Northern network], accessed 15 August 2016, http://news.enorth.com.cn/system/2012/05/05/009169236.shtml.

45 "Don't Take Peaceful Approach for Granted," *Global Times*, 25 October 2011, accessed 4 April 2019, http://www.globaltimes.cn/ content/680694.shtml.

46 As quoted by Mark Lander, "Offering to Aid Talks, U.S. Challenges China on Disputed Islands, *New York Times*, 23 July 2010.

47 Stephen Frost and Mary Ho, "中国大陆的投资浪潮: 国有企业和 在东南亚的国外直接投资" [Mainland China's investment flow: SOEs and China's FDI in Southeast Asia], 《南洋资料译丛》 [Southeast Asian studies] 4 (2006): 1–20.

CHAPTER 6

"Ambiguity is Fun"

CHINA'S STRATEGY IN THE SOUTH CHINA SEA

Donald K. Emmerson, *Stanford University, United States*

T he estimated 3.7 million square kilometer surface of the South China Sea (scs) makes it the third largest of the world's 100-plus seas. According to estimates for years in 2015–17, it accounted annually for one-third — usd $3.4 trillion — of global shipping, and 11 billion barrels of oil and 190 trillion cubic feet of natural gas in proved and probable undersea reserves. More than half of the world's fishing vessels operate there, although they take only 12 percent of the global catch. Nearly 80 percent of the oil that China imported in 2016 came through the Malacca Strait and the scs. But the sea is vital for Southeast Asia's economies as well. Of the five countries that traded the most across its waters as a percentage of their worldwide trade in that year, every one was Southeast Asian — Vietnam at 86 percent, Indonesia 85, Thailand 74, Singapore 66, and Malaysia 58, compared to China at 39 percent — and Southeast Asians are a large proportion of the estimated 3.7 million people officially employed in its fisheries, not to mention the many more whose roles are unrecorded.[1]

The South China Sea's waters encompass some 250 land features. They vary in size, shape, composition, and elevation above or below water at high tide. The Paracel and Spratly Islands account for the great majority of these formations. Outliers such as Mischief Reef make up the rest. China claims all or virtually all of the sea's land features and occupies or otherwise exercises authority over most of them. Under its domestic law, the People's Republic of China (PRC) exerts "sovereign control" and jurisdiction over these real or supposed holdings, which are administered through Hainan Province in the sea's northwestern corner.[2] China has controlled all of the Paracels since 1974, when PRC troops took them in a brief war with the then

Republic of [South] Vietnam on the eve of the latter's defeat and replacement by the Socialist Republic of Vietnam.

In the Spratlys, six different countries have made claims and come to exercise various degrees of control over what they consider theirs. They are Vietnam, the Philippines, China, Malaysia, Taiwan, and Brunei, listed in order from the most to the fewest Spratly land features under the de facto authority of each one.[3] A seventh state, Indonesia, denies being a claimant despite Chinese incursions into its northernmost exclusive economic zone (EEZ). The denial does not reflect Indonesian uncertainty over the validity of China's vague claim in the overlapping area, however. By rejecting claimant status, Jakarta hopes to reinforce Indonesia's sovereign rights in its EEZ as a matter of obvious and acknowledged fact under international law, whereas a mere claim could be debated.

This chapter reviews China's strategy regarding the SCS. Eight tactics employed by Beijing on behalf of that strategy are introduced, of which four are discussed at greater length. The chapter ends by considering some possible scenarios going forward, including four responses to China's strategy that have been tried by one or more of the Southeast Asian claimants, or could be tried in future. The Philippines and Vietnam receive particular attention for reasons to be noted below.

Strategy and Tactics

China's strategic goal is control. China asserts, by admission or action, sovereign jurisdiction or "historic rights" over virtually the entire SCS, including the land features, waters, and resources therein.[4] Yet many or some of those same land formations or waters are claimed, occupied, or used by at least one of the four SCS-coastal states in the Association of Southeast Asian Nations (ASEAN). Nor has Beijing's maritime primacy been widely or consistently endorsed by powers outside Southeast Asia.[5] The future of the SCS will depend in no small measure on the extent to which China is able to reduce if not eliminate the discrepancy between its ambition and its achievement.

In fairness, a judgment that Beijing wishes to control the SCS is compatible with geopolitical empathy for China. Chinese access to the Pacific Ocean is constrained by the natural "fence" of islands that runs from Kamchatka through the Russian-administered Kuriles, past the Japanese and Philippine archipelagoes, and along the coasts of Malaysia and Brunei to where Indonesia almost touches Singapore. But the chance that ASEAN's littoral states would try to block China's egress into the Pacific, absent a prior Chinese attack, is vanishingly small. And crimping geography hardly justifies Beijing's use of domestic law, armed outposts, physical threats, and "frown diplomacy" for the purpose of turning the SCS into a Chinese lake.[6]

Among the tactics China has used to achieve that outcome are *annexation*, *augmentation*, *construction*, *militarization*, *intimidation*, *ambiguation*, *co-optation*, and *prolongation*. Each one warrants a brief introduction.

The doubtful character of China's claim to have exercised jurisdiction over the SCS for thousands of years is noted later in this chapter. Suffice it here to cite far more recent and less disputable instances not of jurisdiction but of seizure, historically justified or not: Beijing's forcible *annexation* of all of the Paracel Islands, several of the Spratly Islands, Mischief Reef, and Scarborough Shoal, respectively, in 1974, 1988, 1995, and 2012.

A second and related tactic is *augmentation*. In the Spratlys in December 2013, soon after Xi Jinping's rise to power, Beijing launched a quick and concerted terraforming campaign. Dredgers were used to suction sand and pulverize coral from the seabed for deposit on reefs and other land features under China's control. The 3,200 new acres (1,300 hectares) of artificial surface thereby created far exceeded the prior expansion of their own holdings by all of the other claimants combined.[7]

Construction and *militarization* followed. On the features in the Spratlys that China had taken, occupied, enlarged, and raised above the water line, Beijing built civilian and/or military outposts and equipped them with infrastructure suitable for use in war. The installations included docks, runways, and hangars; anti-aircraft guns; emplacements for missiles deployable against ships and planes; barracks and bunkers; and multiple radar installations readily evident from the air.[8]

The infrastructure's visibility from above matters because the building and arming were done in secret. Satellite photos of the activity were released by an American think tank in December 2016. Only then did China's defense ministry publicly admit responsibility for erecting "necessary military facilities." Why necessary? Because if "someone was at the door of your home, cocky and swaggering, how could it be that you wouldn't prepare a slingshot?"[9] The metaphor cast China in the role of David defending himself against the American Goliath. Seen from a Southeast Asian shore, however, it was harder to dismiss China's SCS bases as a "slingshot" aimed only at America, and easier to view them as high-tech hard-power platforms that a Chinese Goliath could also use to intimidate its neighbors.

Intimidation can occur by threat or by harassment. It happens by threat whenever littoral states, knowing that Chinese hard power could be deployed against them, censor themselves or otherwise try to please Beijing. The threat is implicit and indirect. Harassment is actual and direct. It occurs when vessels in the People's Liberation Army (PLA) Navy, the China Coast Guard (CCG), or civilian fishing boats mobilized by Beijing physically challenge — shadow, swarm, ram, even sink — the vessels of other littoral states. The abuses are also jurisdictionally egregious when they take place within the maximum 200-nautical-mile breadth of an EEZ that a littoral state is allowed under the UN Convention on the Law of the Sea (UNCLOS).[10] Unlike inferential threats, aggressive harassment quickly stokes anger in the country to which those being harassed belong. Xi Jinping's government knows this. That it persists in bullying its neighbors in such an arguably counter-productive way illustrates how undiminished its desire for control really is.

Ambiguation means being vague about something on purpose. In the SCS, Beijing has been deliberately unclear about two boundaries — one conceptual, one cartographic. The conceptual distinction is between land and sea. Land features in the SCS vary in location, size, shape, and height, as do the coastal formations along its periphery. Traditionally under international law, the boundaries of maritime zones in which a country may exercise certain rights are derived from the location and character of those land features. Not the reverse. Under the provisions of UNCLOS, one cannot claim sovereignty over a stretch of water without reference to a coastline and then infer, from that claim, sovereignty over the land features located inside that particular stretch or within any particular distance from it.

Figure 6.1 features the generously drawn "nine-dash line" that Beijing has used on maps of the SCS to somehow legitimize and maximize its claim without having to specify either the meaning of the line or the exact nature of the claim that it makes. Also shown, for comparison, are the claimed EEZs of China, the Philippines, and Vietnam.[11]

As mapped in Figure 6.1, the sheer size and sweep of the Philippine EEZ, reaching as it does almost to the shores of Taiwan and Malaysia, should not be mistaken for definitive proof that Manila, like China, is inflating its borders in violation of international law. As an archipelagic state, the Philippines is entitled under UNCLOS to link "the outermost points" of its "outermost islands and drying reefs" using straight baselines from which a maximum-200-nm EEZ can be drawn, subject to certain conditions.[12] Not shown in Figure 6.1 are the very small Philippine land features whose outermost locations and resulting proximities to neighboring states have allowed Manila to claim baselines yielding a maximal EEZ that extends almost to the coasts of Taiwan and Malaysia.

The Philippine claim is not uniquely large. Countries routinely outline their EEZs as generously as possible. The EEZs that Taiwan and Malaysia

FIGURE 6.1 The nine-dash line and three exclusive economic Zones (EEZS) in the South China Sea

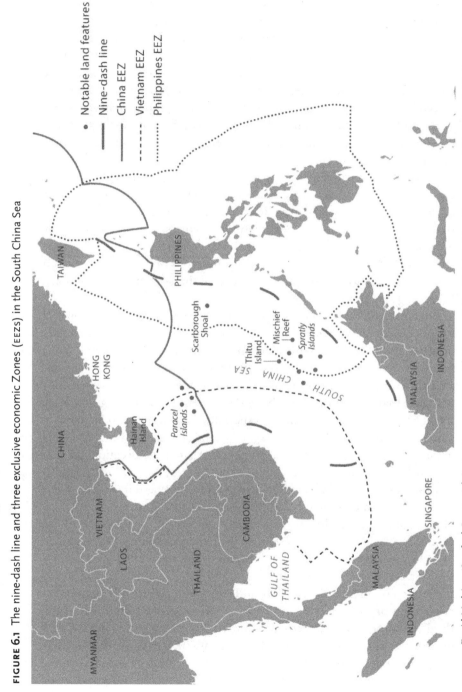

SOURCE: David Medeiros (Stanford Geospatial Center) in cooperation with Gregory Poling (Asia Maritime Transparency Initiative) and this chapter's author.

NOTE: For readability, small land features in and around the SCS are omitted except for those most relevant to the text.

have drawn for themselves both overlap with and to that extent reject the Philippine one. Taiwan's legal limbo as a state whose sovereignty is contested and constrained makes an UNCLOS-based settlement of its EEZ dispute with the Philippines unlikely. Conceivably, however, an UNCLOS-compatible negotiation, arbitration, or bilateral compromise between Malaysia and the Philippines could someday replace their overlapping EEZs with a bilaterally agreed border between them. In contrast, no such solution to the nine-dash line's overlaps with Bruneian, Indonesian, Malaysian, and Philippine EEZs is possible as long as China continues to refuse to explain its dashes while insisting that they are not negotiable at all.

Unlike Manila's archipelagic claim under UNCLOS, China's dashes are drawn in the sea without any clear or consistent reference to land features in the SCS. China appears to be inferring its sovereignty — or sovereign rights — over all of those land features from its asserted sovereignty over the dash-bordered waters around them. If so, that would violate land-border-derived maritime law in the provisions of UNCLOS and the rulings of the International Tribunal of the Law of the Sea and the International Court of Justice.

By refusing to clarify what it wants in the SCS, Beijing has tried to protect the possibility that it really does assert full ownership over the entire body of water, including everything under, in, on, and even above it, without any limiting reference to land features. But that same ambiguity also encourages the contrary speculation: that China's claim is less comprehensively obdurate than its critics in Southeast Asia might think. Beijing may hope thereby to earn from its neighbors, especially those wanting to believe that ambiguity might hide flexibility, some benefit of the doubt — that China might in fact be less hostile to maritime rules than its obfuscation and bullying behavior would suggest.

Co-optation is another tactic in China's strategic repertoire for control of the SCS. This gambit is mainly transactional in nature. Material co-optation occurs, for example, when Beijing trades economic aid to Phnom Penh for Cambodian help in censoring ASEAN on the subject of the SCS. Less crass and often less successful is symbolic co-optation, as in the trading of esteem for support. Xi Jinping likely had that calculus in mind in 2015 when he hosted the leaders of Cambodia and Laos in Beijing at a lavish 70th-anniversary celebration of the end of World War II. Less generally acknowledged is a third variation: preemptive co-optation. That happened when Beijing tried to leverage its economic support for three ASEAN states by presumptively and unilaterally announcing their endorsement of China's stance on the SCS, thereby trapping them between bad choices — false consent or risky objection. That ploy and its failure are discussed in this book's first chapter. Other variations include one that is not a PRC-initiated tactic: self-solicited co-optation. Philippine president Rodrigo Duterte tried out that move when he decided, in effect, to seek his own country's material co-optation by appeasing Beijing with regard to the SCS in the hope of motivating Chinese development aid.

Prolongation is a delaying tactic used by China to ensure that its meetings with the ASEAN states on matters of conduct in the SCS do not make decisions that Beijing does not want. The longer such talks go on, the more entrenched and harder to dial back China's armed maritime presence becomes.

ASEAN has long rationalized its proclivity for dialogue by arguing that "talking is certainly better than fighting," to quote one of its general secretaries, the late Rod Severino. "Only talk," he said, "can lead to understanding, agreement and cooperation."[13] Beijing has tried to turn that logic into a license to keep Southeast Asian diplomats at the table patiently talking and listening while trusting in Chinese goodwill. That trust is damaged when China harasses its littoral rivals in the SCS. But Beijing may calculate that it can, by threatening its neighbors, reinforce their fear of fighting, and thereby replenish their commitment to endless, results-free conversation. China's interest is further served by the contribution to delay that results from discord among the ASEAN states themselves, whether genuine or cultivated by Beijing.

The evidence for the first four tactics mentioned above — occupation, augmentation, construction, and militarization — has been widely acknowledged and is readily available.[14] The rest of this chapter therefore elaborates on the additional four ploys just introduced — intimidation, ambiguation, prolongation, and co-optation — with particular attention to the Philippines and Vietnam. They are respectively the most and second-most populous of the four Southeast Asian countries with self-acknowledged claims to the SCS, and each of their claims is distinctively large. Those attributes and the strikingly different ways in which the Philippines and Vietnam have responded to Chinese behavior warrant their prominence in any space-limited discussion of China's ability to control the SCS.

Intimidation

Chinese intimidation has served different purposes. In 1994–95, for example, it helped China acquire another land feature when, step by step, ignoring Manila's protests, Beijing gained control over Mischief Reef, located inside the Philippines' EEZ (see Figure 6.1). Afraid of war, Manila let it happen. Having absorbed the reef, Beijing enlarged it, built it up, and weaponized it.[15]

Chinese expansion on this and other occasions has benefited from a type of intimidation that PLA Major General Zhang Zhaozhong has candidly and approvingly called a "cabbage strategy." Multiple different civilian and semi-civilian Chinese vessels form circles around a land feature that China has targeted. They wrap it "layer by layer like a cabbage." PLA Navy warships are placed in the outermost ring to block foreign entry, while at the heart of the cabbage, Chinese fishermen continue to ply the feature's waters undisturbed. In 2012 Beijing gained control over Scarborough Shoal, another feature inside Manila's EEZ, in part by executing this version of intimidation with Chinese characteristics.[16]

China has also used intimidation to convey a general sense of peril to a wide audience. Consider the implicit threat launched at the end of June 2019, when China tested six anti-ship ballistic missiles by propelling them from its mainland into portions of the SCS — areas variously claimed by China, the Philippines, and Vietnam. The unannounced rehearsal did no physical harm. But it delivered a warning to anyone who might challenge China's assertion of sole authority over nearly all of the SCS: Whoever you are, look at what we can do to you. The message's priority recipient was likely the US Pacific Fleet, whose repeated enactments of freedom of navigation by sailing near land features controlled by China have infuriated Beijing. But others in the intended audience for Chinese ire could have included Australia, Canada, France, Japan, and New Zealand as well. Their SCS-transiting warships have also angered Beijing. Not to mention the warning that China's missiles seemed to convey to Southeast Asian navies as to the punishment they might face for transgressing supposedly Chinese waters, whether sailing alone or in tandem with ships from outside the region.[17]

The case of Thitu Island in the Spratlys, shown in Figure 6.1, illustrates China's use of intimidation to force a halt to activities that it does not like. Although the Philippines has occupied the feature since the early 1970s, the installations on Thitu are unprepossessing. They consist of a small military garrison and an unpaved airstrip, Manila still not having satisfied the Philippine Navy's wish for a base there. By 2019, the sea had begun to erode the dirt airstrip at both ends, making take-offs and landings dangerous. When Manila announced plans to repair the runway and build a barracks, China responded by "cabbaging" Thitu — swarming the waters around it with a motley flotilla of PLA Navy, coast guard, and supposedly civilian fishing vessels.

By blocking access to Thitu, Beijing hoped to prevent the repairs from taking place and the barracks from being built. The harassment continued for months. A China-based analyst tried to justify the intimidation by noting that upgraded facilities on Thitu could be used by the United States for the purpose of "undermining China's military advantage in the South China Sea."[18] His comment ignored the strategic autonomy of the Philippines to define its own national interest and the location of Thitu just outside Manila's EEZ, far from the Chinese mainland.

China has also targeted Vietnam. Under UNCLOS, a littoral country enjoys sole sovereign rights to natural resources inside its EEZ including not only fish, but oil and natural gas as well. In violation of international law, Beijing has tried to stop Hanoi from accessing resources in Vietnam's coastal EEZ. An undersea gas field in the SCS supplies as much as 10 percent of Vietnam's need for energy. The field is located in Block 06-01 inside Vietnam's EEZ. Within that zone in 2017–18, Beijing coerced Hanoi into halting and finally canceling a Vietnamese-Spanish effort to drill for hydrocarbons under the sea floor.

China found it harder to force Vietnam to stop a joint exploring and drilling venture between PetroVietnam and a Russian firm, Rosneft, in Block 06-01. In July 2019 Beijing sent a group of vessels, including a huge, well-armed, helicopter-carrying CCG ship, to the area to halt the resupply of the venture's Japanese-owned rig. Vietnam responded by sending its own ships to the site. A standoff ensued. This time Hanoi did not back down and the Chinese ship eventually left. Beijing meanwhile continued to explore and exploit hydrocarbon resources for its own benefit in other contested waters in the SCS.[19]

Terminating fishing by China's rivals is another goal of intimidation. One night in June 2019, near Reed Bank inside the Philippines' coastal EEZ, a Chinese trawler rammed and badly damaged a stationary Philippine fishing boat, obliging its 22-member crew to abandon ship. The crew was asleep, but lights on both vessels were on, so the trawler could see the boat before hitting it. Afterwards, the trawler turned its lights off and left the scene without even trying to rescue the crew, who were eventually saved by a Vietnamese ship. Although Filipino protesters later burned 22 PRC flags in honor of the sailors, President Duterte preferred to curry favor with Beijing by downplaying the affair.[20]

In the Paracels in March 2019, inside Hanoi's EEZ, a CCG ship water-cannoned and chased a Vietnamese fishing boat. The boat hit rocks and capsized. Another Vietnamese vessel rescued the crew of five.[21] China had again acted out its desire to control access to "its" resources — fish, oil, gas — and to use physical punishment to that end.

These incidents show how the Philippines and Vietnam have been singled out for vigorous intimidation by Beijing. Inside Malaysia's zone at Luconia Shoals, 1,700 nm from China's coast, CCG ships have harassed Malaysian oil and gas vessels, veering as close to them as 80 meters.[22] But compared with the Philippines (pre-Duterte) and Vietnam, Malaysia and especially Brunei have been less vocal in challenging China's claims. Chinese intimidation has accordingly targeted Philippine and Vietnamese vessels more.

Ambiguation

A map is supposed to replace ambiguity with clarity. That has not been the purpose of the map of the SCS that Beijing has used to warrant its claim. On the contrary, it is precisely the cryptic nature of that map's distinctive feature — the "nine-dash line" drawn around almost all of the sea[23] — that illustrates China's avoidance of clarity as a tactic in its pursuit of control. Beijing has cited that broken line as putative proof of a vast extension of some form or forms of Chinese ownership, authority, rights, impunity, or all of the above. Ambiguation allows China to maximize its claim whenever it is expedient to do so, free of the limits that definitive clarity could impose.

In May 2009, the PRC's mission to the UN officially conveyed Beijing's stance on the SCS to then UN secretary-general Ban Ki-moon. Two identical statements, italicized here for emphasis, declared that

> China has indisputable sovereignty over the islands in the South China Sea and the adjacent waters, and enjoys sovereign rights and jurisdiction over the relevant waters as well as the seabed and subsoil thereof (see attached map).[24]

The "attached map" bore neither a title nor an explanatory caption, and the accompanying notes said nothing about the map except that it was attached. Some baffled and suspicious viewers of the map mentally filled in the blanks between the nine dashes to imagine a giant Chinese "cow's tongue" lapping up the entire SCS.[25]

Having taken part in the negotiations that produced UNCLOS, China did ratify its terms in 1996. As noted earlier, under the treaty's provisions, a coastal, peninsular, or insular country's entitlements to do certain things under, in, or on the sea depend on characteristics of its land or lands as they relate to those waters, especially where land meets water. Among those determining aspects of the land are matters of location, distance, configuration, tide-contingent dry height, and natural versus artificial formation. Before a land feature can be granted the status of an island, for example, it should be economically viable on its own and possess resources, such as fresh water, that can sustain human life.[26]

China's terse submission to the UN in 2009 ignored these criteria and declared "indisputable sovereignty" over "the islands in the South China Sea," presumably all of them, without stating what an "island" is. The *Oxford English Dictionary* says it is a "piece of land completely surrounded by water."[27] By that inclusive definition, Beijing claims as China's property all of the land features in the SCS — atolls, cays, reefs, shoals, and sandbars included. Beijing's failure to define or otherwise qualify the term "island" naturally causes other countries to think that China believes it possesses all of those various features. Whether the original lack of clarity in Beijing's statement was intentional or not, the persistence of that opacity for more than a decade since 2009 attests to its premeditated nature.

The UNCLOS-compliant borders of maritime zones are centrifugal. They are drawn outward from land features. China's UNCLOS-ignoring claim is centripetal. It is inferred inward from the nine-dash line, which encloses waters and land features alike. Could the dashes be meant to signal, at the greediest extreme, three-dimensional Chinese ownership of everything under, on, and above the "tongue"? According to UNCLOS, the near-total sovereignty exercised by a coastal state over its "territorial sea" covers the "bed and subsoil" beneath it and the "air space" above it as well.[28]

Beijing's 2009 declaration of sovereignty did not mention a territorial sea. Instead it proclaimed Chinese sway over the "islands" and "the adjacent waters" and over "the seabed and subsoil" beneath "the relevant waters." Arguably, that self-assigned scope did not include waters that were either not "adjacent" or not "relevant." But the authorities in Beijing declined to say — and a decade-plus later still have not said — how far from any one of the hundreds of land features scattered across the SCS a stretch of water ceases to be adjacent, or what the even more ambiguous notion of relevance is supposed to mean. Nor has Beijing clarified the nine-dash line, including the blanks between its dashes, or bothered to specify the coordinates of the dashes in latitude and longitude. How can a Southeast Asian fishing boat's crew even know if and when they have crossed China's line?

In 2018, a group of researchers in China were reported to have "discovered" a map, first published in April 1951, that connected the dashes to form a single continuous line. The report seemed to augur a measure of clarity after all. But the researchers had an agenda. The solid-line map, they said, indisputably "proves" that the filled-in line is China's "national boundary" and "the border of China's *territorial sea*" (italics added).[29] Under UNCLOS, the breadth of a territorial sea is limited to 12 nm, an infinitesimal width compared to the nearly 1.5 million square nm of water that lie inside the nine-dash line. Labeling virtually the entire SCS a sovereignty-bestowing "territorial sea" grossly violates international maritime law. Doubtless aware of the international backlash the researchers' jingoism could trigger, yet unwilling to risk domestic criticism by calling them out, Beijing has preserved ambiguation as a tactic by neither endorsing nor dismissing the researchers' "discovery," keeping future options open.

The dashes' ambiguity is available for China to use in relations not only with its neighbors, but with the United States as well. In March 2012 at the Jakarta International Defense Dialogue in Indonesia, for instance, this author privately asked a uniformed Chinese naval officer why his government would not clarify the nine-dash line. He replied by saying, in effect, be careful what you wish for. An American naval officer serving in the US Embassy in Beijing at the time later recalled Chinese officers also telling him, "You don't want us to define the line."[30] Vagueness allows China to warn off unwanted outsiders without running the risks that candor might entail.

The SCS is important to China for its living and energy resources, its role in seaborne commerce, and its location. Successfully exercising control over it would help China hold sway over its ASEAN neighbors, protect its southern coast, and project power eastward beyond the Southeast Asian segment of the "first island chain" — Sakhalin to Singapore — that physically hems China in. Ambiguation helps China confuse its littoral rivals and keep them off-balance while rationalizing its acts of intimidation at sea and avoiding heightened opposition. Understandable in this light is what an especially high-ranking PRC official told this author off the record in May 2016. The official, far from regretting the indeterminacy of China's claims, embraced their opacity as marvelous and enjoyable: "Ambiguity is wonderful! Ambiguity is fun!"

Two months later, on 12 July 2016, an international arbitral court, convened under UNCLOS provisions at the behest of the Philippines, unanimously demurred. The enigmatic nine-dash line had "no legal basis" in the Convention.[31] Ambiguity was not fun. It was not even legal.

From Nine Dashes to "Historic Rights"

Compared with the economic and military power that strong states wield, international law is a weapon of the weak. In January 2013, the Philippine government, then led by President Benigno Aquino III, set in motion a process that would lead to a landmark decision in maritime law. Manila wanted clarity. Beijing did not. So Manila unilaterally prompted a legal proceeding, allowable under UNCLOS,[32] to request a ruling that the treaty's terms had been flouted by Chinese claims and actions in the SCS. Alleged diversions and contraventions cited in the petition included the nine-dash line and the assertion of rights based upon it; the occupation and upbuilding of land features in transgression of UNCLOS-authorized Philippine rights; the exaggeration of maritime entitlements; and interference in Philippine fishing.[33] An international arbitral court was duly formed to consider the case.

Consistently from the submission of Manila's request in 2013 to the arbitral court's judgment in 2016, Beijing rejected the legality and content of President Aquino's request for a ruling; attacked the ensuing arbitral process, including the formation, composition, and jurisdiction of the court; and boycotted the court's proceedings. In July 2016, upon reading the tribunal's decision, which upheld nearly every Philippine complaint, Beijing ratcheted its anger higher. A vice foreign minister called the judgment "nothing but a scrap of paper."[34] State Councillor Yang Jiechi, arguably the most influential Chinese official on foreign affairs, denounced it as "full of nonsense" — a "political farce" that could not alter Chinese sovereignty, rights, and interests in the SCS "formed over the course of over two thousand years."[35]

Since the arbitral court's ruling, China has tweaked its position on the SCS in two respects. First, Beijing has downplayed the nine-dash line and emphasized "historic rights" instead, in keeping with Yang's recourse to the ancient past. Second, legal terms used in UNCLOS have shown up more often in PRC statements, but without elucidation, as if to suggest rather than demonstrate conformity with international law. A Chinese statement issued immediately following the arbitral court's decision illustrated both tweaks: "China has, based on Nanhai Zhudao [the South China Sea Islands], internal waters, territorial sea, contiguous zone, exclusive economic zone and continental shelf" — all UNCLOS terms. But the generic wording left unclear whether such entitlements were being drawn individually around each land feature or around all of them together as if they formed one giant archipelago. And the statement continued: "In addition, China has historic rights in the South China Sea."[36] In the treaty, "historic rights" are nowhere to be found.

Realizing that the court would delegitimize the nine dashes, and knowing how controversial those markings were, China stopped mentioning them, but did not abandon them, preserving the opportunity to redeploy them. As for "historic rights," they figured prominently in the rebuttal of the court's ruling issued by the PRC-based Chinese Society of International Law in 2018.

The 39 Chinese authors of that 542-page rejoinder had nothing to say about the nine-dash line. But they spent more than 100 pages defending China's "historic rights" in the scs. "As early as the 2nd century BCE," the authors wrote, "the Chinese people sailed in the South China Sea and discovered Nanhai Zhudao in the long course of [their] activities."[37]

One might think Beijing deserves praise for downsizing its appetite by at least temporarily de-emphasizing the dashed line. But because "historic rights" are abstractions, lacking any fixed location, Beijing can assert them to justify its behavior anywhere in the scs, including in waters beyond the dashes. And even if China's ambitions do not go beyond the line, implementing that already sweeping claim to sovereignty would, by one estimate, transfer to China the following shares of the declared EEZs of its littoral neighbors in Southeast Asia: Brunei 90 percent; the Philippines 80; Malaysian Sarawak and Sabah 80; Vietnam 50; and Indonesia northeast of Natuna 30.[38]

When PRC officials revert to claiming "historic rights" dating back millennia, they commit the fallacy of presentism — anachronistically importing latter-day concepts and rationales back into ancient times when empirical referents for those terms did not yet exist. Not until 1993 was the concept of "historic rights" linked to the scs, by the government in Taipei not Beijing, and not without objection by Taiwanese scholars who doubted such a claim could be established under international law.[39] Only five years later were "historical rights" officially included in the PRC's claim.[40] Included, but not explained.

The notion of importing the present into the past implicates more than historiography. A French scholar has cited possible evidence of "patriotic archeology" by China in the scs that may have included planting backdated Chinese sovereignty markers on land features — false signs of ownership ready to be "discovered" later.[41] To be fair, whether or not and how early China may have existed as a country in the modern sense and exercised recognizably UNCLOS-consonant rights, China and its precursor polities have had a long if intermittent record of maritime activities off its southeastern coast. The question is whether those activities can be retroactively considered to have involved the exercise of "rights" — a modern legal term — and how exclusively they were exercised by ethnic-Chinese seafarers compared with the also "rightful" activities of coastal Arabs, Austronesians, and Malayo-Polynesians, also based in premodern proto-states, who also were sailing the scs.

In those centuries, the scs was a maritime commons. Modern-state sovereignty as a territorial model evolved from the terms of the Peace of Westphalia after it was signed in 1648. The concept of maritime sovereignty as an extension of the Westphalian state grew out of John Selden's *Mare Clausum* (Closure of the Sea), published in 1635. The sea voyages of Zheng He in the first quarter of the 15th century were certainly remarkable. But they hardly epitomized prior millennia of supposed Chinese sea-mindedness even before the Ming dynasty turned its back on the scs. Notably ignored in such Sinocentric accounts, for instance, are the maritime activities of the Sumatra-based scs-facing Srivijaya empire from the 7th to the 14th century.[42]

Co-optation

UNCLOS and its courts are not meant to decide who owns what in maritime space. Allocating contested sovereignty to a particular state is the purview of the International Court of Justice (ICJ). The ICJ can decide a dispute between two parties only if both of them want it to and have declared their acceptance of the compulsory character of its jurisdiction. Manila declared its acceptance in 1972. Beijing never has. China's refusal protects its claim of sovereignty in the scs from being challenged in the ICJ by the Philippines or any other state.[43]

UNCLOS was drawn up to establish and interpret the rules affecting the maritime claims and behaviors of all states party to the convention, including the Philippines and China, without delimiting or allocating sovereignty between specific contending states. The 501-page judgment[44] issued by the UNCLOS court in 2016 neither assigned nor denied sovereignty per se to either the Philippines or China. But in addition to ruling that the convention did not support the nine-dash line, the court concluded that none of the many land features in the Spratlys, regardless of who might or might not legally own them, were "islands" in the UNCLOS sense of warranting up-to-200-nm EEZs. As already noted, inside such a zone, its owner and only its owner is entitled to exercise certain UNCLOS-specified rights, including the right to fish and lift oil and gas.

By ruling that none of the hundreds of land features in the Spratlys deserved EEZs, the court drastically shrank the area within which UNCLOS-compliant rights could be claimed by China, the Philippines, or anyone else. In doing so, the judges bestowed on a major portion of the scs a "high seas" status rendering it legally usable by all — claimants and non-claimants alike.

Had Hugo Grotius (1583–1685) been alive, that advocate of open access in his influential 1609 book *Mare Liberum* (Freedom of the Sea) would have applauded. In his spirit, one might have thought, users of the scs and claimants other than furious Beijing would have endorsed the court's decision and pressed others to do so, given their shared interest in access to passage, fish, and seabed resources free of Chinese interference.[45] The EEZs that Southeast Asian claimant states had drawn in and around the Spratlys had been appraised by the court to Manila's benefit and Beijing's detriment, given the locations of the Philippines and China respectively near and far from the area. In that light, the loudest applause for the ruling should have come from the Philippine president's office in Malacañang.

It did not. In a national election in the Philippines in May 2016, Rodrigo Duterte won a plurality of the vote — 39 percent — and with it, the presidency of his country. He was inaugurated in June, two weeks before the July announcement of the court's ruling that satisfied virtually all of his predecessor's concerns. To the surprise of many observers, however, Duterte downplayed his country's win and focused instead on mending relations with Beijing.

It is tempting to picture Duterte — mercurial, violence-obsessed,[46] and embittered against America[47] — leading his country through a volte-face in the SCS for idiosyncratically personal reasons. His personality and its demons aside, however, he responded to the same China-related structural or situation-based constraints and incentives that have affected the behaviors of other ASEAN states. Compared with most of the region's other rulers, he was merely being more candid in publicly acknowledging China's massive superiority in military might and material wealth, and more nakedly opportunistic in bowing to Chinese power while requesting Chinese aid. He did not bandwagon China in the sense of boarding its juggernaut without recompense. By appeasing Beijing in the SCS in the hope of development aid, he solicited his own country's co-optation.

In July–September 2016, far from welcoming the arbitral court's juristic erasure of China's nine-dash line and urging all states to observe that decision, Duterte stalled Aquino's momentum. Xi Jinping, delighted, sweetened Duterte's October visit to China with a promise of $24 billion in loans, bank credit, and investments. Continued soft-pedaling by Manila yielded further pledges.[48] Actual transfers have fallen far short of China's commitments,[49] however, not to mention the disadvantages of politically contingent Chinese help compared with aid from Japan and other sources. As of June 2018, China accounted for less than 1 percent of total official development assistance received by the Philippines, compared with 40, 21, and 18 percent, respectively, from Japan, the World Bank, and the Asian Development Bank. Lack of follow-through aside, the drawbacks of deals involving Chinese loans have included secrecy, above-concessional interest rates, and China-favoring provisions for procurement.[50]

Manila under Aquino showed principled boldness in challenging Chinese avarice in the SCS by asking the court whether Beijing was or was not in breach of international law. Duterte refused to take the judges' "yes" for an answer. He preferred to accommodate Beijing through a self-co-opting transaction: agreeing not to challenge China's maritime claim and hoping for Chinese aid in return.

Prolongation

It is virtually certain that the overlapping assertions of sovereignty in the SCS will never be negotiated—demarcated, allocated—to the satisfaction of all of the claimants. That impracticality helps to explain the long-running appeal of a less impossible project: rather than deciding who owns what, regulating who does what. Such an effort could, for example, gestate a multilateral agreement not to seize land features, harass fishermen, or initiate conflicts that could turn into wars. Hence the idea of drafting, signing, and implementing a code of conduct (COC) in the SCS: a set of rules that would guide the actions of claimant states, and possibly affect what other states do there as well.

China has helped make that goal elusive by prolonging the rule-making process, keeping Southeast Asians at the table expecting an eventual resolution while ensuring that it does not happen, at least not until China can dictate its terms. Accordingly, for more than a quarter century, to varying degrees, Beijing's strategy in the SCS has featured deliberate delay.

The option to regulate behavior first surfaced officially in 1992 when the foreign ministers of ASEAN recommended "establishing a code of international conduct over the South China Sea." The six countries then comprising ASEAN—Brunei, Indonesia, Malaysia, the Philippines, Singapore, and Thailand—unanimously agreed on the need for such a code and offered the idea for consideration by "all parties concerned."[51]

Short of an attack risking war, China's acquisitions and artificial formations of land in the SCS are surely permanent. The conversion of the larger or enlarged ones into armed platforms outfitted to project threat-based influence, coupled with recurrent rammings, crowdings, and standoffs initiated by Beijing, have made clear and urgent the need for peaceful and stabilizing behavior at sea. Yet a COC in the SCS still does not exist, despite more than a quarter of a century of talking about ASEAN's 1992 proposal. The COC persists instead on ASEAN's agenda as an unmet priority that continues to resurface in Southeast Asia's relations with China, year after year, dialogue upon dialogue.

Intra-ASEAN dissension is partly responsible for the lack of progress. The grouping's enlargement to include Vietnam in 1995, Laos and Myanmar in 1997, and Cambodia in 1999 made intramural consensus less likely, as have tensions between ASEAN-state claimants in the Spratlys. Also divisive has been the disagreement between those wanting a stronger code, which Beijing would dislike, and those uneager to risk Chinese displeasure. The less provocative course has appealed in particular to Laos and Cambodia — the one landlocked, the other not facing the SCS, and both relatively poor and keen to procure Chinese aid. The concerned party most interested in thwarting the birth of an effective COC, however, is still the one littoral state with both the desire and the ability to control the SCS — the PRC itself. The enforceability of any protocol designed to restrain bad behavior is crucial in this context.

In 2002, a decade after ASEAN first raised the idea of a COC, the foreign ministers of ASEAN and China, unable to agree on a code, settled for a statement: a non-binding Declaration on the Conduct of Parties in the South China Sea (DOC). Its signers promised "to work, on the basis of consensus, toward the eventual attainment" of a COC and "to exercise self-restraint" in order not to "complicate or escalate disputes."[52]

The fatal weakness of the DOC was and remains its unenforceability — a flaw made evident by the early, widespread, and ongoing violation of its entirely voluntary terms. The agreement included no mechanism that could even monitor misbehavior, let alone bring misbehavers to account. The clear inference to be drawn from the 17-year-long failure of the DOC is that it should be replaced, if possible, by a COC that does more than simply exhort. Understandably, in light of China's kinetic power and desire for unilateral control, its diplomats kept moving the goal posts of agreement on a code. In 2013 Beijing even tried to make a COC conditional on the prior "full and effective implementation" of the unenforceable 11-year old DOC — an intentionally high bar that would have to be cleared before negotiations toward a COC could even begin.[53]

As if that condition were not retardive enough, it was argued that before all of the DOC's wishful terms could be put into practice by all concerned, guidelines for reaching that outcome would need to be drafted and endorsed. A tentative text was finally drafted in 2005, followed by six more years of discussion before the guidelines were finally announced in 2011. But they were vacuous and made no provision for monitoring or enforcement — the very reason why the DOC had failed. Instead, the guidelines repeated the perfectionist mantra that the declaration deserved "full and effective implementation" and called for unspecified "voluntary" steps to achieve that goal "based on consensus."[54] By thus assuring further delay in putting the DOC into practice, the guidelines postponed the devising of a COC into an even more hypothetical future. Prolongation bought valuable time that Beijing, unbothered by a code, could and did use to entrench and militarize its presence in the SCS.

In 2017, six years after the guidelines were issued, the DOC had still not been implemented. Nor was the credibility of China's commitment to the process helped when in 2018 the government of Hainan Province offered to lease uninhabited land features in the SCS to any "entity or individual" wanting to build and operate infrastructure on them, for durations of rental from 15 to 50 years. That solicitation explicitly violated China's promise not to inhabit uninhabited features under the fifth article in the DOC that China and foreign ministers from all 10 ASEAN states had individually signed.[55]

By 2017 pressure had mounted on Beijing to drop the detour through a DOC and directly negotiate a COC. That may have nudged PRC foreign minister Wang Yi to announce in that year that China and its neighbors had consented to a secret draft "framework" for a COC. But the document's leaked details showed it to be nothing but another wishful listing of norms. As if that were not obstructive enough, Wang laid down four more preconditions for further progress: enhancing "mutual trust"; "deepen[ing] cooperation"; "necessary preparatory work by all parties"; and, pointedly, "get[ting] rid of interference from inside and outside the region." Only then, he implied, would China hold "substantive consultations," linguistically downgraded from actual negotiations, toward achieving a COC at a to-be-determined "proper time."[56]

In 2018, Beijing did appear to have given in to Southeast Asian pressure to step up the pace of COC diplomacy. In August, Foreign Minister Wang joined his ASEAN counterparts in reporting their agreement on a Single Draft Negotiating Text (SDNT) that would serve as the basis for an eventual COC. The SDNT was not released, but an enterprising analyst of the SCS disputes obtained a copy and circulated his summary of the text, including quotes from it.

Despite the "Single Draft" in its name, the SDNT was not a unified document. It included a compilation, article by article, of differing alternative bits of language proposed and submitted by one or more of the negotiating states. The resulting collage-in-progress revealed differences between China and the members of ASEAN and among the latter as well. Notably, Beijing wanted the text of the COC to forbid maritime economic cooperation among littoral states from involving "companies from countries outside the region" and to deny Southeast Asian states the right to hold "joint military exercises with countries from outside the region, unless the parties concerned are notified beforehand and express no objection." Clearly, America is "outside the region," China is a "concerned" party, and the prohibitions would cut back the economic and the strategic freedom of China's neighbors to choose their own partners. Reflecting what is undoubtedly a widespread view in Southeast Asia, Malaysia wanted language in the SDNT ensuring that nothing in the COC would affect the "rights or ability" of the signing states "to conduct activities with foreign countries or private entities of their own choosing."[57]

Also in 2018, to keep the ASEAN states at the table debating a COC, Beijing tried to renew their credulity that someday an agreed-upon code really could exist. While indirectly reminding them of their disunity, Chinese premier Li Keqiang sought to refresh their naïveté. "China and some [unnamed] ASEAN countries," he said, had "put forward a vision [not a deadline] of concluding COC consultations [not negotiations] in three years' time."[58] That "vision," apparently meant to be encouraging news, would propel the birthday of a code forward to 2022, almost one-third of a century after ASEAN first raised the idea.

It is plausible to believe that Beijing still thinks it has time on its side. But the ASEAN states may not be as gullible as China seems to wish they were. They stay at the table more from fear than faith — fear of China, but also fear of being left out of an eventual arrangement that might even benefit them, or at least hurt them less than leaving the table would. Empathy between ASEAN's members remains low. If one Southeast Asian state walked away while the others stayed at the table, the façade of ASEAN consensus would be destroyed, and the stayers might ignore or thwart the interests of the absent party. Other things being equal, an ASEAN state would probably rather meet with China as part of a group if the alternative is a one-on-one bilateral weighted to favor whatever China wants. Beijing meanwhile can tolerate its numerical disadvantage when facing all 10 ASEAN states, first, knowing that the group is divided, and second, having already banned the incendiary topic of sovereignty from DOC- or COC-focused discussions of state behavior.

For these reasons, a meaningful — comprehensive, fair, enforceable — code of conduct in the SCS has become an institutionalized mirage. The mirage is institutionalized because the idea that a COC would be good to have is at least something that the ASEAN states can agree on in principle, however endlessly debatable a draft text might be in practice. The idea of a code has been cemented in ASEAN's agenda to the point that an outright failure to achieve even a platitudinous text could be seen as a failure of the association itself. In those foreign ministries that are most invested in the COC project, that fear of failure may lower the bar for success, and in doing so make an anodyne outcome more likely. An unenforceable code could be preferable, after all, to one that effectively bans naval exercises with outsiders and authorizes China to monitor violations of the agreement's provisions using high-tech methods of surveillance that could be used to extend and deepen Chinese control. If and as pushback by ASEAN states against that prospect weakens over time, Beijing could decide to take advantage of its neighbors' exhaustion and fatalism and push toward a COC that, far from averting Chinese control, helps to bring it about.

From Regulating Conduct to Sharing Resources?

China's futures in the SCS span a spectrum of scenarios. At one far and unlikely end, the influence that China has already gained in the SCS will be decisively reversed, forestalling Chinese dominance once and for all. At the other end, China's control over the sea will expand, deepen, and become permanent.

How control is defined affects the plausibility of any future between these extremes. Were China to exercise full *positive control*, Beijing would be the sole cause of everything that happens above, on, in, and under the SCS. But that combination of enormous scope and thoroughgoing intrusion is beyond Xi Jinping's ability to manage, as he himself likely knows, notwithstanding his ongoing effort to install a surveillance state on the mainland. That scenario also ignores the attention Beijing must pay to challenges on multiple other fronts. More plausible is the prospect that China could someday exercise kinds and degrees of *negative control*, including by surveillance, sufficient to ensure that China is not actually challenged, or is only challenged unsuccessfully, in the SCS. A negative-control strategy would not require China to attack and acquire land features occupied by its Southeast Asian neighbors, for example, so long as they accept China's entitlement to access and use resources throughout the sea while policing its waters and features. If a feature-occupying ASEAN state did resist Chinese negative control, it could risk eviction and replacement were Beijing to decide to transform negative into positive control in that instance.

China's repertoire of tactics intended to achieve negative control already includes transactional co-optation based on limited sharing. Conversations between Xi and Duterte in August and October 2019 seemed to point in that direction. On those occasions, the two presidents discussed a possible agreement whereby Beijing and Manila could jointly seek and extract oil and gas from beneath the Philippines' own EEZ. Reportedly, use of the energy could be split unevenly in Manila's favor — 60 percent to the Philippines, 40 percent to China. Beijing might even be willing to defray the costs of exploration and production. Apparently in return, however, Manila would be expected to ignore or perhaps even disavow the 2016 UNCLOS court's invalidation of the nine-dash line, in addition to surrendering two-fifths of its own energy resources in the area where the joint activity would occur. Of further interest was a decision reportedly reached by Xi and Duterte to establish a joint "steering committee" to coordinate the arrangement.[59]

But the devil is in the details, as it proved to be in the failure of a 2005 Sino-Philippine-Vietnamese agreement to test for the presence of hydrocarbons beneath contested waters in the SCS. Which country's laws should govern a joint Sino-Philippine activity? How should the two partners' contributions, benefits, and roles be allocated? Would the answers appear to validate one partner's claim to maritime sovereignty over that of the other?

In 2019, a Philippine newspaper called the proposed 60-40 Duterte-Xi agreement a "win-win" for both sides.[60] But the Philippines would merely "gain" access to three-fifths of the offshore energy resources that it already possesses in its own EEZ. Beijing would acquire, in addition to the other two-fifths, Manila's complicity in a de facto boosting of the legitimacy of China's claim to own those same resources. The agreement's provisions would not assign sovereignty. But China would be able to argue that it had generously shared its own resources with the Philippines, not the reverse, especially if Manila kept its part of the bargain by repudiating the arbitral court's repudiation of the nine-dash line. The net incremental effect of such a "lose-win" deal would be to normalize Chinese primacy in the SCS. On the other hand, if the Philippines declined the bargain and invited a non-Chinese energy company to locate and lift the oil and gas, Beijing could exert negative control through intimidation by punishing Manila and threatening to stop any such project, whose contribution to future economic growth the Philippines certainly needs.

Nor is Beijing necessarily attracted by what the Philippine government can offer. The Philippine constitution is unequivocal: All lands and waters in the public domain are owned by the state, which exercises "full control and supervision" of the resources therein.[61] Under standard Philippine negotiating practice, a would-be foreign partner in resource exploration and exploitation is treated not as a co-owner but merely as a client who signs a service contract to provide needed technical help to the Philippine owner under Philippine rules. That would meet the requirements of the Philippine constitution and a still-valid 1972 presidential decree.[62] But Beijing could not sign such a contract without impugning its own claim of sovereignty in Philippine waters.

By 2019 in Manila, Aquino's nationalism, his legal success against China, and his cooperation with the United States had been replaced by Duterte's fatalism, his concessionary tilt toward China, and his anti-American temperament. But that considerable shift had not brought the Philippine defense establishment along.[63] Nor had public opinion sided with Duterte. In surveys of Filipino respondents, 93 percent took a Philippine-nationalist view of China's expansion in the scs; 89 percent said the Philippines should trust America; and 74 percent said their country should not trust China. On the other hand, for mainly domestic reasons, 85 percent of Philippine respondents approved of Duterte's performance in office.[64]

Duterte's health is poor. His six-year presidency ends in June 2022 and the current Philippine constitution forbids him a second term. Although that ticking clock may prompt China to accelerate its effort to co-opt the Philippine president, the ranks of the "deep state" underneath Duterte are likely to remain suspicious of China and its motives, not to mention the effects of interaction between Chinese expansionism and Philippine nationalism.

Vietnam is different. The credibility of Hanoi's hard-power deterrent means that China would think more than twice before reprising its 1979 invasion of Vietnam. Hanoi has, however, followed the Philippines in considering legal redress against Chinese ambition in the scs. The option of challenging Beijing's maritime claims was discussed in Hanoi even before Manila won its case.[65] More recently, in 2019, a Vietnamese foreign ministry official acknowledged the possibility of taking legal action against China, including recourse to arbitration. Two days later, a Chinese foreign ministry official responded by blaming Vietnam and China's other rival claimants for causing the scs disputes by "invading and occupying" Chinese islands. Hanoi, he urged, should simply admit "historical reality"—the "reality" of China's sovereignty over the scs and the implied need for Hanoi to bow to superior Chinese power.[66]

Space limits here prohibit exploring the possible requests, outcomes, and juridical complexities that a petition to an UNCLOS court could entail. Rather than choosing to take that route, Vietnam may want to keep legal redress optional but not pursued—a contingent threat meant to lessen Chinese intimidation and, conceivably, motivate China's cooperation. Compared with the expedient ambiguities and suspensions of disagreement that are central to the *resource-concessionary* approach that Xi and Duterte have entertained, the *legal-petitionary* UNCLOS option is more clear-cut and confrontational in nature. But the judicial option, if chosen, will prolong delay. An answer to the Philippine request took three years. Ceding resources risks provoking a nationalist backlash in the compliant country, but it could save time. And these two approaches by no means exhaust the policy alternatives available to Southeast Asians.

The massive imbalances of hard power between China and its southern neighbors would seem to preclude a traditional *deterrent-military* approach. But the cost to China of waging an armed conflict with a Southeast Asian state would depend on which one it is. A war with Vietnam, Indonesia, or Singapore would be harder for China to win than one with Laos, Cambodia, or Brunei.[67] A decision whether and how to attack a particular ASEAN state would likely take into account how severe-to-trivial the incurred damages could turn out to be. Conversely, in a more strategically minded state such as Vietnam or Singapore, an equivalent calculus could guide military spending, force modernization, and the cultivation of defense partnerships with extra-regional actors.

Just as China has tried to exclude outsiders from involvement in maritime-security diplomacy and rebuffed their freedom-of-navigation sail-throughs, the ASEAN claimants are aware of the counterbalancing value of trying to internationalize the SCS. The appeal of such an *outsider-inclusionary* approach, however, has been limited by the ASEAN countries' differing engagements and stakes in the SCS and its resources, together with fears of losing strategic autonomy to foreigners on the one hand, or overestimating their reliability on the other. ASEAN's leaders know that verbal assurances by President Trump in particular could be ignored or withdrawn at any time.

The US-ASEAN and East Asia Summits, convened annually in Southeast Asia, are useful occasions for American presidents and diplomats to meet their counterparts in the region. Especially productive are the more selective and focused conversations typically held on the sidelines of these two largely symbolic main events. But showing up matters. In November 2019, for the second year in a row, President Trump failed to attend either meeting. The Trump administration further downgraded its representation at the 2019 summits in Bangkok, despite the status of their host, Thailand, formally an American treaty ally. Southeast Asian impressions of American disregard for the region were amplified accordingly. ASEAN's leaders, embarrassed, retaliated with their own downgrading of the US-ASEAN Summit. They substituted foreign ministers for seven of the 10 heads of government who would normally have attended the event. The American side, in turn, accused the Southeast Asians of damaging US-ASEAN relations by embarrassing Trump.[68]

Two months before, in September, a first-ever US naval exercise with all 10 ASEAN countries had traversed part of the SCS, ostensibly to train the crews in humanitarian assistance and disaster relief. But the losses of diplomatic face in Bangkok in November undercut the outsider-inclusionary approach favored by those among Southeast Asia's leaders who had hoped the American president would, by his presence and support, help them resist being absorbed into a Chinese sphere of influence.

The above four Southeast Asian responses to Beijing — *resource-concessionary*, *legal-petitionary*, *deterrent-military*, and *outsider-inclusionary* — should be viewed in the light of ASEAN's fruitless but persisting decades-long search for a COC in the SCS. That quixotic endeavor took up too much of the professional bandwidth of Southeast Asian diplomats, academics, and analysts — time that could have been spent not only on improving the responses reviewed here but on brainstorming other unilateral and, especially, collaborative approaches to the China challenge.

Closing Thoughts

China will not be disarmed in, let alone dislodged from, the SCS, barring an unlikely war that China would have to lose. But there are different kinds, degrees, and limits of Chinese control. This chapter has argued that China will not be able to ensure that whatever happens in the SCS will have been caused by Beijing. But if positive control is unrealistic, negative control is not. Using combinations of tactics including those reviewed in this chapter, China could institutionalize its maritime primacy and be able to prevent or defeat challenges to it. But that outcome is by no means inevitable, and it may not be fully achievable unless China proves able to cultivate, in its own discourse and demeanor, the one kind of power that it lacks the most in its dealings with Southeast Asians: soft power.

Economic power is less than fully soft if it is used to induce reluctant deference and involuntary self-censorship in a recipient country; co-optation and coercion can go together. But transactional "win-win" promises in PRC propaganda and public relations cannot compensate for the lack of empathy toward China in Southeast Asia. Beijing cannot expect its models of government and development "with Chinese characteristics" to captivate societies that are not "Chinese," whatever that term may mean. If China were more open to outsiders and more attractive to them, it would not have granted, in 2016, only 1,576 permanent residency cards to foreigners — one-thousandth of one percent of the estimated 1.2 million issued that year by the United States.[69]

Maritime control by China or any other single power is not foreordained. The South China Sea's claimants and users could cooperate in many ways to protect and share its resources. Multilateral pacts are not impossible. Jointly written and implemented, or delegated to impartial actors, their provisions could help to mitigate overfishing, pollution, and the damage done by global warming, even if shared development proves a bridge too far.

Some if not all of the Southeast Asian states with overlapping EEZs in the SCS could jointly acknowledge the urgency of independently negotiating their overlays among themselves, with UNCLOS criteria in mind, and begin discussions to that effect, while promising Beijing reciprocal recognition of a UNCLOS-compatible Chinese EEZ. The fact that the EEZs claimed by the Philippines and Vietnam do not overlap could make it easier for non-governmental experts on maritime affairs in those two countries to begin someday laying the basis for such an EEZ-clarifying and tension-reducing process.

It is encouraging to recall that in 2014 Indonesia and the Philippines managed to reach a historic agreement defining the maritime boundary between their overlapping EEZs in the Mindanao Sea and Celebes Sea. Admittedly harder to imagine are agreed-upon EEZ borders in the SCS, given how much more diplomacy, patience, and luck their achievement would require.

Other steps are possible. For instance, a single Southeast Asian state could issue, all by itself or jointly with other claimants, this one-sentence statement: *No single country should control the South China Sea.* The declaration would then be opened for signature by any other state, in Asia or elsewhere, including China and the United States. If enough countries endorse the avowal, it could be submitted for approval to the UN General Assembly and, if China signs it, the Security Council as well.[70]

Proposals are easier to invent than execute. But Southeast Asians cannot be stopped from rethinking their options and imagining new ones — ideas that could, if implemented, help them live with China, not under it. The states in Southeast Asia's northern tier, Vietnam likely excepted, could someday become the integrated southern extension of a "greater China."[71] But even if that were to occur, the culturally distinctive SCS-littoral states in ASEAN's maritime south and east will not easily relinquish to Beijing their stakes in the SCS. Maintaining maritime access is a visceral interest of trade-dependent Singapore and geographically bifurcated Malaysia, to cite but two cases in point. The next Philippine president may not continue

Duterte's courtship of China or share his antipathy toward the United States. Nor will the United States, Japan, India, and Australia, among other major outside powers, readily tolerate the establishment of exclusionary Chinese control over the sea and its features.

The strategic autonomy of Southeast Asia is not doomed. The dragon is not fated to swallow the deer. The heartwater of Southeast Asia has not been irrevocably lost to dominance by China or any other would-be overlord. Not yet.

Notes

1 Relative size: "The World's Largest Oceans and Seas," The Travel
Almanac, https://www.thetravelalmanac.com/lists/oceans.htm. Shipping
data: "How Much Trade Transits the South China Sea?," China
Power Project, Center for Strategic and International Studies (CSIS),
Washington, DC, https://chinapower.csis.org/much-trade-transits-south
-china-sea. Fishing data: Gregory B. Poling, "Illuminating the South
China Sea's Dark Fishing Fleets," Asia Maritime Transparency Initiative
(AMTI), CSIS, Washington, DC, 9 January 2019, https://ocean.csis.org
/spotlights/illuminating-the-south-china-seas-dark-fishing-fleets.
Hydrocarbon data: "South China Sea Energy Exploration and
Development," AMTI, CSIS, https://amti.csis.org/south-china-sea-energy
-exploration-and-development.

2 Sarah Lohschelder, "Chinese Domestic Law in the South China Sea,"
New Perspectives in Foreign Policy 13 (Summer 2017), https://www.csis
.org/npfp/chinese-domestic-law-south-china-sea.

3 "Occupation and Island Building," AMTI, CSIS, Washington, DC,
accessed 22 July 2019, https://amti.csis.org/island-tracker. Also see
Alexander L. Vuving, "South China Sea: Who Occupies What in the
Spratlys?," *The Diplomat*, 6 May 2016, https://thediplomat.com/2016/05
/south-china-sea-who-claims-what-in-the-spratlys.

Not dealt with in this chapter is the sixth claimant, Taiwan, which has
occupied the largest land feature in the Spratlys since 1956. Taiwan
formally supports the extent of the mainland's maritime claim to the SCS,
but it does so in its PRC-challenged capacity as the self-named Republic
of China.

4 At international conferences attended by this author, Chinese officials
have gone so far as to "guarantee" freedom of navigation in the SCS,
without acknowledging that in order to do that, China would have to
control its waters. Such officials often note that commercial shipping
within established sea lines of communication continues uninterrupted,
implying that China would never interfere with that traffic. As discussed
later in this chapter, however, Beijing has not clarified the vast and
proprietary scope of its own "nine-dash" line. Nor has it clearly located
either the "relevant" or the land-"adjacent" waters that it also claims.
Barring blind trust in its self-restraint, Beijing's avoidance of candor
effectively confirms the grand scope of the control that it wishes to
possess. China does specify its objection to "certain Western politicians"

who "flex their military muscles" by sending naval vessels into China's "adjacent" waters. A ban applied to the US Navy by China could, however, be enlarged to interdict any navy in Southeast Asia. The statement about "Western politicians" was made by China's ambassador to the United Kingdom, Liu Xiaoming, in a 20 March 2019 *Daily Telegraph* editorial, "'Gunboat Diplomacy' Does Not Promote Peace," republished by *China Daily* the next day, http://www.chinadaily.com.cn/a /201903/21/WS5c92c091a3104842260b1aca.html.

5 Compare the generous listing by Chinese analysts in Beijing with the different and far less favorable to China evidence from CSIS, respectively, in Wang Wen and Chen Xiaochen, "Who Supports China in the South China Sea and Why," *The Diplomat*, 27 July 2016, https://thediplomat .com/2016/07/who-supports-china-in-the-south-china-sea-and-why; and "Who Is Taking Sides after the South China Sea Ruling?," AMTI, CSIS, 15 August 2016, https://amti.csis.org/sides-in-south-china-sea. CSIS also found that countries were more likely to support China's position if they were less well governed, more corrupt, and had less regard for the rule of law.

6 Donald K. Emmerson, "China's 'Frown Diplomacy' in Southeast Asia," *PacNet*, no. 45, 6 October 2010, https://pacforum.org/publication /pacnet-45-chinas-frown-diplomacy-in-southeast-asia.

7 "Occupation and Island Building."

8 See, for example, Steven Stashwick, "China's New Missiles in the Spratlys May Be a Turning Point," *The Diplomat*, 14 June 2018, https:// thediplomat.com/2018/06/chinas-new-missiles-in-the-spratlys-may-be-a -turning-point; and Alexander Neill, "China's Radar Installations in the Spratly Islands: What Do They Tell Us about Its Ambitions for the South China Sea?," International Institute for Strategic Studies, London, 19 February 2018, https://www.iiss.org/blogs/analysis/2018/02/china-radar.

9 Stephen Feller, "Beijing Admits It Has Installed Weapons on Islands in the South China Sea," United Press International, 16 December 2016, https://upi.com/6469979t.

10 United Nations Convention on the Law of the Sea (UNCLOS), part V ("Exclusive Economic Zone"), article 57, https://www.un.org/depts/los /convention_agreements/texts/unclos/unclos_e.pdf. For evidence of China's harassment of Vietnam, for example, see Gregory B. Poling and Murray Hiebert, "Stop the Bully in the South China Sea," *Wall Street Journal*, 28 August 2019, https://www.wsj.com/articles/stop-the-bully -in-the-south-china-sea-11567033378.

11 Figure 6.1 omits the EEZs of Indonesia, Malaysia, and Brunei due to the relative importance of Philippine and Vietnamese claims and roles, the need for readability on the printed page, and the accessibility of comprehensive graphics elsewhere. An excellent interactive map showing claims, EEZs, and other features can be found at "Who's Claiming What?," AMTI, CSIS, https://amti.csis.org/maritime-claims-map. Also included there is Taiwan's claim, which matches the PRC's inasmuch as the nine dashes evolved from a map drawn by the Republic of China in 1947 that Taipei does not disavow.

12 UNCLOS, part IV ("Archipelagic States"), article 47 (1).

13 Rodolfo C. Severino, "Asia Policy Lecture: What ASEAN Is and What It Stands For," The Research Institute for Asia and the Pacific, University of Sydney, 22 October 1998, https://asean.org/?static_post=asia-policy -lecture-what-asean-is-and-what-it-stands-for-by-rodolfo-c-severino -secretary-general-of-asean-at-the-research-institute-for-asia-and-the -pacific-university-of-sydney-australia-22-october-1.

14 See, for example, "Occupation and Island Building," AMTI; and Tom Phillips, "Photos Show Beijing's Militarisation of South China Sea in New Detail," The Guardian, 6 February 2018, https://www.theguardian .com/world/2018/feb/06/photos-beijings-militarisation-south-china-sea -philippines.

15 For more, see Steve Mollman, "How a 'Fishermen's Shelter' on Stilts Became a Chinese Military Base in the South China Sea," Quartz, 15 December 2016, https://qz.com/863811; and "Mischief Reef," Wikipedia, accessed 3 August 2019, https://en.wikipedia.org/wiki/Mischief_Reef.

16 Craig Hill, "China Boasts of Strategy to 'Recover' Islands Occupied by Philippines," China News, 28 May 2013, https://chinanewsstories. com/2013/05/28/china-boasts-of-strategy-to-recover-islands-occupied -by-philippines; and Rodel Rodis, "China's Salami-slicing Cabbage Strategy to Seize PH Islands and Reefs," Inquirer.net, 3 June 2013, https:// globalnation.inquirer.net/76323/chinas-cabbage-strategy-to-recover -chinese-islands-reefs-illegally-occupied-by-ph#ixzz6DmtwwDPw.

17 Sebastian Roblin, "China's Aircraft Carrier Killer Missiles Splashdown in the South China Sea," National Interest, 14 July 2019, https://nationalinterest.org/blog/buzz/chinas-aircraft-carrier-killer-mis siles-splashdown-south-china-sea-66927.

18 Said by Jinan University professor Zhang Mingliang as quoted in Zhenhua Lu, "Beijing Tried to Block Philippine Military Facilities on

Disputed Island 'over Fears US Could Use Them,'" *South China Morning Post*, 13 April 2019, https://www.scmp.com/news/china/diplomacy/artic le/3006012/beijing-tried-block-philippine-military-facilities-disputed.

19 "China Risks Flare-up over Malaysia, Vietnamese Gas Resources," AMTI, CSIS, Washington, DC, 16 July 2019, https://amti.csis.org/china -risks-flare-up-over-malaysian-vietnamese-gas-resources; and Liu Zhen, "China and Vietnam in Stand-off over Chinese Survey Ship Mission to Disputed Reef in South China Sea," *South China Morning Post*, 12 July 2019, https://www.scmp.com/news/china/diplomacy/article/3018332 /beijing-and-hanoi-stand-over-chinese-survey-ship-mission.

20 Raissa Robles, "Chinese Vessel Mainly to Blame for Sinking of Philippine Boat in South China Sea, but Filipino Crew Had 'Deficiencies': Leaked Report," *South China Morning Post*, 8 July 2019, https://www .scmp.com/week-asia/geopolitics/article/3017757/chinese-vessel-mainly -blame-sinking-philippine-boat-south.

21 "Vietnam Protests to China about Local Boat Sinking in South China Sea," Reuters via CNBC, 21 March 2019, https://www.cnbc.com/2019 /03/22/vietnam-protests-to-china-about-local-boat-sinking-in-south -china-sea.html.

22 Teddy Ng, "China Blocking Malaysian and Vietnamese Oil and Gas Vessels Shows Greater Willingness to Intimidate, Says Think Tank," *South China Morning Post*, 17 July 2019, https://www.scmp.com/news /china/diplomacy/article/3018951/china-blocking-malaysian-and -vietnamese-oil-and-gas-vessels.

23 Since 2013, the line has had 10 dashes. The first map drawn in 1947 by China's Nationalist Party (Kuomintang) showed 11. Over the ensuing years, dashes at the northeastern and northwestern ends of the line were removed or added. In 2013, soon after Xi Jinping's rise to power, the northeastern-most dash east of Taiwan was reinstated, as if China's interest in controlling the South China Sea were an extension of its non-negotiable "core interest" in controlling that island. In the light of common usage and because that tenth dash lies outside Southeast Asia, the boundary is referenced in this book as the "nine-dash line."

24 Dated 7 May 2009, the notes are identified as CML/17/2009 (http:// www.un.org/Depts/los/clcs_new/submissions_files/mysvnm33_09 /chn_2009re_mys_vnm_e.pdf) and CML/18/2009 (http://www.un.org /depts/los/clcs_new/submissions_files/vnm37_09/chn_2009re_vnm.pdf).

25 For example, DeathByChina, "Beijing's Hungry Cow's Tongue in the South China Sea," YouTube, 28 February 2016, https://www.youtube.com/watch?v=6i0zlQcx0b8.

26 Inferred from the specification of a "rock" in UNCLOS, part VIII ("Regime of Islands"), article 121(3).

27 2nd ed. (Oxford: Clarendon Press, 1989).

28 UNCLOS, part II, section 1, article 2(2).

29 Richard Javad Heydarian, "China's 'New' Map Aims to Extend South China Sea Claims," National Interest, 30 April 2018, https://national interest.org/blog/the-buzz/chinas-new-map-aims-extend-south-china -sea-claims-25628.

30 Personal communication, 9 September 2019.

31 Permanent Court of Arbitration, "The South China Sea Arbitration (The Republic of the Philippines v. the People's Republic of China)," The Hague, 12 July 2016, summarizing the tribunal's finding, p. 6, https://pca -cpa.org/wp-content/uploads/sites/6/2016/07/PH-CN-20160712-Press -Release-No-11-English.pdf.

32 See UNCLOS, part XV, section 2 (Compulsory Procedures Entailing Binding Decisions), esp. articles 286–87; and annex VII, esp. article 1.

33 "Philippines Submits South China Sea Disputes with China to UNCLOS Annex VII Arbitration," Boundary News, IBRU, Centre for Borders Research, Durham University, Durham, UK, 22 January 2013, https://www.dur.ac.uk/ibru/news/boundary_news/?itemno=16498. For the text of the initiating request, see Republic of the Philippines, Department of Foreign Affairs, "Notification and Statement of Claims," Manila, 22 January 2013, https://assets.documentcloud.org/documents/2165477/phl -prc-notification-and-statement-of-claim-on.pdf.

34 Charles Clover and Wan Li, "Beijing Warns Neighbours after South China Sea Ruling," Financial Times, 12 July 2016, https://www.ft.com /content/6a6e831a-48bd-11e6-8d68-72e9211e86ab.

35 Ministry of Foreign Affairs, People's Republic of China, "Yang Jiechi Gives Interview to State Media on the So-called Award by the Arbitral Tribunal for the South China Sea Arbitration," 15 July 2016, http://www .fmprc.gov.cn/nanhai/eng/wjbxw_1/t1382712.htm. See also "Arbitration Award More Shameless than Worst Prediction," Global Times [Beijing], 12 July 2016, http://www.globaltimes.cn/content/993855.shtml.

36 The full text of the statement, a white paper issued by the PRC's State Council Information Office and titled in English "China Adheres to the Position of Settling through Negotiation the Relevant Disputes between China and the Philippines in the South China Sea," is available in "History and Law Back China's Sovereignty," *China Daily USA*, 14 July 2016, http://usa.chinadaily.com.cn/epaper/2016-07/14/content_26088 896.htm.

37 See Chinese Society of International Law, "The South China Sea Arbitration Awards: A Critical Study," *Chinese Journal of International Law* 17, no. 2 (June 2018): 207–748, including 255, 422, 455, 465, 684, 686, 699 ("the long course of history"), and 455 ("2nd century BCE"), https://academic.oup.com/chinesejil/issue/17/2.

38 Antonio T. Carpio, *The South China Sea Dispute: Philippine Sovereign Rights and Jurisdiction in the West Philippine Sea* (self-pub., 2017), 30, https://su.edu.ph/sc-assoc-justice-publishes-book-on-ph-sover eign-rights-and-jurisdiction-in-the-west-ph-sea/.

39 Keyuan Zou, *Law of the Sea in East Asia* (Abington, UK: Routledge, 2005), 148–49; and Bill Hayton, "China's 'Historic Rights' in the South China Sea: Made in America?," *The Diplomat*, 21 June 2016, https:// thediplomat.com/2016/06/chinas-historic-rights-in-the-south-china-sea -made-in-america/.

40 Exclusive Economic Zone and Continental Shelf Act, adopted at the third session of the Standing Committee of the Ninth National People's Congress, Beijing, 26 June 1998, https://www.un.org/Depts/los/LEGISLA TIONANDTREATIES/PDFFILES/chn_1998_eez_act.pdf.

41 François-Xavier Bonnet, "Archeology and Patriotism: Long Term Chinese Strategies in the South China Sea," conference paper, Ateneo Law Center, Makati, 17 March 2015, https://seasresearch.files.wordpress .com/2015/04/archeology-and-patriotism.pdf.

42 Instructive on the recent origin of China's supposedly long-standing claim and its empirical basis are these works by Bill Hayton: "The Modern Creation of China's 'Historic Rights' Claim in the South China Sea," *Asian Affairs* 49, no. 3 (September 2018): 370–82, https:// doi.org/10.1080/03068374.2018.1487689; "The Modern Origins of China's South China Sea Claims: Maps, Misunderstandings, and the Maritime Geobody," *Modern China* 45, no. 2 (2019): 127–70, https:// doi.org/10.1177/0097700418771678; and *The South China Sea: The Struggle for Power in Asia* (New Haven, CT: Yale University Press, 2014). For a non-China–centered or "Nusantarian" understanding of relevant

maritime history, see Philip Bowring, *Empire of the Winds: The Global Role of Asia's Great Archipelago* (London: I. B. Taurs, 2019).

43 UN members are automatically parties to the statute that created the ICJ. But acceptances of compulsory jurisdiction that are still in effect have been made by only two Southeast Asian countries other than the Philippines: Cambodia in 1957 and Timor-Leste in 2012. The United States rejected the provision in 1986 and, unlike China, has not ratified UNCLOS.

44 In the Matter of the South China Sea Arbitration (Philippines v PRC) (12 July 2016), case no. 2013-19, Permanent Court of Arbitration, The Hague, https://pcacases.com/web/sendAttach/2086.

45 For instances of such interference from 2009 up to the 2016 ruling, see "Timeline of the South China Sea Dispute," Wikipedia, https://en.wikipedia.org/wiki/Timeline_of_the_South_China_Sea_dispute.

46 During his presidential campaign, Duterte promised to order the Philippine police and military to find criminals and drug pushers "and kill them." "The funeral parlors will be packed," he said; "I'll supply the dead bodies." He planned to stamp out the drug problem within his first six months as president. "But if I fail, kill me." Quoted in Richard Javad Heydarian, *The Rise of Duterte: A Populist Revolt against Elite Democracy* (Singapore: Palgrave Macmillan, 2018), 94.

47 Prashanth Parameswaran, "Why the Philippines' Rodrigo Duterte Hates America," *The Diplomat*, 1 November 2016, https://thediplomat.com/2016/11/why-the-philippines-rodrigo-duterte-hates-america/.

48 Ralph Jennings, "Once-distrusted China Pledges Millions More to Philippines," *VOA News*, 13 April 2018, https://www.voanews.com/a/philippines-china-investment/4346430.html.

49 Jason Koutsoukis and Cecilia Yap, "China Hasn't Delivered on Its $24 Billion Philippines Promise," *Bloomberg*, 2 July 2018, https://www.bloomberg.com/news/articles/2018-07-25/china-s-24-billion-promise-to-duterte-still-hasn-t-materialized.

50 Bienvenido S. Oplas, Jr., "The Meager Truth of China's Aid to the Philippines," *Asia Times*, 5 December 2018, https://www.asiatimes.com/2018/12/article/the-meager-truth-of-chinas-aid-to-the-philippines. Corruption has also been a problem, although apportioning responsibility for it between the Philippines and China is itself problematic.

51 1992 ASEAN Declaration on the South China Sea, CIL Document Database, Centre for International Law, National University of

Singapore, https://cil.nus.edu.sg/wp-content/uploads/2017/07/1992
-ASEAN-Declaration-on-the-South-China-Sea.pdf.

52 Declaration on the Conduct of Parties in the South China Sea, 4
November 2002, https://asean.org/?static_post=declaration-on-the-con
duct-of-parties-in-the-south-china-sea-2.

53 In PRC foreign minister Wang Yi's words, "You can't have a COC
without a DOC." Xinhua, "China, ASEAN to Hold Meetings on S China
Sea," *China Daily*, 1 July 2013, http://www.chinadaily.com.cn/china/2013
-07/01/content_16692273.htm.

54 "Guidelines for the Implementation of the DOC," 2011, https://www
.asean.org/wp-content/uploads/images/archive/documents/20185
-DOC.pdf.

55 Jesse Johnson, "China's Hainan Province Invites 'Individuals' to
Develop Uninhabited Islands in South China Sea," *Japan Times*, 7 July
2018, https://www.japantimes.co.jp/news/2018/07/07/asia-pacific/chinas
-hainan-province-invites-individuals-develop-uninhabited-islands-south
-china-sea.

56 Gregory Poling, "This Isn't the COC You're Looking For," AMTI,
CSIS, Washington, DC, 15 June 2017, https://amti.csis.org/isnt-coc-you
re-looking.

57 The SDNT quotes are taken from Carl Thayer, "A Closer Look at the
ASEAN-China Single Draft South China Sea Code of Conduct," *The
Diplomat*, 3 August 2018, https://thediplomat.com/2018/08/a-closer-look
-at-the-asean-china-single-draft-south-china-sea-code-of-conduct.

58 Ministry of Foreign Affairs, PRC, "Full Text of Premier Li Keqiang's
Speech at the 13th East Asia Summit," State Council, PRC, 16 November
2018, http://english.www.gov.cn/premier/speeches/2018/11/16/content
_281476392673224.htm.

59 Details as reported by James Patterson, "Duterte Says China's
Xi Offered Deal for Ignoring South China Sea Ruling," *International
Business Times*, 12 September 2019, https://www.ibtimes.com/duterte
-says-chinas-xi-offered-deal-ignoring-south-china-sea-ruling-2825744;
and Darryl John Esguerra, "60-40 Sharing 'Fair' as China Will Spend for
WPS Exploration—Esperon," Inquirer.net, 25 October 2019, https://
globalnation.inquirer.net/181480/60-40-sharing-fair-as-china-will-spend
-for-wps-exploration-esperon#ixzz64GTu9iNV.

60 "A 'Win-win' Approach to Tapping SCS Resources," editorial, *Manila Bulletin*, 27 July 2019, https://news.mb.com.ph/2019/07/27/a-win-win -approach-to-tapping-scs-resources.

61 The 1987 Constitution of the Republic of the Philippines, article XII, section 2, http://www.officialgazette.gov.ph/constitutions/the-1987 -constitution-of-the-republic-of-the-philippines/the-1987-constitution -of-the-republic-of-the-philippines-article-xii/.

62 Presidential Decree No. 87, Malacañang, Manila, 31 December 1972, Section 8(2), https://www.officialgazette.gov.ph/1972/12/31/presidential -decree-no-87-s-1972/.

63 Jim Gomez, "Philippine Defense Chief Hits China for South China Sea Acts," AP News, 30 July 2019, https://apnews.com/e0bfb7f82df94474 a51d02a04bfa76a7.

64 Andrea Chloe Wong, "Philippine Public's Perception on Duterte's China Policy," *PacNet*, no. 48, Pacific Forum, 22 August 2019, https:// pacforum.org/publication/pacnet-48-philippine-publics-perception-on-dutertes-china-policy; Pathricia Ann V. Roxas, "Pulse Asia: Most Filipinos Distrust China, Russia; US, Canada Trusted," Inquirer.net, 26 July 2019, https://globalnation.inquirer.net/178338/pulse-asia-most-filipinos-distrust -china-russia-us-canada; and Melissa Luz Lopez, "Duterte's Approval, Trust Ratings Steady in June — Pulse Asia," CNN Philippines, 17 July 2019, https://cnnphilippines.com/news/2019/7/17/Duterte-Pulse -Asia-June-2019.html.

65 Zachary Keck, "Vietnam Threatens Legal Action against China," *The Diplomat*, 2 June 2014, https://thediplomat.com/2014/06/vietnam -threatens-legal-action-against-china.

66 "China Hopes Vietnam Does Not 'Complicate' South China Sea Issue," Reuters, 8 November 2019, https://reut.rs/2rklf6Y.

67 See "Military Capability" in *Asia Power Index 2018*, Lowy Institute [Sydney], accessed 9 November 2019, https://power.lowyinstitute.org.

68 Kyodo News and AP, "US Upset by Asean's 'Effort to Embarrass' Trump via Partial Boycott," *Bangkok Post*, 4 November 2019, https:// www.bangkokpost.com/world/1786919/us-upset-by-aseans-effort-to -embarrass-trump-via-partial-boycott.

69 Hepeng Jia, "China's Science Ministry Gets Power to Attract More Foreign Scientists," *Nature Index*, 23 March 2018, https://www .natureindex.com/news-blog/chinas-science-ministry-gets-power-to -attract-more-foreign-scientists. In fairness, the 1,576 permanent

residencies that China granted to all foreigners (not just scientists) represented an increase of 163 percent over the number issued the previous year. Trump's xenophobic nationalism also attenuates the comparison with America.

70 For more, see Donald K. Emmerson, "'No Sole Control' in the South China Sea?," *Asia Policy* 13, no. 4 (October 2018): 67–73, https://muse .jhu.edu/article/708154.

71 For this and other speculations, see Donald K. Emmerson, "Mapping ASEAN's Futures," *Contemporary Southeast Asia* 39, no. 2 (August 2017): 280–87.

CHAPTER 7

Re-enlisting the Diaspora
BEIJING AND THE "OVERSEAS CHINESE"

Geoff Wade, *Independent Scholar, Canberra, Australia*

In Kuala Lumpur on 25 September 2015, China's ambassador to Malaysia, Huang Huikang, caused a furor. On Petaling Street in the city's Chinatown, in an atmosphere of racial tension between the ethnic-majority Malays and the ethnic-minority Chinese, he warned against "the infringement" of "China's national interests" and noted possible "violations of [the] legal rights and interests of Chinese citizens and businesses, which may damage the friendly relationship between China and the host country." Were such things to happen, he said, invoking his role as the representative of the People's Republic of China (PRC), "we will not sit idly by."[1]

A few days later, at an event in Kuala Lumpur held to celebrate China's national day, addressing Malaysians of Chinese origin in the Chinese language, Ambassador Huang reasserted the tie between his listeners and his country: "Zhongguo yongyuan shi haiwai Huaren ji Huaqiao wenxin de niangjia" (China is forever the warm parental home of the ethnic Chinese abroad and the overseas Chinese).[2] The Chinese term *niangjia* (parental or natal home) refers to the familial household where a woman lived before leaving it to marry into another family. By asserting the permanence of intimate relations between China and Malaysia's ethnic Chinese, the ambassador implied that they could always find refuge in China should their status or safety be threatened in Malaysia.

That China has a role to play in protecting the "overseas Chinese"[3] (OC) in Southeast Asia is not a new idea. The "parental home" metaphor was used early in the PRC's existence. In April 1955 in Jakarta, China's then premier Zhou Enlai told an audience of OC that for them to leave Indonesia and return to China would be like a married woman going back to her natal home, and that China would always welcome their return.[4] What is remarkable about the present renewal of ties between Beijing and the ethnic Chinese in Southeast Asia is the scope and the vigor of the efforts by China to re-enlist "its" diaspora in pursuit of the current "China Dream" of Xi Jinping.[5] Before exploring those efforts, however, it will be helpful to briefly review earlier endeavors in the 20th century.

From "Revolutionary Mother" to "Backbone Force"

"The Overseas Chinese are the Mother of the Revolution." This iconic phrase has long been associated with Sun Yat-sen and his efforts to rally the OC as supporters and funders of the intended revolution against the rulers of the Qing Empire in the early 20th century. While the use of the phrase has a checkered history,[6] there can be no doubt that the OC were at this time being drawn on for political purposes within the Chinese polity.

Subsequently, from the early 1920s onwards, in the years of contention for political control of China between the Kuomintang (KMT) and the Communist Party of China (CPC), the ethnic Chinese in Southeast Asia were key elements as the two parties vied for their political and financial support. The KMT, as the governing party of China until 1949, established "a network of extraterritorial organisations in the countries of residence" of the OC.[7] The CPC meanwhile developed diverse underground organizations and ostensibly broad but Communist-led "united fronts" of ethnic-Chinese supporters across Southeast Asia, purposely including those who were not members of the CPC — hence the "united front" name. During this period, for both parties, the roles of the OC were perceived in terms of the domestic politics of China.

In 1949 the PRC was launched with the CPC at its helm. The new state's relations with the OC became an immediate issue. That same year an Overseas Chinese Affairs Commission was created to oversee the affairs of ethnic Chinese abroad and has continued to exist in various forms until today. During the early years of the PRC, "the two major issues on which the CPC regularly called for support were Korea and Taiwan. The Chinese abroad were asked to explain and propagate Chinese policy on these two questions."[8]

In light of the burgeoning nationalism of Southeast Asian states at that time and the processes of decolonization then underway, citizenship became a key issue for the Chinese of Southeast Asia. Some held Chinese citizenship, some were dual citizens, and some had no citizenship at all. At the Asian-African Conference in Bandung, Indonesia, in 1955, Premier Zhou Enlai renounced the idea of OC holding dual citizenship; China would no longer claim that any person with a Chinese patriline was automatically a citizen of China. At the same time, the Sino-Indonesian Treaty on Dual Nationality called for ethnic Chinese living in Indonesia to choose one nationality or the other.[9] Indeed, by 1957, China was urging ethnic Chinese in Southeast Asia to become host-country citizens: "The broad masses of Overseas Chinese resident abroad must now put aside any reservations and, on the principle of free choice, choose local nationality. They must live and work in peace in the countries of residence. . . . This will be of assistance in promoting friendly relations between China and the countries of residence."[10]

That did not mean, however, that China would stop using the OC. They had long played major roles in the revolutionary movements that the CPC had assisted and, in some ways, directed across Southeast Asia, beginning even before the PRC's birth in 1949. Overseas Chinese were active in Malayan, Indonesian, Sarawak, Burmese, Thai, and Philippine revolutionary forces — the armed wings of local Communist parties that China's party-state supported into the 1970s. Concurrently the KMT-affiliated Chinese in the region developed organizations and parties, such as the Malayan Chinese Association, aimed at countering Communist influence in their countries of residence. We thus see during this period a different role for OC in the eyes of Beijing — their enlistment in actions affecting the politics of states outside of China.

In the late 1970s and early '80s in the PRC, Deng Xiaoping assumed and then consolidated prime political power. Those years of economic reform and opening were also marked by changes in China's foreign policy, including a decision to stop aiding revolutionary movements in Southeast Asia. This withdrawal of support from the ideological and cultural center that was Beijing brought disillusionment among the many OC for whom "New China" had been a beacon of hope and aspiration. The change did, however, significantly lessen political violence in the region, and to that extent it did, as desired, improve relations between China and Southeast Asia.

Deng also allowed Guangdong and Fujian — the provinces from which the ancestors of most Southeast Asian Chinese had come — to gain privileged rights to solicit overseas trade and investment. With the creation of China's first four special economic zones (SEZs) in 1980, incoming investment burgeoned. Funds from OC, particularly those in Southeast Asia, flowed through the traditional emigrant ports in Guangdong and Fujian. The zones were novel in practice, but not in purpose. "[W]hile Deng and his reform allies may have been innovators in the context of recent PRC history," historian Glen Peterson has written, "seen from a longer perspective they were reverting to a strategy that was consistent with that of every Chinese national government since the late nineteenth century: wooing the wealth and business acumen of Chinese overseas for China's modernization."[11]

In tandem with that reversion, the Chinese state began to portray the OC in an apparently novel way by launching "a new state discourse glorifying the allegedly primordial and enduring ties of Overseas Chinese to their *qiaoxiang* (ancestral villages)."[12] An old purpose was being revived: to strengthen China's own economy by attracting capital from OC.[13] The diaspora was again being used by the Chinese state as a means to domestic ends.

By the 1990s this policy focus had expanded beyond long-standing overseas communities to encompass more recent emigrants as well. In 1996 China's State Council described these "new migrants" as already "becoming an important rising force" inside the diaspora. The council envisaged them, especially those who had gone to study in the United States or other developed Western countries and decided to stay on, as a future "backbone force" friendly to China.[14] Not coincidentally, a historian in Singapore, Liu Hong, has associated this "new migrant" phenomenon with a revival of Chinese nationalism among ethnic Chinese abroad.[15]

Increasingly since the State Council's projection of a "backbone force," Beijing has been using the OC in pursuit of economic and political goals abroad. Members of OC business associations and representatives of regional hometown associations are encouraged to become local advocates of China's foreign policy positions. Beijing is emphasizing again an attributed affiliation of Southeast Asians of Chinese descent with China and presenting the PRC as the ultimate defender of their rights and interests. China's economic objectives are especially apparent in that context, not only for economic reasons but also for the leverage toward geopolitical primacy that material ties can provide.

China's efforts do not run only one way from Beijing to the region. Many in the diaspora, especially those trained in local Chinese-language schools, are inclined or even eager to identify with China as it asserts itself more and more vigorously in Southeast Asia and around the globe. Since announcing its "Going Out" policy in 1999, Beijing has urged PRC firms and entrepreneurs to move offshore and enlist foreign resources, markets, labor, and technology in productive activity to their own and China's advantage. President Xi Jinping's signature Belt and Road Initiative (BRI, initially called "One Belt, One Road" or OBOR) dramatically extends this policy through financing and infrastructure — PRC-tied loans and investments meant to spin a vast skein of roads, railroads, port nodes, and industrial structures spanning Eurasia and the Indo-Pacific.[16]

The reach and pursuit of these ambitions raises the question of ultimate intent. It is not hard to argue that strategic primacy if not outright dominion may well be their long-run aim.[17] Nor is it implausible to suggest that the OC will have roles to play in this scaled-up "creative involvement" of Xi Jinping's China in regional and global affairs.[18]

Inside China:
Agency, Activity, and the Administration of Influence

A number of agencies and organizations inside China administer the work of influencing Southeast Asia's OC. Foremost among them is the State Council's Overseas Chinese Affairs Office (OCAO), which oversees, coordinates, and monitors the PRC's plans for and policies toward not only the more than 50 million ethnic Chinese who reside abroad, but also toward those who have returned to China. James Jiann Hua To has produced the most detailed study of the OCAO and its activities.[19] The United Front Work Department[20] of the CPC Central Committee, through which the OCAO is now administered, also plays other major roles in influencing the OC through "united front" organizations that recruit and encompass sympathetic non-party groups.[21] President Xi illustrated that strategy in May 2015 in a speech that advocated the "broadest patriotic united front" for "achieving the China Dream" and implicitly assigned to the OC an important role in that campaign.[22] But these supervisory and "front work" agencies hardly exhaust the range of entities and activities that influencing the diaspora entails.

Business associations and meetings to promote China's economic policies are a case in point. In July 2015, for example, following China's announcement of the BRI (OBOR) in October 2013,[23] the government convened a huge meeting of OC businesspeople. At this First Global Conference of Overseas Chinese Industry and Commerce, China's premier Li Keqiang urged the diaspora "to contribute to the country's economic growth."[24] Responding to his call, the state-sponsored China Overseas Chinese Entrepreneurs Association issued a statement exhorting OC entrepreneurs to boost China's economic renaissance by building commercial networks transnationally across their communities.[25]

Notable among these mechanisms of enlistment, suasion, and control are the media.[26] The authorities guide and tutor the Chinese-language press outside China to report on issues in ways that support PRC positions and projects. In early 2016, for instance, the Xiamen city government invited, hosted, and educated reporters from Chinese-language newspapers that circulate in countries through which the BRI's maritime "One Road" is expected to pass. Malaysian, Philippine, Singaporean, and Indonesian Chinese-language journalists were given briefings on the initiative by the Xiamen city government's press office and attended related sessions with government and party economic and propaganda units and the local Federation of Returned Overseas Chinese.[27]

Alongside such initiatives, state-owned or state-directed bodies are moving to control Chinese-language media beyond China's borders, including through ownership.[28] Such efforts are reviving a record of intervention dating back to the earliest days of the PRC.[29] China itself also broadcasts Chinese-language television and radio programs to Chinese speakers overseas and others around the world via the China Global Television Network and China Radio International.

Another way of influencing OC communities is by creating or supporting local, regional, and global "origin associations" and "affinity groups." An instance of the latter at the global level is the World Chinese Entrepreneurs Convention (WCEC, *shijie huashang dahui*), usually held outside of China and aimed at "bringing together Chinese business organizations from all places around the world."[30]

Such groups have burgeoned since the 1980s, as have their links to China.[31] Consider, among origin associations, those whose members trace their ancestry to Fuzhou, on the mainland coast opposite Taiwan. A PRC-sponsored gathering of people of Fuzhou origin called the Fourth Mindu Culture Forum was held in Malaysia in December 2015. Members of various Fuzhou-related associations in Southeast Asia took part.[32] The president of the World Federation of Fuzhou Associations, Abdul Alek Soelystio (a.k.a. Zhang Jinxiong), took the occasion to say that while the Fuzhou people in Southeast Asia have deep affection for their countries of residence, they have never forgotten that their roots are in Fuzhou. He also advertised the BRI's "One Road" linking maritime Southeast Asia westward to the Indian Ocean. "The Maritime Silk Road that symbolizes peace and amiability has been inherited [as a legacy] for several centuries," he said. "Today, unleashing strong thriving vitality, [the renewed route] is moving toward the world with China's vision for a harmonious neighborhood and friendship, and cooperation for win-win results."[33] Endorsement of Chinese foreign policies at PRC-sponsored OC events is seen by Beijing as a major propaganda gain.

Recent efforts to enlist the OC also involve their legal status and legal rights. China does not recognize dual citizenship. Yet in 2015 reports circulated that China was planning to implement some kind of "Chinese Card" for ethnic Chinese born abroad, including in Southeast Asia, that would equip its holders with many of the rights of PRC citizens. The apparent intent of such a measure would be to entice more OC to invest in the mainland and bring their talents "home." Some suggested that the card would also be available to former citizens of the PRC who had assumed other nationalities abroad. As advertised on a website based in Malaysia, the project would greatly enhance solidarity among the OC and strengthen their feelings of attraction toward China.[34]

The pilot-project regulations "for safeguarding the rights and interests of overseas Chinese" issued by Guangdong's provincial government in October 2015 were the first efforts in this direction. These regulations, if implemented, would initially apply only to Chinese who have origins in Guangdong. They would provide treatment of the OC similar to what is accorded to PRC citizens in many spheres, allow for reimbursement of family property confiscated in the past, and encourage OC to invest in the mainland and set up businesses and charities there.[35]

Enlistment also occurs through ties of identity—language and culture. Chinese is taught at Confucius Institutes that have been established in nine of the 10 ASEAN member states.[36] The very first overseas university campus opened anywhere with the approval of Beijing is Xiamen University Malaysia (XUM). A branch campus of Xiamen University, XUM opened its doors in Sepang near Kuala Lumpur's international airport in 2016.[37] Targeted are ethnic-Chinese Malaysian students who have been in effect excluded from state-sponsored higher education in Malaysia.[38] XUM also provides a platform where students from China can study in Southeast Asia and help disseminate Chinese culture.[39]

Inside China, the OC are extolled in diaspora-dedicated museums in Beijing and in southern coastal cities such as Guangzhou, Xiamen, and Quanzhou.[40] Museums showcasing the history of Chinese communities abroad and stressing their ties to the PRC are also being built outside the PRC. An example is the Malaysian Chinese Museum in Kuala Lumpur, opened in 2018 on the ground floor of the Federation of Chinese Associations of Malaysia's 12-story building, whose façade was built to resemble that of the Great Hall of the People in Beijing.[41] Meanwhile China's foreign ministry, OCAO, and other PRC and CPC agencies cultivate and incentivize influential OC individuals and groups in Southeast Asia to play roles as local advocates of policies that favor, or are favored by, the PRC.

The next paragraphs look beyond the apparatus of enlistment inside China to survey in brief the associations and activities that the PRC-CPC fosters in particular Southeast Asian countries. The snapshots begin in the northern tier of states physically nearest to China and unfold south and east through maritime Southeast Asia. Space sharply limits the attention given to any one country, Malaysia partly excepted due to the controversial importance of the ethnic-Chinese minority in that country, as already noted in the opening reference to Ambassador Huang's implied threat to intervene.

Inside Southeast Asia:
Countries, Cases, and the Implementation of Influence

Laos

Among Southeast Asian states, Laos hosts the smallest number of OC — perhaps 200,000 or a little more[42] — and they constitute less than 3 percent of the country's estimated seven million total population. But Laos abuts China, and its leaders have increasingly tied their own economy with southern China's. An influx of new migrants into Laos has both accompanied and furthered these links.[43]

Beijing actively supports OC organizations in Laos. Even an incomplete sampling of entities and events in a single year, 2015, conveys the point. A main channel of influence over the Laotian economy is the China Chamber of Commerce in Laos (CCCL), most of whose members are recent arrivals from the PRC. Headquartered in the capital Vientiane, the CCCL broadened its footprint in 2015 by establishing a branch in the historic city and tourist mecca Luang Prabang.[44] The CCCL has also grown branches tied to provincial authorities within China, as when it created a local presence for the Guangdong Chamber of Commerce (GCC), also in 2015.[45] In Laos that same year, at the launching of an Overseas Chinese Mutual Help Center, OCAO deputy director He Yafei described it as an important program sponsored by China's State Council in Beijing to support the ethnic-Chinese diaspora.[46] That the linkage from Guangdong to Laos was publicized on the website of the Ministry of Commerce in Beijing suggests the extent to which these and other long-distance-but-local-branch initiatives instantiate the reach of Chinese state power.

Cambodia

China exerts massive influence over the political economy of Cambodia. Beijing is a powerful supporter of recent Chinese business migrants to Cambodia and the key force behind the Chinese Chamber of Commerce in Cambodia (CCCC). At the chamber's annual meeting in 2015 its chairman clearly acknowledged Beijing's role when he located the CCCC "under the correct leadership of the PRC Embassy in Cambodia." He praised the Chinese ambassador and counselor for giving "much attention to the work of the chamber," "often participating" in its activities, and "making many valuable suggestions" regarding its work, and for using the chamber to help "China-funded enterprises to resolve their problems."[47] Even more tellingly than in the case of the GCC in Laos, the featuring of these comments on the website of the Ministry of Commerce in Beijing leads one to believe that the seemingly private CCCC may in fact be a PRC state organ located in Phnom Penh.

Myanmar

Here too an influx of new Chinese migrants over the last decade has spurred the formation of PRC-tied OC business associations that facilitate mainland agendas and interests. In 2015 the Zhejiang Chamber of Commerce in Myanmar (ZCCM) was born, linking that ASEAN country to China's Zhejiang Province. Attending and lauding the occasion were representatives of the China-Myanmar Friendship Association, the Myanmar Chinese Chamber of Commerce, and the Zhejiang Chamber of Commerce. Later that year a delegation from the PRC led by a member of the Standing Committee of the National People's Congress, Zhang Shaoqin, arrived to promote and obtain local help in furthering Beijing's priority extension project, the BRI.[48]

A 14th World Chinese Entrepreneurs Convention, endorsed and supported by the PRC, was held in mid-September 2017 in Myanmar's commercial center, Yangon. The convention's website featured hyperlinks to four chambers of commerce. Three were OC organizations in Singapore, Hong Kong, and Thailand, named as having co-founded WCEC. The fourth link was to the China Overseas Chinese Entrepreneurs Association, a United Front body headquartered in Beijing.

Thailand

The WCEC secretariat's location in Bangkok is not coincidental. No Southeast Asian country has more overseas Chinese than Thailand does — as many as nine million or 14 percent of the total population, depending upon the criteria used.[49] Among them are many in the country's socioeconomic and political elite who identify as being of Chinese descent.[50] This Sino-Thai elite dominates business and politics along the entire north-south Chao Phraya basin, including Bangkok. The degree to which these individuals feel any affiliation with Chinese culture or with the PRC varies greatly. One of Beijing's aims in Thailand is to inculcate or revive such feelings among the Sino-Thai. The spread of Confucius Institutes across Thailand — no

ASEAN country hosts more — and their endorsement by Thai royalty are key elements to that end.[51]

The individuals who helm such organizations are also worthy of note. A key China-linked body in Thailand is the Thai-Chinese Culture and Economy Association.[52] Its chairman is Dr. Bhokin Bhalakula, a Thai of Chinese descent and former president of Thailand's National Assembly.[53] He often leads cultural delegations to China, having been hosted by the International Department of the CPC Central Committee (2015),[54] the Chinese People's Association for Friendship with Foreign Countries (2013, 2014, 2015),[55] the Xiamen Municipal People's Congress (2014),[56] and the China Association for International Friendly Contact (2013).[57]

His ongoing support for China and its policies is manifest in the speeches that Dr. Bhalakula gives. His remarks at the ASEAN-China Strategic Seminar in Shenzhen in 2015 exemplified his view of the PRC: He congratulated "China under the leadership of the Communist Party" for its "great success" and for resolutions by the CPC and its Politburo that "will help to stop conflicts and steer peace and development" in Asia and the world. He praised the prospect of a "21st Century Maritime Silk Road" — the BRI's southern route through Southeast Asia — as being "of great benefit to the region and the world, and not for any particular nation" — the latter remark likely made with China in mind. He urged "all nations" to "unite" and "push" for the road to be realized; he predicted it would bring "sustainable trust and peace."[58] Beijing encourages such exaltations of its policies, and rewards them through commendation, commercial access, and financial favor.

The Philippines

Compared with its counterpart in Thailand, the Philippine OC is smaller in absolute and proportional terms — less than 1.5 million in a population of slightly over 100 million — but they are politically and economically influential nonetheless. Chinese-descended Filipinos tend to be "old migrants." Historically, many had close ties with the KMT. In this century, however, many belong to "patriotic groups" of OC who support the PRC and Xi's "China Dream," including Taiwan's return to the mainland, and share Beijing's antipathy to Japan. Such groups include the Federation of Filipino-Chinese Associations of the Philippines and the Federation of Filipino-Chinese Chambers of Commerce & Industry and the 200-plus OC organizations in the Philippines mobilized by the Chinese embassy in 2015 to commemorate the "70th anniversary of the victory in the global anti-fascist war and the Chinese people's war against the Japanese."[59]

At an event in Manila attended by China's ambassador and representatives from OCAO in February 2016, the honorary chairman of the Philippines Association for the Promotion of the Reunification of China, Lu Zuyin, put it this way: "[China's] unification is a historical necessity as the Chinese nation moves toward its great revival. Promoting the peaceful unification of China, and helping to achieve the China Dream of the great revival of the Chinese nation, is the duty-bound mission of the overseas Chinese."[60]

Malaysia

As in the Philippines, China's officials also welcome and encourage the promotion of PRC policies by ethnic-Chinese politicians and businesspeople in Malaysia. When OC functionaries from Beijing visited the influential Federation of Chinese Associations of Malaysia in 2015, its president Pheng Yin Huah ardently backed China's efforts to counter US naval patrols in the South China Sea and urged the Malaysian Chinese to join him in doing so.[61] A month later the ethnic-Chinese president of the Malaysian Iron and Steel Industry Federation sided with Beijing against Kuala Lumpur by urging the Malaysian government to cancel its anti-dumping duties on the import of hot-rolled steel coils from China.[62]

PRC positions and policies are also promoted by prominent OC politicians. The National Front that ruled Malaysia until 2018 comprises three political parties that are supposed to represent, respectively and in declining order of size, the country's ethnic-Malay, ethnic-Chinese, and ethnic-Indian communities. The second of these components is the Malaysian Chinese Association (MCA). In 2016, MCA's president, Liow Tiong Lai, concurrently transport minister in the government, spoke at the start of construction of a Malaysia-China Friendship Building designed to headquarter the Malaysia-China Friendship Association (MCFA). The MCA, he said, would continue to promote the BRI and to ensure that the Malaysia-China Friendship Association "continues to play a positive facilitator role in promoting friendly relations between Malaysia and China through politics, economics, culture, education, and other fields in order to strengthen the friendly ties between the two countries."[63] The speech was widely publicized on PRC media sites. Other influential ethnic-Chinese politicians and businesspeople in Malaysia have publicly urged greater use of China's currency — renminbi — in trade-settlement transactions, visa-free entry to Malaysia for PRC citizens, China-friendly industrial policies, and tie-ups between Chinese and Malaysian ports, among other PRC-backed ideas.

Chinese-language education in Malaysia is another channel for influence from Beijing. China's leaders know that Malaysian OC who are literate in

Chinese are more likely to have and to value a cultural affinity with China. PRC ambassadors to Malaysia have understood their assignments to include lauding and funding Chinese-language education throughout the country.[64] Accordingly, PRC diplomats extend financial or other support to a variety of ethnic-Chinese organizations, schools, media, and individuals in Malaysia. Accounts of these activities are featured on the PRC embassy's website only in its Chinese-language section; they are not detailed in the English-language part of the site.[65] Visitors to the site who are not versed in Chinese are thus kept from realizing that increasingly the PRC depicts itself as the core defender of the interests of the ethnic-Chinese minority in Malaysia, albeit in the face of discriminatory treatment by the Malaysian state.

Such discrimination reinforces the inclination of PRC officials to make OC Malaysians aware of opportunities with and in the PRC that might be less available to OC in Malaysia itself. One can perhaps sense this logic in a speech by Chinese ambassador Huang Huikang delivered in 2016 a few months after he made the controversial comments noted at the beginning of this chapter. Speaking before an audience of Malaysian OC, he encouraged them "to boost their communications and exchanges with Chinese enterprises to create more opportunities for business."[66]

The pioneering importance of Xiamen University Malaysia in Sino-Malaysian relations was noted earlier in this chapter. In September 2019, "China's first university in Malaysia" awarded bachelor of arts degrees in Chinese studies, journalism, and other fields to the 371 students in its very first graduating class. Two-thirds of the graduates were from Malaysia, one-third from China.[67]

One of the speakers at the convocation ceremony was the chair of the Malaysia-China Business Council, Tan Kok Wai. He had been named a "special envoy" to China to "complement" the work of Malaysia's ambassador to China, Datuk Zainuddin Yahya.[68] In his speech, Tan praised XUM, calling it the brainchild of Malaysian-Chinese cooperation in China's Belt and Road Initiative. The "Greater China region" and the countries taking part in the BRI were "tremendous rooms" in which the graduates could "shine brilliantly." The PRC's ambassador to Malaysia also spoke. He lauded the university as a "pearl" along the BRI's 21st Century Maritime Silk Road, urged the graduates to contribute to Sino-Malaysian friendship, and noted that more than 50,000 students from China were studying in Malaysia while nearly 10,000 from Malaysia were studying in China.[69]

Finally worth noting is suggestive evidence of Beijing's interest in influencing if not controlling Chinese-language media in Malaysia. Media Chinese International (MCI), incorporated in Bermuda, describes itself as "the leading Chinese news and information provider in Malaysia."[70] Daily readers of the 22 newspapers and magazines published under its auspices in Malaysia reportedly include, on average, a third of the country's six million ethnic Chinese. In 2016–17, MCI was controlled by Malaysia's controversial timber baron Tiong Hiew King. In April 2016, Tiong was accused of "curry[ing] favor with China" and "apparent subservience to Beijing" in light of his likely role in punishing another of his properties, the well-regarded Hong Kong daily *Ming Pao*, for carrying news critical of PRC leaders and their families.[71] Was it purely coincidental that in 2016 a company controlled by China's state-owned Qingdao West Coast Development Group, incorporated in the British Virgin Islands, began making plans to acquire a 70 percent stake in MCI?[72]

Singapore

Ethnic-Chinese immigrants or the descendants of immigrants make up three-fourths of the population of this small but prosperous nation. As in Malaysia and other Southeast Asian societies, Beijing also cultivates links with groups and individuals in Singapore. The annual celebration of Chinese New Year is a favored occasion for Chinese diplomats to reaffirm ties between the PRC and organizations such as the Singapore-China Business Association, the Singapore Chinese Chamber of Commerce and Industry, the Singapore Federation of Chinese Clan Associations, the Singapore Metal and Machinery Association, and the Tan Kah Kee Foundation.

As mentioned above regarding the Philippines, in 2015 Beijing orchestrated a militant and scathingly anti-Tokyo commemoration of the victory that had ended the "Global Anti-Fascist War" and the "Chinese People's War Against the Japanese" 70 years before. Attending as invited guests were 1,779 prominent individuals from OC communities around the world including Southeast Asia. Eight prominent OC guests from Singapore observed the military parade held to mark the anniversary.[73] On 31 August, prior to the delegation's departure for Beijing, the PRC's ambassador to Singapore, Chen Xiaodong, hosted them at a farewell dinner. Chen took the opportunity to lambaste the Japanese militarists for the pain they had inflicted on to Asia. He recalled the suffering shared at that time by the peoples of China and Singapore. Chen also stressed the key role that modern Singapore could play in realizing the "China Dream." The OC delegates were reported to have replied to the speech with "patriotic" statements emphasizing how China always loves peace and how the OC are drawing ever closer to China.[74]

A Singapore portal dedicated to China's BRI strategy was launched in March 2016, the first such website in Southeast Asia. Its sponsors were

Singapore's state-owned Chinese-language newspaper *Lianhe Zaobao* and the Singapore Business Federation.[75] The federation's chair, Teo Siong Seng, had been among Beijing's OC guests at the World War II victory commemoration six months before.

As it does in some other ASEAN states, China uses interviews with OC scholars in Singapore to push PRC policies and propound the mainland's views. In 2015, for instance, China's news mouthpiece Xinhua interviewed the Singapore historian Liu Hong. According to Xinhua, he suggested ways in which China might strengthen its media and cultural footprint regionally, how the OC could play a bridging role in promoting the BRI, and how the Chinese state might influence the OC toward those ends. "In the sphere of cultural propagation," he was reported to have said, "I believe there is a need to stress through various channels the friendly relations that have existed for thousands of years between China and the countries along the Maritime Silk Road, and to affirm that this mutual-benefit win-win model has existed from days of yore."[76]

Indonesia

The BRI has also become a priority topic in Beijing's efforts to mobilize ethnic-Chinese Indonesians on behalf of Chinese goals. In December 2015 the Chinese government sent the chair of the China Overseas Exchange Association to Indonesia to enlist the help of Indonesian OC in promoting the 21st Century Maritime Silk Road. During his visit he noted the go-between role of Indonesians of Chinese descent. Their ability to understand the peoples and mores of China and Indonesia alike, he said, made them "a very valuable trans-border cultural resource," well suited to becoming "key participants in strengthening links between Indonesia and China in the 'One Belt, One Road' [BRI] project, in achieving strategic interfaces, and in promoting cooperation." What those "strategic interfaces" might be, he did not say.[77]

The China Chamber of Commerce in Indonesia, in which more recent Chinese migrants are prominent, is another venue where Beijing can further its objectives. In early 2016, for example, at a meeting with chamber leaders, including many representing China-funded enterprises, China's ambassador to ASEAN Xu Bu urged them to do more to integrate China's and ASEAN's economies, and promised to help the chamber to those ends.[78] Provincial governments inside China use the chamber to pursue economic engagements with Indonesia, [79] and the OCAO in Beijing is also active in the Indonesian OC community.[80] Prominent members of the ethnic-Chinese community in Indonesia were invited to Beijing to watch the "anti-fascist"

September 2015 military parade, but the names of those who attended were not made publicly available.

On 19 December 2015 on the Indonesian island of Bintan near Singapore, a foundation stone was laid for a planned new institution of higher education—the ASEAN Nanyang University.[81] Ambassador Xu Bu took part, but the ceremony was premature. As of 2018, the endeavor remained no more than notional, due in part to anti-OC prejudice in majority-Muslim Indonesia. But it is reasonable to think that some enterprising Indonesian and Singaporean Chinese may still hope to develop a Chinese-language university for the OC in Southeast Asia and thereby strengthen and foster connections between China, the OC, and the region.[82]

Conclusions

Enlistment is a process of cultivation and involvement. Enlistees—a population, group, or person—are approached, appreciated, and motivated to help the enlister pursue certain ends. The purpose of this chapter has been to demonstrate and illustrate the extent of China's enlistment of the overseas Chinese in Southeast Asia on behalf of China's goals.

This is not new. In the 20th century, successive Chinese leaders and agencies engaged the OC in order to influence them. At times, the OC were drawn on to contribute to activities and purposes inside China. At other times, China used them on behalf of its goals abroad. What is new today, of course, is the dramatic economic rise of China and its arrival as a major actor on the global stage. A manifestation of that ascent is the diverse range of Chinese initiatives to enlist the OC in realizing the "China Dream." Detailing that range, however briefly, country by country, has been the aim of this chapter.

Enlistment can of course benefit the enlistee. OCs who accept offers to contribute to China's economic growth may thereby gain better lives. Depending on the implications of what they do, they may also thereby further the development of the countries where they reside. Chinese-language instruction can help satisfy the understandable desire of a later-generation OC to work with the burgeoning economy that is China today. Successful enlistment may reflect, alongside China's "pull," a sincere and voluntary "push" on the part of enlistees already disposed to support what the PRC is and does.

These caveats do not render China's behavior uncontroversial, however. Beijing is waging a major campaign to influence Southeast Asia's overseas

Chinese and, through them, the societies they live in and the governments they live under. It is up to Southeast Asians themselves, including the OC, to assess and manage the balances of benefit and detriment attributable to China's uses of "its" diaspora in "its" neighborhood. The quote marks reflect the ambiguity of China's role. At its most intrusive, Beijing's rhetoric can be interpreted as a jurisdictional claim — an identification with the OC that demotes their local nationality and promotes a presumed extraterritorial commitment to the motherland.

The argument made here is *not* that Beijing is bent on creating a subversive ethnic "fifth column" abroad. It is rather a call for more scholarly attention to the causes, contents, effects, and implications of China's enlistment of support from the overseas Chinese in Southeast Asia across the many domains noted above — Chinese identity, Chinese culture, Chinese education, Chinese enterprise, Chinese policy, and Chinese authority. Ultimately, for the people and the leaders of Southeast Asia and China alike, the question must arise: Whose dream is the "China Dream"?

Notes

1 "China's Envoy to Malaysia Visits Petaling Street Day before Rally,"
Malay Mail, 25 September 2015, https://www.malaymail.com/news
/malaysia/2015/09/25/chinas-envoy-to-malaysia-visits-petaling-street-day
-before-rally/976463.

2 "黄惠康：李克强11月来马料带来惊喜" [Huang Huikang: Li Keqiang
will visit Malaysia in November and will bring a surprise]. See 《诗华日
报》 [SeeHua Online], 29 September 2015, http://news.seehua
.com/?p=97023. Translation by author, as are all subsequent translations
from Chinese in this chapter.

3 A minimalist definition of the "overseas Chinese" (OC) would describe
them as persons of Chinese descent who live outside the People's Republic
of China (PRC) and Taiwan. People of wholly or partly Chinese ancestry
living outside that area, however, may or may not include themselves in
that category. And a person may self-identify or be identified by others as
belonging to the category based on any of several criteria, such as lineal
descent from groups originating in China, affinity with Chinese culture,
or acknowledgment of Chinese origin however defined. This chapter's
broad use of the term "OC" includes persons classified by Beijing as
huaqiao, huaren, or *huayi.* It is also important to state that the chapter's
focus on the PRC's efforts to assert and promote cultural and political
connections with OC persons and associations and to enlist them in
support of PRC foreign policy is in no way meant to underestimate their
heterogeneity, their ability to resist such enlistment, or the extent of their
typically long-standing and thorough integration into the societies where
they reside.

4 See Paul J. Bolt, *China and Southeast Asia's Ethnic Chinese: State and
Diaspora in Contemporary Asia* (Westport: Praeger, 2000), 20.

5 Frank Ching, "China Vies for Hearts and Minds of 'Sons and
Daughters' Overseas," *Ejinsight*, 9 May 2016, http://www.ejinsight.com
/20160509-china-vies-for-hearts-and-minds-of-sons-and-daughters
-overseas.

6 See Huang Jianli, "Umbilical Ties: The Framing of the Overseas
Chinese as the Mother of the Revolution," *Frontiers of History in China*
6, no. 2 (2011): 183–228.

7 Stephen Fitzgerald, *China and the Overseas Chinese: A Study of Peking's Changing Policy 1949–1970* (Cambridge: Cambridge University Press, 1972), 14.

8 Fitzgerald, *China and the Overseas Chinese*, 89.

9 Philip A. Kuhn, *Chinese among Others: Emigration in Modern Times* (Lanham, MD: Rowman and Littlefield, 2008), 330.

10 Fitzgerald, *China and the Overseas Chinese*, 142.

11 Glen Peterson, *Overseas Chinese in the People's Republic of China* (Abingdon, UK: Routledge, 2012), 171–72.

12 Peterson, *Overseas Chinese,* 173.

13 See Paul J. Bolt, "Looking to the Diaspora: The Overseas Chinese and China's Economic Development," *Diaspora: A Journal of Transnational Studies* 5, no. 3 (1996): 467–96.

14 Mette Thunø, "Reaching Out and Incorporating the Chinese Overseas: The Trans-territorial Scope of the PRC by the End of the 20th Century," *China Quarterly* 168 (2001): 922.

15 Liu Hong, "New Migrants and the Revival of Overseas Chinese Nationalism," *Journal of Contemporary China* 14, no. 43 (2005): 291–316.

16 Scott Kennedy and David A. Parker, "Building China's 'One Belt, One Road,'" CSIS Blog, 3 April 2015.

17 See Geoff Wade, "China to Move Production Capacity Offshore," *Flagpost*, Australian Parliamentary Library blog, 7 August 2015, http://www.aph.gov.au/About_Parliament/Parliamentary_Departments /Parliamentary_Library/FlagPost/2015/August/China_to_move _production_capacity_offshore.

18 王逸舟 [Wang Yizhou],《创造性造性介入:中国外交新取向》 [Creative involvement: New orientations in China's diplomacy] (Beijing: Peking University Press, 2013). For a review of the book, see "Creative Involvement in Global Order Can Leave Clearer Chinese Imprint," *Global Times* (Beijing), 15 August 2013, http://www.globaltimes.cn/content /804152.shtml.

19 James Jiann Hua To, *Qiaowu: Extra-Territorial Policies for the Overseas Chinese* (Leiden: Brill, 2014).

20 "The Hard and Soft Faces of China's 'United Front' Work," *Radio Free Asia*, 22 May 2015, http://www.rfa.org/english/news/china/united -05222015124837.html.

21 Gerry Groot, "The United Front in an Age of Shared Destiny,"
in *Shared Destiny*, eds. Geremie R. Barmé, Linda Jaivin, and Jeremy
Goldkorn (Canberra, Australia: ANU Press, 2015), 129–35, https://press
.anu.edu.au/publications/china-story-yearbook/shared-destiny. See also
Gerry Groot, *Managing Transitions: The Chinese Communist Party,
United Front Work, Corporatism and Hegemony* (Abingdon, UK: Taylor
& Francis, 2003).

22 "巩固发展最广泛的爱国统一战线, 为实现中国梦提供广泛力量支
持" [Strengthen and develop the broadest patriotic united front in order
to provide broad strength and support for achieving the China dream],
People's Daily, 21 May 2015, http://politics.people.com.cn/n/2015/0521
/c1024-27032155.html.

23 *"One Belt, One Road": An Economic Roadmap* (London: The
Economist Intelligence Unit, 2016).

24 "Premier Calls on Overseas Chinese to Contribute to Economy,"
China Daily, 7 July 2015, http://www.chinadaily.com.cn/business/2015
-07/07/content_21199276.htm.

25 "中国侨商投资企业协会向全球华商发出倡议书" [A proposal by the
China Overseas Chinese Entrepreneurs Association directed to overseas
Chinese business people throughout the world], *China News Service*
(Beijing), 7 July 2015, http://www.chinanews.com/hr/2015/07-07/7390725
.shtml.

26 An especially useful study of PRC efforts in these regards is
Wanning Sun and John Sinclair, eds. *Media and Communication in
the Chinese Diaspora: Rethinking Transnationalism* (Abingdon, UK:
Routledge, 2015).

27 "一带一路 商机处处 厦门与东盟浓情化不开" [One Belt One Road:
Business opportunities abound, the great affection between Xiamen
and ASEAN will never be broken], *Kwong Wah Yit Po* (George Town,
Malaysia), 4 Jan 2016, http://www.kwongwah.com.my/?p=72518.

28 "China SOEs Snap Up Overseas Chinese Media," *Asia Sentinel*, 8
March 2016, http://www.asiasentinel.com/econ-business/china-soe-snap
-up-overseas-media/.

29 Fitzgerald, *China and the Overseas Chinese*, 43–44, 49.

30 The 13th World Chinese Entrepreneurs Convention was held in Bali in
September 2015. Chinese organizations from around the world took part
in the meeting.

31 As described by Kuhn, *Chinese among Others*, 374–78.

32 Among them, the PRC state-directed Mindu Cultural Studies Association; the World Federation of Fuzhou Associations; the Federation of Foochow Associations of Malaysia; and the Sarawak Foochow Association.

33 "張錦雄：雖深愛居住國・南洋福州人沒忘根" [Zhang Jinxiong: Although they deeply love the countries in which they live, Nanyang Fuzhou persons will never forget their roots], *Sinchew Jit Poh* (Selangor, Malaysia), 18 December 2015, http://news.sinchew.com.my/node/4577 54?tid=1.

34 "China's Pilot Green Card Plan to Attract More Overseas Chinese," PREC Edu Services, Kuala Lumpur, 2016, http://www.studyinchina.com .my/web/page/green-card-to-attract-more-overseas-chinese/. See also Kor Kian Beng, "China to Ease Green Card Rules to Draw Foreign Talent," *Straits Times*, 13 January 2016, http://str.sg/ZHEy.

35 "中国首部保护华侨权益综合性地方法规明起实施 哪些权益从此有法可依" [China's first comprehensive local laws for safeguarding the rights and interests of overseas Chinese: Which rights and interests are protected by these laws?]《缅华网》[Myanmar Chinese net], 3 October 2015, http://www.mhwmm.com/Ch/NewsView.asp?ID=13221.

36 "About Confucius Institutes," Hanban (Beijing), http://english.han ban.org/node_10971.htm. Among ASEAN members as of 2018, only Brunei did not have one.

37 See XUM's website, http://www.xmu.edu.my/about/index.html.

38 See "A Never Ending Policy," *The Economist*, 27 April 2013, http:// www.economist.com/news/briefing/21576654-elections-may-could-mark -turning-point-never-ending-policy.

39 "First Chinese University Opens Campus in Malaysia," China Central Television, 3 March 2016, http://english.cntv.cn/2016/03/03/VIDExgWo MGeX0BaAryZPWjWK160303.shtml. English is the language of instruction in most subjects at XUM. In Singapore six decades earlier (1956), a Chinese-language institution, Nanyang University, opened and stayed open until 1980. Although it was not sponsored by Beijing, it was seen by the Lee Kuan Yew government as a breeding ground for Chinese chauvinism and pro-PRC political activism. Observers suggested that the English-educated elite saw the university as a threat to their domination of Singapore. See Wong Ting-Hong, *Hegemonies Compared: State Formation and Chinese School Politics in Postwar Singapore and Hong Kong* (New York: Routledge, 2002); and Huang Jianli, "Nanyang

University and the Language Divide: Controversy over the 1965 Wang
Gungwu Report," in《南大图像：历史河流中的省视》[Imagery of
Nanyang University: Reflections on the river of history], ed. Lee Guan
Kin (Singapore: NTU Centre for Chinese Language and Culture and
Global Publishing, 2007), 137–220.

40 See Mette Thunø, "Newly Established Emigration Museums in
Beijing and Shanghai: Reasserting the Chinese Nation State by the
Representation of Those Leaving It," paper presented at ISSCO 2016
International Conference, University of British Columbia, Canada, 6–8
July 2016.

41 Ho Wah Foon, "Huazong Status Lifted by New Home," *The Star*
(Kuala Lumpur), 14 February 2016, https://www.thestar.com.my/news
/nation/2016/02/14/huazong-status-lifted-by-new-home-the-spanking
-rm80mil-wisma-huazong-is-a-reflection-of-the-associat/.

42 Calvin Yang, "Young Laotians Learn Chinese to Improve Job
Prospects," *New York Times*, 9 February 2014, https://nyti.ms/1f6T2Od.

43 For more, see Danielle Tan, *Chinese Engagement in Laos: Past,
Present, and Uncertain Future* (Singapore: Institute of Southeast Asian
Studies, 2015), https://www.iseas.edu.sg/images/pdf/trends_in_sea
_2015_7.pdf.

44 "老挝中国总商会琅勃拉邦中国商会成立" [Luang Prabang China
Chamber of Commerce established under the China General Chamber
of Commerce in Laos], *Laowo Tong* (Vientiane, Laos), 20 October 2015,
http://www.laowotong.com/thread-7214-1-1.html.

45 "老挝中国总商会广东商会举行成立大会" [Meeting to establish
Guangdong Chamber of Commerce under the China Chamber of
Commerce in Laos], Ministry of Commerce, Beijing, 12 May 2015, http://
www.mofcom.gov.cn/article/i/jyjl/j/201505/20150500968599.shtml.

46 "驻老挝大使关华兵出席'老挝海外华侨华人互助中心'揭牌
仪式" [PRC ambassador to Laos Guan Huabing participates in the
naming ceremony for the "Overseas Chinese Mutual Help Center of
Laos"], Embassy of the People's Republic of China in the Lao People's
Democratic Republic, 10 December 2015, http://la.china-embassy.org/chn
/dssghd/t1327426.htm.

47 "柬埔寨中国商会举行2015年度工作会议" [Chinese Chamber of
Commerce in Cambodia holds 2015 work meeting], Economic and
Commercial Counsellor's Office of the Embassy of the People's Republic

of China in the Kingdom of Cambodia, 14 December 2015, http://
cb.mofcom.gov.cn/article/catalog/201512/20151201209557.shtml.

48 "中国海上丝绸之路经贸考察团到访缅甸中华总商会" [Chinese
Maritime Silk Road economic and trade delegation meets with Myanmar
Chinese Chamber of Commerce], 《金凤凰报》 [Golden phoenix news]
(Myanmar), 21 December 2015, http://www.mmgpmedia.com/sino-mm
/11662.

49 Jeffrey Hays, "Chinese in Thailand and Luk Krueng (People of Mixed
Thai Blood)," Facts and Details, May 2014, http://factsanddetails.com
/southeast-asia/Thailand/sub5_8b/entry-3225.html.

50 See Tong Chee Kiong and Chan Kwok Bun, eds., *Alternate Identities:
The Chinese of Contemporary Thailand* (Singapore: Times Academic
Press, 2001); and G. William Skinner, *Chinese Society in Thailand: An
Analytical History* (Ithaca, NY: Cornell University Press, 1957).

51 Ruji Auethavornpipat, "Revealing China's Hegemonic Project in
Thailand: How the Confucius Institute Furthers the Chinese State's
International Ambitions," paper presented at the 12th International
Conference on Thai Studies, Sydney, Australia, 22–24 April 2014. In
Thailand in 2016 there were 14 Confucius Institutes and 11 Confucius
Classrooms, compared with only six institutes and no classrooms in the
ASEAN country with the next greatest concentration, Indonesia; see
"About Confucius Institutes," Hanban, http://english.hanban.org/node
_10971.htm.

52 It was founded by an ex-prime minister of Thailand of Chinese
descent, Chavalit Youngchiyudh; its website is http://www.thaizhong
.org/zh/.

53 For biographical details, see "关于协会" [About the association],
Thai-Chinese Culture and Economy Association, http://www.thaizhong
.org/index.php?option=com_content&view=article&id=5602&Itemid
=104&lang=zh.

54 "Wang Jiarui Meets with Head of Thai-Chinese Culture and
Economy Association," International Department, Central Committee of
the Communist Party of China (Beijing), 1 July 2015, http://www.idcpc
.org.cn/english/news/201507/t20150702_75688.html.

55 "President Li Xiaolin Meets Delegation of Thai-Chinese Culture and
Economic Association," 4 November 2013, http://en.cpaffc.org.cn/content
/details20-22914.html; "President Li Xiaolin Meets Delegation of
Thai-Chinese Culture and Economy Association," 29 October 2014,

http://en.cpaffc.org.cn/content/details20-47633.html; and "President Li Xiaolin Meets with Delegation of Thai-Chinese Culture and Economy Association," 29 June 2015, all at the Chinese People's Association for Friendship with Foreign Countries (Beijing) website.

56 "Mr. Zheng Daoxi, Chairman of the Standing Committee of Xiamen Municipal People's Congress Met with Dr. Bhokin Bhalakula, Former President of Thai National Assembly," Foreign Affairs Office of Xiamen Municipal People's Government, 26 September 2014.

57 "A Delegation of Thai-Chinese Culture and Economy Association Visits China," China Association for International Friendly Contact (Beijing), 1 December 2013, http://www.caifc.org.cn/en/content.aspx?id =3396.

58 Bhokin Bhalakula, "Maritime Silk Project — A Road to Peace and Development," *The Nation* (Bangkok), 23 May 2015, http://www.nation multimedia.com/opinion/Maritime-Silk-project--a-road-to-peace-and -develop-30260683.html.

59 "驻菲律宾使馆联合侨界召开世界反法西斯战争暨中国人民抗日战争胜利70周年纪念大会" [Philippines embassy and overseas Chinese organizations convene meeting to commemorate the 70th anniversary of the victory in the global anti-fascist war and the Chinese people's war against the Japanese], Embassy of the People's Republic of China in the Republic of the Philippines, 17 August 2015, http://ph.chineseembassy .org/chn/sgdt/t1289267.htm.

60 "菲律宾统促会新届职员就职 国侨办电贺" [New committee of the Philippines Association for the Promotion of the Reunification of China is installed; State Council's Overseas Chinese Affairs Office sends congratulatory telegram], *China News Service*, 29 February 2016, http:// www.chinaqw.com/hqhr/2016/02-29/80984.shtml.

61 "北京侨辦訪華總 了解華社情況"[Beijing overseas Chinese officials visit Malaysia to understand the situation of the Chinese community], *Orient Daily News*, 5 November 2015, http://www.orientaldaily.com.my /amp/111588.

62 "钢铁工联驳美佳·征倾销税起作用 中印钢价廉没不合理" [Malaysian Iron and Steel Industry Federation rebuts Megasteel: Antidumping duties effective: Cheap Chinese and Indonesian steels not unreasonable], *Nanyang Siang Pau*, 30 December 2015, http://www .enanyang.my/?p=469813.

63 "廖中莱：马来将扮演好'一带一路'建设战略伙伴角色" [Transport Minister Liow Tiong Lai: MCA makes effort to promote China's "One Belt, One Road" construction], *Sinchew Jih Pao*, 12 January 2016, http://www.yfcnn.com/news/world/20160112/3416334.html.

64 "黃惠康：成中馬友誼橋樑·中文教育是大馬寶藏" [Huang Huikang: A bridge of friendship between China and Malaysia / Chinese-language education is a national treasure], *Sinchew Jih Pao*, 11 March 2016, http://news.sinchew.com.my/node/469497?tid=1.

65 Compare http://my.china-embassy.org/chn/sgxw/ (in Chinese) and http://my.china-embassy.org/eng/ (in English).

66 He spoke to the Tawau Chinese Chamber of Commerce, the Tawau Federation of Chinese Associations, and six major Chinese clan organizations. "黃惠康大使考察沙巴州斗湖仙本那" [Ambassador Huang Huikang inspects Tawau and Semporna in Sabah State], 16 February 2016, http://my.china-embassy.org/chn/sgxw/t1340901.htm.

67 Loh Foon Fong, "First Batch of Xiamen University Students Conferred Their Degrees," *The Star*, 28 September 2019, https://www.thestar.com.my/news/nation/2019/09/28/first-batch-of-xiamen-university-students-conferred-their-degrees.

68 Bernama, "'Special Envoy' Tan Kok Wai to Complement Ambassador to China, Foreign Minister Says," *Malay Mail*, 1 September 2018, https://www.malaymail.com/news/malaysia/2018/09/01/special-envoy-tan-kok-wai-to-complement-ambassador-to-china-foreign-ministe/1668380

69 Loh, "First Batch of Xiamen University Students Conferred."

70 Media Chinese International Limited, "Announcement of Final Results for the Year Ended 31 March 2017," 29 May 2017, 20, http://www.mediachinesegroup.com/pdf/ew00685_mci_annual_announcement_20170529.pdf.

71 "Malaysian Tycoon Dismembers HK Paper for Beijing," *Asia Sentinel*, 21 April 2016, https://www.asiasentinel.com/politics/malaysia-tycoon-dismembers-hongkong-paper-for-beijing/.

72 "China SOEs Snap Up Overseas Chinese Media," *Asia Sentinel*, 8 March 2016, http://www.asiasentinel.com/econ-business/china-soe-snap-up-overseas-media/.

73 The invitees are listed in "新加坡华人代表启程前往北京出席二战胜利纪念活动" [Singapore's ethnic-Chinese representatives prior to their departure for Beijing to participate in the victory in World War II commemorative activities], *Nanyang Post* (Singapore), 31 August 2015,

http://news.nanyangpost.com/2015/08/31_57.html, as well as in "驻新加坡大使陈晓东在新加坡华人代表赴华出席中国人民抗日战争暨世界反法西斯战争胜利70周年纪念活动送行会上的讲话" [Speech by Ambassador Chen Xiaodong at the Singapore National People's Congress in Singapore to attend the commemoration of the 70th anniversary of the victory of the Chinese People's War of Resistance against Japanese Aggression and the World Anti-Fascist War], Ministry of Foreign Affairs of the People's Republic of China, 30 August 2015, http://www.fmprc.gov.cn/web/gjhdq_676201/gj_676203/yz_676205/1206_677076/1206x2_677096/t1292272.shtml. The 17-strong Malaysian contingent in Beijing included media magnate Tiong Hiew King.

74 "新加坡华人代表启程前往北京出席二战胜利纪念活动" [Singapore's ethnic-Chinese representatives prior to their departure for Beijing to participate in the victory in World War II commemorative activities].

75 "Lianhe Zaobao and Singapore Business Federation Launch 'One Belt, One Road' Portal," *Straits Times* (Singapore), 8 March 2016, http://str.sg/ZFpA.

76 "刘宏：海外华人华侨可发挥'一带一路'桥梁作用" [Liu Hong: Overseas Chinese can play a bridging role in the "One Belt, One Road" initiative], *Xinhuanet Singapore*, 14 March 2015, http://sg.xinhuanet.com/2015-03/14/c_127580964.htm.

77 "何亚非就'一带一路'与欧亚联通在印尼发表演讲" [He Yafei speaks in Indonesia on "One Belt, One Road" and Europe-Asia linkage], Chinese Embassy in Indonesia, 7 December 2015, http://id.chineseembassy.org/chn/zgyyn/t1322098.htm.

78 "驻东盟使团与印尼中国商会新一届理事会举行新春座谈会" [PRC Mission to ASEAN holds Chinese New Year Forum with new board of the China Chamber of Commerce in Indonesia], Chinese Mission to ASEAN, 16 January 2016, http://asean.chinamission.org.cn/chn/stxw/t1332424.htm.

79 "浙江省商务厅代表团访印尼中华总商会" [Zhejiang Provincial Commercial Bureau delegation visits China Chamber of Commerce in Indonesia], *Guo Ji Ri Bao* [International daily news] (Jakarta), 9 June 2015, http://www.guojiribao.com/shtml/gjrb/20150609/221844.shtml.

80 See, for example, "中国侨联副主席乔卫率团访问印尼中华总商会" [Delegation led by Qiao Wei, deputy chairman of China's Overseas Chinese Affairs Office, visits Indonesian Chinese Entrepreneur

Association], *China News Service*, 28 June 2015, http://www.chinanews
.com/hr/2015/06-28/7370125.shtml.

81 "China ASEAN Expo," 23 December 2015, http://www.gxlxg.net
/dongmengbolanhui/2015/1223/322.html.

82 See and compare China News Service, "东盟南洋基金会主席：亚
投行开业将促进印尼基础设施建设" [ASEAN Nanyang Foundation
chairman: AIIB will promote Indonesia's infrastructure development], 10
January 2016, http://www.chinanews.com/gj/2016/01-10/7709451.shtml;
and Pearl Lee, "Reviving Dreams of Nantah in Bintan 'Wellness' Village,"
Straits Times, 20 November 2016, http://str.sg/4Msm.

CHAPTER 8

Coping with the Dragon
VULNERABILITY AND ENGAGEMENT IN SINGAPORE-CHINA RELATIONS

See Seng Tan, *Nanyang Technical University, Singapore*

Are we not vulnerable? If we are not vulnerable, why do we spend 5 to 6 per cent of GDP [gross domestic product] year after year on defence? Are we mad? This is a frugal government, you know that well. . . . We are not vulnerable? They can besiege you. You'll be dead. Your sea lanes are cut off and your business comes to a halt. . . . We've got friendly neighbors? Grow up.
— Minister Mentor Lee Kuan Yew, Singapore, 2010[1]

Singapore-China relations have come a long way. We are old friends, and China knows that Singapore will always remain steadfast to our old friends.
— Foreign Minister Vivian Balakrishnan, Singapore, 2016[2]

This chapter examines Singapore's relations with China and the consequences for Singapore's policy choices. As noted by Singapore's founding prime minister, Lee Kuan Yew, in the above quotation, China has had — it is safe to say, continues to have — a profound and politically sensitive influence on Singapore. In deference to its adjacent neighbors, Singapore chose not to establish normal diplomatic relations with the People's Republic of China (PRC) until October 1990. A decent interval thus followed Jakarta's full recognition of the PRC in July alongside signs of warming Malaysia-China relations. But Singapore's relations with China had begun to improve much earlier, in the wake of Beijing's 1970 decision to halt its relentless dissemination of anti-Singapore propaganda. Following the death of Mao Zedong in 1976, Sino-Singaporean relations benefited as successive Chinese leaders — notably Deng Xiaoping and reportedly Xi Jinping as well — looked to Singapore as a model of governance that China might wish to emulate.[3]

In the decades after Mao, Singapore basically welcomed deeper relations with China. Singapore's ties with Beijing were relatively free of the suspicions regarding Chinese strategic motives that had tended to shape the early perspectives of other Southeast Asian countries. As Lee reportedly told Deng when the latter visited Singapore in late 1978, the other member countries of the Association of Southeast Asian Nations (ASEAN) did not fear the "Russian bear" as much as they did the "Chinese dragon."[4] Economically and politically beneficial as closer links with China have been for Singapore, however, in more recent years they have brought to the city-state a measure of uncertainty and insecurity.

Although Singapore did purposely delay diplomatic recognition of the PRC until after the end of the Cold War in 1989, it has become more apparent in recent years that neither Singapore, nor or any other country, can determine on its own the terms and tenor of its relations with China.[5] For the most part, what Singapore and other Asian countries have done is to pursue relations with China that benefit them commercially while looking for their security to the United States.

China supplanted Japan as the world's second-largest economy in 2011. By 2012, for the first time, the Fortune Global 500 listed more Chinese companies than Japanese ones. Signs grew that China expected other countries to relate to it on its terms rather than theirs. Nowhere has this trend been more evident, in the eyes of some Southeast Asian states, than in Beijing's "assertive" augmentation and militarization of islands and reefs in the South China Sea.[6] At the same time, however, the deepening of material interdependence has created leverage for possible use in reducing the freedom of action of the weaker party in those relationships.

Have Sino-Singaporean ties grown so close that, as a necessary result of interdependence or a contingent effect of Chinese pressure, Singapore's policy options have become constrained to the point of rendering the city-state significantly vulnerable to China? For reasons of size and location, vulnerability has long defined and driven much of Singapore's economic and political life, especially from the standpoint of its leaders.[7] Are the risks of economic intimacy with the PRC a new but manageable variation on vulnerability as usual? Or are China's material ties with Singapore more and more worrisomely tying the latter's hands?

Singapore's Strategy

It is often said of Asian countries that they share a propensity to hedge against great powers such as China and the United States.[8] Most Asian states maintain fairly robust trade and investment ties with China while variously relying on the security implied by American military might. Singapore generally enjoys vibrant economic relations with China and an equally strong partnership with the United States, not only in security terms but economically as well. This dualistic strategy is usually attributed to a uniquely realist-cum-neoliberal outlook ostensibly preferred by Singapore's key decision-makers.[9] But the literature on the foreign policies of small states[10] suggests that Singapore behaves in ways that are not so exceptional when compared with what other ASEAN members do. Like many of its Asian neighbors, Singapore relates to the Chinese and American behemoths on different levels in differing versions of engagement and without sacrificing the flexibility that the city-state's leaders have cherished. Thus, for the most part and with qualifications, Singapore has been content to continue the regional status quo with America as the top Pacific power and main strategic guarantor, while at the same time harnessing the commercial opportunities provided by a rising China that has been principally interested, especially during the 1980s and 1990s, in the growth of its own economy.

The reasons for the success of Singapore's strategy are many. Not least among them is the city-state's physical distance from China compared with the nearer-to-China locations of ASEAN's fully mainland states such as Cambodia, Laos, Thailand, and Vietnam. If Southeast Asian countries live under China's long shadow, Singapore inhabits a penumbral area where a measure of flexibility is more readily enjoyed — and jealously guarded. In a sense, Singapore has hitherto engaged China because it can, while Cambodia and Laos have done so because they must.[11] But the explanatory power of geography is limited. Actual interactions matter as much if not more. As Singapore's engagements with its huge and increasingly powerful neighbor have multiplied, have they affected the relative latitude that its domestic and foreign policies have enjoyed?

Consider the role of interdependence. In matters of diplomacy, economy, and society, Singapore and China have become more interdependent than ever before. Yet the smaller partner prizes the autonomy and flexibility — the independence — with which its policy decisions are made, as all states do. Political communities that grow interdependent experience a rising sensitivity toward one another, whether by their own will or because one tries to coerce the other. For one partner if not both, beyond a certain point, that sensitivity can turn into a sense of exposure, of being at risk. Pertinent in this connection are distinctions between different types of interdependence defined by their differing ramifications for power relations between and among increasingly interconnected states.[12]

Thus, for Keohane and Nye, "sensitivity interdependence" (SI) refers to the ability of country A to affect co-interdependent country B significantly, but not enough to limit the policy options available for B to consider when choosing a course of action to overcome whatever negative effects its interdependent relationship with A might have entailed. In contrast, when "vulnerability interdependence" (VI) prevails, the power that A has over B is strong enough to constrain B's policy alternatives, such that B has effectively "no way out" of its disadvantageously interdependent relationship with A. Its vulnerability in the latter case leaves B with little choice other than to remain interdependent with A and bear the consequences.[13]

Few published works on Singapore's foreign policy are as memorable as a monograph by Michael Leifer published in 2000.[14] In it, he defined the fundamental security challenge confronting Singaporean leaders as one of coping with perceived vulnerabilities, foreign and domestic. Domestic risk was particularly acute during the city-state's early struggles with communism and communalism — homegrown strife in which Beijing nevertheless played an indirect role, although the extent of China's involvement has long been a matter of debate.[15] Leifer argued that Singapore's key decision-makers reinforced these perceived risks and turned them into pillars of legitimacy for the state — a "cult of vulnerability" including a "siege mentality" necessitating constant vigilance against all manner of threats and dangers that Singapore purportedly faced.[16]

Apart from Lee Kuan Yew's above-quoted worry about unfriendly neighbors, presumably including China, Singapore's sense of insecurity has been fed, justifiably or not, by other phenomena as well. Examples include the Asian Financial Crisis of 1997, the terrorist bombings in Bali in 2002, the Boxing Day tsunamis of 2004, and growing anxiety over possible shortages of energy and food.[17] Yet such fears have hardly paralyzed the city-state. On the contrary, despite its small size, Singapore has been lauded by hard-power realists in international affairs for "punching above its weight" in interstate relations.[18] So, politically useful perceptions aside, how truly vulnerable is Singapore?[19]

The country's name in Malay is *Singapura* — the Lion City. Singapore's informal "mascot," however, is the *merlion* — a composite creature with the head of a lion and the body of a fish. The combined allusion to prowess on both land and sea fits the Merlion City's location at the juncture of continental and maritime Southeast Asia. The merlion is physically far enough from the dragon to imply, by this crude criterion, more policy autonomy for Singapore than Laos enjoys, for instance, being right on China's border. Yet Singapore's interactions with China cannot be reduced to distance. They are many, diverse, and nuanced, spanning as they do all three spheres of interest: economy, society, and security.

Economic Engagement

Although diplomatic ties between Singapore and China were normalized only in 1990, economic interchange began in the wake of the merlion's independence in 1965. Even without full mutual recognition, Sino-Singaporean relations had already begun to warm with the advent of big-power détente in the 1970s,[20] and would remain more or less cordial ever since.[21] In the troubled years preceding and immediately following independence, Singapore's rulers cracked down on left-wing opposition at home and worried about the ideological influence that the PRC might bring to bear on the city-state's largely ethnic-Chinese population.[22] Yet Singapore's leaders felt comfortable engaging in "enlightened economic pragmatism" — part of a broader pragmatism encompassing security as well that continues to inform the country's foreign policy.[23] Incongruously, Singapore-China trade during the Mao period peaked at the height of the Cultural Revolution in 1967–69.[24] In the post-Mao era, Singapore vigorously pursued economic engagement with China in an effort to develop a "second wing" of regional and global market expansion to complement its existing "first wing" of involvement with the West.[25] The complementarity of Singapore's and China's very different economies helped to incentivize the merlion to exploit economic opportunities with the dragon.[26] Except for a few years here and there, Singapore has long been China's largest trading partner among the ASEAN economies, and was the first Asian country to sign a free trade agreement with the PRC.[27]

Bilateral economic cooperation has not focused on trade alone. It has also fostered the transfer of varieties of investments and managerial skills, exemplified by government-to-government projects such as the Suzhou Industrial Park, the Tianjin Eco-city, and the Chongqing Connectivity Initiative — the latter an effort to contribute to and benefit from China's Belt and Road Initiative. Singapore has also pursued privately driven but officially supported projects to serve China's development needs, including the Guangzhou Knowledge City, the Sichuan Hi-tech Innovation Park, the Nanjing Eco Hi-tech Island, and the Jilin Food Zone. Despite the extent of such bilateral collaboration, however, it has been argued that hitherto the two countries have not fully reaped the expected gains in terms of capital inflows and outflows.[28]

Under Deng Xiaoping's leadership, the dragon began looking to the merlion as a possible model: a well-managed country from which China could learn. In 1992, pointing to the city-state along with Japan and South Korea, Deng is said to have praised Singapore's social order as "rather good. Its leaders exercise strict management. We should learn from their experience, and we should do a better job than they do."[29] To that end, during the Deng era, thousands of China's best and brightest were sent to Singapore to be educated, a practice that has more or less persisted to the present. For years Beijing has been sending officials of the Communist Party of China (CPC), including top brass from the party's central, provincial, and local governments and state-owned enterprises, to study at Singapore's tertiary educational and training institutions.

Of these arrangements, the most formalized is probably the Nanyang Centre for Public Administration (NCPA), a specialist graduate-level school for senior Chinese officials at the Nanyang Technological University. Established as a joint initiative in 2010 by the Chinese and Singaporean governments, the NCPA administers a one-year course taught entirely in Mandarin with tuition and ancillary costs wholly covered by the Chinese side.[30] In October 2012 in Beijing, three weeks before the start of the 18th National Congress of the CPC, a commentary appeared in its Central Party School's leading policy journal, *Study Times*, stating that the CPC could learn a great deal from the semi-authoritarian practices of Singapore's long-ruling People's Action Party (PAP). A Chinese political scientist, Zhang Min, was quoted as saying of "the Singapore model" that it had been "admired by most Chinese leaders" and that Xi Jinping might "see Singapore's success as the dreamed accomplishments of his rule in [the] coming decade."[31]

Given the extreme disparity in spatial and demographic size between Singapore and China, it is all too tempting to assume that, far from being to some degree interdependent economically, the merlion depends wholly on the dragon in material terms, while the latter can easily do without the former at little or no cost to itself. The data on trade and investment yield a more nuanced view. Admittedly, in 2016, by value, Singapore traded more with China than with any other country, but despite its diminutive physical size, the city-state ranked tenth among China's trading partners.[32] And while most Southeast Asian countries ran dependence-suggesting deficits in trade with China, Singapore's balance of trade with the behemoth was (modestly) positive.[33] Indeed, as of 2018, among all of the ASEAN states' trade balances with China since 2011, Singapore's alone had remained positive year by year.[34]

Compared with trade deficits and surpluses, balances of outward versus inward foreign direct investment (FDI) are harder to know. Compared with trade flows, flows of FDI from one country to another tend to vary more sharply year by year and to be harder to trace back to an actual country of origin. A country-specific stock of inward FDI is the total accumulated value of investment that country A has received from country B as of one point in time, normally the end of a year. The size of the accumulation in A that has come from B indicates a commitment to A — and arguably, by implication, a roughly corresponding degree of influence over A — that B may possess. In principle, other things being equal, the plausibility of inferring B-over-A influence from cumulative B-in-A FDI is strengthened to the extent that the value of that stake dwarfs the value of A's stock of FDI in B. By the same suggestive logic, the more balanced in value these two stocks of investment are and the more diverse the composition of A's FDI partners is, the less vulnerably dependent is A on B.

Based on official Singapore data on FDI stocks, the merlion appears to be less vulnerable to the dragon than one might think. The origins of FDI in Singapore are diverse. The city-state is not proportionally overdependent on inward FDI from China proper. The value of those investments at the end of 2016, for example, was a mere 1.8 percent of Singapore's total inward stock of FDI, compared with the 15.8 percent of all outward stock from Singapore that had accumulated in China proper.

"China proper" excludes Hong Kong. If that "autonomous territory" is added to China proper's share, the inward-to-Singapore and outward-from-Singapore percentages change, respectively, to 5.7 and 22.7. Further adding the capital stock received from and by the British Virgin Islands and the Cayman Islands — places notorious for allowing disguised transfers of money — increases the respectively inward-to-Singapore and outward-from-Singapore figures to 18.4 and 33.1 percent. Despite the opacity regarding exact origins and destinations, these positive balances of outward-over-inward stocks of FDI in Singapore's favor are evidence against the idea that the city-state is vulnerably dependent on China as either the predominant origin or the main destination of FDI in or from Singapore. As for the United States, its contribution to Singapore's total inward stock of FDI in 2016, at 20.6 percent, exceeded that of any other country or territory, while the American share of Singapore's entire outward stock was only 3.9 percent. If a negative balance indicates vulnerability, or makes it more likely, by the purely statistical and thereby limited logic of this disparity, Singapore might worry more about America than about China, especially insofar as US president Donald Trump wants foreigners to invest in America rather than the reverse.

As for flows rather than stocks, Singapore also does relatively well in that regard. Independently generated data for 2016 show that while the merlion received more investment from the dragon than did any other country in that year,[35] suggesting Chinese influence over Singapore, Singapore was also the second-largest source of investment into China,[36] implying proportional leverage in the opposite direction. The kinds and causes of influence, of course, are too many and too contingent to be inferred from any pattern of investment considered outside of its socioeconomic and political contexts.

Despite the complementary nature of their two economies, Singaporean firms faced serious competition from China's large domestic pool of low-cost labor.[37] To tackle this problem, Singapore opted to retrain its labor force and reduce its manufacturing sector while expanding its service sector.[38] Singapore's policymakers and business leaders are not about to take the dragon on head-to-head in an economic slugfest they would likely lose. They are better off creating niche markets for Singapore inside China by emphasizing the city-state's comparative advantages, including promoting Singapore as a trustworthy brand name synonymous with integrity in business.[39] As one market analyst put it, "Singapore has to do things that the Chinese can't do."[40]

Even so, Singapore today finds itself confronted with a problem that Japan has long faced: having its business model and related knowledge and ideas voraciously plagiarized by China. To cite a notorious instance, shortly after the Suzhou Industrial Park was established, the Suzhou city government created a rival park based on Singapore's ideas, christened it the "Suzhou New District Industrial Park," and set it to competing directly with Singapore's project and for the same investors.[41] Singaporeans who lamented this development only needed to recall Deng's pointed observation that China should learn from Singapore — but then aim to overtake it.[42] The Suzhou case especially discomforted Singaporeans who had naïvely assumed that sharing with Beijing an ostensibly common Chinese culture and a joint interest in doing business would somehow ensure "win-win" cooperation.[43]

Social Overlap and Irritation

Although 76 percent of Singaporeans are ethnically Chinese,[44] that social fact has never implied the city-state's economic, cultural, or political immersion in a Sinosphere centered on Beijing. Singapore's history is rife with evidence of its autonomy in these regards. Off and on through the 1950s and '60s, China supported communist insurgencies in Southeast Asia, Singapore included. "Southeast Asia was chosen as a center of [the] PRC's revolutionary activities," according to one scholar, "because of its strategic location, geographical proximity, [the] lesser presence of major powers, and [the] still weak colonial or newly independent governments" therein.[45] In the late 1970s, under Deng Xiaoping and his more accommodating foreign policy, the CPC scaled down its support for insurgent communism in Southeast Asia. In Lee Kuan Yew's view, part of the reason for this apparent change of heart could have been Deng's desire to garner support from the ASEAN states for a united front with China against the Soviet Union and Vietnam—a rationale that would hardly appeal to Southeast Asia's leaders if Beijing kept on waging ideological war against them.[46]

Since those turbulent times, China's cultural encounters with Singapore have been considerably more placid and positive. Instances include China's participation in Singaporean cultural occasions such as the large and elaborate Chinese New Year-related Chingay Parade and River Hongbao celebrations; the Chinese Festival of Arts (Huayi); and the completion and opening of a China Cultural Centre in Singapore in 2015. Three years earlier, in 2012, Beijing had given Singapore a pair of giant pandas—only the seventh country to have been so honored (after the United States, Japan, Spain, Austria, Australia, and Thailand).[47]

Nowadays, the sense of being socially related to China that Singapore's ethnically Chinese citizens share reflects less their ongoing ethnic-majority status in the city-state, or the stories or memories of their own families' migration, than how they feel about the growth of current and recent arrivals from the PRC. Mainland China has long been a major source of tourism and immigration for Singapore.[48] In the late 1980s and early 1990s, Singapore's economic boom and labor shortage facilitated inflows of thousands of mainland Chinese professionals who were officially welcomed as needed additions to the country's pool of talent. By 2004, foreigners had become 27 percent of Singapore's population. A decade later the figure had risen to 39 percent.[49]

Understandably in this burgeoning context, Singapore's search for "foreign talent" attracted criticism from residents.[50] Domestic objections had grown caustic enough by 2012 to prompt Prime Minister Lee Hsien Loong, in that year's "state of the nation" address, to warn his fellow citizens against xenophobia.[51] To the extent that these local critics were ethnically Chinese and the newcomers were from the PRC, the locals were less inclined to embrace that shared cultural past than to question the visitors' behavior when it seemed un-Singaporean.

Concerns over status differences and job competition aside, some Singaporeans even suggested, fairly or not, that the government's pro-immigration policy could have been driven by the desire of the ruling PAP to enlarge its electoral base. That political suspicion presumed that incoming Chinese immigrants might reward the party's welcome by acquiring Singaporean citizenship, and with it the right to vote. Other locals with hidden intentions in mind improbably attributed to the government a demographic motive: that expanded ethnic-Chinese immigration could counter the proportional effects of fertility rates, the rates of the Malay and Indian minorities being higher than that of Chinese Singaporeans.[52] Notwithstanding the appreciation of China's readiness to help Southeast Asia recover from the Asian Financial Crisis in 1997–98,[53] the issue of foreign Chinese talent and corresponding job competition grew into an important source of frustration among Singaporeans.[54] That said, to be fair, one researcher did argue, contrary to media reports, that Singaporeans were not particularly bothered by perceived Chinese-immigrant competition for jobs, and that Chinese nationals living in Singapore, while aware of the reported resentment of newcomers by the homegrown, did not feel especially stigmatized by it.[55]

When incidents occur or resentments are voiced, social media can magnify them. Two cases from July 2012 come to mind. In the first, a USD $1.4 million Ferrari driven well above the speed limit in early morning hours ran a red light and struck a taxi, killing its two occupants. Also dead was the Ferrari's driver, Ma Chi, a young financial investor and PRC citizen who had moved to Singapore just four years before. A different taxi's dashboard camera captured the horrific event. Uploaded to the web, the video went viral. Quickly and unfairly, the crash became a lightning rod for all kinds of local gripes against newcomers from mainland China. Stereotypes circulating on line included the *nouveaux riches* flaunting their wealth in vulgar ways; the hyper-industrious students tutored by their "study mamas" outperforming local pupils, including ethnic-Chinese Singaporeans, in the city-state's competitive school classrooms; and "gold-digging" mainland-Chinese women derogatorily labeled *wuya* (Mandarin for "crows") for allegedly preying on local men. Not unrelated to these signs of social stress was the success of the Singapore government's effort to encourage immigration, evident in the near-doubling of the country's population since 1990 to 5.2 million in 2012.[56]

Compared with local anger over the fatalities on a Singapore street, the second case was a matter of opinion more than provocation. When Singapore's athletes paraded in the opening ceremony of the 2012 Olympics in London, the honor of carrying their country's flag was given to a PRC-born table tennis player, Feng Tianwei. Singapore's Foreign Sports Talent Scheme, hoping she would improve the city-state's performance in her sport, had sponsored Feng's move to Singapore in 2007. A mere year later, at the 2008 Olympics in Beijing, she and her teammates earned the first (silver) medal ever won by Singapore in any sport at any Olympic Games since the country's independence in 1965.[57] Feng went on to win an individual bronze in table tennis in London in 2012. Yet her achievements and the honor of carrying Singapore's flag did not sit well with many of her adopted compatriots, according to a popular blog on sociopolitical issues.[58]

Also offensive to some locals is the way some PRC nationals in Singapore call themselves *zhongguoren* ("China Chinese") rather than *huaren* ("ethnic Chinese"), thereby identifying with the People's Republic of China rather than with the more inclusive and trans-political status of being Chinese.[59] Objections to Singapore's "China Chinese" are not hard to find, especially in cyberspace.[60] So far, however, the government has kept such sentiments, justified or not, from undermining the basic pragmatism of its policies toward China. In this respect, the relative unpopularity of "PRCs," as the newcomers from the mainland are sometimes called, has not exceeded a manageable level of sensitivity. Nor does the problem imply a sense of Singaporean vulnerability so drastic as to induce the merlion to comply with whatever the dragon wants. The issue of army exercises on Taiwan raised in the next section illustrates the point.

Security Issues

Prime Minister Lee's three-day visit to China in September 2017 marked the ostensible end of an unusually turbulent period in the two countries' diplomatic interactions. Lee had not been included on the long list of heads of state invited to the "summit" convened in Beijing in May 2017 to support Xi Jinping's signature foreign-policy innovation — the Belt and Road Initiative. Only in January had a set of Singapore Army vehicles finally been repatriated from Hong Kong, where they had been seized and detained en route home from Taiwan, apparently at the behest of Beijing. Singapore had long been conducting military exercises in Taiwan (among other places) despite China's disapproval. Singapore had earlier infuriated Beijing by, in effect, endorsing the July 2016 international-legal nullification of China's "nine-dash line" in the South China Sea by an arbitral court in The Hague.

Viewed in historical context, such bilateral flare-ups have been rare. Singapore's military ties with China are not long-standing and have been relatively minor in nature.[61] They have been growing, however, especially in the form of defense diplomacy broadly defined.[62] Examples include high-level visits, policy dialogues, staff training, educational exchanges, and collaboration on non-military security issues such as interdicting cross-border crime.[63] In May 2007, the two countries' naval vessels first joined those from six other countries in a combined maritime exercise in waters off Singapore under the framework of the Western Pacific Naval Symposium (WPNS). Annual bilateral defense consultations, however, began only the following year.

The most powerful ships in Singapore's navy are frigates. In August 2008, one of them — the RSS *Steadfast* — became the first to visit China. China's navy has visited Singapore, but those visits have been far fewer than port calls to Singapore by vessels in the US Navy or in Japan's Maritime Self-Defense Force, for example.[64] Singapore Armed Forces (SAF) personnel have taken part periodically in bilateral exercises with the People's Liberation Army (PLA), beginning on a small scale with an uncontroversial counterterrorist rationale. Not until 2014 were conventional armed forces involved, and the upgrade in that year surprised some observers. Considering that Singapore had supported Washington's "rebalance" of its forces to favor the Asia-Pacific, news that SAF soldiers were playing live-fire war games using tanks and artillery alongside PLA counterparts in China's Nanjing Military Region raised eyebrows across the region.[65]

Lifted eyebrows did not lower Singapore's commitment to its American security partner. Singapore has retained its durable and robust security ties with the United States. Weapons are a case in point. China has had minor success selling arms to some Southeast Asian states — portable surface-to-air missiles (SAMs) and air defense systems to Indonesia, grenade launchers and offshore patrol vessels to Thailand, and portable SAMs to Malaysia, among other transfers. But Singapore has bought its arms exclusively from Western countries, especially the United States.[66] The two countries share a bilateral free trade agreement and a security framework accord that, for all intents and purposes, make them near-allies in kind though not in name. In regional security terms, Singapore still sees America as indispensable in balancing against revisionist powers — the Soviet Union during the Cold War, China since then — and in restraining potentially revisionist ones, notably Japan, with which Singapore maintains a bilateral security alliance.[67]

When President Barack Obama formally served notice of the American rebalance toward Asia in late 2011, Singapore had already decided to facilitate the rotational deployment to the city-state of up to four of the US Navy's littoral combat ships. Crucially, Singapore's generally warm response to the rebalance was more than military in character; it included support for broader American engagement in the region. Singapore's leaders worked assiduously to cultivate continuing trans-Pacific involvement of the United States through America's membership in the East Asia Summit and its leadership in planning the Trans-Pacific Partnership (TPP) trade pact. Until President Donald Trump's January 2017 announcement of intent to pull his country out of the TPP, Washington and Singapore shared policy priorities on maintaining access to markets, navigational freedom, and global financial stability.[68] Arguably, market access aside, they still do.

The rebalance angered Beijing, and Sino-American tensions have worsened since. China reclaimed land in the South China Sea at an alarming rate — over 2,900 acres by June 2015, according to a Pentagon report. Beijing built military facilities on the land features under its control.[69] Some claimant states have done likewise, but not at the tremendous pace and scale of China's effort.[70] The US Navy for its part ran "freedom of navigation" exercises. Beijing condemned them as destabilizing and hypocritical in the light of Washington's criticism of China's military buildup in the same disputed waters.[71]

These developments complicated Singapore's role as the country coordinator for ASEAN-China dialogue relations from mid-2015 to mid-2018 and as ASEAN's chair in 2018. Singapore is not a territorial claimant in the South China Sea. But it has urged Beijing to clarify China's claims for the sake of ensuring the observance of international law and freedom of navigation for all.[72] At least until Lee Hsien Loong's fence-mending trip to Beijing in 2017, if not since, China has continued to suspect Singapore of harboring anti-China views, notwithstanding the merlion's continuing assurance that it sides with neither power — not the dragon, nor the eagle.

Must Singapore Choose?

In his 2012 book *The China Choice*, Australian strategic thinker Hugh White argued that China deserves to be treated as a major power and that the United States should share power and responsibility with China.[73] Singapore and other Southeast Asian countries still face differing specific versions of White's abstract "China choice," with particular reference to how their typically growing engagement with China may affect the autonomy of their foreign policies. Notwithstanding the benefits that Singapore gains from its China ties, are there costs that make the merlion vulnerable to pressures from the dragon — pressures that can no longer be relieved by recourse to cooperation and partnership with other countries including the United States? Bluntly put, is Singapore so dominated by China that it has few choices left but to line up with Beijing, like it or not? With these questions in mind, the next paragraphs briefly revisit in summary fashion the three spheres in which the two countries interact — economy, society, and security.

Economy Singapore is appropriately sensitive to the leverage that its Chinese involvements may cede to Beijing. But the case for significant Singaporean vulnerability is poor. The city-state's trade and investment linkages are diverse and reasonably balanced. Compared with its bilateral vulnerability with China, the greater risk may come from the global environment, especially the chance of collateral damage from American protectionism under Trump, Chinese mercantilism under Xi, and worsened relations between those two big powers.

Society Singaporeans do not think of their country as an outpost of China. Many of them have disapproved of newcomer "PRCs" with mainland ways and resented their government's efforts to attract "foreign talent," students and scholars from China included.[74] Yet most Singaporeans understand that the city-state's small population makes attracting and developing human capital a priority, or indeed a necessity.[75] Anti-immigrant sentiments among Singaporeans not having seriously jeopardized PAP rule, the country's policies on immigration are likely to continue, although more attention may be paid to upgrading the skills of the existing resident workforce.[76]

Security It is in this third and final sphere that both sensitivity and vulnerability are most evident. China has pursued its claims to the South China Sea assertively — to some, aggressively. Singapore's roles in 2015–18 at the interface of ASEAN-China relations and as the chair of ASEAN itself required the city-state's leaders to deal with China's maritime ambition. Beijing knew that Singapore was not a rival claimant to the South China Sea. But in 2016, already angered by Singapore's support for the arbitral court's rejection of China's nine-dash line in July, Beijing apparently prompted the detention in Hong Kong of Singapore Army vehicles being shipped home from military exercises on Taiwan.

PRC leaders had long resented the training of Singaporean soldiers on Taiwan, and the city-state had tried to mollify China by downsizing the exercises. At one point as many as 15,000 soldiers from Singapore had traveled to Taiwan to train at three different bases on the island, but that number was reduced to about 7,000, and later cut further to 3,000. Reportedly, the exercises will continue.[77] But they could someday be shrunk to the point of being purely symbolic in nature. Yet another frustration for Singapore has been the attempts by Beijing to undermine the unity and thus the efficacy of ASEAN. A case in point was the "four-point consensus" that Beijing incorrectly claimed to have reached with Brunei, Laos, and Cambodia in 2016.[78] Finally and notably, Singapore's evident sensitivity toward China's influence and actions has not stopped the merlion from freely engaging in a security partnership with the eagle.

As this chapter has shown, Singapore's rulers have long emphasized their country's vulnerability, arguably in part to ensure their relevance as keepers of its security. In fact, however, constraints on the city-state's foreign policy specifically regarding what China says, or does, or could do have not rendered Singapore as broadly vulnerable as its leaders may claim.

Singapore does not face an either-or "China choice." Its policy autonomy has survived both despite and because of its close ties with China. Singaporeans have willingly engaged with China and drawn benefit therefrom. The engagement has been problematic at times, but sensitivity has not blossomed into fear based on vulnerability. Notwithstanding the uncertainties attached to the presidency of Donald Trump, Singapore's leaders do not expect Beijing to replace Washington anytime soon as the internationally acknowledged guarantor of security in Asia.[79] In their view, China is neither ready nor willing to be responsible for managing the international order. Nor is China seeking what the late American foreign-policy advisor Zbigniew Brzezinski called a "G2" partnership with the United States, especially not if it entails a burdensome role for Beijing as a global provider of public goods.[80] Caveats regarding Donald Trump aside, as of 2018, events had still not refuted Lee Kuan Yew's case for the regional indispensability of America — rather than China — whether the region is called the Asia-Pacific, the Indo-Pacific, or the Indo-Asia-Pacific.[81]

Of necessity and from rational desire, Singapore will remain sensitive to Beijing. But China's rise has by no means foreordained a progression from understandable concern to a vulnerability so perilous as to call for acquiescence in Chinese control.

Notes

1 Quoted in an interview with the *Straits Times* on 16 January 2010, available as "ST: We Are Not Vulnerable? They Can Beseige [*sic*] You. You'll Be Dead," SLOW Movement, 16 January 2011, https://chutzpah .typepad.com/slow_movement/2011/01/st-we-are-not-vulnerable -they-can-beseige-you-youll-be-dead.html. For this and other *Straits Times* interviews with Lee, see Han Fook Kwang et al., eds., *Lee Kuan Yew: Hard Truths to Keep Singapore Going* (Singapore: Straits Times Press, 2011).

2 Vivian Balakrishnan, "Singapore-China Relations: A Progressive Partnership," *China Daily*, 29 February 2016, republished the same day in the *Straits Times*, https://www.straitstimes.com/singapore/singapore -china-ties-a-progressive-partnership-says-singapores-foreign-minister.

3 Cary Huang, "Communist Party Journal Suggests It Could Learn from Singapore's PAP," *South China Morning Post*, 23 October 2012; "China's Top Officials Study at Singapore's Knee," *Asahi Shimbun*, 29 June 2010, http://news.asiaone.com/News/Education/Story/A1Story20100629 -224342.html.

4 Lee Kuan Yew, *From Third World to First* (New York: Harper Business, 2011), 663–64.

5 See Seng Tan, "Faced with the Dragon: Perils and Prospects in Singapore's Ambivalent Relationship with China," *Chinese Journal of International Politics* 5, no. 3 (Autumn 2012): 245–65.

6 Carlyle A. Thayer, "Southeast Asia's Autonomy under Stress," in Malcolm Cook and Daljit Singh, eds., *Southeast Asian Affairs 2016* (Singapore: ISEAS Yusof Ishak Institute, 2016), 3–18.

7 Michael Leifer, *Singapore's Foreign Policy: Coping with Vulnerability* (London: Routledge, 2000). The subtitle of this work says it all.

8 Evelyn Goh, "Great Powers and Hierarchical Order in Southeast Asia: Analyzing Regional Security Strategies," *International Security* 32, no. 3 (Winter 2007/08): 113–57.

9 See Alan Chong, "Singapore's Foreign Policy Beliefs as 'Abridged Realism': Pragmatic and Liberal Prefixes in the Foreign Policy Thought of Rajaratnam, Lee, Koh, and Mahbubani," *International Relations of the Asia-Pacific* 6, no. 2 (2006): 269–306; Narayana Ganesan, *Realism and Interdependence in Singapore's Foreign Policy* (London and New York:

Routledge, 2005); Amitav Acharya, *Singapore's Foreign Policy: The Search for Regional Order* (Singapore: World Scientific, 2008).

10 Miriam Fendius Elman, "The Foreign Policies of Small States: Challenging Neorealism in Its Own Backyard," *British Journal of Political Science* 25, no. 2 (April 1995): 171–217; Jeanne A. K. Hey, *Small States in World Politics: Explaining Foreign Policy Behavior* (Boulder, CO: Lynne Rienner, 2003).

11 Granted, "can" and "must" here are idealized categories. The reality, as is often said, lies somewhere in between.

12 Robert O. Keohane and Joseph S. Nye, *Power and Interdependence*, second edition (Boston, MA: Scott, Foresman and Co., 1989).

13 Keohane and Nye, *Power and Interdependence*, 11–19.

14 Leifer, *Singapore's Foreign Policy*.

15 For an analysis of the ideological and political ties between the Chinese and Malayan Communist Parties and their impact on Singapore in the prewar, wartime, and postwar periods, see *The Malayan Communist Party in the Federation of Malaya*, a report prepared in April 1956 by a British government intelligence agency and filed with "The Cold War in Asia (1945–1990)" documentary database, a project of the Asia Research Institute, National University of Singapore, accessed 3 November 2012, http://www.ari.nus.edu.sg/docs/SEA-China-interactions -Cluster/TheColdWarInAsia/1956%20Report%20on%20Malayan%20 Communist%20Party%20in%20the%20Federation%20of%20 Malaya.pdf.

16 The emphasis by Singapore's leaders on its alleged vulnerability to threats did, to be sure, have "productive" uses beyond general legitimation, notably in mobilizing support for economic development and nation-building. These implications are discussed in See Seng Tan and Alvin Chew, "Governing Singapore's Security Sector: Problems, Prospects and Paradox," *Contemporary Southeast Asia* 30, no. 2 (August 2008): 241–63.

17 Ralf Emmers, Mely Caballero-Anthony, and Amitav Acharya, eds., *Studying Non-traditional Security in Asia: Trends and Issues* (Singapore: Marshall Cavendish, 2006).

18 Andrew T. H. Tan, "Punching above Its Weight: Singapore's Armed Forces and Its Contribution to Foreign Policy," *Defense Studies* 11, no. 4 (2011): 672–97. Likewise, the US ambassador to Singapore, David Adelman, had this to say in 2010 when he assumed that role: "Singapore

is a country that punches above its weight. They are a relatively
small country, but they have a very powerful economy." See "New US
Ambassador David Adelman Praises Singapore," Pressrun.net, 20 March
2010, accessed 2 November 2012, http://www.pressrun.net/weblog/2010
/03/new-us-ambassador-david-adelman-praises-singapore.html.

19 The history of Singapore's dependence on fresh water from Malaysia
is an instance of Singapore's success in becoming less vulnerable to its
neighbors. The city-state managed to diversify its sources to include
desalinated water and highly purified recycled water (whose potable
version is called Newater), in addition to gathering local-catchment water
in more than a dozen reservoirs. In Keohane-Nye terms, Singapore is still
sensitive to Malaysian pressure as a contingency of concern, but the city-
state is no longer structurally as vulnerable as it would have remained had
it not multiplied its sources. For the details, see Tim Huxley, "Singapore
and Malaysia: A Precarious Balance," *Pacific Review* 4, no. 3 (1991): 204–
13; Joey Long, "Desecuritizing the Water Issue in Singapore-Malaysia
Relations," *Contemporary Southeast Asia* 23, no. 3 (December 2001):
504–32; Kog Yue Choong, Irvin F.J. Lim, and Joey S.R. Long, *Beyond
Vulnerability? Water in Singapore-Malaysia Relations*, Monograph No.
3 (Singapore: Institute of Defence and Strategic Studies, 2002); and Ming
Hwa Ting, "Singapore-Malaysia Relations Revisited: An 'English School'
IR Analysis," *New Zealand Journal of Asian Studies* 11, no. 2 (December
2009): 172–98.

20 Poon Kim Shee, "Singapore's Foreign Policies towards the People's
Republic of China since 1965," in *China ASEAN Relations: Political,
Economic and Ethnic Dimensions*, ed. Theresa C. Carino (Manila: China
Studies Program, De La Salle University, 1991), 111.

21 John Wong, "Sino-Singapore Relations: Looking Back and Looking
Forward," Singapore China Friendship Association, http://www.singapore
-china.org/profile/selected2.shtml.

22 Edwin Lee, *Singapore: The Unexpected Nation* (Singapore: ISEAS,
2008), 417–52. Lee's book on the history of Singapore's nation-building
efforts includes a fascinating analysis of the ethnic-Chinese population's
divided loyalties: between identifying with the Chinese community and
possibly heeding the siren calls of Chinese chauvinism and China-inspired
communism, on the one hand, and the vision of a multiracial and multi-
religious nation on the other.

23 Kenneth Paul Tan, "The Ideology of Pragmatism: Neo-liberal Globalization and Political Authoritarianism in Singapore," *Journal of Contemporary Asia* 42, no. 1 (2012): 67–92.

24 Poon Kim Shee, "Singapore-China Special Economic Relations: In Search of Business Opportunities," *Ritsumeikan International Affairs* 3 (2005): 154.

25 Shee, "Singapore-China Special Economic Relations," 151.

26 Audrey Chia, "Singapore's Economic Internationalization and Its Effects on Work and Family," *Sojourn: Journal of Social Issues in Southeast Asia* 15, no. 1 (2000): 123–38; Kuik Cheng-chwee, "The Essence of Hedging: Malaysia and Singapore's Response to a Rising China," *Contemporary Southeast Asia* 30, no. 2 (August 2008): 159–85. Economic engagement with advanced economic and industrial powers and markets has indeed long been a key strategy for Singapore, as elucidated by Lee Kuan Yew in a speech he gave in India in 1996: "We had decided soon after independence to link Singapore up with the advanced countries and make ourselves a hub or nodal point for the expansion and extension of their activities." Cited in Leifer, *Singapore's Foreign Policy*, 12.

27 "Singapore, China to Sign Free Trade Pact in Beijing," Channel News Asia, 21 October 2008, http://www.channelnewsasia.com/stories/singa porelocalnews/view/384360/1/.html.

28 Luyao Wang, "China's Expanding Outward Investment in Singapore," *East Asia Policy* 4, no. 2 (April and June 2012): 73–84.

29 Cited in Nicholas Kristof, "China Sees Singapore as a Model for Progress," *New York Times*, 9 August 1992.

30 "China's Top Officials Study at Singapore's Knee."

31 Huang, "Communist Party Journal Suggests It Could Learn from Singapore's PAP."

32 Daniel Workman, "China's Top Trading Partners," WTEx, 24 March 2018, http://www.worldstopexports.com/chinas-top-import-partners.

33 "Overall Exports and Imports for Singapore 2016," WITS, World Bank Group, https://wits.worldbank.org/CountrySnapshot/en/SGP /textview.

34 "Singapore's International Trade," Department of Statistics, Singapore (see under infographic "Merchandise Trade Performance with Major Trading Partners, 2018"), accessed 16 February 2019, https:// www.singstat.gov.sg/modules/infographics/singapore-international-trade;

and OH Yun Ah, "China's Economic Ties with Southeast Asia," *World Economy Brief* 7, no. 18 (4 September 2017): 4, Figure 6a.

35 Stephanie Luo, "Singapore Top Destination for China Investments," *Straits Times*, 8 December 2017, http://www.straitstimes.com/business /economy/spore-top-destination-for-china-investments.

36 Catherine Wong, "From Trade to Trains, China and Singapore Boost Their Economic Ties," *South China Morning Post*, 20 September 2017, www.scmp.com/news/china/diplomacy-defence/article/2112051/trade -trains-china-and-singapore-boost-their-economic.

37 Liu Yunhua and Ng Boey Kui, "Impact of a Rising Chinese Economy and ASEAN's Responses," Working Paper No. 2007/03, Economic Growth Centre, Nanyang Technological University, Singapore: 2007, 1.

38 Peck Ming Chuang, "SM Lee — S'pore Must Remake Itself," *Business Times*, 16 October 2001.

39 "China Races to Replace US as Economic Power in Asia: NY Times," *PeopleDaily.com*, 28 June 2002, accessed 7 November 2012, http://english .peopledaily.com.cn/200206/28/eng20020628_98737.shtml.

40 "China Races to Replace US as Economic Power in Asia."

41 Hui Yin Loh, "Singapore 'to Finish Only Portion of Suzhou Park'," *Straits Times*, 10 June 1999; Michael Richardson, "Singapore Industrial Park Flounders: A Deal Sours in China," *New York Times*, 1 October 1999.

42 Kristof, "China Sees Singapore as a Model for Progress."

43 Leifer, *Singapore's Foreign Policy*, 121.

44 Government of Singapore, *2014 Population in Brief* (Singapore: National Population and Talent Division, September 2014), 11 (Chart 6), http://www.nptd.gov.sg/portals/0/news/population-in-brief-2014.pdf.

45 Stanislav Myšička, "Chinese Support for Communist Insurgencies in Southeast Asia during the Cold War," *International Journal of China Studies* 6, no. 3 (December 2015): 203–30.

46 Yew, *From Third World to First*, 665.

47 Leong Weng Kam, "Completed China Cultural Centre to Boost Arts Exchange," *Straits Times*, 1 September 2015, http://www.straitstimes .com/singapore/completed-china-cultural-centre-to-boost-arts-exchange; John Wong and Lye Liang Fook, "China-Singapore Relations: Looking Back and Looking Forward," in *Singapore-China Relations: 50 Years*,

eds. Zheng Yongnian and Lye Liang Fook (Singapore: World Scientific, 2016), 1–29.

48 See Ng Jing Yng, "Chinese Tourists, Marketing Blitz Lift Singapore Tourism," *TODAY*, 12 February 2016, http://www.channelnewsasia.com/news/singapore/chinese-tourists/2508652.html; and Brenda Yeoh and Weiqiang Lin, "Rapid Growth in Singapore's Immigrant Population Brings Policy Challenges," *Migration Policy Institute*, 3 April 2012, http://www.migrationpolicy.org/article/rapid-growth-singapores-immigrant-population-brings-policy-challenges.

49 Government of Singapore, *2014 Population in Brief* (Singapore: Prime Minister's Office, September 2014), 14 (Table 1). "Foreigners" for this purpose are nonresidents and permanent residents but not (or not yet) citizens.

50 Hing Ai Yun, Lee Kiat Jin, and Sheng Sixin, "Mainland Chinese 'Foreign Talents' in Singapore," *Asian Journal of Social Science* 37, no. 5 (2009): 757–77.

51 "PM Lee Speaks Out against Xenophobia," *AsiaOne*, 26 August 2012, http://www.asiaone.com/News/Latest%2BNews/Singapore/Story/A1Story20120826-367701.html.

52 In 2011 the fertility rate in Singapore, by ethnicity, was 1.08 for the Chinese, 1.09 for Indians, and 1.64 for Malays. "S'poreans Respond to LKY's Comments on Birth Rate," *Today Online*, 13 August 2012, http://www.todayonline.com/Voices/EDC120813-0000029/Sporeans-respond-to-LKYs-comments-on-birth-rate.

53 Richard Halloran, "China's Decisive Role in the Asian Financial Crisis," Global Beat Issue Brief, No. 24, 27 January 1998, http://www.bu.edu/globalbeat/pubs/ib24.html.

54 Andrew Jacobs, "In Singapore, Vitriol against Chinese Newcomers," *New York Times*, 26 July 2012; Mark Fenn, "Singapore's Foreigner Problem," *The Diplomat*, 21 February 2014, http://thediplomat.com/2014/02/singapores-foreigner-problem.

55 Er-Xin Lee, *Chinese Nationals Among "Overseas Chinese" in Singapore* (Ann Arbor, MI: UMI Microform, 2007), 14–17.

56 Jacobs, "In Singapore, Vitriol against Chinese Newcomers."

57 "Outcry over China-born Feng Tianwei Being Singapore's Flag-bearer at the London Olympics," *Temasek Times*, 29 July 2012, http://temasektimes.wordpress.com/2012/07/29/outcry-over-china-born-feng-tianwei-being-singapores-flag-bearer-at-the-london-olympics.

58　"Majority of Singaporeans Not Proud of Bronze Medal Won by
China-born Feng Tianwei," *Temasek Times,* 2 August 2012, accessed 8
November 2012, http://temasektimes.wordpress.com/2012/08/02/majority
-of-singaporeans-not-proud-of-bronze-medal-won-by-china-born-feng
-tianwei. According to this article, "77 percent" of respondents to an
"online poll by Yahoo News" were "not proud of a foreign import
winning a medal" for Singapore in Beijing. The piece also stated that Feng
was "widely criticized by Singaporeans for throwing flowers at cheering
PRC fans after her victory over Japan's Kasumi Ishikawa, a clear sign
that she [Feng] has not forgotten her motherland which is China and not
Singapore." Embedded in the piece is a video clip showing what may well
have been Feng throwing a bunch of flowers to a crowd, but that is hardly
a "clear sign" of disloyalty to Singapore. Nor could the veracity of the
"77 percent" be independently determined.

59　Lee, *Chinese Nationals among "Overseas Chinese" in Singapore.*

60　In the angst-ridden words of one Singaporean netizen: "Native
Singaporeans are losing out in every sector of the economy — jobs,
housing, education, etc. [—] to this huge influx of new immigrants.
They take over most of the jobs in the service industries [—] hotels,
food courts, retail centers, hawker centers, etc. [—] and now native
Singaporeans have to speak their language in order to get any service or
anything done. Most local food [*sic*] are no longer authentic but blended
with Mainland Chinese cooking flavor. Native Singaporeans are losing
their identities, culture, local cuisine and very soon their Singlish and
future." See Wing Lee Cheong, "The Last of the Native Singaporeans,"
SG-Quitters, 1 May 2012, accessed 31 March 2018, http://sg-quitters.blog
spot.sg/2012/05/last-of-native-singaporeans.html. Singlish is distinctively
Singaporean — a colloquial, English-based amalgam of adaptations from
various languages including Malay and several Chinese dialects.

61　Maria Siow, "Singapore-China Military Ties Not Mutually Exclusive,
Says Ng Eng Hen," Channel News Asia, 21 June 2012, accessed 8
November 2012, http://www.channelnewsasia.com/stories/singaporelocal
news/view/1209073/1/.html.

62　See Seng Tan and Bhubhindar Singh, "Introduction: Defense
Diplomacy in Southeast Asia," *Asian Security* 8, no. 3 (2012): 221–31.

63　"Chinese, Singapore Discuss Defense Ties," *Daily Mail Online
Edition*, accessed 8 November 2012, http://dailymailnews.com/0511/17
/ChinaPage/index.php?id=2 ().

64 Ian Storey, "China's Bilateral Defense Diplomacy in Southeast Asia," *Asian Security* 8, no. 3 (2012): 287–310.

65 Janice Tai, "SAF and People's Liberation Army Carry Out Bilateral Exercise in Nanjing," *Straits Times*, 2 November 2014, accessed 20 May 2016, http://www.straitstimes.com/news/singapore/more-singapore-stories/story/saf-and-peoples-liberation-army-carry-out-bilateral-exer#sthash.AryEAnDM.dpuf.

66 Storey, "China's Bilateral Defense Diplomacy in Southeast Asia."

67 See Seng Tan, "Mailed Fists and Velvet Gloves: The Relevance of Smart Power to Singapore's Evolving Defense and Foreign Policy," *Journal of Strategic Studies* 38, no. 3 (2015): 332–58.

68 Richard Sokolsky, Angel Rabasa, and C. Richard Neu, *The Role of Southeast Asia in U.S. Strategy Toward China* (Santa Monica, CA: RAND, 2001), 33.

69 *Asia-Pacific Maritime Security Strategy: Achieving U.S. National Security Objectives in a Changing Environment* (Washington, DC: US Department of Defense, August 2015), 16.

70 Gordon Lubold, "Pentagon Says China Has Stepped Up Land Reclamation in South China Sea," *Wall Street Journal*, 20 August 2015, http://www.wsj.com/articles/pentagon-says-china-has-stepped-up-land-reclamation-in-south-china-sea-1440120837.

71 Laura Zhou, "United States to Remain World's Number 1 Power 'for a Fairly Long Time': Beijing," *South China Morning Post*, 21 May 2016, http://www.scmp.com/news/china/diplomacy-defence/article/1948896/united-states-remain-worlds-number-1-power-fairly-long.

72 Jane Chan, "Singapore and the South China Sea: Being an Effective Coordinator and Honest Broker," *Asia Policy*, no. 21 (January 2016): 41–46.

73 Hugh White, *The China Choice: Why America Should Share Power* (Melbourne, VIC: Black Inc. Publishing, 2012).

74 Peidong Yang, *International Mobility and Educational: Chinese Foreign Talent Students in Singapore* (New York: Palgrave Macmillan, 2016).

75 "Majority Say Foreign Talent Is the Way to Go," *New Chapter*, 8 August 2012; see also S. Ramesh, "S'pore Cannot Do without Foreign Talent: Ex-MM Lee," Channel News Asia, 22 July 2011, http://www

.tremeritus.com/2012/08/03/foreign-sports-talent-policy-and-political
-repercussion-to-pap/.

76 Chia Yan Min, "Singapore Budget 2018: That Missing Debate on
Singapore's Foreign Talent Policy," *Business Times*, 6 March 2018, http://
www.businesstimes.com.sg/government-economy/singapore-budget-2018
/singapore-budget-2018-that-missing-debate-on-singapores.

77 Reuters, "Singapore Military Juggles Ties with Taiwan, China,"
Epoch Times, 25 August 2006, http://www.theepochtimes.com/news
/6-8-25/45307.html; and Lawrence Chung, "Singapore 'Assures' Taiwan
that Military Training Agreement Will Stay, Taipei Says," *South China
Morning Post*, 2 October 2017, http://www.scmp.com/news/china
/diplomacy-defence/article/2113687/singapore-assures-taiwan-military
-training-agreement.

78 For example, Singaporean senior diplomat Ong Keng Yong, who
served as secretary-general of ASEAN from 2003 to 2007, criticized
the consensus statement made by Chinese foreign minister Wang Yi as
amounting to China meddling in the internal affairs of ASEAN. Francis
Chan, "China Criticised for Apparent Attempt to Divide Asean," *Straits
Times*, 26 April 2016, http://www.straitstimes.com/asia/china-criticised
-for-apparent-attempt-to-divide-asean.

79 Robert G. Sutter, *China's Rise in Asia — Promises, Prospects and
Implications for the United States*, Occasional Chapter Series (Honolulu,
HI: Asia-Pacific Center for Security Studies, 2005), 5.

80 François Godement, "Introduction," in *No Rush into Marriage:
China's Response to the G2*, China Analysis no. 22, European Council
on Foreign Relations/Asia Centre at SciencesPo., June 2009. Chinese
State Councilor Dai Bingguo later counter-proposed a "C2" whereby
the two powers would somehow "coordinate" with each other in global
governance. Wang Qi, "China and U.S. Not G2, but C2," *Sina English*, 4
May 2012, accessed 16 February 2019, http://english.sina.com/china/2012
/0503/464519.html.

81 Chua Chin Hon and Tracy Quek, "MM Calls on US to Retain Key
Role in East Asia," *Straits Times*, 29 October 2009.

CHAPTER 9

Underbalancing the Dragon
UNSTRATEGIC INDONESIA

Yohanes Sulaiman, *General Ahmad Yani University, Indonesia*

This chapter assesses Indonesian foreign policy toward China with particular reference to the South China Sea. The assessment supports an argument. The argument is that, in the realm of security, Jakarta lacks a coherent plan for dealing strategically with China, due in part to the inward orientation of the Indonesian military. The chapter analyzes Indonesia's traditionally "free and active" foreign policy and its association with the decade-long administration of President Susilo Bambang Yudhoyono (2004–14), known as "SBY." Featured are the insularity of the Indonesian military and Yudhoyono's reliance on the Association of Southeast Asian Nations (ASEAN) as a site for hoped-for constructive dialogue regarding the South China Sea disputes and China's role therein. The chapter then considers the China policy preferred by the follow-on administration of President Joko ("Jokowi") Widodo. Elected to his first five-year term in 2014, Jokowi was re-elected in 2019 for another five years. His and Yudhoyono's policies are found to have differed more in style than in substance regarding the South China Sea. Both presidents avoided or downplayed criticism of Beijing's military assertions there. The chapter ends by projecting that continuity into the future insofar as things remain more or less equal over the course of Jokowi's second presidential term.

Pressing Issues and Lagging Forces

Indonesian decision-makers have not always given China the benefit of the doubt. In a survey of Indonesian leaders in 1966, for instance, a majority viewed China as "aggressive" and "a serious threat to Indonesia." Navy officers even worried that Beijing could launch an invasion of Indonesia from the Chinese island of Hainan in the northwestern corner of the South China Sea.[1] During the Cold War, twin fears of China and communism rationalized Jakarta's only foreign adventure under the authoritarian presidency of General Suharto (1968–98), the 1975 invasion of East Timor, justified as forestalling the creation of a "Southeast Asian Cuba" inside Indonesia.[2]

Sino-Indonesian relations have improved greatly since then, especially following the resumption of diplomatic ties in 1990. Yet many in Indonesia's elite circles still see China as a threat, notably in view of the ongoing upgrading of its military power, a trend used in Jakarta as evidence of Indonesia's need to respond in kind.[3] As for the notion of a "Chinese invasion," it remains a potent issue, available for use by unscrupulous political actors hoping to score partisan gains in a country whose population was estimated in the 2010 census to be 87 percent Muslim and only 1 percent ethnically Chinese.[4]

The 2017 election for governor of Jakarta offers more evidence of concern. In that contest, the ethnically Chinese Christian incumbent, Basuki "Ahok" Tjahaja Purnama, ran and lost, despite his enviable 70 percent approval rating[5] and his close association with the popular president, Jokowi. The campaign was tainted by ethno-religious slanders to the point of being called one of the most divisive electoral competitions Indonesia had ever seen.[6] Opponents of Ahok maligned him by suggesting that Beijing was trying to inflate his support by providing false identity cards to people who would then illegally vote for him. Such purveyors of fake news cast him as a Chinese "Manchurian candidate" preparing to steal the election.[7] Even Jokowi had to address the rumor that Beijing might be sending 10 million Chinese to work illegally in Indonesia[8] as an advance invasion force in a plot to colonize the country.[9]

Suspicion and fear aimed at Ahok and Beijing did not, however, redirect Indonesian foreign policy against China. Rather than alienate Beijing, Jokowi's administration preferred to engage it. That practice had been maintained, with mixed results, by all of Indonesia's presidents since the country's latest experiment with democracy began following President Suharto's resignation in 1998.

Engagement is one thing; coherence is another. Neither Yudhoyono (SBY) in his two presidential terms, nor Jokowi in his first term, was able to fashion and pursue a clear, consistent, comprehensive strategy for dealing with China's growing influence in Southeast Asia, including in the South China Sea. Indonesia's diplomacy under these leaders was not inactive, but it was more reactive than proactive. There were differences. SBY and his foreign minister Marty Natalegawa strongly favored a multilateral approach. In contrast, Jokowi's interactions with China have been more bilateral, and he has been willing, on occasion, to act unilaterally as well. But these are differences of means not ends, related more to the two leaders' personal styles than to a consistently planned and purposeful way of dealing with Beijing.

One of the reasons for the absence of a full-spectrum strategy beyond diplomatic interchange is simply that the weakness of Indonesia's military has precluded its use as leverage in relations with China. Indonesia's armed forces have difficulty just keeping their equipment up to date, let alone purchasing more, given the absence of adequate budgets. In 2014, Yudhoyono's deputy minister of defense noted that the military budget could fund only 40 percent of what was needed to develop a "minimum essential force"—merely to protect Indonesia's own physical integrity,[10] never mind projecting power beyond its borders.

Most of the military's budget is spent on personnel.[11] Little money is left to replace aging weaponry, let alone to try challenging China. Relevant, too, is the vast difference between Chinese and Indonesian military outlays. In 2014, China's annual budget for its armed forces stood at USD $200 billion compared to Indonesia's $6.5 billion. In other words, Asia's third biggest country in physical size and the world's fourth largest by population was willing to commit to its defense a mere 3 percent of what China was willing to spend. Compared to Yudhoyono, Jokowi did allocate more to the military,[12] despite slower economic growth. But that was a far cry from Jokowi's promise to triple the amount.[13]

From 2017 to 2018, Indonesian military spending actually declined by 6.2 percent, while Chinese commitments continued to grow—7.0 percent in 2017 and 8.1 percent in 2018 based on official figures, and probably faster in reality.[14] There was no reason for Indonesia to wage an arms race it could not win. But it did not follow from that futility that the weakened state of its armed forces should be ignored.

Yudhoyono understood the importance of military power, as does Jokowi. Their approaches differed. Yudhoyono tried to make the armed forces more professional; Jokowi raised their budgets. But neither president entertained major reforms, and it could be argued that Jokowi did not even try minor ones. For both men, other priorities intervened. Yudhoyono, obsessed with the need to maintain political stability, avoided changes that he thought would upset the status quo and invite conflict and controversy.[15] His reluctance ignored recommendations to reorient the military away from domestic security by slashing the number of troops and thereby releasing more money for weapons procurement and the externally cautionary if not deterrent effect that could have had.[16]

Jokowi has had bigger fish to fry. These pressing issues have included Indonesia's deteriorating infrastructure, neglected during the Yudhoyono administration and needing funds for repair and replacement estimated to run as high as 27 percent of the country's gross domestic product.[17] Among Jokowi's other challenges have been the global slowdown that has depressed commodity prices and hurt Indonesia's economy; the persisting high rate of poverty; and the inhibiting effect of red-tape bureaucracy on economic growth.[18] These predicaments have taken the lion's share of the president's attention.

In addition, the previously mentioned defeat of the president's ally Ahok in the Jakarta gubernatorial election in 2017 cast doubt on Jokowi's chances for re-election in 2019. (The Jakarta governor's contest came to be seen as a virtual dress rehearsal for the presidential contest.)[19] Hard-line nationalists and Islamists have targeted Jokowi, falsely accusing him of communist ties and sympathies. [20] Such charges make it politically harder for him to reform the military by reducing its size.

Jokowi's anti-communist opponents might want him to challenge China directly. But he knows that could jeopardize badly needed Chinese investment in Indonesia's sluggish economy. China's construction of military bases on seven artificially built-up islands in the South China Sea is concerning.[21] But Jakarta only pushes back when it thinks Beijing's behavior goes too far. Chinese incursions in waters off Indonesia's Natuna Island have, to a limited extent, been a case in point.[22] Domestic problems have nevertheless continued to upstage foreign ones as priorities for presidential attention.

Free and Active between Two Reefs

The philosophy of Indonesia's foreign policy can be traced clear back to the perilous years of the country's struggle for independence. Notably, in a speech on 2 September 1948, then vice president Mohammad Hatta argued that Indonesia should not align itself with either the Soviet Union or the United States, but should instead be energetic and autonomous: "an *active agent* entitled to decide its own standpoint."[23]

Hatta's administration at that time was extremely vulnerable. His nascent republic was besieged and blockaded by the Dutch, who wanted to get their former colony back by inducing its economic collapse. The republic's armed forces were shambolic for lack of training and equipment.[24] At the same time, Hatta's leftist opponents, hoping to align Indonesia with the Soviet Union, were busy denigrating his administration for what they saw as his obeisance to the United States.

It is important to note that Hatta drafted and delivered his remarks in response to mounting domestic pressures. He was trying to blunt the arguments of Indonesians who wanted the beleaguered republic to side with the USSR. In Hatta's reasoning, that step would further imperil the newborn state: Aligning with Moscow would only confirm Dutch accusations that the insurgent republic was controlled by communists. That would in turn alienate Washington at a time when an American role as an honest broker between rebelling Indonesians and the returning Dutch was badly needed. Hatta's "free and active" policy was a desperate effort to allay domestic fears and refute domestic accusations by endorsing Indonesia's autonomy in foreign policy. Hatta knew that Indonesia was then, in fact, too weak to be autonomous and that it needed American support if the nascent republic were to become independent in a more than rhetorically "free and active" sense.[25]

Hatta's coinage was soon taken from this specifically domestic context and enshrined as a guiding principle of Indonesian foreign policy. First published in 1951 under the title *Mendajung antara dua karang* (Rowing between two reefs),[26] the idea of a "free and active" role for Indonesia in the larger world became an institutionalized fixture in the country's policy culture. The centrality and longevity of the idea would be assured a few years later, in 1955, when then Prime Minister Ali Sastroamidjojo oversaw a major international triumph by hosting the Asia-Africa Conference in Bandung,[27] a key precursor of the Non-aligned Movement.

As time went by, the entrenched symbolic importance of "free and active" obliged successive Indonesian administrations to adhere to such a policy, at least in principle, lest they be denounced by political opponents as willing to surrender the republic's independence in foreign affairs.[28] Yet the phrase has been criticized for elevating symbol above substance,[29] and it can be constraining as well. That risk arises to the extent that the "free and active" slogan is used to recommend actively seeking autonomy without taking into account Indonesia's actual economic and military capacity to be and remain fully autonomous and, by implication, entirely non-aligned. One can also ask how helpful it still is, two decades after the end of the Cold War, for Indonesia to picture itself navigating, freely and actively, a course equidistant from two equally dangerous Chinese and American "reefs" in the South China Sea.

The Indonesian military cannot avoid this tension between autonomy and capacity. A defining characteristic of the country's military officers is their aversion to involving their country in a military alliance. They acknowledge the benefits of alliances, especially when one partner helps the other one modernize its forces.[30] But they also know that a military pact would likely violate the "free and active" rule. Worse, an alliance could sacrifice the very autonomy that an ally's assistance in capacity-building might have helped to enable. An alliance, they fear, could trap Indonesia in debilitating webs of dependence and entanglement.[31]

Reinforcing this ethos of self-reliance in Indonesia's armed forces is their commanders' commitment to *resilience*, including the idea that the strength of one's spirit is more important than the strength of one's hard power in funds and arms — that with sheer will and courage one can and must keep struggling against one's enemies, regardless of which side is better armed and trained.[32] This fixation on resilience inspires the military's desire to rely solely on its own strength when facing outside threats.

To illustrate: In 1971, during the Cold War, Malaysia proposed the creation of a zone of neutrality in Southeast Asia whose non-alignment would be guaranteed by the United States, the Soviet Union, and China. Indonesia objected, arguing that rather than allocate such a role to outsiders, the ASEAN states should develop and rely on the inner strength of their own resilience. In essence, "the only way to guarantee security in Southeast Asia was for each nation to strengthen itself internally" first, especially by growing its domestic economy so as to afford the modernization of its armed forces using its own resources.[33]

A lack of trust in the militaries of other countries bolsters this outlook. An ally may not stay allied. Defense cooperation may provide cover for the ally's spies to operate in Indonesia.[34] The risk of external reliance was brought home when Washington curtailed military relations with Jakarta in the aftermath of a 1991 massacre of civilian demonstrators in East Timor by Indonesian troops. All US military ties were suspended in 1999 following further bloodshed in the wake of Indonesia's defeat in that year's referendum on Timorese independence. Many Indonesian officers saw the American embargo as a betrayal of the close military relations that Washington had built with Jakarta during the Cold War.[35] In Indonesian military circles, the suspension of those ties bolstered the belief that the country could rely only itself and augmented local support for developing a strong indigenous defense industry with that goal in mind.[36]

As a general proposition, up to a point, growing one's economy before improving one's military makes sense. But it does not necessarily follow that the resulting material gains will then be invested in defense, as Indonesia's experience has shown.

Sovereignty versus Contingency?

Aware of their country's vulnerability to outsiders, the armed forces zealously guard the Indonesian nation and oppose entering agreements perceived as jeopardizing its territorial integrity.

Consider the 2004 Malacca Strait Security Initiative (MSSI). Indonesia, Malaysia, and Singapore fashioned the agreement ostensibly to counteract incidents of piracy and terrorism that had come to threaten the security of commerce in that crucial maritime lane. In reality, however, that was not the threat that Jakarta and Kuala Lumpur cared most about. What bothered them most was the chance that Singapore might join an American-proposed regional maritime security initiative. Indonesia and Malaysia feared that Singapore's close ties with the United States could facilitate the involvement of Americans and potentially other outsiders in co-managing the Malacca Strait. In the eyes of Indonesian and Malaysian leaders, sharing that responsibility with international actors risked inviting threats to the territorial integrity of their own respective countries.[37] In rejecting the American proposal and instead joining Singapore to create an indigenous, three-state MSSI, Jakarta and Kuala Lumpur sought to preempt American interference in ensuring the security of a crucial waterway whose borders they shared.[38]

Further illustrating these nationalist concerns, the MSSI disallowed "hot pursuit." One country in the trio could not freely chase pirates across the border between its territorial waters and those of another member of the trio. The pursuer was required to contact the other country and let it take over the chase. Such operations were coordinated, but they were not jointly conducted, so that each of the three partners would be safe from unilateral incursion by either of the other two, despite the interest they all shared in keeping their common borders secure.[39]

A conviction that Indonesia must be the sole and sovereign master of its own house creates a quandary for its armed forces as to what Jakarta should say or do about the disputes over the South China Sea. Indonesian officers are well aware of their unpreparedness should these rivalries someday kindle a war, and they also know that sooner or later such a conflict would likely drag them in. The 2008 edition of the defense ministry's *White Book* already viewed regional disputes over sovereignty as potential triggers of confrontations in which Indonesia might not be able to avoid involvement.[40]

The quandary arises from a contingency: the possibility that in such a conflict scenario, one of the contending states, notably China, might need to be treated as an adversary of Indonesia. Civilian officials in Jakarta, and to an extent even military leaders, have basically denied that contingency. They have accepted the idea that no country should be considered a potential enemy. Accordingly, as noted later in this chapter, Indonesia has officially described itself as having only friends, not enemies. But if everyone is a friend and no one is an enemy, and treating a friend as a could-be enemy would be unfriendly, the reason for contingency planning backed by hard power disappears.[41] So does the incentive to identify what threats exist, or are likely to arise, and to think about how to deal with them.

The 2015 *White Book* did cite the South China Sea disputes. But it avoided acknowledging China's role therein. Unmentioned, for example, was Beijing's "nine-dash line," which cuts into the exclusive economic zones (EEZs) of Indonesia and other littoral countries and bears major responsibility for the associated maritime tensions.[42] A 2012 defense ministry regulation on Indonesia's need for a "minimum essential force" might have been expected to focus on foreign threats, but it mainly featured domestic threats to domestic security. These included separatism, natural disasters, illegal activities, energy shortages, financial turmoil, and pollution of the environment. "Foreign military aggression" was mentioned, but not further defined.[43] As noted by one analyst, the "minimum essential force" that the defense ministry had in mind was designed less to develop Indonesia's ability to defend itself in a possible conflict with China than simply to meet existing requirements while improving the administration of defense.[44]

One might think that Indonesia's military establishment would want to be prepared for a possible physical clash with China, and would cultivate partnerships with other countries, including the United States, with that contingency in mind. But the officers in charge of Indonesia's armed forces continue to stress self-strengthening and diplomacy instead. They are not averse to cooperation with the militaries of other countries. The Indonesian Navy, for example, is interested in interoperability and coordination with foreign navies. But fully integrated maritime operations are avoided lest they be taken as rehearsals for an alliance.[45] In keeping with such restraint, Indonesia's 2018 defense policy paper reaffirms the importance of self-defense and self-strengthening along with cooperation through diplomatic dialogue and improved satellite communication.[46]

Yudhoyono's "Zero Enemies" and ASEAN's Disarray

A "free and active" foreign policy suitable for navigating "between two reefs" during the Cold War meant siding neither with the United States nor with its Soviet or Chinese opponent. Toward the end of his first presidential term, Yudhoyono (SBY) advanced a new rationale for ruling out alliances. In November 2008, noting that his country had established partnerships with diverse countries including China, India, Japan, and Russia, he described Indonesia as pursuing an "all direction foreign policy" whereby Jakarta has "a thousand friends and zero enemy."[47] At the inauguration of his second term, he boosted that already lopsided ratio to "a million friends and zero enemy."[48]

According to SBY's foreign minister, Marty Natalegawa, by practicing a no-enemies foreign policy, he and the president were "aggressively waging peace,"[49] including building diplomatic relations with virtually every member of the United Nations[50] — Israel excepted, due to the domestic outcry recognition would trigger in a nearly 90 percent Muslim country. The aim and the logic were clear: Indonesia seeks partnerships with as many countries as possible; the more friends it has, the more secure it becomes.

Alongside "zero enemies," the concept of "dynamic equilibrium" also entered Indonesian political discourse. As developed by Natalegawa, this notion acknowledged that the region's international relations were constantly in flux. The influence exercised by different states necessarily waxed and waned, modifying the balance of power. But this pattern was not to be feared as a cause of regional instability. That would risk triggering muscular moves to counter a rising state, moves that would only trigger further confrontations. Instead, changes in the balance of power should be viewed in a positive light as opportunities for peaceful cooperation in areas such as trade and investment. Responding to the region's dynamics required a comprehensive approach including efforts to foster "a virtuous circle of confidence-building steps" fostering socioeconomic cooperation and progress sufficient to smooth political and security frictions.[51]

China was not singled out as a power whose rise could unbalance the region's "dynamic equilibrium." But SBY's and Natalegawa's neo-liberal argument had China very much in mind. Socioeconomic cooperation could generate interdependence and mutual trust, peacefully involve China in an ASEAN-hosted regional system, and thereby ensure the security of the region. Soft power would succeed where hard power could not. In tune with this logic, regarding tensions over sovereignty in the South China Sea, SBY's government reasoned that a "code of conduct" that states could observe in that body of water was needed above all to build their confidence in one another's peaceful intentions.[52]

Foreign policy generally and ASEAN in particular ranked high on Yudhoyono's list of priorities. This was partly a matter of personality. He relished the attentions of the international community and the respectful treatment he received from world leaders. Unlike his domestic critics, they praised him and appeared to value his accomplishments, making him all the more keen to make time for regional and global issues.[53] ASEAN was prominent on his policy horizon. He worked to strengthen what he saw as a vehicle well suited to contributing to peace and security not just in Southeast Asia but also in the wider world. He hoped other states could cultivate the habits of consultation on display at ASEAN meetings where leaders who would not otherwise be talking to one another could meet, discuss, and agree.[54]

Yet SBY's emphasis on ASEAN was not as disinterested as it might seem. As Dewi Fortuna Anwar argued more than two decades ago, if ASEAN were held in high regard as an influential grouping, its individual members would benefit as well. ASEAN could, in effect, magnify the ability of any one Southeast Asian state to make a difference in the region.[55] Although ASEAN and Indonesia have of course changed since she wrote, her argument is still pertinent. By playing up ASEAN, Yudhoyono could hope to compensate for the relative lack of influence Indonesia could exert by itself, given the evident weaknesses of Indonesia's economy and military — compared, for example, to the commercial centrality of Singapore and the hard-power prowess of China and the United States. An ASEAN-featuring foreign policy would also capitalize on Indonesia's status as by far the largest Southeast Asian country and therefore, by implication, the association's natural leader.

But how successful did Yudhoyono's and Natalegawa's approach to foreign affairs turn out to be? Its strategic purpose was unclear to critics inside and outside Indonesia. Broad hopes of friendship aside, the administration's conduct of foreign policy from day to day seemed haphazard. A high-ranking Indonesian naval officer said as much when this author interviewed him in October 2014. In an article published that same month, Australian analyst Aaron Connelly argued that "SBY's foreign policy vision was often short on details" and "avoided hard choices." An "all directions foreign policy" of making "a thousand friends and zero enemies" by definition avoided hard choices, he wrote. SBY had "prioritised the promotion of Indonesia's profile overseas ahead of progress on thorny issues in world affairs."[56]

The president's unwillingness to tackle hard choices not only marred Indonesian policy. Ironically in light of his emphasis on ASEAN, it hurt the association itself. Ironic, too, was the inadvertent creation of a leadership vacuum within ASEAN for lack of leadership by its natural leader. SBY's ASEAN was often aimless for being rudderless, especially when problems of regional security called for early warnings, creative thinking, and preventive diplomacy.[57]

A dramatic case in point unfolded in July 2012 in Phnom Penh when the 45th ASEAN Foreign Ministers Meeting, for the first time in the long history of that event, could not agree on the wording of its usual joint communiqué.

The background: In the South China Sea in February 2011, Chinese patrol vessels, apparently bent on implementing Beijing's expansive claim to land features within its infamous nine-dash line, fired shots at Philippine fishermen plying their trade within the Philippines' 200-nautical mile EEZ. Three months later, inside Vietnam's EEZ, Chinese vessels cut the underwater cables being used by a Vietnamese ship to survey for oil and gas, followed a month later by another such incident. In April 2012, a standoff between Beijing and Manila at Scarborough Shoal inside the Philippine EEZ grew into a full-blown crisis. As it intensified, China halted tourist travel to the Philippines and blocked Philippine fruit imports, ostensibly on health grounds by claiming that they carried 104 different types of "harmful organisms."[58] Beijing barred entrance to the shoal in July and soon thereafter seized sole control.

At the gathering of ASEAN foreign ministers in Phnom Penh that same month of July, Cambodia, already by then a Chinese client state, vetoed any mention of what it called "bilateral disputes" in the South China Sea, restating Beijing's argument that the disputes were not regional issues and therefore did not and should not involve ASEAN at all.[59] Indonesia's Natalegawa among other foreign ministers tried to convince their Cambodian host that the confrontation at Scarborough Shoal should at least be mentioned in the communiqué. Cambodia refused, its veto held, and silence ensued.

To his and Indonesia's credit, Natalegawa managed to contain the damage done to ASEAN's reputation. His shuttle diplomacy after the debacle yielded a face-saving "common position" comprising six broad principles to which even Cambodia agreed.[60] But that did not alter the shared responsibility for the fiasco in Phnom Penh. The ASEAN foreign ministers, one analyst wrote, had "acquiesced to Cambodia's high-handedness in vetoing the draft joint communiqué" despite its having been drawn up by four of their own ministerial colleagues. The regional interest of ASEAN had "played second fiddle to its relations with China."[61]

In the end, SBY's idea of Indonesia having a thousand friends and no enemies could not overcome the weaknesses of Indonesia's and ASEAN's geostrategic position vis-à-vis China. Since 2014, when Jokowi's presidency began, he has had to face the same limitations.

Jokowi's "Maritime Fulcrum" and the South China Sea

On 22 June 2014, during his third presidential debate with Prabowo Subianto, the rival he would defeat at the polls on 9 July, Jokowi acknowledged the shifting of geopolitical and economic power from the West to Asia then underway. Indonesia, located between the Indian and Pacific Oceans, needed to face the challenges posed by that shift and develop its all-round sea-related character as a "global maritime fulcrum," so that "our country will be respected." He recalled the glory that Indonesia had gained by hosting the Asia-Africa Conference in 1955. As a global maritime fulcrum, Indonesia could renew that acclaim. Other countries would respect Indonesia, and they would come to it, wanting to enter its seas.[62]

Twice during his debate with Prabowo and again in its aftermath, Jokowi mentioned the "global maritime fulcrum" — sometimes translated as a "nexus" or an "axis." The idea was hailed as the new president's signature foreign policy, designed to revive the country's identity as an archipelagic state while hewing closely to its traditional "free and active" stance."[63]

Even in 2018, however, four years into Jokowi's first five-year term, no one could be sure exactly what playing the role of a "global maritime fulcrum" was supposed to mean. Jokowi's administration did announce a presidential regulation on sea policy, including a Sea Policy Action Plan, "in the context of accelerating" the fulcrum's implementation.[64] But the plan was criticized as "effectively a 'bureaucratic umbrella' document" that merely gathered and relabeled already existing policies and programs. Rather than venturing a new approach to Indonesia's international role, the announcement skewed the fulcrum inward, toward domestic conditions and needs.[65]

Jokowi's view of the fulcrum role also prioritized its economic aspects rather than its strategic value for national or regional security. More generally, one might even say that he has focused on foreign affairs mainly if not solely to further his economic goals. "Our diplomatic approach," he has said, must not be "the sort of diplomacy that spends money, but one that makes money."[66] As for SBY's "many friends" preference, Jokowi has favored a more transactional policy geared more to Indonesia's own economic needs. He once rhetorically asked, "What's the point of having many friends but we only get the disadvantages? Many friends should bring many benefits."[67]

Yudhoyono's presidency was globalist in outlook. He relished the opportunity for Indonesia to shine regionally and worldwide through its and his participation in international organizations and forums. Jokowi has been more unilateralist, wanting most to do things that materially benefit Indonesia. For Jokowi, foreign policy has been an afterthought. Most of his energy and political capital have been spent on domestic matters, economic development in particular.

SBY loved his and by implication Indonesia's global role and was thought to aspire to be chosen UN secretary-general.[68] Jokowi has been known for his reluctance to attend international gatherings. In October 2014, Jokowi's hesitation to commit to joining other leaders at a G20 summit in Australia the following month led to speculation that he might skip the event altogether,[69] though in the end he did go. SBY would have welcomed the opportunity.

Jokowi's priorities have affected Jakarta's relations with Beijing. His desire to grow Indonesia's economy and upgrade its infrastructure have made him eager to attract Chinese investment. SBY visited China only twice during his two five-year terms.[70] Jokowi, in contrast, from his inauguration in October 2014 to May 2017, met six times with Chinese president Xi Jinping, five of them in Beijing.[71] In the first half of 2017 compared with the first half of 2016, Chinese investment in Indonesia grew by 93 percent, to $2 billion.[72] In April 2018, the two countries signed contracts worth $23 billion under China's infrastructure-focused Belt and Road Initiative.[73]

Closer Sino-Indonesia relations have had political repercussions. Jokowi's domestic opponents, including conspiracy theorists, have pictured him as a Chinese puppet and closet communist selling out his country to Beijing.[74] Such smears dogged him during the election of 2014 and were kept alive thereafter by his political rivals, including General Gatot Nurmantyo, who headed the Indonesia's armed forces in 2015–17.[75]

The political damage done to Jokowi had strategic consequences. Jokowi needed to burnish his credentials as a nationalist who would not kowtow to China. Accordingly, in 2016, he brought several of his ministers to a cabinet meeting purposely held on an Indonesian navy warship in Indonesian waters off Indonesia's Natuna Islands in the South China Sea, where incidents with China had occurred.[76] As if to follow up, in July 2017, his deputy minister for maritime affairs, Arif Havas Oegroseno, announced that the northernmost waters in Indonesia's EEZ off Natuna would henceforth be called the "North Natuna Sea," reportedly "to make it sound more Indonesian."[77]

The "North Natuna Sea" did not last long. In August, China formally objected to the new name.[78] But rather than demonstrate its refusal to kowtow to Beijing, Jakarta quietly backtracked. In September, Indonesia's coordinating minister for maritime affairs, retired general Luhut Binsar Pandjaitan, who outranked Oegroseno, said that he (Pandjaitan) had never approved the name.[79] It was, in effect, withdrawn. In February 2018, Oegroseno was confirmed as Indonesia's new ambassador to Germany,[80] a location pointedly far from the South China Sea.

To dampen tension with Beijing, Jakarta has denied claiming sovereignty in the South China Sea beyond its EEZ; limited its actions against China to protecting the zone against poaching by Chinese or other fishermen; and politely called for more "concrete cooperation" between states involved in the South China Sea dispute. As for China's unilateral construction and militarization of land features in the sea, Jakarta has remained silent on that sensitive issue.[81]

Jokowi's focus on illegal fishing shows not only how important Indonesia's domestic economy is to him, but how little he cares about the regional security implications of Chinese expansion in the South China Sea, including the related diminishing of ASEAN's centrality as a regional actor. In the words of one senior foreign analyst, Jakarta's "attempts to reframe the EEZ problem as a bilateral Indonesia-China fisheries issue ignore the core of the problem," namely, "China's ultimate objectives in the region."[82] Nor is that problem alleviated by Jokowi's lack of interest in leading ASEAN and his indifference to its loss of centrality as an actor in the South China Sea.

These worries are not limited to the writings of foreign observers. Already in July 2016, mounting concern over Jokowi's unconcern regarding ASEAN and foreign affairs generally prompted 20 Indonesian foreign-policy professionals, including this chapter's author, to prepare and post a joint critique of their country's foreign policy in those regards.[83]

Conclusion

In the course of the third Jokowi-Subianto debate during the 2014 presidential campaign, each man was asked, if elected, what his policy on the South China Sea would be. Subianto said that because Indonesia's and China's claims off Natuna overlapped, Indonesia was involved in the disputes over sovereignty, like it or not. Jokowi disagreed: Indonesia need not be involved, especially insofar as it had no solution to the problem. Pressed further, Jokowi simply said that the matter should be settled through additional diplomacy.[84] That answer affirmed and continued Yudhoyono's and Natalegawa's previous emphasis on trust-building through dialogue. "Through ASEAN," Natalegawa had said three years before, "we are projecting the norms by which these big countries [China, the United States, India, Japan] should conduct themselves in a more peaceful and benign manner."[85] Despite the expectations raised by Jokowi's "global maritime fulcrum," at the end of the day, Jokowi and his foreign minister Retno Marsudi basically pursued the same status quo policies in foreign and military affairs they had inherited from Yudhoyono and Natalegawa.

It is true that, compared with his predecessor, Jokowi can be seen as having acted more forcefully in defense of Indonesia's maritime sovereignty. This impression has been strengthened by his willingness to let his minister of maritime affairs and fisheries Susi Pudjiastuti not only capture foreign fishermen poaching in Indonesian waters but blow up their vessels as well. What is more, in December 2018, the head of Indonesia's armed forces inaugurated a military base on Natuna Island.

Yet Jakarta remains unwilling to risk seriously offending Beijing. That is a line that Jokowi will not cross. Maritime security does concern him, and the base on Natuna has burnished his administration's nationalist credentials.[86] The opening of the base was likely related in part to Jakarta's concern regarding Beijing's intentions off Natuna in the slice of the South China Sea that is inside Indonesia's EEZ and on China's side of the nine-dash line. As this chapter has argued, Indonesia's fear of China is not something new.

That said, the build-up on Natuna neither augurs nor reflects a clear or decisive strategic decision to address Beijing's ambition in the South China Sea. As Evan Laksmana has noted, planning for such a base has been underway for at least a decade, and it is still a work in progress. As if to illustrate the military's inward orientation, the base is part of an archipelago-wide project "to develop greater tri-service integration and joint operational capabilities and to relieve internal organizational pressures" — pressures caused by the growing severity of promotional logjams created by a mismatch between too many officers and too few available posts.[87]

It is past time to retire the Yudhoyono doctrine. Hoping for "a thousand friends and no enemies" is not a foreign policy. It is wishful thinking. Indonesian foreign policy is unstrategic because it lacks clear and realistic goals along with plans to achieve them. Such goals and plans cannot be drafted and pursued effectively without a prior analysis of the distribution of hard power in the region, its impact on the security of the South China Sea, and the implications not only for the prosperity of Indonesia but for Indonesian autonomy as well. Military parity between Indonesia and China is out of the question. But the Indonesian military needs to — and can — acquire a greater deterrent capacity if it wants to be taken seriously as a strategic actor with a more than mainly insular outlook.

The Indonesian government should calculate both the strategic risks and the material benefits of encouraging Chinese aid and investment. Indonesian diplomats should be less complacent about ASEAN's ability to matter without a leader. Indonesia's own ability to be simultaneously "free" and "active" will not be served if it continues to undervalue foreign policy, underbalance China, and remain more or less indifferent to Beijing's strategy of enlarging and deepening its primacy in Southeast Asia.

Notes

1 Franklin B. Weinstein, *Indonesian Foreign Policy and the Dilemma of Dependence* (Cornell: Cornell University Press, 1976), 93-94.

2 Michael Richardson, "Ford and Kissinger Had Bigger Problems/'We Will Understand and Will Not Press You': How U.S. Averted Gaze When Indonesia Took East Timor," *New York Times*, 20 May 2002, http://www.nytimes.com/2002/05/20/news/20iht-timor2_ed3_.html.

3 Daniel Novotny, *Torn between America and China: Elite Perceptions and Indonesian Foreign Policy* (Singapore: ISEAS, 2010), 219.

4 "Religion in Indonesia" and "Ethnic Groups in Indonesia," Wikipedia, https://en.wikipedia.org/wiki/Ethnic_groups_in_Indonesia and https://en.wikipedia.org/wiki/Religion_in_Indonesia, sourcing the 2010 census. On how to interpret the ethnicity figure, see "Chinese in Indonesia," Facts and Details, accessed 14 May 2018, http://factsanddetails.com/indonesia/Minorities_and_Regions/sub6_3a/entry-3993.html.

5 Jewel Topshield, "Battle for Jakarta: Ahok under Siege despite High Approval Rating in Office," *Sydney Morning Herald*, 10 February 2017, https://www.smh.com.au/world/the-battle-for-jakarta-governor-ahok-under-siege-despite-high-approval-rating-in-office-20170210-gu9y9i.html.

6 Fergus Jensen and Tom Allard, "'Dirty' Jakarta Election Looms as Religious Politics Resurfaces," Reuters, 18 April 2017, https://www.reuters.com/article/us-indonesia-election/dirty-jakarta-election-looms-as-religious-politics-resurfaces-idUSKBN17K15Z.

7 Yohanes Sulaiman, "Religious Warfare and the Jakarta Election," *New Mandala* (Canberra), 13 February 2017, http://www.newmandala.org/religious-warfare-jakarta-election.

8 Ihsanuddin, "Penjelasan Jokowi soal tenaga kerja China di Indonesia" [Jokowi's explanation on the question of Chinese workers in Indonesia], *Kompas* (Jakarta), 23 December 2016, https://nasional.kompas.com/read/2016/12/23/11211181/penjelasan.jokowi.soal.tenaga.kerja.china.di.indonesia.

9 Lutfy Mairizal Putra, "Di balik isu banyaknya tenaga kerja China, benarkah China akan jajah Indonesia? Ini jawabannya" [Behind the rumor of so many Chinese workers, is it true that China is going to colonize Indonesia? This is the answer], *TribunNews.com*, 24 December 2016, http://www.tribunnews.com/nasional/2016/12/24/di-balik-isu-ban

yaknya-tenaga-kerja-china-benarkah-china-akan-jajah-indonesia-ini
-jawabannya.

10 Berni Moestafa and Sharon Chen, "China's Advance Spurs Indonesian
Military Shift: Southeast Asia," *Bloomberg*, 29 May 2014, http://www
.bloomberg.com/news/2014-05-28/china-s-advance-spurs-indonesian
-military-shift-southeast-asia.html.

11 Evan Laksmana, "Is Southeast Asia's Military Modernization
Driven by China? It's Not That Simple," *Global Asia* 13, no. 1 (Spring
2018): 42–47.

12 Annually on average from 2007 to 2012 (in constant 2015 dollars)
Yudhoyono spent only USD $4.2 billion on the armed forces, although the
figure rose to $7.3 billion in 2013, compared with Jokowi's average of $7.2
billion in 2015–16. "SIPRI Military Expenditure Database," Stockholm
International Peace Research Institute, https://www.sipri.org/sites/default
/files/Milex-constant-2015-USD.pdf.

13 Sita W. Dewi, "Jokowi Promises to Triple Defense, Security Budget,"
Jakarta Post, 3 June 2014, http://www.thejakartapost.com/news/2014/06
/03/jokowi-promises-triple-defense-security-budget.html.

14 Conversions from rupiah and yuan were made at the exchange rates
then in effect. See "APBN 2018: Kementerian Pertahanan masih menjadi
prioritas" [2018 National Income and Expense Budget: the Ministry of
Defense is still a priority], *Katadata Indonesia*, 7 February 2018, https://
databoks.katadata.co.id/datapublish/2018/02/07/apbn-2018-kementerian
-pertahanan-masih-menjadi-prioritas; and Christian Shepherd and
Michael Martina, "China Boosts Defense Spending, Rattling Its
Neighbors' Nerves," Reuters, 4 March 2018, https://www.reuters.com
/article/us-china-parliament-defence/china-boosts-defense-spending
-rattling-its-neighbors-nerves-idUSKCN1GG072.

15 Edward Aspinall, Marcus Mietzner, and Dirk Tomsa, "The
Moderating Presidency: Yudhoyono's Decade in Power," in *The
Yudhoyono Presidency: Indonesia's Decade of Stability and Stagnation*,
eds. Edward Aspinall, Marcus Mietzner, and Dirk Tomsa (Singapore:
ISEAS, 2015), 12–13.

16 Jacqui Baker, "Professionalism without Reform: The Security Sector
under Yudhoyono," in Aspinall, Mietzner, and Tomsa, *The Yudhoyono
Presidency,* 120.

17 "World Bank's State of Logistics Indonesia 2013 Report," The World Bank, August 2013, http://documents.worldbank.org/curated/en/2013/09 /18197499/state-logistics-indonesia-2013.

18 "OECD Economic Surveys: Indonesia," OECD, October 2016, https:// www.oecd.org/eco/surveys/indonesia-2016-OECD-economic-survey -overview-english.pdf.

19 Tom Allard, "Indonesian President Faces Twin Threats from Jakarta Poll," Reuters, 19 April 2017, https://www.reuters.com/article/us-indo nesia-election-islam-analysis/indonesian-president-faces-twin-threats -from-jakarta-poll-idUSKBN17L235.

20 Tom Allard and Agustinus Beo Da Costa, "'Red Scare' Puts Pressure on Indonesian President," Reuters, 28 September 2017, https://www .reuters.com/article/us-indonesia-politics-military/red-scare-puts-pressure -on-indonesian-president-idUSKCN1C21AQ.

21 Kyodo, "China Has Built Seven New Military Bases in South China Sea, US Navy Commander Says," *South China Morning Post*, 15 February 2018, http://www.scmp.com/news/china/diplomacy-defence /article/2133483/china-has-built-seven-new-military-bases-south-china.

22 Joe Cochrane, "Indonesia, Long on Sidelines, Starts to Confront China's Territorial Claims," *New York Times*, 10 September 2017, https://www.nytimes.com/2017/09/10/world/asia/indonesia-south-china -sea-military-buildup.html.

23 Mohammad Hatta, "Indonesia's Foreign Policy," *Foreign Affairs* 31, no. 3 (April 1953): 441-52.

24 Telegram from the Consul General at Batavia (Livengood) to the Secretary of State, November 17, 1947, in *Foreign Relations of the United States, 1947, The Far East, Volume VI*, ed. John G. Reid (Washington, DC: United States Government Printing Office, 1972), 1073.

25 Yohanes Sulaiman, "The Banteng and the Eagle: Indonesian Foreign Policy and the United States during the Era of Sukarno 1945–1967" (PhD diss., Ohio State University, 2008), 77–79.

26 Mohammad Hatta, *Mendajung antara dua karang: Keterangan pemerintah diutjapkan oleh Drs. Mohammad Hatta di muka sidang B.P.K.N.P di Djokja pada tahun 1948* [Rowing between two reefs: Government declaration by Drs. Mohammad Hatta at the B.P.K.N.P. meeting in Djokja in 1948] (Jakarta: Kementerian Penerangan Republik Indonesia, 1951), compiled in August 2011 by Shohib Masykur, http://

www.academia.edu/36758395/Drs._Mohammad_Hatta_MENDAJUNG
_ANTARA_DUA_KARANG.

27 Ide Anak Agung Gde Agung, *Twenty Years Indonesian Foreign Policy* (The Hague: Mouton, 1973), 210–11.

28 Sulaiman, "The Banteng and the Eagle," 80, 247.

29 Shunmugam Jayakumar, *Diplomacy: A Singapore Experience* (Singapore: Straits Times Press, 2011), 242.

30 Republic of Indonesia, Ministry of Defense, *Postur pertahanan negara* [National defense posture] (Jakarta: Ministry of Defense, 2007), 31.

31 Dewi Fortuna Anwar, *Indonesia in ASEAN: Foreign Policy and Regionalism* (Singapore: Institute of Southeast Asian Studies, 1994), 132, 134.

32 Yohanes Sulaiman, "Indonesia's Strategic Culture: The Legacy of Independence," in *Strategic Asia 2016–17: Understanding Strategic Cultures in the Asia-Pacific*, eds. Michael Wills, Ashley J. Tellis, and Alison Szalwinski (Seattle and Washington, DC: The National Bureau of Asian Research, 2016), 176–87.

33 Weinstein, *Indonesian Foreign Policy*, 187.

34 Trimulyono Hendradi, "Isu internasionalisasi Selat Malaka sebagai ancaman terhadap kedaulatan Indonesia" [The issue of internationalizing the Malacca Strait as a threat to Indonesia's sovereignty] (thesis, Indonesian Defense University, 2010), 5, 9, 36.

35 Rizal Sukma, "Strength in Numbers: Indonesia's Multiple Defense Relationships," *Strategic Review* (Jakarta) 3, no. 2 (April–June 2013): 18–19.

36 Republic of Indonesia, Ministry of Defense, *Buku putih pertahanan Indonesia 2008* [White book on the defense of Indonesia] (Jakarta: Ministry of Defense, 2008), 156–58.

37 Hendradi, "Isu internasionalisasi Selat Malaka," 35.

38 Frederick Situmorang, "The Need for Cooperation in the Malacca Strait," *Jakarta Post*, 19 July 2012, accessed 24 October 2014, http://www.thejakartapost.com/news/2012/07/19/the-need-cooperation-malacca-strait.html.

39 Bill Tarrant, "Balancing Powers in the Malacca Strait," Global News Journal, Reuters, 7 March 2010, http://blogs.reuters.com/global/2010/03/07/balancing-powers-in-the-malacca-strait.

40 Ministry of Defense, *Buku putih pertahanan Indonesia 2008*, 16.

41 Catur Sulasdiarso, "Kebijakan pembelian alutsista 2009–2013 dalam upaya menghadapi ancaman militer negara asing" [Defense materiel procurement policy in 2009–13 for confronting foreign military threats] (thesis, Indonesian Defense University, 2014), 75–76.

42 Republic of Indonesia, Ministry of Defense, *Buku putih pertahanan Indonesia 2015* [White book on the defense of Indonesia 2015] (Jakarta: Ministry of Defense, 2015), 7–8, https://www.kemhan.go.id/wp-content /uploads/2016/04/BPPI-INDO-2015.pdf.

43 Republic of Indonesia, Ministry of Defense, "Kebijakan penyelarasan minimum essential force komponen utama" [Policy regarding the alignment of the main components of the minimum essential force], Peraturan [Regulation] 19 (2012), 8, https://www.kemhan.go.id/ppid /wp-content/uploads/sites/2/2016/10/Permenhan-Nomor-19-Tahun-2012 -Lampiran-1.pdf.

44 Evan A. Laksmana, "Why There Is No 'New Maritime Dispute' between Indonesia and China," *The Strategist* (Barton, Australia), 2 April 2014, accessed 10 September 2018, https://www.aspistrategist.org.au /why-there-is-no-new-maritime-dispute-between-indonesia-and-china.

45 Amarulla Octavian, "It's Time for Joint ASEAN Naval Exercises," *Strategic Review* 3, no. 2 (April–June 2013): 8–9.

46 Republic of Indonesia, Ministry of Defense, "Kebijakan pertahanan negara tahun 2018" [National defense policy 2018], *WiRA* 70, no. 54 (January–February 2018), Puskom Publik Kemhan, Jakarta, https://www .kemhan.go.id/wp-content/uploads/2018/03/wirajanfeb18-website-kemh anOK.pdf.

47 Susilo Bambang Yudhoyono, "Indonesia and America: A 21st Century Partnership," 14 November 2008, Washington, DC, accessed 10 September 2018, http://usindo.org/wp-content/uploads/2010/07/SBY -Speech-at-USINDO-Nov-20081.pdf. In this and the following quote, the plural — "enemies" — was implied.

48 Susilo Bambang Yudhoyono, "Pidato lengkap Presiden SBY 20 Oktober 2009" [Full text of President SBY's speech on 20 October 2009], *Kompas*, 20 October 2009, accessed 10 September 2018, http://sains .kompas.com/read/2009/10/20/1324076/pidato.lengkap.presiden.sby.20 .oktober.2009.

49 Marty M. Natalegawa, "Waging Aggressive Peace: ASEAN and the Asia-Pacific," *Strategic Review* 1, no. 2 (November–December 2011): 42.

50 "Indonesia buka 21 hubungan diplomatik 2011" [Indonesia opens diplomatic relations with 21 countries in 2011], *ANTARA News* (Jakarta), 7 January 2011, accessed 11 September 2018, http://www .antaranews.com/berita/240945/indonesia-buka-21-hubungan -diplomatik-2011.

51 Natalegawa, "Waging Aggressive Peace," 44–45.

52 Yuliasri Perdani, "Jakarta Dialogue Aims at Easing Tension in Asia," *Jakarta Post*, 21 March 2013, accessed 11 September 2018, http://www .thejakartapost.com/news/2013/03/21/jakarta-dialogue-aims-easing -tension-asia.html.

53 Evi Fitriani, "Yudhoyono's Foreign Policy: Is Indonesia a Rising Power?," in *The Yudhoyono Presidency*, eds. Edward Aspinall, Marcus Mietzner, and Dirk Tomsa (Singapore: ISEAS, 2015), 85, 88.

54 Natalegawa, "Waging Aggressive Peace," 43, 45.

55 Anwar, *Indonesia in ASEAN*, 85.

56 Aaron L. Connelly, *Indonesian Foreign Policy under President Jokowi* (Sydney: Lowy Institute for International Policy, October 2014), 3–4, accessed 11 September 2018, https://www.lowyinstitute.org/sites/default /files/indonesian-foreign-policy-under-president-jokowi_0_0.pdf.

57 Bradley N. Nelson, "Can Indonesia Lead ASEAN?," *The Diplomat*, 5 December 2013, http://thediplomat.com/2013/12/can-indonesia -lead-asean.

58 Andrew Higgins, "In Philippines, Banana Growers Feel Effect of South China Sea Dispute," *Washington Post*, 10 June 2012, https://www .washingtonpost.com/world/asia_pacific/in-philippines-banana-growers -feel-effect-of-south-china-sea-dispute/2012/06/10/gJQA47WVTV _story.html.

59 Jeremy Grant, Ben Bland, and Gwen Robinson, "South China Sea Issue Divides Asean," *Financial Times*, 16 July 2012, https://www.ft.com /content/3d45667c-cf29-11e1-bfd9-00144feabdc0#axzz3GRoDiyCs.

60 Vikram Nehru, "Collision Course in the South China Sea," *National Interest*, 23 August 2012, http://nationalinterest.org/commentary /collision-course-the-south-china-sea-7380.

61 Carlyle A. Thayer, "ASEAN's Code of Conduct in the South China Sea: A Litmus Test for Community-Building?," *Asia-Pacific Journal: Japan Focus* 10, issue 34, no. 4 (20 August 2012), https://apjjf.org/2012 /10/34/Carlyle-A.-Thayer/3813/article.html.

62 "Transkrip lengkap jalannya debat capres iii 22 juni 2014—lebih runut untuk dicermati" [Complete minute-to-minute transcript of the course of the presidential candidates' third debate on 22 June 2014], Simomot, 23 June 2014, accessed 12 September 2018, http://simomot.com /2014/06/23/transkrip-lengkap-jalannya-debat-capres-iii-22-juni-2014 -lebih-runut-untuk-dicermati.

63 Evan A. Laksmana, "Indonesia's New President Can Deepen Cooperation with Europe and the United States," German Marshall Fund of the United States, 15 August 2014, http://www.gmfus.org/blog /2014/08/15/indonesia's-new-president-can-deepen-cooperation-europe -and-united-states.

64 "Peraturan Presiden Republik Indonesia nomor 16 tahun 2017 tentang kebijakan kelautan Indonesia" [Republic of Indonesia presidential regulation 16, year 2017, on Indonesia's maritime policy], accessed 12 September 2018, http://www.bkipm.kkp.go.id/bkipmnew/public/files /regulasi/PERPRES_NO_16_2017.pdf.

65 Evan Laksmana, "Indonesian Sea Policy: Accelerating Jokowi's Global Maritime Fulcrum?," Asia Maritime Transparency Initiative, Center for Strategic and International Studies, Washington, DC, 23 March 2017, https://amti.csis.org/indonesian-sea-policy-accelerating/.

66 Sheany, "Indonesia to Boost Efforts in Economic Diplomacy," JakartaGlobe, 12 February 2018, http://jakartaglobe.id/news/indonesia -boost-efforts-economic-diplomacy/.

67 Robertus Wardhy, "Jokowi Signals Break with 'Thousand Friends' Foreign Policy," JakartaGlobe, 17 November 2014, http://jakartaglobe.id /news/jokowi-signals-break-thousand-friends-foreign-policy/.

68 "Indonesian President Yudhoyono Offered Leading Position at United Nations: Report," Straits Times, 2 September 2014, http://www.straits times.com/asia/se-asia/indonesian-president-yudhoyono-offered-leading -position-at-united-nations-report.

69 Aaron L. Connelly, "Will Jokowi Skip the G20 in Brisbane?," The Interpreter, 20 October 2014, https://www.lowyinstitute.org/the-inter preter/will-jokowi-skip-g20-brisbane.

70 Cheng Guanjin and Li Jiabao, "China, Indonesia Push Ties," China Daily, 24 March 2012, http://www.chinadaily.com.cn/china/2012-03/24 /content_14902840.htm. SBY did not visit China after his second trip in 2012.

71 Ina Parlina, "Jokowi Has Fifth Meeting with China's Xi," *Jakarta Post*, 3 September 2016, http://www.thejakartapost.com/news/2016/09 /03/jokowi-has-fifth-meeting-with-chinas-xi.html; and Heru Purwanto, "President Jokowi Concludes Work Visit in Beijing," *Antaranews.com*, 15 May 2017, https://en.antaranews.com/news/110920/president-jokowi -concludes-work-visit-in-beijing.

72 Anton Hermansyah, "Investment from China Grows by 92.79 Percent: Board," *Jakarta Post*, 27 July 2017, http://www.thejakartapost.com/news /2017/07/27/investment-from-china-grows-by-92-79-percent-board.html.

73 Rachmadea Aisyah, "Chinese Investments Trending in Indonesia," *Jakarta Post*, 2 May 2018, http://www.thejakartapost.com/news/2018/05 /02/chinese-investments-trending-in-indonesia.html.

74 "Rumors There Are Already 10 Million Chinese Workers in Indonesia on the Rise, Jokowi Tells Police to Catch Hoax Spreaders," *Coconuts Jakarta*, 23 December 2016, https://coconuts.co/jakarta/news/rumors -there-are-already-10-million-chinese-workers-indonesia-rise-jokowi -tells-police/.

75 Hendra Friana, "Salim Said: Pemutaran film G30S/PKI langkah politik Jokowi hadapi Gatot" [Salim Said: the screening of the movie about the 30 September Coup by the Indonesian Communist Party is Jokowi's political maneuver against Gatot], *Tirto.id*, 25 September 2017, https:// tirto.id/pemutaran-film-g30s-pki-langkah-politik-jokowi-hadapi-gatot -cw7Y.

76 Kanupriya Kapoor and Fergus Jensen, "Indonesia President Visits Islands on Warship, Makes Point to China," Reuters, 23 June 2016, http:// www.reuters.com/article/us-southchinasea-indonesia-idUSKCN0Z909D.

77 Joe Cochrane, "Indonesia, Long on Sidelines, Starts to Confront China's Territorial Claims," *New York Times*, 10 September 2017, https://www.nytimes.com/2017/09/10/world/asia/indonesia-south-china -sea-military-buildup.html.

78 John McBeth, "China Drags Indonesia into South China Sea Morass," *Asia Times*, 7 September 2017, http://www.atimes.com/article/china -drags-indonesia-south-china-sea-morass/.

79 Kurnia Sari Aziza, "Luhut pastikan tak ada pengubahan nama Laut China Selatan menjadi Laut Natuna Utara" [Luhut assures that the South China Sea has not been renamed the North Natuna Sea], *Kompas.com*, 13 September 2017, http://ekonomi.kompas.com/read/2017/09/13/193437026

/luhut-pastikan-tak-ada-pengubahan-nama-laut-china-selatan-menjadi
-laut.

80 Ray Jordan, "Jokowi lantik 17 dubes baru, Foke diganti Arif Havas"
[Jokowi inaugurates 17 new ambassadors, Foke is replaced by Arif
Havas], *detikNews* (Jakarta), 20 February 2018, https://news.detik.com
/berita/d-3875591/jokowi-lantik-17-dubes-baru-foke-diganti-arif-havas.

81 Zuraidah Ibrahim, "Exclusive: Widodo's Peace Formula for South
China Sea," *South China Morning Post*, 29 April 2017, http://www.scmp
.com/week-asia/geopolitics/article/2091549/exclusive-widodos-peace
-formula-south-china-sea.

82 Donald E. Weatherbee, "Re-Assessing Indonesia's Role in the South
China Sea," *Perspective* (Singapore), no. 18 (21 April 2016), https://www
.iseas.edu.sg/images/pdf/ISEAS_Perspective_2016_18.pdf.

83 Evan Laksmana (initiator), "Indonesia Foreign Policy Community
Concerned over South China Sea," *ipetitions* (New York), 25 July 2016,
https://www.ipetitions.com/petition/indonesian-foreign-policy-south
-china-sea. Ten more analysts signed the statement after its circulation.

84 Yohanes Sulaiman, "Foreign Affairs a Stranger to Indonesia's
Presidential Hopefuls," *New Mandala*, 23 June 2014, http://asiapacific
.anu.edu.au/newmandala/2014/06/23/foreign-affairs-a-stranger-to-indo
nesias-presidential-hopefuls/.

85 James D. Zirin, "A Conversation with Marty Natalegawa," *Council
on Foreign Relations* (New York), 27 September 2011, https://www.cfr
.org/event/conversation-marty-natalegawa-1.

86 "Indonesia Opens Up Military Base on Edge of South China Sea to
'Deter Security Threats,'" *South China Morning Post*, 20 December 2018,
https://www.scmp.com/news/asia/southeast-asia/article/2178741/indo
nesia-opens-military-base-edge-south-china-sea-deter.

87 Evan Laksmana, "Why Indonesia's New Natuna Base Is Not about
Deterring China," *Asia Maritime Transparency Initiative*, 25 January
2019, https://amti.csis.org/indonesias-natuna-base-not-about-deterring
-china/.

CHAPTER 10

Who Wins in China's "Win-Win" Relations with Cambodia?

A SKEWED ILLUSION

Daniel C. O'Neill, *University of the Pacific, United States*

The government of the People's Republic of China (PRC) likes to call its bilateral foreign economic relations "win-win" (*gongying* or *shuangyingde*). As Chinese president Xi Jinping wrote in the Cambodian daily *Rasmei Kampuchea* in October 2016: "Our two countries enjoy deep political trust and win-win economic cooperation.... China and Cambodia are devoted friends. On issues concerning each other's core interests and major concerns, our two countries have stood together and supported each other."[1] Sino-Cambodian engagement has indeed benefited Cambodian elites. However, the fundamental question for understanding the politics of bilateral relations is not whether each state wins, but who wins in each state. It is in this sense that the inclusively "win-win" rhetoric of state-to-state diplomacy is a skewed illusion.

China's bilateral ties with all of the states of Southeast Asia are asymmetric. The Chinese side is significantly more powerful — economically, militarily, diplomatically — than any of the 10 members of the Association of Southeast Asian Nations (ASEAN). Yet these relations are rarely zero-sum. There are winners on both sides.

For any given ASEAN state, this bilateral asymmetry, combined with the domestic distribution of gains from cooperation with China, creates local beneficiaries. They typically include officials and members of the ruling elite, who are then subject to Chinese influence. Presently no ASEAN government is more influenced by China than is Cambodia's. Whether it be Phnom Penh's approval of domestically unpopular Chinese hydropower projects or its role as Beijing's proxy inside ASEAN regarding the disputed sovereignties in the South China Sea, the government of Cambodia often says and does what the government of China prefers. This chapter will appraise Cambodia's political economy and its ties with China to identify the Cambodians who benefit, how Beijing uses them to influence their country, and how authoritarian institutions facilitate this process.

The extent of Chinese influence in Cambodia is a function of several factors. Among them are historical ties between the two countries and, in Cambodia, ethnic-Chinese networks and the relative scarcity of capital for investment. More important, however, are Cambodia's authoritarian political institutions, both formal and informal. They provide the context in which political actors make decisions, including influencing choices as to who will rule and how they will stay in power. Institutions thus determine who is or is not among the Cambodian winners whom China can use to influence the country's policies and direction. Among these local winners are actors in government, business, and the security sector, many with close personal ties to Cambodia's long-ruling prime minister, Hun Sen.

What Each Country Needs from the Other

Three assumptions underlie this chapter's analysis of Cambodia's relations with China. First, as is true of all great powers, one of China's foreign economic policy goals is to reward those in a partner country who can influence its government's positions and actions. Second, China's decision-making process is motivated less by altruism and more by rational self-interest; Beijing's promotion of "development" abroad is more instrumental than benevolent. Third, whereas self-defined "realist" scholars reify the state as the primary actor in international affairs, the analysis here features individual Cambodian actors and the particular groups that they form. Cambodia's needs in general are reviewed in the next section, but the policy-influencing interplay of domestic politics occurs among particular individuals pursuing their various interests. For the purpose of this analysis, for example, groups such as business firms can be treated as interchangeable with those who lead them. As for the usage of "Cambodia" and "China," unless stated otherwise, these terms will denote their respective governments and, more specifically, the executive authorities therein.

Cambodia's economy is poorly developed and its state is militarily weak. The country's needs are to these extents self-evident. For the state to become more powerful and the government to become more popular, Cambodia needs to increase employment, lift incomes, lower poverty, improve education and health care, expand infrastructure, generate more energy, and acquire the means to defend its borders. China can help Cambodia meet all of these needs, especially the capital outlay that each one requires. The export of capital is already among the key drivers of China's "Go Out" (*zouchuqu*) and Belt and Road Initiative (BRI) policies and the associated internationalization of Chinese firms. China is also a regional military power, and a global diplomatic power as well, if only because of its permanent and veto-equipped seat on the UN Security Council. Despite not participating in military alliances, China can protect the Cambodian state.

Beijing is already a key patron of the Phnom Penh regime, albeit rhetorically guided by "non-interference in each other's internal affairs," the third of China's Five Principles of Peaceful Coexistence. China protects Hun Sen's government from regime change by counterbalancing the strong pressure for liberal reforms coming from Western countries and international bodies including non-governmental organizations (NGOs). As one Cambodian scholar has written, "When Cambodia falls under pressure from international bodies to reform its human rights abuses, corruption, oppression of its people, or misuse of power, it turns to the Chinese for financial support."[2] Hun Sen does so knowing that Chinese leaders have what he needs to help ensure the survival of his regime.

Cambodia has much to offer China in return: strategic location, investment opportunities, natural resources, and regional membership. First, Cambodia borders China's long-time regional rival, Vietnam. It was Vietnamese invaders who in 1979 swept the genocidal Khmer Rouge out of Phnom Penh and swept in Cambodia's current leaders, including Hun Sen, Heng Samrin, and their Kampuchean People's Revolutionary Party, the precursor to the ruling Cambodian People's Party (CPP). There is no stronger evidence of the authoritarian nature of Cambodia's political institutions than the three-decade length of their rule.[3] Second, less developed and energy-scarce Cambodia, where businesses commonly rely on generators for electricity, is attractive to major Chinese state-owned enterprises (SOEs) whose domestic opportunities are increasingly limited. Notable among these investors are state-owned hydropower firms that have built seven major dams in Cambodia with amounts totaling more than USD $2.4 billion in value.

Third, Cambodia has resources that China needs, such as timber and land for agricultural production. Accordingly, the Chinese firm Tian Rui has been developing a 300-hectare, $2 billion special economic zone in the province of Kampong Speu for agricultural processing to support food exports to China. Another Chinese company, Rui Feng, opened a $360 million sugar mill, among the largest in Asia, as part of a planned $1.5 billion industrial development in Preah Vihear Province in late 2016. Fourth and finally, Cambodia belongs to ASEAN, which operates by consensus. An outside state that manages to gain decisive influence over just one ASEAN member can exercise a proxy veto over what the organization can do. Cambodia, beholden to China, can and does prevent ASEAN from criticizing China's claim to the South China Sea. Thus weakened from within, the multilateral organization cannot oppose Beijing's insistence on separate bilateral — hub-and-spokes — negotiations with each and only each of the four ASEAN members whose claims to both land features and sea space in the South China Sea conflict with China's. By maximizing the skew of power and leverage in China's favor, such bilateral discussions take on a "win-lose" character that belies the positive-sum language in Beijing's rhetoric.

Exercising Chinese Power

If influence is essentially "the exercise of power," power is "the ability of A to make B do what it would otherwise not do."[4] Clearly, given the extreme asymmetry between them, it is China (A) that has the greater ability to make Cambodia (B) do what it would not otherwise do — and China has not hesitated to use that power. It is no coincidence that the statements and actions of the Hun Sen government frequently mimic Chinese preferences, strong domestic and international incentives to the contrary notwithstanding. Some of the many examples include the permanent closing of the Taipei Economic and Cultural Representative Office (the de facto Taiwanese embassy in Phnom Penh) and official Cambodian approval of a wide range of locally unpopular Chinese investment proposals. Among the latter are hydropower and other projects involving the forced relocation of citizens. Some of these proposals and projects have been variously opposed by the World Bank, the United Nations, domestic and international environmental NGOs, and Cambodian opposition politicians. Other instances where Phnom Penh has aligned its preferences with Beijing's include the forced repatriation of 20 Uighurs from China's restive Xinjiang Province in 2009, despite condemnations by the UN High Commissioner for Refugees, NGOs such as Human Rights Watch, and various foreign governments; Cambodia's shift from supporting to opposing a permanent seat for Japan on the UN Security Council, copying China's objection while ignoring Japan's historical role as a major aid donor to Cambodia; and the already mentioned role of Cambodia as a proxy for China inside ASEAN on the South China Sea disputes, despite counterpressure from some other ASEAN states.

As these cases suggest, Beijing aims to influence Phnom Penh particularly in two issue areas key to the incumbency and survival of the Communist

Party of China (CPC): economic growth on the one hand, state sovereignty on the other. Since Deng Xiaoping began his "opening and reform" (*gaige kaifang*) policies at the end of the 1970s, replacing Mao's brand of Marxism, which had given the party ideological legitimacy, CPC leaders have relied on a form of performance legitimacy grounded in economic development.[5] Their choice has improved the lives of Chinese citizens while greatly enhancing the power of the Chinese state, allowing the government to pursue more aggressively its disputed claims to sovereignty along its periphery. Beijing tries to influence foreign governments to support not only China's "One China" policy, which is now a widely held norm in international relations, but also China's efforts to repress ethnic separatism in the provinces (technically "autonomous regions") of Xinjiang and Tibet. More recently, China has assertively pursued its territorial claims in the South China Sea, referring to them in talks with US officials as a "core national interest" (*hexin liyi*), a term previously limited to Taiwan and the ostensibly autonomous regions. Beijing has also challenged Japanese control of the Diaoyu/Senkaku Islands in the East China Sea and asserted its claims to a large portion of the Indian state of Arunachal Pradesh.

In pursuit of the Chinese party-state's other priority concern, economic development, Beijing seeks to influence foreign governments to provide access to the resources and opportunities that the Chinese state and its firms require to continue rapid domestic economic growth. In addition to exporting capital abroad, BRI policies are designed to keep the Chinese economy growing by creating globally competitive firms; enlarging their access to foreign markets; helping them acquire advanced technology and natural resources; and fostering their global growth potential. Because of Cambodia's less developed economy and small domestic market, it is primarily resources and opportunities to develop infrastructure that Chinese firms seek there, apart from the substantial participation of private Chinese firms in Cambodia's garment manufacturing sector, which is dominated by ethnic Chinese from around the region.

The major economic component of Sino-Cambodian bilateral relations in recent years has been foreign direct investment (FDI) in Cambodia by Chinese SOEs with funding provided, at least in part, by the Chinese government, including through its Export-Import Bank and other "policy banks." This state-led character of FDI is likely only to increase, propelled by Xi Jinping's Belt and Road Initiative. Chinese decisions to invest are often attributed to entrepreneurial Chinese firms. But when such commitments are funded indirectly by Chinese state lending to the Cambodian government, they can also be accurately thought of as investments by the Chinese state itself.

Beijing cultivates and grows its leverage over Cambodia among many other economically developing states by using aid and loans to finance investments and trade. Its greatest leverage comes from funding for major investments by China's SOEs. China's trade with Cambodia is substantial in quantity but skewed in favor of Cambodian imports from China, including inputs into Cambodia's booming construction industry. These imports far outweigh Cambodia's exports to China, which are mainly agricultural.[6] In 2016 Cambodian exports comprised only $830 million of the $4.8 billion in trade between the two countries that year.[7]

Admittedly, Cambodia's main export markets are not in China but in the United States and Europe, which import the bulk of the products of Cambodia's larger garment sector. Exports to the United States in 2016 were a robust $2.8 billion, although down from $3 billion the previous year.[8] Yet US-Cambodian ties are otherwise weak. China, not the United States, is Cambodia's major foreign partner, and this is because Chinese firms shape and dominate the flow of FDI in Cambodia and, increasingly, Beijing furnishes most of the "aid" to Hun Sen's regime.[9]

Hun Sen and other high-ranking members of his government have expressed a strong preference for Chinese loans and investments. The predilection is unsurprising. The opaque nature of Sino-Cambodian negotiations and their outcomes prevents opposition politicians, the press, and civil society from identifying precisely who benefits from these agreements, as well as how, and how much. Hun Sen also greatly values the apparently "no strings attached" character of the funding, in contrast to the provisos for political or economic reforms often required by Western governments and associated international financial institutions, conditions that might threaten the political survival of the receiving regime. Hun Sen also appreciates the Chinese policy of so-called non-interference (*bu ganshe*) in the domestic affairs of other countries, whereby Beijing refrains from public criticism of the Cambodian government. High-level officials in Phnom Penh have lauded the Chinese for providing aid, in Hun Sen's words, "without attaching any condition such as telling us to do this or that."[10] Or, as a secretary of state in the Council of Ministers put it,

> In terms of money ... we choose China because [Chinese investment] does not come with conditions. ... A number of [W]estern investments come with attachments ... we have to be good in democracy. We have to be good in

human rights. But in Cambodia we went through a civil war and we understand that if you have no food in your stomach, you cannot have human rights.[11]

Gaining Influence

If China's inputs into Cambodia's economy are to enlarge Beijing's influence over Phnom Penh, they need to reach the right people. Given the authoritarian character of Cambodia's political system and Hun Sen's paramount role therein, two sets of "the right people" — Cambodians with the power to slant Cambodia's policies in China's favor — warrant priority Chinese attention. Beijing can acquire influence by providing benefits, first, to the prime minister himself and his family; and second, to those in his ruling group, the "winning coalition" whose support is necessary and, China hopes, sufficient for the Cambodian leader to maintain power.[12] The benefits are designed to incentivize their recipients to say and do what China wants.

In a democracy, this ruling coalition is a subset of the electorate. In authoritarian Cambodia, however, it is a subset of what political scientists have called the "selectorate": those that have "a formal role in expressing a preference over the selection of the leadership" and "some chance of becoming an essential supporter of the incumbent."[13] In a true democracy, every adult, with few exceptions, can vote for a candidate for public office; the candidate needs a majority, or at least a plurality, to win; and incumbents commonly provide public goods to a large part of the electorate whose support is required for re-election. Leaders in autocracies, in contrast, are incentivized to bestow private goods on a relatively small but potentially "winning and ruling coalition" inside the selectorate. Behind a façade of seemingly democratic institutions, Cambodia is ruled by just such a group of elites in government, security, and business, many of whom are interlinked through financial dealings and intermarriage.

Political Institutions and the Winners in Cambodia

Douglass North defined institutions as "the rules of the game."[14] Who wins a game may depend on the rules, and the winners in political economy are no different; institutions matter for them as well. We can think of institutions, formal or informal, as roads toward opportunities. A winner is someone who can and does take advantage of such paths. For some, to be sure, the roads are blocked, but for others, they are open, while others can access the road if they pay a toll.

Chinese winners on the opportunistic "roads" that Beijing has opened in Cambodia are many and diverse. They include the leaders of the CPC; the ministers of commerce and foreign affairs, among others in the state bureaucracy; the heads of outward-investing state-owned firms at national and provincial levels; provincial leaders and bureaucrats; importers of Cambodian resources; and Chinese workers in Cambodia. In contrast, Cambodians who benefit from Sino-Cambodian cooperation disproportionally belong in, or are closely involved with, the ruling group around Hun Sen. Among them are high-level politicians and bureaucrats, politically connected businesspeople, and authorities in the security and military spheres. Notably absent from this list is the monarchy.

Of these Cambodian winners, some gain directly from Chinese favors, including material assistance. Others enjoy indirect access to Chinese loans and business profits via joint ventures with Chinese firms or are beneficiaries of rents linked to inflows of Chinese capital. Hun Sen can be thought of as the gatekeeper to the avenues of opportunity pointing toward such benefits. He can open the gate for those whose support he needs to retain power — the winning coalition inside the selectorate. To reward and retain their support and trust, he offers access to resources and income, including the rents available through partnering with Chinese counterparts and tapping the aid, loans, and investments they provide. Intermarriage among members of Hun Sen's family and security and economic elites further enhances that support and trust. Hun Sen thus augments the probability of his political survival.

Although no leader possesses literally absolute power, clearly Hun Sen is a dictator. Some Cambodians call him, behind his back, Saddam Hun Sen.[15] He himself shaped the authoritarian institutions that he continues to lead. Heuristically, one could think of him as the Mafia-style "godfather" of Cambodia's political economy. He is the prime minister of an elected government. But his authoritarian control of the rules of game — institutions that only weakly constrain his behavior — allows him to distribute access to resources and opportunities in ways that maximize his personal gain, that of his family, and that of others in the winning coalition, not least those who operate the apparatus of security.

Cambodia's legislature and courts are largely rubber stamps.[16] This is especially true of the Phnom Penh Municipal Court, which Hun Sen often uses to punish his opponents. The dictator also controls the relevant bureaucracies, most importantly the Ministry of Commerce, which promotes and regulates trade; the Ministry of Environment, which is supposed to conserve natural resources and remedy their contamination; and the Ministry of Mines and Energy, whose tasks include overseeing mineral extraction and hydropower. Hun Sen also chairs the Council for the Development of Cambodia. Described as "the highest decision-making level of the government for private and public sector investment," its potentially lucrative duties include "review[ing] investment applications and grant[ing] incentives to investment projects."[17]

For Hun Sen, the greatest benefits from Sino-Cambodian ties are political; they yield resources and opportunities that he can wield to maintain support within the ruling coalition. As Wintrobe has written, "the distribution of rents in exchange for loyalty" is a dictator's "major avenue for developing political support or trust."[18] Among other government officials and businesspeople (and the many who are both), major winners from these bilateral relations include three CPP members of Cambodia's senate: Mong Reththy, chairman of the Mong Reththy Group; Lao Meng Khin, who together with his wife, Yeay Phu (aka Choeung Sopheap), owns the Pheapimex Company; and Ly Yong Phat, president of the LYP Group, vice president of the Cambodia Chamber of Commerce (CCC), and special economic adviser to Prime Minister Hun Sen. Other tycoons who profit from their country's ties to China include Royal Group chairman and CCC president Kith Meng, and the Try Pheap Group's sole proprietor, Try Pheap. In addition to their titles as government officials and business leaders, each of these moguls holds a distinctive Khmer title: *oknha*.[19]

Oknha was formerly a royal title bestowed by the king on very few. Roughly 20 Cambodians held the title in 2004, but just a decade later that number had grown to some 700.[20] The expansion reflects the increase in wealth among business elites in Cambodia as well as the co-opting of business elites into the CPP. Evoking wealth and loyalty to the party, the title has become a tool used by Hun Sen and his party-state to legitimate their power in Cambodia's patronage system.[21] King Sihanouk gave the title sparingly to those who had, in his eyes, improved the country, but later the requirement became a $100,000 donation to the state. In 2017, Hun Sen raised the minimum contribution to $500,000.

According to the executive director of Transparency International in Cambodia, Preap Kol, many Cambodians who are entitled to call themselves oknha use the honorific to obtain business advantages or special official favors on the one hand, while they "violate human rights or abuse poor or marginalized people" on the other.[22] A CPP spokesman, Cheam Yeap, has claimed that the monarchy alone decides who gets the title. But according to a spokesman for the royal family, Om Daravuth, the king merely confirms what Hun Sen requests — and paying the fee to the state is enough to earn the accolade. As for the prior king, Norodom Sihanouk, his secretary recalled that in his last two decades Sihanouk himself only chose "three or four people" to receive the title.[23]

Many of the Chinese-funded investment projects in Cambodia are joint ventures with firms owned by oknha who are well positioned to gain needed access to the government, especially to acquire concessions of land for investment.[24] Among the uses of such land are hydropower, timber and mineral extraction, food production, and real estate development. Official access is indispensable, especially in view of the abolition of private ownership of land under the Khmer Rouge and its appropriation by the state. The state allocates concessions of land in various settings — forests, fisheries, mineral deposits, heritage sites — and in various deals, including "land swaps" involving state-owned buildings. A 2007 report by Global Witness found that many of these transactions violated Cambodian law and turned over valuable public assets for private control by tycoons "who are themselves part of the shadow state structure," where business and politics overlap.[25]

China Courts the Oknha, and Vice Versa

Hun Sen's immediate family has interests in at least 114 private Cambodian companies with a once-listed value totaling more than $200 million.[26] That reckoning, however, excludes the likely far greater value of the family's holdings in land. Unverified estimates of the family's total assets range from $500 million to $4 billion, and this in the poorest country in Southeast Asia.[27] Even less clear is the size of the wealth that opaque Sino-Cambodian agreements have afforded the prime minister and his near kin. For other members of the winning coalition, however, such gains are more apparent.

Ly Yong Phat   Consider, for instance, the fortunes of tycoon-cum-senator Oknha Ly Yong Phat and his LYP Group, headquartered on Mao Tse Toung Boulevard in Phnom Penh. In December 2016, Ly penned a $1.5 billion agreement with the China Minsheng Investment Group to build a "Cambodia-China Friendship City," including hotels, schools, and amusement parks, just north of the capital. The senator's company was also chosen by Hun Sen and Beijing for the first phase of construction of the Morodok Techno National Sports Complex, which will cost $157 million by the time it is completed for the 2023 Southeast Asia Games in Phnom Penh. At a groundbreaking ceremony in April 2017, Hun Sen proudly claimed that the Chinese ambassador had told him "this is the biggest fund that the Chinese government never [*sic*!] granted to any country in the world."²⁸ Oknha Ly and his LYP Group will further benefit from spillovers due to the sports complex's location near the proposed Friendship City.

Lao Meng Khin   Of the oknha-tycoon-senators, however, it is Lao Meng Khin and his wife, Yeay Phu, who have most effectively used political connections to take advantage of the opportunities that Sino-Cambodian economic ties present. Evidence abounds: Registration papers list the CPP senator and his wife as "governors" of Sinohydro (Cambodia) United Ltd, a Cambodian subsidiary of Sinohydro Corporation, the Chinese state hydropower giant.²⁹ Lao and his fellow CPP senator Sy Kong Triv co-direct Pheapimex, which has been engaged in a Sino-Cambodian joint venture with the (Chinese) Wuzhishan L.S. Group. In 2004 the group received from the Cambodian government a concession "in principle" to establish a pine-tree plantation in Mondulkiri Province on 199,999 hectares of land — far beyond the legal limit of 10,000 hectares.³⁰ Five hundred members of the local Phnong minority were prevented by police from marching in protest against the plantation project, which they said was destroying their ancestral lands. According to Global Witness, as of 2007 Pheapimex had received concessions equal to over 7 percent of Cambodia's entire land area.³¹

Senator Lao also owns the Cambodia International Investment Development Group and Shukaku, Inc. These firms joined a Chinese SOE, Mongolia Erdos Hongjun Holding Group, to build a 700-megawatt coal-fired power plant in the Sihanoukville area. The National Assembly obligingly passed a law guaranteeing the price of the energy produced. These examples illustrate how business and government overlap in Cambodia, and how a Chinese state firm working with well-connected local partners can gain economic access, including a protected price for its investment.³²

In 2010 Mongolia Erdos Hongjun also joined with Lao's Shukaku in what may be the most controversial Chinese investment in Cambodia: a luxury apartment and retail development on what had been Phnom Penh's Boeung Kak Lake. Some 1,500 families were moved from homes around the lake as it was filled and "reclaimed" as land for development. The lease agreement stated that the project would impact 4,252 families.³³ Protests and arrests soon followed. In 2011, due to the scheme's highly controversial nature — the evictions, the environmental destruction — the World Bank ceased lending to Cambodia until the government and the firms involved addressed the rights of relocated residents.³⁴ Mongolia Erdos pulled out of the project in 2014, but a year later Beijing-based Graticity Real Estate Development began building the first section of the project, a six-story condominium and apartment complex.³⁵ Thus was Chinese involvement continually linked to the displacement of thousands of poor people, the destruction of their livelihoods, and the ruin of a natural resource.

Kith Meng   Another billionaire close to Hun Sen is Oknha Kith Meng. He, too, owes his political influence to his decade-plus term as president of the state-created Cambodia Chamber of Commerce. In 2016, a memorandum of understanding (MOU) to boost Sino-Cambodian trade and investment was co-signed by Meng as head of the CCC and by Zhang Li, the similarly wealthy Chinese chair of the China Council for the Promotion of International Trade, an official organ of the PRC.[36] In January 2017, a $3 billion joint project between Meng's Royal Group and Li's Guangzhou R&F Properties to build luxury ("six-star") hotels in Cambodia received Hun Sen's approval at a meeting between Li and the prime minister. In welcoming the plan, the prime minister praised Li's choice of Meng as a partner because Li had capital and Meng had land, adding that the investment would also support China's BRI.[37]

Meng has been a frequent member of Cambodian government delegations to China. Those trips, his links to Hun Sen (who attended his million-dollar wedding), and his CCC presidency have rendered him best placed among the oknha to profit from the BRI. At the BRI summit in Beijing in May 2017, for example, he signed an MOU with the China Railway 17 Bureau Group and Sino Great Wall International Engineering to invest in Cambodian railway construction, including a high-speed rail project from the capital to the port city of Sihanoukville.[38]

In February 2014, the Beijing-based China Huaneng Group took a 51 percent share in a controversial $870 million Lower Sesan 2 project to build a dam for hydropower in northeastern Cambodia. Payments to the Chinese side and to its partner, Meng's Royal Group, had been guaranteed by Cambodia's rubber-stamp Senate, including its oknha-tycoon members in 2013.[39] Following the vote, the Senate Secretary General Oum Sarith cited two studies in assuring the public that the dam's impact would be "minor compared to the benefit," yet those studies anticipated that 10,000 families would have to be relocated.[40] Hun Sen has also defended the project.[41] Cambodia watchers in the NGO community disagreed. They accused Meng's company of using its right to clear the site as a cover for laundering illegally cut timber from elsewhere in Cambodia. In May 2017, to the surprise of many, the National Police even posted on its website a condemnation of Kith Meng's Royal Group for having engaged in such unlawful activities. Predictably, within a week, the police removed the post and issued a retraction: that it had been "published because of a technical mistake and unintentionally" by a "tired" employee.[42] In the eyes of some observers, the present author included, the seemingly inadvertent posting could have been an effort by the National Police to improve their bargaining position for securing rents from such a lucrative project.

These examples — Ly Yong Phat, Lao Meng Khin, and Kith Meng, and their dealings — illustrate how wealthy and politically connected business-people benefit from Sino-Cambodian ties, which are multiplying as China's Belt and Road Initiative expands. Such men act as brokers between Chinese officials, firms, and official firms (i.e., SOEs) on the one hand, and Cambodian authorities on the other. The brokers deal in access, favors, approvals, and payments on the side, which may be especially helpful to would-be investors from China seeking partnered entry into questionable projects requiring massive transfers of land.[43] While seeking Chinese partners, these oknha elites provide political support for Hun Sen and financial support for the CPP. For Hun Sen, however, that is not enough. Still more important to him and his entourage is that the regime also be supported by the security sector — the military and the police — which enhances the regime's control of the economy as well. In the latter realm, China helps to enhance his support within the coercive apparatus of the state.

The Security Sector

A primary task for the police and military security apparatus in Cambodia is to protect the leaders of the regime and the businesspeople associated with it, including by suppressing their opponents. For this to be done, security officials must be loyal to Hun Sen. One method he has used to ensure and enhance their fealty is through intermarriage. One of his sons and two of his daughters have married into the families of high-ranking security personnel.[44] Another method is by rewarding the custodians of the armed forces and co-opting them into the CPP. In 2010, he announced a corporate sponsorship program drawing on the wealth of politically reliable oknha to fund security units. Ostensibly meant to improve the capabilities of the country's armed forces, the program also strengthened military support for the regime and its winning coalition.[45] Five years later, in 2015, the CPP enlarged its central committee to include a number of National Police commissioners and senior military officers.[46]

This government-military-business complex was ripe for abuse even before Hun Sen formalized it in 2010. As early as 1995, the military was already calling for private funders and sponsors. Poorly paid soldiers and policemen were moonlighting as guards for companies whose land concessions had triggered opposition. The guards evicted residents and tried to halt protests when told to do so.[47] That happened at Boeung Kak Lake, as discussed above. At another massive land-concession site, in Koh Kong Province, villagers were forcefully removed from their homes by military and police forces working for China's Tianjin Union Development Group (UDG). UDG had secured a 99-year government lease on a 45,000-hectare expanse of land partially in Botum Sakor district, home of the largest national park in Cambodia and the site of a "$5 billion mega-tourism zone" and hydropower project. According to the firm, the lease also includes exclusive rights to build an airport in the area during those 99 years.[48] The concession was estimated to involve the displacement of more than 1,000 families.[49] In February 2014, UDG warned residents that if they did not end their protests, "paratroopers" would be brought in.[50] Nor could the firm's concessionary success be attributable merely to the skill or luck of one Chinese company. Zhang Gaoli, a member of China's single most powerful executive body, the Standing Committee of the Politburo, attended the joint signing of the document authorizing the projects. Also notably, military leaders in both countries have endorsed the arrangements.[51] UDG is also building a deepwater port among other projects along the one-fifth of Cambodia's coastline that the company controls based on its 2008 agreement to that effect with the Hun Sen regime. Unsurprisingly in this clearly strategic context, Cambodian defense minister Tea Banh made sure to spend time at the headquarters of UDG during his five-day "military-to-military" visit to Beijing in July 2015.[52]

Another example involves the Rattanak Stone mine, which began operating in Preah Vihear Province in 2005. The owner of the site is the commander-in-chief of Cambodia's armed forces and simultaneously a high-ranking CPP official, General Pol Saroeun. The mine itself is a joint venture between Pheapimex and a Chinese SOE, the China National Machinery Corporation.[53] In 2016, on the seventh anniversary of the formation of Hun Sen's personal bodyguard unit, General Saroeun professed his "100 percent" loyalty to the prime minister and the first family and promised to "prevent a color revolution from happening in Cambodia."[54] Cambodian soldiers are paid to guard the mine. Such officially authorized corporate sponsorships have expanded in recent years, from 42 when the program began to 100 today.[55] The counterterrorism unit commanded by Hun Sen's son, Hun Manet, for example, is sponsored by Oknha Suy Sophan, owner of Phanimex Development Company and beneficiary of a concession of residential land in Phnom Penh. Displaced residents who protested were attacked by a motley force carrying truncheons, electro-shock batons, and sidearms.[56]

The creation of a hybrid party-army-business security network linking oknhas to the regime was a logical step for Hun Sen and for the CPP, which has always viewed the military as belonging to the party in a relationship that seems to resemble the formal subordination of the People's Liberation Army (PLA) to the CPC in China. Arguably unlike the Chinese case, however, to cite one analyst, "there has been no real effort to either demilitarize Cambodia's politics or truly nationalize the military."[57] Another analyst concurs, describing the Cambodian military as "a partisan, corporate arm" of the CPP while noting that the subordination is not institutional in character but reflects instead the personalized primacy of Hun Sen.[58] In 2015, General Chea Dara, who along with several other high-ranking officers had recently been made a member of the Central Committee of the CPP, said this to an audience of military and civilian officials and businesspeople: "I speak frankly when I say that the army belongs to the Cambodia People's Party." More telling, however, was the reason: because of Hun Sen — the real "feeder, caretaker, commander and leader of the army." In response, opposition parliamentarian Son Chhay stated that the CPP had "declared that the army belongs to them, which is contrary to our constitution."[59]

Chinese Military Charm?

Sino-Cambodian military ties have expanded rapidly during the presidency of Xi Jinping. That the purposely coercive PLA should be taking part in a "charm offensive" seems ironic, but Beijing has indeed mobilized hard power in pursuit of the softer kind on behalf of increased Chinese influence in Southeast Asia. Given Cambodia's strategic location and already friendly ties to China, Phnom Penh has been the target of much of this security diplomacy. A researcher at the Center for Naval Analyses in Washington, DC, has identified these fruits of Chinese military charm and their reciprocation by Hun Sen as "relationship building" thanks to military aid from Beijing, including education and training for Cambodian military personnel, dialogues between senior military officials, and operational outreach including port visits and bilateral exercises.[60]

Cambodia's security sector has benefited most tangibly from transfers of materiel. To cite but a few examples: In 2010, China donated 250 military jeeps and trucks after the United States canceled the delivery of 200 vehicles following Hun Sen's decision to deport 20 Uighur refugees back to the PRC. In 2013, the PLA gave a dozen military helicopters to Cambodia's armed forces. China also donated more than 1,000 handguns with ammunition to the National Police. In 2014, China's Ministry of Public Security agreed to supply, free of charge, a $3 million surveillance system for Phnom Penh; it became operational the following year. China has also paid the construction and operational costs of Cambodia's Army Institute, which trains about half of Cambodia's future officers and whose four-year program of instruction includes half a year in China.[61]

Concomitantly with the expansion of Sino-Cambodian military ties, relations between the Cambodian and American armed forces have shrunk. Hun Sen initially downgraded cooperation with the US military following American criticism of voting irregularities in the 2013 election. In 2017, a mobile construction unit of the US Navy left Cambodia at the government's request, ending nearly a decade of humanitarian assistance and terminating 20 projects including the building of schools and hospitals.[62] Also in 2017, Phnom Penh canceled an annual bilateral military exercise with the United States, Angkor Sentinel, in what would have been its eighth year. The revocation occurred just one month after Cambodia held its first-ever Golden Dragon exercise with the PLA Navy. [63]

One Patron, One Client, Few Winners — For Now

Bilateralism is based on reciprocity: "the simultaneous balancing of specific quid-pro-quos by each party."[64] When such a relationship reflects an asymmetry of power between its two participants, however, they can come to play, respectively, the roles of patron and client.[65] Colloquially such a relationship could be termed a fundamentally unequal or "lop-sided friendship."[66] The clientelist dynamic involves the provision of political support for the patron in return for material goods for the client.[67] As this chapter has endeavored to show, that dynamic not only drives how Hun Sen and members of his ruling coalition relate to each other — increasingly it also animates relations between Xi Jinping's China and its Cambodian client state.

In the past, Hun Sen's regime could be said to have tried, as the weaker state, to balance its relations with more powerful states, to avoid becoming too dependent on any single would-be patron while playing them off, one against another. But rather than cultivating China as merely one among various sources of military, financial, and diplomatic support, Hun Sen has apparently decided to place all of his foreign-policy eggs in a single "Made in China" basket. Facilitating this shift away from the West and Japan toward greater and greater reliance on China is the relative irrelevance of Cambodia's export markets to its domestic politics. Most investors in Cambodia's garment sector, which dominates exports, are private, foreign firms that do not offer the funds or the access to rents to the massive extent that these are obtainable via Chinese state loans and investments. China furnishes these resources free of conditions requiring reforms whose implementation might threaten Hun Sen's rule. So far, in accessing these resources, the oknha-business-military-party-bureaucracy complex has remained sufficiently beholden to Hun Sen and his Chinese backers to prolong his longevity in power.

The political institutions of a country can constrain its executive head. Cambodia's do not. That lack of constraint augments China's ability to influence Hun Sen and his government. China's also, if differently, authoritarian polity caters, in return, to Hun Sen's desire for a reliable, long-haul patron unhampered by domestic checks on power.

Which side gains more from its patron-client ties, Cambodia or China? Hun Sen's long-time chief opponent, Sam Rainsy, would answer: China. "The net benefit for Cambodia is unclear," he has said, "because China takes back [in resources] with one hand what she gives with the other."[68] But whether China's or Cambodia's economy gains more from bilateral ties is not the important *political* question for Cambodians. That question is, inside their country, who gains, who loses, and how much? The Cambodians who win are those with access to the opportunities that ties with China provide: Hun Sen, his family, the regime, the party, the business elite, the security sector — in brief, the winning coalition. As long as these winners continue to win, the trajectory of Sino-Cambodian relations is likely to remain fairly stable. If, however, for some reason, Cambodia's political institutions should be revamped or nudged toward a more genuinely democratic regime, the country's future will no longer depend on a small ruling group inside the selectorate but on a broader coalition within the even broader electorate. At that turning point, if it arrives, China may realize that its venally deferential Cambodian asset has become a liability. Cambodians, in turn, will understand what many of them already know: that inside their country, between its oknha and its people, China's "win-win" rhetoric was an all too skewed illusion.

Notes

1 Xi Jinping, "China and Cambodia: Good Neighbors and Trusted Friends," also published as "Full Text of Chinese President's Signed Article in Cambodian Newspaper," Xinhua, 12 October 2016, accessed 31 May 2017, http://news.xinhuanet.com/english/china/2016-10/12/c_135749070.htm.

2 Sophal Ear, *Aid Dependent in Cambodia: How Foreign Assistance Undermines Democracy* (New York: Columbia University Press, 2013), 29–30.

3 The most recent positions still held by Hun Sen and Heng Samrin as of 2018 were, respectively, prime minister (since 1998) and national assembly president (since 2006).

4 Robert A. Dahl, "The Concept of Power," *Systems Research and Behavioral Science* 2, no. 3 (1957): 201, quoted in David Shambaugh, *China Goes Global* (Oxford: Oxford University Press, 2013), 7.

5 Mary E. Gallagher, "'Reform and Openness': Why China's Economic Reforms Have Delayed Democracy," *World Politics* 54, no. 3 (2002): 338–72.

6 Tsz-Kwan Ho and Kang Sothear, "Cambodia-China Trade to Top $5 Billion by 2017," *Cambodia Daily*, 23 June 2015, accessed 15 May 2017, https://www.cambodiadaily.com/business/cambodia-china-trade-to-top-5-billion-by-2017-86222.

7 May Kunmakara, "PM Backs China's Key Role," *Khmer Times*, 12 April 2017, accessed 20 May 2017, http://www.khmertimeskh.com/news/37454/pm-backs-china---s-key-role.

8 "Trade in Goods with Cambodia," United States Census Bureau, accessed 21 May 2017, https://www.census.gov/foreign-trade/balance/c5550.html.

9 China's lending abroad often is not concessional enough to meet the definitional requirement by the Organisation for Economic Co-operation and Development that official development assistance have a "grant element of at least 25%"; "DAC Glossary of Key Terms and Concepts," https://data.oecd.org/oda/net-oda.htm.

10 "Hun Sen Praised China for Providing Unconditional Aid to Cambodia," Everyday.com.kh, 8 June 2007, translation by Heng Soy, accessed 1 May 2017, http://ki-media.blogspot.com/2007/06/hun-sen-praised-china-for-providing.html.

11 Phay Siphan, quoted in James Kynge, Leila Haddou, and Michael Peel, "FT Investigation: How China Bought Its Way into Cambodia," *Financial Times*, 8 September 2016, accessed 2 May 2017, https://www .ft.com/content/23968248-43a0-11e6-b22f-79eb4891c97d.

12 Milan Svolik, "Power Sharing and Leadership Dynamics in Authoritarian Regimes," *American Journal of Political Science* 53, no. 2 (April 2009): 478.

13 Bruce Bueno de Mesquita and Alistair Smith, *The Logic of Political Survival* (Cambridge, MA: MIT Press, 2003), 38; see also Susan Shirk, *The Political Logic of Economic Reform in China* (Berkeley: University of California Press, 1993).

14 Douglass North, *Institutions, Institutional Change and Economic Performance* (Cambridge, UK: Cambridge University Press, 1990).

15 As told to the author by long-time leader in the opposition and then member of parliament Son Chhay, Phnom Penh, February 2009.

16 See, for example, "Polity IV Country Report 2010: Cambodia," Center for Systemic Peace, accessed 2 May 2017, http://www.systemic peace.org/polity/Cambodia2010.pdf.

17 Council for the Development of Cambodia, "Who We Are," accessed 3 May 2017, http://www.cambodiainvestment.gov.kh/about-us/who-we -are.html.

18 Ronald Wintrobe, *The Political Economy of Dictatorship* (Cambridge: Cambridge University Press, 2000), 155.

19 Still other entitled "tycoon-senators" include Oknha Sy Kong Triv, chairman of the KT Pacific Group; Oknha Men Sarun, president of Men Sarun Co. LTD; and Oknha Kok An, managing director of ANCO Brothers Company Ltd.

20 Sek Odom and Simon Henderson, "As Oknha Ranks Grow, Honorific Loses Meaning," *Cambodia Daily*, 21 June 2014, accessed 5 May 2017, https://www.cambodiadaily.com/archives/as-oknha -ranks-grow-honorific-loses-meaning-62057/.

21 Michiel Verver and Heidi Dahles, "The Institutionalisation of Oknha: Cambodian Entrepreneurship at the Interface of Business and Politics," *Journal of Contemporary Asia* 45, no. 1 (2015): 48–70.

22 Quoted in Odom and Henderson, "As Oknha Ranks Grow."

23 Quoted in Odom and Henderson, "As Oknha Ranks Grow."

24 Verver and Dahles, "The Institutionalisation of Oknha." Also: Sophal
Ear, "Sowing and Sewing Growth: The Political Economy of Rice and
Garments in Cambodia," working paper no. 384, Stanford Center for
International Development, Stanford University, April 2009, accessed 2
June 2017, http://scid.stanford.edu/sites/default/files/publications/384wp
.pdf.

25 Global Witness, *Cambodia's Family Trees: Illegal Logging and the
Stripping of Public Assets by Cambodia's Elite* (Washington, DC: Global
Witness Publishing Inc., June 2007), 10, https://www.globalwitness.org
/documents/14689/cambodias_family_trees_low_res.pdf.

26 Global Witness, *Hostile Takeover: The Corporate Empire of
Cambodia's Ruling Family* (London: Global Witness, July 2016), 4,
https://www.globalwitness.org/en/reports/hostile-takeover/. Online access
to the listing has since been restricted.

27 For wealth estimates, see Luke Hunt, "How Rich Are Cambodia's
Hun Sen and His Family?," *The Diplomat*, 7 July 2016, https://
thediplomat.com/2016/07/how-rich-are-cambodias-hun-sen-and-his
-family/. For per capita incomes, see International Monetary Fund,
World Economic Outlook (Washington, DC: IMF, April 2017), http://
statisticstimes.com/economy/countries-by-projected-gdp-capita.php.

28 Quoting Hun Sen: "Morodok Techno National Sports Complex
Financially Funded by Chinese Government," Swift News, April 2017,
accessed 2 June 2017, http://swiftnewsdaily.com/en/morodok-techo
-national-sports-complex-financially-funded-by-chinese-government.

29 "Power Couple Linked to Sinohydro Project," *Phnom Penh Post*, 13
March 2014, accessed 1 May 2017, http://www.phnompenhpost.com
/national/power-couple-linked-sinohydro-project.

30 "Contract for Pine Plantation between the Ministry of Agriculture,
Forestry and Fisheries and Wuzhishan L.S. Group Co., Ltd," Kingdom of
Cambodia, 30 December 2005, accessed 2 June 2017, https://data.open
developmentmekong.net/en/dataset/contract-for-pine-plantation-between
 the-minsitry-of-agriculture-forestry-and-fisheries-and-wuzhish/resource
/8b750bdc-5c4e-4433-9d0b-a4141c15470c?type=agreement.

31 Global Witness, "Cambodia's Family Trees."

32 Daniel O'Neill, "Playing Risk: Chinese Foreign Direct Investment in
Cambodia," *Contemporary Southeast Asia* 36, no. 2 (2014): 173–205.

33 "Boeung Kak Lake Lease Agreement: Some Questions for
Discussion," Cambodia Development Watch, [2008?], http://www.cam

bodia.org/downloads/pdf/DPP_CambodiaDevelopmentWatchJune07Final
_English.pdf.

34 "World Bank Blocks Cambodia Loans amid Boeung Kak Row," BBC
News, 9 August 2011, http://www.bbc.co.uk/news/world-asia-pacific
-14457573.

35 Peter Ford and Aun Pheap, "Chinese Firm Begins Construction
at Boeng Kak," *Cambodia Daily*, 1 October 2015, accessed 2 June
2017, https://www.cambodiadaily.com/news/chinese-firm-begins
-construction-at-boeng-kak-96025.

36 Prashanth Parameswaran, "Cambodia, China Ink New Economic
Pact," *The Diplomat*, 12 September 2016, accessed 2 June 2017, http://
thediplomat.com/2016/09/cambodia-china-ink-new-economic-pact.

37 "Chinese Real Estate Developer to Invest $3 Bln in Luxury Hotels in
Cambodia," Xinhua, 5 January 2017, accessed 2 June 2017, http://www
.chinadaily.com.cn/business/2017-01/05/content_27868204.htm.

38 Phan Soumy, "Chinese Companies to Develop New
Cambodian Railways," *Cambodia Daily*, 17 May 2017, accessed
2 June 2017, https://www.cambodiadaily.com/news/chinese
-companies-to-develop-new-cambodian-railways-129841.

39 RGC (Royal Government of Cambodia), "Draft Law on Authorization
of Payment Warranty of the Royal Government of Cambodia for the
Hydro Power Lower Sesan 2 Company," RGC, Phnom Penh, 10 January
2013, accessed 10 May 2018, https://www.internationalrivers.org/sites
/default/files/attached-files/draft_law_on_rgc_approval_of_lower_sesan
_2_eng-2.pdf.

40 Kuch Naren, "Senate Oks Sesan Dam Payment Deal," *Cambodia
Daily*, 23 February 2013, 10.

41 Ben Sokhean and Janelle Retka, "Dam Will Not Damage the
Environment, Hun Sen Says," *Cambodia Daily*, 16 May 2017, accessed 2
June 2017, https://www.cambodiadaily.com/news/dam-will-not-damage
-environment-hun-sen-says-129792.

42 Phak Seangly, "Report Fingering Tycoon in Timber Crime Taken
Down," *Phnom Penh Post*, 23 May 2017, accessed 5 June 2017,
http://www.phnompenhpost.com/national/report-fingering-tycoon
-timber-crime-taken-down; Chhorn Phearun, "Police Link Kith
Meng to Illegal Wood Racket," *Cambodia Daily*, 17 May 2017,
accessed 5 June 2017, https://www.cambodiadaily.com/news/police
-link-kith-meng-to-illegal-wood-racket-129845.

43 Pal Nyiri, "Managers, Brokers and Culture Workers," in *Chinese Encounters in Southeast Asia: How People, Money and Ideas from China are Changing a Region*, eds. Pal Nyiri and Danielle Tan (Seattle: University of Washington Press, 2017).

44 See O'Neill, "Playing Risk," 183.

45 Global Witness, "Cambodia's Family Trees."

46 Kevin Ponniah and Vong Sokheng, "CPP Bigger, Not Better, Say Foes," *Phnom Penh Post*, 3 February 2015, accessed 5 June 2017, http://www.phnompenhpost.com/cpp-bigger-not-better-say-foes.

47 Jody Ray Bennett, "Cambodia: Military, Inc." ETH Zurich Center for Security Studies, n.d., accessed 5 June 2017, https://thenonstateunlimited.wordpress.com/2010/08/17/cambodia-military-inc.

48 Sen David, "Developer, Soldiers, 'Destroyed 29 Homes,'" *Phnom Penh Post*, 28 January 2017, accessed 3 May 2017, http://www.phnompenhpost.com/national/developer-soldiers-%E2%80%98destroyed-29-homes%E2%80%99.

49 Say Mony, "On Coast, Chinese Development Pushes Thousands from Land," VOA Cambodia, 24 July 2013, accessed 3 May 2017, http://www.voacambodia.com/a/on-coast-chinese-development-pushes-thousands-from-land/1708815.html.

50 Kuch Naren, "Threat to Unleash 'Paratroopers' in Land Dispute," *Cambodia Daily*, 8 February 2017, accessed 3 May 2017.

51 Kynge, Haddou, and Peel, "FT Investigation."

52 Cheang Sokha, "Defence Minister to Meet UDG in China," *Phnom Penh Post*, 9 July 2015, accessed 9 April 2019, http://www.phnompenhpost.com/national/defence-minister-meet-udg-china.

53 "Country for Sale: How Cambodia's Elite Has Captured the Country's Extractive Industries," Global Witness, February 2009, accessed 12 February 2010, http://www.globalwitness.org/sites/default/files/import/country_for_sale_high_res_english.pdf.

54 Ben Sokhean, "Hun Sen's Bodyguard Unit Marks Seven Years," *Cambodia Daily*, 5 September 2016, accessed 3 May 2017.

55 Vong Sokheng and Daniel Pye, "In Praise of RCAF Inc," *Phnom Penh Post*, 30 July 2017, accessed 3 May 2017, http://www.phnompenhpost.com/national/praise-rcaf-inc.

56 Luke Hunt, "Cambodia's Well-Heeled Military Patrons," *The Diplomat*, 10 August 2015, http://thediplomat.com/2015/08/cambodias

-well-heeled-military-patrons/; "Cambodia: Security Forces Beat Housing Rights Protestors," Human Rights Watch, 14 February 2014, accessed 3 May 2017, https://www.hrw.org/news/2014/02/14/cambodia -security-forces-beat-housing-rights-protesters.

57 Ou Virak, quoted by Hunt, "Cambodia's Well-Heeled Military Patrons."

58 Paul W. Chambers, "'Neo-Sultanistic Tendencies:' The Trajectory of Civil-Military Relations in Cambodia," *Asian Security* 11, no. 3 (2015): 179–205.

59 Sokheng and Pye, "In Praise of RCAF Inc."

60 "Jeffrey Becker, "What Is the PLA's Role in Promoting China-Cambodia Relations," *The Diplomat*, 29 April 2017, http://thediplomat .com/2017/04/what-is-the-plas-role-in-promoting-china-cambodia -relations.

61 "Chinese Influence in Cambodia Grows with Army School, Aid," Reuters, 2 April 2015, http://www.reuters.com/article/us-cambodia -china-military-idUSKBN0MT0SW20150402.

62 "U.S. Navy Aid Unit Told to Leave Cambodia," Reuters, 4 April 2017, http://www.reuters.com/article/us-cambodia-usa-navy-idUSKBN1760TA.

63 Sopheng Cheang, "Cambodia Cancels Military Exercise with U.S." *Seattle Times*, 16 January 2017, https://www.seattletimes.com/nation -world/cambodia-cancels-military-exercise-with-us/.

64 John Gerard Ruggie, "Multilateralism: The Anatomy of an Institution," *International Organization* 46, no. 3 (1992): 572.

65 John D. Ciorciari, "China and Cambodia: Patron and Client?," working paper, no. 121, International Policy Center, University of Michigan, Ann Arbor, http://ipc.umich.edu/working-papers/pdfs/ipc-121 -ciorciari-china-cambodia-patron-client.pdf.

66 Julian Alfred Pitt-Rivers, *The People of the Sierra* (New York: Criterion Books, 1954), 140.

67 Susan C. Stokes, "Political Clientelism," in *The Oxford Handbook of Comparative Politics*, eds. Carles Boix and Susan Stokes (Oxford: Oxford University Press, 2009).

68 Cristina Maza, "Rainsy Says China Aid to Blame for Rights Abuses," *Phnom Penh Post*, 17 October 2016, accessed 3 May 2017, http://www .phnompenhpost.com/national/rainsy-says-china-aid-blame-rights-abuses.

CHAPTER 11

High Modernism in a Small Country
CHINA "DEVELOPS" LAOS

Kearrin Sims

China under President Xi Jinping is not only rising. It is reaching out. An array of Chinese initiatives, vigorously pursued, are carrying the country's economic and political presence throughout Southeast Asia and to the broader world.

Beijing's massive Belt and Road Initiative (BRI) has begun building and financing physical infrastructure westward by land and sea from China, across Southeast, South, and Central Asia, all the way to Europe. In 2017 negotiations were underway to upgrade China's 2002 Free Trade Agreement (FTA) with the 10-country Association of Southeast Asian Nations (ASEAN).[1] By 2017 China could count 19 FTAs underway between itself and other countries or regions — 14 "signed and implemented" plus five "under construction."[2] China has greatly enlarged its regional financial footprint as well, by innovating the Asian Infrastructure Investment Bank (AIIB), partly meant to finance the BRI, and a New Development Bank jointly with Brazil, Russia, India, and South Africa. Headquartered respectively in Beijing and Shanghai, they began operations in 2015.

By thus leveraging its domestic economic "rise" into a full-spectrum "going out" into the larger world, China is exporting its approach to development into the political economies of poor recipient countries on a major scale. The approach is best summarized as "high modernist" in character.

"High modernism," in the words of the Southeast Asianist James Scott,

is best conceived as a strong, one might even say muscle-bound, version of the beliefs in scientific and technical progress that were associated with industrialization in Western Europe and in North America from roughly 1830 until World War I. At its core was a supreme self-confidence about continued linear progress, the development of scientific and technical knowledge, the expansion of production, the rational design of social order, the growing satisfaction of human needs, and, not least, an increasing control over nature.[3]

Scott has chronicled the failures of development plans based on high-modernist presumptions and ambitions — state-driven, top-down, technocratic, and interested neither in learning from local knowledge nor in applying local practice. Yet it is just this approach that China has adopted in Laos, this chapter's country of concern.

Over nearly three decades, from 1989 through 2015, Laos registered an annual average 6.96 percent rate of economic growth — among the highest of any country in the world.[4] To the extent that China's economic involvements in Laos contributed to that record, they were successful in aggregate terms. That said, the evidence gathered over nearly a year of fieldwork in Laos plus additional research[5] yields a far more cautionary conclusion: that China's high-modernist way of doing development has disproportionally favored the country's elite to the disadvantage of its poor people, thereby furthering their marginalization.

Development Aid — From the OECD to the PRC

A small, mountainous, land-locked state in the heart of mainland Southeast Asia, Laos is a "least developed country" in the parlance of the UN Development Programme (UNDP). "Human development" scores for Laos are among the lowest in Southeast Asia. Laos's indicators in 2015 included a per capita gross national income of USD $5,049, an average life expectancy of 67 years, and a mere 5.2 years of schooling per adult. Of the 11 Southeast Asian states listed on the UNDP's Human Development Index for that year, only Cambodia and Myanmar ranked lower than Laos.[6] Nevertheless, Laotian[7] authorities and a diverse, changing, and sometime competing set of donors have made the country's development a national and international priority, not without some success. Most notably, from 1992 to 2015, absolute poverty in Laos was cut in half — from 46 to 23 percent.[8] But the country continues to face major socioeconomic challenges, including food insecurities, vulnerability to natural disasters, high infant and maternal mortality rates, and weak public infrastructure.

As a former French colony and the site of intense violence on the ground and from the air during the First and especially the Second Indochina War, Laos and its people have long had to contend with clashing beliefs about development, modernity, and progress. Following the cessation of interstate conflict in mainland Southeast Asia, and especially since the mid-1980s, Laotian leaders have sought to cultivate economic and diplomatic relations with countries from across the geopolitical spectrum. Two events were noteworthy in this context: In 1986 Laos announced a "New Economic Mechanism" to encourage economic liberalization including the deregulation of trade. In 1992 the Asian Development Bank launched a program to develop what it called a "Greater Mekong Subregion" linking Laos to Thailand, Myanmar, Vietnam, and two adjacent parts of China (Yunnan and Guangxi). In Vientiane — the Laotian capital, located on one side of the Mekong opposite Thailand on the other — the authorities welcomed foreign aid and investment from any source.

Laos and Vietnam share a legacy of close if sometimes troubled relations between their respective nationalist-communist political movements-turned-parties dating from the colonial era through the Indochina Wars to the present day. Nationalism is still an important pillar of legitimacy for Laos's rulers, who still describe their system as communist — a Lao People's Democratic Republic led by the Lao People's Revolutionary Party. But since the crisis-and-implosion of the Soviet Union in 1989–91 deleted what had been Vientiane's number-one source of foreign aid, globalizing economic trends and corresponding economic reforms have increasingly fostered and sustained narratives of development that value the state's ability to attract foreign economic support.[9]

Laos has been receiving foreign assistance for more than half a century. Few countries have received more aid per capita than has Vientiane.[10] The landscape of economic aid in Laos, as in all developing countries, is a highly politicized field on which foreign donors try to use their ostensible largesse to advance their own national interests. The purposes and terms of aid to Laos, since at least the end of the Cold War, have been dominated by the objectives and activities of three sets of donors: the 29 industrial-country governments (and the European Union) that belong to the Development Assistance Committee (DAC) of the Organisation for Economic Co-operation and Development (OECD); the relevant multilateral institutions in those member countries; and the pertinent non-governmental organizations also based there. In 2010–14, for example, DAC-member governments provided development assistance to Laos totaling more than $1.4 billion.[11]

Formed in 1961, the OECD's DAC is the leading international forum for suppliers of bilateral aid. Its guidelines are meant to ensure that the aid that its members provide is effective, efficient, and takes into account issues of poverty, gender, and the environment, among other criteria. These priorities have remained in place with little objection for more than two decades. DAC members must maintain the transparency of their aid, including its provisos, and their cooperation is subject to regular peer review. In Laos, as elsewhere, DAC donors have disbursed substantial portions of their aid funds through international non-governmental organizations (INGOS) that run community programs to alleviate poverty. More than six dozen INGOS are included in one non-exhaustive directory of civil society organizations working in Laos.[12]

The flows of aid to Laos from within this established and monitored DAC framework have begun to weaken, however, as new, "partners" for "development" in Laos have arisen, beyond DAC's purview, with their own motives and methods of operation. Of foremost importance in this non-DAC setting has been the burgeoning presence of one actor in particular — China.

Since the 1980s, China has grown its economy more rapidly and for longer than just about any country in history. This feat has enabled China to transition from merely receiving aid to providing it as well. Previously, China's contributions to the development of other countries lagged behind the efforts of many DAC donors. But growing flows of Chinese aid and investment have now challenged the agenda-setting dominance of traditional donors, especially in Asia. There, in 2013, China was the leading non-DAC provider of aid not only to Laos, but to Cambodia, Indonesia, Mongolia, Myanmar, Philippines, Timor-Leste, and Vietnam.[13]

Beijing's heightened influence in impoverished nations has attracted sometimes polarized scholarly debate. On the favorable side, for example, Woods has argued that China's greater participation in aid to developing countries has helpfully exposed Western "standards and processes that are out of date and ineffectual." Fullbrook has concluded that all of the less developed countries in Southeast Asia would be worse off without Chinese aid and investment.[14] In an African context, China has been commended for funding aid projects more quickly and cheaply than traditional providers, and for introducing healthy competition among them.[15]

On the negative side, Chinese-donor funding has been criticized as mercantilist, exploitative, resource-driven, and supportive of authoritarian or rogue states. Beijing has been condemned for a lack of transparency regarding aid funding, little concern for social and environmental standards, and poor safety conditions for workers on China-funded aid projects.[16] Beijing has also been faulted for its opacity. In contrast to DAC donors, China has opted out of global reporting systems such as the International Aid Transparency Initiative — arrangements that were put in place to facilitate coordination and improve the accountability of donors and recipients alike. By "blending" aid with investment, Beijing has "blurred" the distinction between them in a way that, many argue, undermines hard-fought norms of international aid provision that distinguish development needs from commercial desires.[17]

As this chapter will show, many of these assessments are relevant to Laos. Of foremost significance to the argument featured here, however, is the technocratic and high-modernist nature of China's development contributions.[18] In Laos, as elsewhere, Beijing has emphasized building infrastructure to facilitate industrialization and urbanization. China's approach also emphasizes top-down state planning as the appropriate means to bring about "progress."[19] As Banks and Hulme have argued, this is a "romanticised and naturalised" interpretation of development that ignores in-built structural inequalities within the global economy and advances the belief that through enhanced modernization, the Global South will somehow catch up to the Global North.[20] Chinese development narratives are already more high-modernist than many contemporary Western discourses, the latter having to an extent relinquished what Nyíri calls "the idea of the continual improvability of the human condition" that China continues to propagate.[21]

Aid with Chinese Characteristics

China-Laos interactions are hardly a recent phenomenon. Substantial migratory flows, trade networks, and sociocultural exchanges between the two peoples can be traced at least as far back as the birth of the first unified Lao kingdom, Lan Xang, in the 14th century CE. This history of interchange underwent periods of expansion and contraction, including times of indifference or hostility. Most recently, however, from at least the 1990s onwards, Sino-Lao relations have trended toward greater and greater mutual engagement and official amity. From 2000 to 2010, for example, trade between the two countries rose at an annual rate of more than 25 percent, reaching $3 billion by 2016. No country provides more foreign direct investment (FDI) to Laos than China does — inflows that are likely to increase further in the wake of Laos's 2015 entry into the ASEAN-China Free Trade Area.[22]

China's growing economic presence, felt throughout Laos, is especially evident in the country's north, where investors (mainly from China's Yunnan Province) have capitalized on the opportunities afforded by close geographic proximity along a shared international border. The main investors in Laos have been Chinese: state-owned enterprises (SOEs) and large private companies principally engaged in agribusiness, mining, hydropower, and construction.[23] Chinese markets, shops, hotels, restaurants, and motor-vehicle dealerships are also now widespread in all of Laos's major central and northern cities, their commerce buoyed by the blossoming of Chinese immigrants and tourists. The trips of Chinese tourists to Laos soared more than 70 percent in 2013–14, reaching 422,440 arrivals, while over the past decade the Chinese diaspora population is believed to have more than tripled.[24]

In addition to its private-sector activities and people-to-people linkages, China has become one of Laos's most important donors of aid. Reportedly, as early as 2012, China's input equaled that of Japan, for decades the top supplier of aid to Laos.[25] In tandem with this expansion, the "synergy" between Laotian and Chinese development priorities has also grown. Illustrations include the establishment of a China-Lao Joint Cooperation Commission as a permanent division of the Laos's Ministry of Planning and Investment, and the growth of uniquely close and informal interactions between the two governments.[26]

If Chinese aid in Laos is prominent and exceptional, it is also opaque. Contrary to DAC guidelines, neither Beijing nor Vientiane has been transparent about the influx of Chinese assistance or investment. And despite the DAC criteria, both governments have allowed private commercial interests to dilute the ostensibly shared idea that aid should provide public goods. Worthy of attention in this constraining context are two valuable sources of information about specific aid contributions and the broader conceptual frameworks that inform Chinese aid policy: a Chinese-drafted development plan for the north of Laos, and a free-and-open-access dataset compiled by AidData, a research lab in Virginia. Both are cited below.

In 2008, Chinese specialists working for the government of Yunnan Province in its capital city, Kunming, prepared a comprehensive 12-year plan for the development of northern Laos. Originally written in Chinese and translated into English as a "mid-term draft" to be circulated for comment, the document affords unique access into official Chinese thinking about development in Laos. The plan covered multiple aspects of development, as reflected in its title, "2008–2020 Planning for *Industrial* Economic Development and *Cooperation* in [the] *Northern* Part of [the] Lao People's Democratic Republic" — italics added.[27] But its main theme was the need to *industrialize* northern Laos. The plan's authors recommended in principle that Vientiane seek foreign aid from various countries, including China, but they specifically wanted Laos to *cooperate* with their own Yunnan Province, adjacent as it was and is to *northern* Laos. In this regard, the plan offered Beijing's model of development and Kunming's willingness to help implement it.[28]

The ideas expressed in this Chinese "northern plan" for Laos were thoroughly "high modernist" by Scott's criteria.[29] The plan upheld Scott's "scientific and technical progress" as a crucial requisite to the efficiency that northern Laos would need in order to accelerate the desired arrival of its industrial future.[30] The plan championed mining and "the expansion of production" to achieve economies of scale in the export of iron, steel, copper, tin, and gold, among other commodities.[31] It projected "linear progress" in statistical scenarios of increased production and the expansion of manufacturing through 2020–21.[32] With the rapidity of China's own economic growth likely in mind, the authors stressed the need "to speed up industrial development" by "foster[ing] backbone industries" — four in particular: mining metals, generating electricity, processing agricultural and forestry products, and promoting tourism and trade.[33] Thus could northern Laos "march forward" to modernity, including an expected average rate of growth in total trade with China exceeding 15 percent per year,[34] with much of that stellar pace to be accounted for, presumably, by trade with Yunnan.

As for poverty reduction, treatment of that topic was postponed until near the end of the main report. There it was covered in under three pages and not considered further. Public health fared even worse; apart from passing mentions of the matter, it earned just one paragraph, the second-to-the-last in the main report. The paragraph mainly recommended attracting help from "neighboring countries" (such as China) in providing health services "for the local people, foreign investors and tourists." The Yunnan authors' high-modernist priorities were for northern Laos "to introduce technologies"; "develop medicine products"; gain economies of "enlarge[d] scale"; "promote exports"; and organize "production according to international standards."[35] As one analyst would later note, rather than "emphasize bottom-up, community-identified development initiatives," the Chinese plan for northern Laos envisaged the area's "intensified industrial[ization] . . . by the state and large enterprises."[36]

It is hard to know the exact extent to which China's plan for northern Laos shaped the actual policies pursued by Vientiane. The available document (henceforth "2008–2020") is a wholly Chinese product, with no indication of any Laotian input. Its stated purpose "is to establish an industrial system with the characteristics of North Laos," as if to adapt for Laotian soil Beijing's familiar call for "development with Chinese characteristics,"[37] but to do so without explaining what those north-Laotian equivalents might be. The authors of "2008–2020" did label it a "Mid-term Draft for Opinions." But what the Laotian government thought of the plan, or if their views were even sought, is unclear.

Unclear, too, is the extent to which Vientiane followed the plan's advice. Laos-China ties are a highly sensitive matter in official Laotian eyes. In numerous interviews with Laotian government officials, this chapter's author asked about the plan. Respondents either denied knowledge of the document or, more often, said they were not authorized to comment on it. A no longer accessible Chinese source did, nevertheless, report that the Chinese plan was adopted at the 9th Congress of the ruling Lao People's Revolutionary Party in March 2011 and would provide a framework for the preparation of Vientiane's 7th National Socio-Economic Development Plan (NSEDP) for 2011–15. And a still available official Chinese-media report in 2011 did credit a "Yunnan–Northern Laos Working Team" with having made "steady progress" in Sino-Laotian cooperation for local development.[38] So some or all of the many projects listed in the "2008–2020" plan may have been wholly or partly implemented with Chinese funds, whether loaned or given, but in keeping with the high-modernist priorities so clearly preferred by Beijing, Kunming, and plausibly Vientiane as well, as argued below.

Confirming these sectoral priorities are the allocations of Chinese financing for development in Laos. AidData offers the most comprehensive available dataset on these inputs. While not exhaustive, the set reflects AidData's effort to record all Chinese aid and "aid-like" transfers to Laos from 1997 until 2014. Over that period of time, these data show, the total of these transfers exceeded $5 billion. Just two sectors accounted for 93 percent of that amount: infrastructure for transportation (58 percent) and infrastructure for energy (35 percent). Compared to these outlays, the combined allocation for health and education was a negligible .0025 percent.[39]

China's high-modernist focus in Laos on infrastructure for aggregate economic growth serves the PRC's economic and political goals in Southeast Asia — access to natural resources, increased trade, opportunities for Chinese firms, and leverage against rival powers such as the United States and Japan. Does Vientiane share Beijing's orientation? Relevant to the answer are the contents of Laos's development plan for the most recently completed five-year period.

The seventh quinquennial NSEDP, for 2011–15, was designed to create a strategic framework for achieving the Laotian government's top development goal: to "graduate" from its UN-bestowed status as a least developed country (LDC) by 2020.[40] At 270 pages, the seventh NSEDP ranged widely across sectors. Consistently throughout the document, however, economic growth and infrastructural modernization were given pride of place. Nor were those priorities treated as possible if partial components of a more inclusive and socially beneficial approach. Growth and modernity were portrayed as the whole essence and outcome of development itself.

The number-one "overall target" of the northern plan was to keep the Laotian economy growing "at more than 8% per year" — a "general direction" toward rapid macroeconomic growth first and foremost.[41] To this end, the plan advised Laos to increase its engagement with "other socialist countries," specifically China and Vietnam, described as Laos's "good neighbours, friends and trustworthy partners" in contrast to the "economically leading countries" that "aggressively interfere [in] and impose unequal conditions [on]" LDCs such as Laos.[42]

Objects of High Modernization

Vientiane's cooperation with Beijing privileges tangible things: physical infrastructure, natural resources, hydropower facilities, and urban construction, considered sequentially below.

Infrastructure   Building cross-border links between Laos and its neighbors has been a priority of regional rulers since the French colonial era. The difficult terrain in Laos and its isolation from the Gulf of Thailand or the South China Sea have restricted foreign investment, hampered international trade, and slowed industrial modernization. Overcoming these obstacles of geology and distance has long been a high-priority policy concern.[43] Numerous steps by Laos and its aid partners have been taken to implement this priority by promoting regional connectivity — upgrading Laos's infrastructures of transportation and communication to boost the flows of trade and investment, people and information, across the country's borders.[44]

China has come to play a leading role in the enhancement of Laos's links with the larger world. China has funded the building of roads and airports, the dredging of the Mekong River, and the unfinished laying of the country's first high-speed railway. Building and bettering transportation infrastructure in Laos supports Chinese trade with ASEAN, improves Chinese access to natural resources, and helps to establish land routes that can lessen Chinese reliance on sea lanes patrolled by the US Navy. Specific Chinese investments in Laotian connectivity are too many to discuss here. But their typically high-modernist tenor can be seen in the following brief scan of China's work-still-in-progress on the intra-Laos segment of the railway that Beijing hopes will someday link Kunming through Vientiane clear to Singapore.

At an estimated cost of at least $5.8 billion, China's proposal to fund and construct this high-speed rail link across Laos is by far the grandest and most expensive, if not also the most grandiose, aid project ever attempted in the history of that small country. Corruption scandals in the railway industry inside China and protracted negotiations over the terms of the project have delayed the work. An estimated 16 percent of the section from the China-Laos border to Vientiane was reported to have been completed by the Chinese SOE in charge as of January 2018.[45] Due for completion by 2022, the project is both a key component of Beijing's expansively geostrategic Belt and Road Initiative and a priority project in Vientiane's seventh NSEDP.

The many aid donors who blame Laos's historically low economic growth and underwhelming industrial output on its land-locked location and mountainous terrain are inclined to support the railway as, in effect, an exit from local poverty. From the idea that poverty results from isolation, these experts derive the advice that infrastructures of connectivity will, by stimulating industry and tourism, generate economic growth with beneficial trickle-down effects for communities adjacent to the new or improved rails, roads, and transportation hubs.[46] China's rail project has symbolic appeal as well. In the eyes of many Laotians, officials and citizens, the sheer scale of the effort and the ostensibly cutting-edge technology involved evoke an exciting prospect of high modernity previously available only to people in the most prosperous Asian nations.[47]

Resources   Land for plantations and mining has also been exploited with Chinese aid. Beginning in the early 2000s the Laotian government and many of its development partners blessed land-utilizing FDI as a way to transform "untapped natural resources" into "productive assets" while curbing opium production and slash-and-burn agriculture.[48] These efforts resulted in the allocation to foreign investors, by 2010, of more than a quarter of Laos's total land area — some 3.5 million hectares.[49] Land concessions in support of agribusiness ventures introduced market practices to subsistence farming communities, sped economic growth, boosted export revenues, and reduced opium production.[50] Often situated in rural peripheries populated by ethnic minorities, Chinese agribusiness ventures helped enable the Laotian state to pursue "distance-demolishing technologies" such as roads, telephone lines, electricity, and airports. These networks in turn facilitated the integration, monetization, and control of "the people, lands, and resources of the periphery" by the center, Vientiane, with help from Beijing.[51] Rubber plantations figured prominently in this process.

The history of Chinese rubber plantations includes most of Southeast Asia.[52] In northern Laos in 1994–2006, rubber cultivation expanded quickly to cover 7,341 hectares by the latter year.[53] The Yunnan plan for northern Laos ("2008–2020") cites rubber as an important commodity to export for economic growth. As of 2003, the Chinese state-owned Yunnan Natural Rubber Industrial Company had already planted 66,000 hectares of rubber in Laos and planned to expand its hold more than fivefold by 2015.[54] Not all Chinese rubber plantations can be linked so directly to Beijing. It is nevertheless apparent, first, that the Chinese government has funded road upgrades and authorized import-tax concessions on Laotian rubber to feed the growth of China's own booming industrial sector; and second, that such incentives have accelerated the expansion of rubber cultivation in Laos. Similarly with regard to the mining sector, Chinese companies have been operating at least 57 such projects in Laos, including a $2 billion bauxite and aluminum mine and the country's largest copper and gold mine.[55]

Hydropower   Across all sectors from 1988 to 2009, Chinese ventures, alone or with Lao partners, were reported to have received official permits to invest in 318 projects valued at some $3.57 billion.[56] Of the estimated $11 billion of all foreign investment in Laos across all sectors during that period, hydropower production accounts for the largest share — 35 percent — followed by mining at 25 percent.[57] That seems impressive, but Laos had barely begun to tap its theoretical 26,500-megawatt potential for hydropower development, a prospect that distinguishes Laos as the could-be "battery" of northern Southeast Asia. As of 2015, the actually installed hydropower capacity, at 4,168 megawatts, represented merely 16 percent of that theoretical potential.[58] The large implied margin for further development explains why Vientiane hopes to generate 10,000 megawatts of hydropower by 2020, with up to three-quarters of that output earmarked for export to Southeast Asian countries as far south as Malaysia.[59]

Fourteen of the 20 cross-border transmission lines operating in 2017 linked Laos to Thailand; only one ran to China.[60] But Chinese involvement in generating Laotian hydropower has burgeoned. That growing engagement comes at a time when many traditional (DAC) donors have shied away from the sector due to mounting critiques by NGOs and development scholars highlighting the damaging impacts of large-scale hydropower dams on fisheries and the environment. Nevertheless, building such dams remains a policy priority for Laos's leaders. The energy tapped thereby is an attractively renewable export, an input to domestic industrialization, and a symbolic marker of high modernity showcasing the technological prowess of the Laotian state.[61] As for Chinese officials and investors, they view hydropower projects as chances to strengthen Beijing-Vientiane relations, lucrative targets for investment by Chinese SOEs, and means to the exercise and strengthening of China's own capacity and prowess as a user and exporter of hydropower.

Urbanism   With the global spread of neoliberal ideas, state resources and private funds have flowed increasingly into globally integrated corridors and nodes. In tandem with this trend, many governments have focused on enlarging and upgrading urban centers.[62] In Laos, urban development is crucial to the country's ability to attract capital and talent and become more than a passive intersection for flows of value between neighboring countries. Yet many traditional donors have continued to channel most of their aid funding toward rural areas. China has quickly seized the opportunity created by this relative neglect and taken the lead in supporting and shaping urbanism in Laos — the development of its cities and towns.

In Vientiane, for example, Chinese aid and investments have funded the construction of government buildings, convention centers, hotels, shopping malls, apartment complexes, and projects such as sports stadiums meant to enhance the national image. In northern Laos near the China border, Chinese investors have financed two casino-equipped special economic zones. In Luang Prabang, Chinese money has erected new hotels and other tourist facilities following a $86 million upgrading of the city's airport thanks to China's Export-Import Bank. As is typical of Chinese development cooperation, these projects have blended public with private interests in support of joint ventures by Laotian and Chinese firms. Such undertakings often lack transparency, however, and are therefore viewed as designed more to maximize profit than alleviate poverty.

Chinese Extractions, Laotian Concessions

Given the size and scope of Chinese aid and investment funding in Laos, the two countries' growing economic and political intimacy has triggered considerable debate. Participants in the debate include scholars, NGOs, media, and ordinary citizens of Laos. In popular discourse, China is commonly if privately portrayed as a new imperial or neo-colonial actor unsustainably consuming Laos's natural resources, leveraging development aid to further the commercial interests of Chinese SOEs, and undermining Lao culture and values.

In Laos, Cambodia, and Vietnam, natural resource extraction has indeed become the leading purpose of Chinese FDI — extractions made feasible by Chinese aid to build the infrastructure needed to forward the resources to the PRC.[63] Nor is China's footprint merely material in nature. In some parts of northern Laos, Chinese migration, tourism, and investment have been associated with the forced resettlement of local residents. In such places,

Mandarin has spread to the point of becoming nearly as commonly spoken as Laos's indigenous and official language, Lao.[64] Close ties between China and Laos have also caused tensions inside ASEAN, and between Laos and many of its traditional aid partners. Some members of ASEAN worry that Beijing's influence over Vientiane has weakened the regional association's ability to speak with one voice on contentious matters such as the territorial disputes over the South China Sea.

Controversial, too, are the high-modernist aspects of China-Laos cooperation. Some of Laos's DAC donors were notably unhappy when, in 2015, Beijing designed, built, and orbited Vientiane's first-ever telecommunications satellite. They worried that within the short 15-year life of Lao Sat-1, its operation might not earn enough to pay its considerable price — $341 million in fresh Laotian debt.[65] In a country designated "least developed," where health and education were severely under-resourced, such a project suggested to DAC that Vientiane cared more about acquiring prestige than lessening poverty. Also concerning were the far larger financial obligations associated with Chinese terms for the high-speed railway. Some wondered whether China's costly technocratic lending might send Laos back into the World Bank's "high risk" debt category from which it had only exited in 2012.[66] The silence of China in the face of Laotian abuses of human rights rankled as well.

If China has been widely criticized for its possibly hegemonic intentions in Laos, the country's leaders have generally welcomed Chinese aid and investment. It is also important to note that such a small country, so dependent on foreign help, has managed to negotiate more than four decades of ongoing foreign support from various sources. Despite a population one two-hundredth the size of China's and an estimated nominal GDP of just $15 billion in 2017, Laos's strong economic performance, wealth of natural resources, and geostrategic location have equipped its leaders with some leverage in dealings with foreign powers.[67] Laos's rulers merit much critique, but they deserve commendation for having avoided dependence on any one foreign country. Notable in this regard was the 2016 removal from office of then foreign minister Somsavat Lengsavad, also known as Ling Xu Guang. Perhaps with his Chinese ethnicity partly in mind, many believed he was fired for ceding too much to Beijing. While raising the level of Vientiane's engagement with Beijing, Laos's leaders have monitored the process so as not to lose control. Provincial authorities, too, have sought to regulate China's economic presence, albeit mainly to benefit their own interests and ambitions.[68]

It is important here to distinguish two inequalities — the one between China and Laos, and the one between Laos's government and its people. Although Vientiane is not a puppet of Beijing, the latter's impact cannot be ignored. Inside Laos, Chinese high modernism has abetted state control and enriched local elites, while helping to propel Laos forward toward its goal of outgrowing, by 2020, the stigma of being a "least developed country."[69] China further obliges and indulges Laotian authorities by not making its aid conditional on environmental protection or political reform.

China's role in Laos has been less kind to the country's vulnerable and impoverished citizens. In these communities, Chinese technocratic impulses have induced residential displacement, environmental degradation, food insecurity, and the consolidation of authoritarian and sometimes violent rule. By placing neoliberal rationality over social empathy while privileging elite interests at the expense of the disadvantaged, Chinese high modernism has translated the politics of development into seemingly apolitical matters of technique.[70]

Development, Damage, and Dispossession

This chapter argues that rapid economic growth in Laos has occurred in tandem with environmental damage, contestation over resources, and various forms of marginalization, exclusion, and disadvantage.[71] Correspondingly, in Laos, Chinese-style high modernist development has lacked transparency, privileged corporate profits over community needs, and unsustainably harvested natural resources.[72]

Infrastructure for transportation is a case in point. The scholarly literature documents the socioeconomic problems that cross-border linkages have posed for poor and vulnerable communities in Laos.[73] One such instance has been the China-financed upgrading and expansion of the North South Economic Corridor (NSEC) that runs through the Greater Mekong Subregion (GMS). Of the nine trade-facilitating "economic corridors" that crisscross the GMS, NSEC is the most important, with the heaviest traffic.[74] The highway's development has been linked to the competitive commercial exploitation of natural resources and associated land seizures, food precarity, and environmental degradation, among other threats.[75]

The ADB has praised NSEC for having driven economic growth while alleviating poverty and enlarging access to hospitals, schools, and other facilities. Yet these services remain beyond the reach of many who need them. Modern Chinese-built corridors serve business needs, but do little for poor villagers who lack the land or capital to produce marketable — transportable — goods.[76] What the locals need are smaller-scale community roads, and these have barely figured in Sino-Laotian high-modernist plans. NSEC and the high-speed railway are meant to advance the transactions of large and medium-scale firms that are mostly headquartered outside of Laos.[77] Passageways such as NSEC have integrated Laos more tightly into East Asian economic networks. But such corridors have done little to move Laos from the periphery toward the center of the activities those networks sustain — and toward the possible leverage for more inclusionary development that such centrality might serve.[78]

These conditions have prompted concern even among some Laotian officials, as in comments made to the author by a director in the Department of Transport. He noted that Laos had been "given a lot of money" to build border-crossing highways, but regretted that they were "only being used" — and damaged — "by trucks from Thailand and Vietnam." Foreign investors, he lamented, "only come to Laos for raw materials" that are not processed in Laos but are sent "straight to their final destination[s]" abroad. "We have private short-term benefits, but no long-term benefits" for the public good. "We are only becoming a transit country," he concluded.[79]

Positive correlations between Chinese aid funding and natural-resource extraction are well documented across the developing world.[80] "State-orchestrated market capitalism" in China has buoyed rapid growth in such locations for two decades, but energy security is required to sustain the pace.[81] China is not the only foreign investor guilty of unsustainably exploiting Laos's natural resources. What does distinguish China's role, however, is the acceleration of its rate of extraction over time, and its disregard for the environmental protocols of traditional (DAC) donors. The social and environmental challenges brought about by China's approach to development contributions are nowhere more evident than in its investments in the production of rubber.

Often promoted as an alternative to the farming of opium, rubber plantations have had wide-ranging deleterious effects. These include increased soil erosion in upland areas, threatened watersheds, diminished biodiversity, food insecurity including damage to edible forest products, and the death of livestock exposed to pesticide.[82] Plantations have often been implemented on communal land without the prior consent of local communities, whose subsistence-level members are turned into underpaid wage-laborers. For many communities, the net result of such outcomes has been not only the worsening of impoverishment, but possibly an increased risk of human trafficking as well.[83]

In the Mekong area, inland fisheries rank among the world's largest — a source of nutrition and income for millions of people in China, Vietnam, Thailand, Cambodia, and Laos.[84] An estimated 87 per cent of Mekong fish species are migratory, and that food source is accordingly exposed to the "serious negative impact" of hydropower.[85] While Chinese hydropower investors tap a valuable resource — water — for aggregate economic growth, they show little regard for the well-being of poor residents of affected sites, notably including their access to food.[86]

Due partly to pressure from civil society organizations, many traditional (DAC) donors no longer fund hydropower dams. Yet their withdrawal has done little to slow the pace of dam building, thanks to an influx of new Chinese and other Asian investments in drawing energy from the flowing of water down the Mekong and its tributary rivers. Notably in this context, Vientiane's decision to build a dam at Xayaburi in Laos has caused major tensions with Hanoi and Phnom Penh.

Alongside damages, displacements are another concerning result of Chinese-enabled mineral extraction, rubber cultivation, hydropower generation, and urban construction in Laos. Increasingly, as Chinese capital has poured into the country, local elites have gained control over land and other resources previously owned and tended by vulnerable communities and groups. Meanwhile, as allocations of land by Laotian authorities to Chinese investors have prompted the forced dispossession and resettlement of people living in or working on the allocated plots, "development" by such means has become more and more controversial.[87]

China is hardly the only foreign investor to have capitalized on Vientiane's concessionary approach to development. But China has pursued its land-hungry high-modernism with particular vigor. The former National Land Management Authority of Laos has concluded that over half of land concessions in the country — more than 2,000 in all — have been "detrimental" to the environment and local residents.[88] Analysts have noted an "assertiveness and enthusiasm to the promotion of concessions as engines of modernization . . . that is peculiar to Chinese projects" — and has fostered new forms of marginalization and detriment including insufficient financial compensation and losses of livelihood and public services, not to mention physical discomfort and emotional stress.[89] Dispossession of land has been particularly characteristic of private investments by Chinese firms in urban areas. "Most resettlement programs that are linked to private investments," one official observed, stem "from Chinese projects."[90]

Processes of possession by some through the dispossession of others — illustrated by the fortunes of Chinese corporate interests abroad, whether state or private, and the misfortune of those who are made to move — have grown increasingly common in developing countries.[91] "Visions of development and modernity" are used in this context as discursive tools to legitimize the appropriation of land and the removal of its poor and vulnerable users.[92] Undoubtedly, Chinese development cooperation has benefited the macroeconomy of Laos. But it has also fueled "logics of expulsion" that "coexist" with that aggregate material growth. Such logics have ratcheted up the numbers of people in poor countries worldwide who are being sidelined or left behind by the high modernism of the increasingly Chinese or like-minded promoters of development with Chinese characteristics.[93] Relevant to China's contribution to the spread of these "logics of expulsion" is the indifference of Beijing toward abuses of human rights and acts of political suppression.

Laos badly needs political reform. The level of repression there, as measured by Freedom House in 2017, was exceeded in only 17 of the 210 countries and territories covered in the comparison. In the same year, only 10 of the 180 jurisdictions ranked by Reporters Without Borders had less press freedom than Laos did.[94] Laos's police force and judicial system are under tight party control, political corruption is endemic, and at every one of its congresses, the ruling Lao People's Revolutionary Party (LPRP) has repeated its vow to ensure that economic growth does *not* incubate democracy.[95] Development plans are made and implemented top-down, while those who oppose them are put down. Laotians who contest state-approved projects are subject to attack, imprisonment, even disappearance.

Since gaining power in 1975, the LPRP has often abused the human rights of its citizens. Of these incidents, the most widely known and still criticized occurred in December 2012 when an internationally admired community development worker, Sombath Somphone, was "disappeared" off a street in Vientiane. Despite video evidence implicating the police, criticism from democratic countries, and requests for information on the case from nearly four dozen NGOs around the world, authorities remain unforthcoming and Sombath's fate is unknown. More recently, in 2017, three young Laotians were sentenced respectively to 12, 18, and 20 years in prison for having criticized their government on Facebook for violating human rights, engaging in corrupt behavior, and abetting the destruction of the country's forests.[96]

Deforestation illustrates how China and corruption are related to the decimation of Laos's natural environment. Investigative researchers with the World Wildlife Foundation implied as much when they determined that in 2013 Laos had in fact exported 1.4 million cubic meters of timber to China and Vietnam, a figure more than 10 times greater than the officially

reported amount.[97] In the light of China's arms sales to Laos, likely including the transfer of otherwise unspecified Chinese "office equipment" to the
defense ministry in Vientiane in 2017, it is also hard to ignore Beijing's role
in strengthening the repressive capacity of the Laotian state.[98] Environmental
predation aside, Chinese largesse also buffers its Laotian recipient against
Western pressure for political reform.

Conclusions

As the 21st century has unfolded, the People's Republic of China has
loomed ever larger in the political economy of the Lao People's Democratic
Republic. Trade relations between the two countries have grown; diplomatic
ties have tightened; flows of tourists and migrants have swelled; and China
has become one of the country's leading providers of aid and investment.
This chapter has sought to describe and appraise China's impact on Laos.

The analysis supports these conclusions: High modernism marks China's
profile in Laos's development. China's contributions have furthered its interests, economic and political. Chinese involvements in Laos — technocratic
and trickle-down — have bolstered the growth of the Laotian economy and
the power of its state while marginalizing and disadvantaging the most vulnerable among its people.

High modernism assumes that welfare is naturally fostered by economic
growth and overlooks the structural inequalities and mechanisms through
which the poor are "economically exploited, socially subordinated and
politically marginalized."[99] China's outlook is not unique in this respect.
Longstanding donors have also projected high-modernist and technocratic
assumptions about development that have privileged physical construction and aggregate growth over the needs of poor communities in Laos.
Increasingly, however, DAC donors have approached development aid with
more socially humane and ecologically sustainable priorities in mind.
Beijing, in contrast, still favors top-down, target-focused, engineer-driven
projects that bypass society, cater to the state, and fortify authoritarian rule.

Development is one thing. Empowerment is another. Barring significant
reforms inside both countries, China's help will be of little help to those in
Laos who need help the most.

Endnotes

1 Stanley Loh, "Taking Asean-China Ties to the Next Level," *Straits Times*, 15 September 2017, http://www.straitstimes.com/opinion/taking-asean-china-ties-to-the-next-level.

2 "China FTA Network," Ministry of Commerce, Beijing, http://fta.mofcom.gov.cn/english/.

3 James C. Scott, *Seeing like a State: How Certain Schemes to Improve the Human Condition Have Failed* (New Haven, CT: Yale University Press, 1998), 89.

4 "Laos GDP Annual Growth Rate," *Trading Economics*. In 2016, the GDP growth rates of Laos and Cambodia — each estimated at 6.90 percent — exceeded those of any of the nine other Southeast Asian countries. Also higher than 6 percent in 2016 were the rates estimated for China (6.70), Myanmar (6.30), and Vietnam (6.21). See "GDP Annual Growth Rate [GAGR]," "China GAGR," "Vietnam GAGR," and the list in https://tradingeconomics.com/country-list/gdp-annual-growth-rate, accessed 13 March 2018.

5 The chapter relies in part on fieldwork in Laos (May 2011–March 2012 and July–August 2015).

6 United Nations Development Programme (UNDP), *Human Development Report 2016: Human Development for Everyone* (New York: UNDP, 2016), 198–201 (Table 1), http://hdr.undp.org/sites/default/files/2016_human_development_report.pdf.

7 Laos is a multicultural country; more than half of its population is ethnically Lao. In this chapter, therefore, "Laotian" is used when citizenship is meant or the country as a whole is referred to.

8 UNDP, "About Lao PD," accessed 14 March 2018, http://www.la.undp.org/content/lao_pdr/en/home/countryinfo.html.

9 For more on the history of Laos, see Martin Stuart-Fox, *Buddhist Kingdom, Marxist State: The Making of Modern Laos* (Bangkok: White Lotus, 1996); Vatthana Pholsena and Ruth Banomyong, *Laos: From Buffer State to Crossroads?* (Chiang Mai: Mekong Press, 2006); and Pholsena, *Post-war Laos: The Politics of Culture, History, and Identity* (Ithaca, NY: Cornell University Press, 2006).

10 Viliam Phraxayavong, *History of Aid to Laos: Motivations and Impacts* (Chiang Mai: Mekong Press, 2009).

11 Organisation for Economic Co-operation and Development, "Query Wizard for International Development Statistics," accessed 14 March 2018 https://stats.oecd.org/qwids/.

12 Internet Directory of iNGOs in Lao PDR, 2016, "List of iNGOs," iNGO Network, accessed 1 June 2016, http://www.directoryofngos.org/ingo2/index.php.

13 The Asia Foundation (TAF), *The Changing Aid Landscape in East Asia: The Rise of Non-DAC Providers* (San Francisco: TAF, May 2014), http://asiafoundation.org/publication/the-changing-aid-landscape-in-east-asia-the-rise-of-non-dac-providers/. For an evaluation of Chinese aid to one Southeast Asian country, see Jin Sato, Hiroaki Shiga, Takaaki Kobayashi, and Hisahiro Kondoh, "'Emerging Donors' from a Recipient Perspective: An Institutional Analysis of Foreign Aid in Cambodia," *World Development* 39, no. 12 (2011): 2091–104, https://www.sciencedirect.com/science/article/pii/S0305750X11000842?via%3Dihub.

14 Ngaire Woods, "Whose Aid? Whose Influence? China, Emerging Donors and the Silent Revolution in Development Assistance," *International Affairs* 84, no. 6 (2008): 1206; and D. Fullbrook, "Hedging Southeast Asia: China's Relations with Burma, Cambodia and Laos," unpublished thesis, School of Oriental and African Studies, University of London, 2006. Also favorable to China, though not about Laos, is Deborah Bräutigam, *The Dragon's Gift: The Real Story of China in Africa* (Oxford: Oxford University Press, 2009).

15 Dambisa Moyo, *Dead Aid: Why Aid Is Not Working and How There Is a Better Way for Africa* (New York: Farrar, Straus and Giroux, 2009), 120–22.

16 See Chris Lyttleton and Pál Nyíri, "Dams, Casinos and Concessions: Chinese Megaprojects in Laos and Cambodia," in *Engineering Earth: The Impacts of Megaengineering Projects*, ed. Stanley D. Brunn (Dordrecht, Netherlands: Springer, 2011), 1243–65. Also see, e.g., Joshua Eisenman, Eric Heginbotham, and Derek Mitchell, *China and the Developing World: Beijing's Strategy for the Twenty-first Century* (Armonk, New York: M. E. Sharpe, 2007); and Joshua Kurlantzick, *Charm Offensive: How China's Soft Power Is Transforming the World* (New Haven, CT: Yale University Press, 2007).

17 Emma Mawdsley, *From Recipients to Donors: Emerging Powers and the Changing Development Landscape* (London: Zed Books, 2012).

18 For more on these terms, see James C. Scott, *Seeing Like a State: How Certain Schemes to Improve the Human Condition Have Failed* (New Haven, CT: Yale University Press, 1998).

19 Pál Nyíri, "Enclaves of Improvement: Sovereignty and Developmentalism in the Special Zones of the China-Lao Borderlands," *Comparative Studies in Society and History* 54, no. 3 (2012): 533–62. See also Marcus Power, "Angola 2025: The Future of the 'World's Richest Poor Country' as Seen through a Chinese Rear-View Mirror," *Antipode* 44, no. 3 (2012): 993–1014.

20 Nicola Banks and David Hulme, "New Development Alternatives or Business as Usual with a New Face? The Transformative Potential of New Actors and Alliances in Development," *Third World Quarterly* 35, no. 1 (2014): 193.

21 Nyíri, "Enclaves of Improvement," 557.

22 "China Pours Billions in Aid and Investment into Laos," Radio Free Asia, 12 January 2018, https://www.rfa.org/english/news/laos/billions -01122018160501.html.

23 Danielle Tan, "'Small Is Beautiful': Lessons from Laos for the Study of Chinese Overseas," *Journal of Current Chinese Affairs* 41, no. 2 (2012): 72.

24 Lao National Tourism Administration, *2015 Statistical Report on Tourism in Laos* (Vientiane: Government of Laos, 2015); and Martin Stuart-Fox, "Laos: The Chinese Connection," in *Southeast Asian Affairs 2009*, ed. Dalijit Singh (Singapore: Institute of Southeast Asian Studies, 2009): 141–69.

25 P. Khennavong, "Aid to Laos in the Twenty-First Century," doctoral dissertation, Crawford School of Public Policy, Australian National University, Canberra, 2014.

26 Overseas Development Institute (ODI), *Age of Choice: Lao People's Democratic Republic in the New Development Finance Landscape* (London: ODI, 2015), 25.

27 "2008–2020 Planning for Industrial Economic Development and Cooperation in Northern Part of Lao People's Democratic Republic — (Mid-term Draft for Opinions)," Northern Laos Industrial Economic Development and Cooperation Planning Preparation Group, May 2008, 175 pp. including appendices, https://mqvu.files.wordpress .com/2009/03/masterplan_econimic1.pdf; original published in Chinese. Hereafter "2008–2020"; page references are to the PDF of the English

version and because the page numbering is confusing, section names and numbers are included when possible. On AidData, see http://aiddata .org/about.

28 Echoing the Chinese Communist Party's use of "leading groups," for example, the plan ("2008–2020") recommends their establishment under state auspices in Laos to handle industry and tourism (section 9.6.1, 91; attachment 3, section 6.2, 4, respectively); "2008–2020" also touts the "development experiences" of Yunnan, noting the importance of "seeking truth from facts" in (unacknowledged) reference to the rather different uses of that traditional phrase by Mao Zedong and Deng Xiaoping. The document also credits Yunnan Province, unironically, with having made "great leaps forward" (see attachment 5, 10–15, especially section 1.1, 10).

29 The quoted phrases in this paragraph's second, third, and fourth sentences are Scott's as cited in the text above, whereas the fifth and sixth sentences solely reference the "2008–2010" report.

30 References relevant to "scientific and technical progress" can be found in "2008–2020" at preface, 2; section 9.2.3, 82–83; section 9.6.1, 91; and attachment 5, section 1.3, 11.

31 See "2008–2020": preface, 4; and sections 4.1.2 to 4.1.4, 26–27.

32 See attachment 2 in "2008–2020": 9 (Table 1); section 2, 10–12; and section 4, 16.

33 See "2008–2020": preface, 2, and section 3.4.1, 20.

34 See "2008–2020": section 3.4.1, 20.

35 See "2008–2020": section 9.7.4, 95–96.

36 Weiyi Shi, "Summary and Analysis: Plan for Industrial Economic Development and Cooperation in Northern Lao PDR," 2009, unpublished manuscript, 15.

37 See, e.g., Xinhua, "China Focus: CPC to Amend Party Constitution," Xinhuanet, 19 September 2017, http://www.xinhuanet.com/english/2017 -09/19/c_136619106.htm; or Charlotte Gao, "China Promotes Human Rights 'With Chinese Characteristics' Ahead of Human Rights Day," *The Diplomat*, 12 December 2017, https://thediplomat.com/2017/12 /china-promotes-human-rights-with-chinese-characteristics/.

38 Xinhua, "Country Report on China's Participation in Greater Mekong Subregion Cooperation," *ChinaDaily USA*, updated 16 December 2011, http://usa.chinadaily.com.cn/china/2011-12/16/content _14279772.htm.

39 These figures were generated by the author using data available at http://aiddata.org as of 13 August 2016. The third and fourth largest allocations were respectively to infrastructure for communications and to infrastructure for industry, mining, and construction.

40 Lao People's Democratic Republic (LPDR), *The Seventh Five-Year National Socio-Economic Development Plan (2011–2015) — Full Version* (Vientiane: Ministry of Planning and Investment, 7 October 2011), 8, 56, 86, 99, 100, 110, 115, 231, 267, http://www.wpro.who.int/countries/lao /LAO20112015.pdf.

41 LPDR, *Seventh Five-Year Plan*, 100. Economic growth as an "overall target" was to be achieved in "a progressive manner," but "progressive" was never defined.

42 LPDR, *Seventh Five-Year Plan*, 221, 98.

43 LPDR, *Seventh Five-Year Plan*, 128ff; and Asian Development Bank (ADB), *Greater Mekong Subregion: Twenty Years of Partnership* (Manila: ADB, 2012), 7.

44 Randi Jerndal and Jonathan Rigg, "From Buffer State to Crossroads State: Spaces of Human Activity and Integration in the Lao PDR," in *Laos: Culture and Society*, ed. Grant Evans (Chiang Mai: Silkworm Books, 1999), 35–60; and Pholsena and Banomyong, *Laos*.

45 "Laos-China Railway Project 16% Complete," *Laotian Times*, 9 January 2018, https://laotiantimes.com/2018/01/09/laos-china-railway -project-16-complete/.

46 For more, see Kearrin Sims, "The Asian Development Bank and the Production of Poverty: Neoliberalism, Technocratic Modernization and Land Dispossession in the Greater Mekong Subregion," *Singapore Journal of Tropical Geography* 36, no. 1 (2015): 112–26.

47 On these symbolic aspects, see Simon Creak, "Laos: Celebrations and Development Debates," in *Southeast Asian Affairs 2011*, ed. Daljit Singh (Singapore: Institute of Southeast Asian Studies, 2011), 105–28.

48 Oliver Schönweger and Peter Messerli, "Land Acquisition, Investment, and Development in the Lao Coffee Sector: Successes and Failures," *Critical Asian Studies* 47, no. 1 (2015): 97.

49 M. B. Dwyer, "Building the Politics Machine: Tools for 'Resolving' the Global Land Grab," *Development and Change* 44, no. 2 (2013): 309–33.

50 Ian G. Baird, "Land, Rubber and People: Rapid Agrarian Changes and Responses in Southern Laos," *Journal of Lao Studies* 1, no. 1 (2010): 2.

51 See James C. Scott, *The Art of Not Being Governed: An Anarchist History of Upland Southeast Asia* (New Haven, CT: Yale University Press, 2009), xii, 4–5, 253; and Ian G. Baird, "Turning Land into Capital, Turning People into Labour: Primitive Accumulation and the Arrival of Large-Scale Economic Land Concessions in the Lao People's Democratic Republic," *New Proposals: Journal of Marxism and Interdisciplinary Inquiry* 5, no. 1 (November 2011): 10–26.

52 See Noboru Ishikawa, *Between Frontiers: Nation and Identity in a Southeast Asian Borderland* (Athens, OH: Ohio University Press, 2009); Anna Lowenhaupt Tsing, *Friction: An Ethnography of Global Connection* (Princeton, NJ: Princeton University Press, 2004); and Geoffrey Wade, *China and Southeast Asia* (Abingdon, UK: Routledge, 2009).

53 Stuart-Fox, "Laos," 144.

54 United Nations, *An Investment Guide to the Lao People's Democratic Republic: Opportunities and Conditions* (New York: UN, 2010), 43, citing a field report by Laos's National Agriculture and Forestry Institute.

55 Rosmarie Sommer, unpublished paper, 7.

56 Rosmarie Sommer, "Analysis of Investments of China and Other Neighboring Countries and Their Influence on the Development Context in Lao PDR," SDC issue paper, Vientiane, 25 February 2010, 1, citing Phouthonesy (9 September 2009), http://rightslinklao.org/wp-content/uploads/downloads/2014/05/SDC-Mandate_China-in-Lao-PDR_-SHORT_February2010-2.pdf.

57 Sommer, "Analysis of Investments," 1, citing Phouthonesy.

58 International Hydropower Association, "Laos," updated May 2016, https://www.hydropower.org/country-profiles/laos.

59 GE Reports Staff, "Laos, the Minnow Nation with Gigantic Development Ambitions," 21 August 2017, https://www.ge.com/reports/laos-minnow-nation-gigantic-development-ambitions/.

60 "LAOS: Electricity Facts," *Laotian Times*, 10 January 2017, https://laotiantimes.com/2017/01/10/laos-latest-electricity-facts/.

61 Cf. James Ferguson, *Expectations of Modernity: Myths and Meanings of Urban Life on the Zambian Copperbelt* (Berkeley, CA: University of California Press, 1999), 243.

62 Neil Brenner, *New State Spaces: Urban Governance and the Rescaling of Statehood* (Oxford, UK: Oxford University Press, 2004); Tim Bunnell,

Malaysia, Modernity and the Multimedia Super Corridor: A Critical Geography of Intelligent Landscapes (London, UK: RoutledgeCurzon, 2004); Saskia Sassen, *Global Networks, Linked Cities* (London, UK: Routledge, 2002).

63 Leeber Leebuapao and Sykham Voladet, "Impacts of China on Poverty Reduction in Laos," in *Assessing China's Impact on Poverty in the Greater Mekong Subregion,* ed. Hossein Jalilian (Singapore: Institute of Southeast Asian Studies, 2013), 385–428.

64 Pholsena and Banomyong, *Laos,* 183.

65 Vientiane Times, "Lao Sat-1 Excites Local, Foreign Companies," The Nation (Bangkok), 14 January 2016, https://www.nationthailand.com /noname/30276926.

66 ODI, *Age of Choice,* 13.

67 ODI, *Age of Choice,* 30.

68 M. B. Dwyer, 2011, "The Internal Frontier: Chinese Extraterritoriality in Northern Laos?," *New Mandala,* 11 February 2011, http://asiapacific .anu.edu.au/newmandala/2011/02/11/the-internal-frontier-chinese-extra territoriality-in-northern-laos/.

69 Danielle Tan, *Chinese Engagement in Laos: Past, Present, and Uncertain Future* (Singapore: Institute of Southeast Asian Studies, 2015), 3.

70 See Arturo Escobar, "Discourse and Power in Development: Michel Foucault and the Relevance of His Work to the Third World," *Alternatives* 10, no. 3 (2000): 388. Also see Tania Murray Li, *The Will to Improve: Governmentality, Development, and the Practice of Politics* (Durham, NC: Duke University Press, 2007); and Timothy Mitchell, *Rule of Experts: Egypt, Techno-politics, Modernity* (Berkeley: University of California Press, 2002).

71 See Derek Hall, Philip Hirsch, and Tanya Murray Li, *Powers of Exclusion: Land Dilemmas in Southeast Asia* (Honolulu: University of Hawai'i Press, 2011); Tania Murray Li, "Indigeneity, Capitalism, and the Management of Dispossession," *Current Anthropology* 51, no. 3 (2010): 385–415; Jonathan Rigg, *Challenging Southeast Asian Development: The Shadows of Success* (London, UK: Routledge, 2016).

72 Keith Barney, "Laos and the Making of a 'Relational' Resource Frontier," *The Geographical Journal* 175, no. 1 (2009): 146–59.

73 Lyttleton and Nyíri, "Dams, Casinos and Concessions."

74 National Transport Facilitation Committees, "North-South Economic Corridor," Australian Aid and ADB, 2013, http://www.gms-cbta.org /north-south-economic-corridor.

75 See Asian Development Bank, *Emerging Asian Regionalism: A Partnership for Shared Prosperity* (Manila: ADB, 2008), 53; ADB, *Build It and They Will Come: Lessons from the Northern Economic Corridor: Mitigating HIV and Other Diseases* (Manila: ADB, 2009); Serge Doussantousse, Bounchanh Sakounnavong, and Ian Patterson, "An Expanding Sexual Economy along National Route 3 in Luang Namtha Province, Lao PDR," *Culture, Health & Sexuality* 13 (2011): 279–91; Melody Kemp, "Roads to Destruction: ADB's Contradictory Roads, Biodiversity and Plantations Activities in Lao PDR or How Did You Know We Wanted Ecocide?," NGO Forum on the ADB, Quezon City, Philippines, 2017, https://issuu.com/ngoforumonadb/docs/roads_to _destructionadb___s_contrad.

76 James R. Chamberlain, *Participatory Poverty Assessment II (2006): Lao People's Democratic Republic* (Manila: National Statistics Center ADB, October 2007), 77, https://www.yumpu.com/en/document /view/24323441/participatory-poverty-assessment-ii-2006-lad-nafri.

77 Jim Glassman, *Bounding the Mekong: The Asian Development Bank, China, and Thailand* (Honolulu, HI: University of Hawai'i Press, 2010).

78 See Glassman, *Bounding the Mekong*; Pholsena and Banomyong, *Laos*; and Jonathan Rigg, *Southeast Asia: The Human Landscape of Modernization and Development* (London: Routledge, 1997), 174.

79 Personal communication, 9 February 2012.

80 For instance: Bräutigam, *The Dragon's Gift*; Eisenman, Heginbotham, and Mitchell, *China and the Developing World*; Dorothy McCormick, "China & India as Africa's New Donors: The Impact of Aid on Development," *Review of African Political Economy* 35, no. 1 (2008): 73–92; and Lyttleton and Nyíri, "Dams, Casinos and Concessions."

81 Giles Mohan, "Beyond the Enclave: Towards a Critical Political Economy of China and Africa," *Development and Change* 44, no. 6 (2013): 1259.

82 See Baird, "Land, Rubber and People"; Paul T. Cohen, "The Post-opium Scenario and Rubber in Northern Laos: Alternative Western and Chinese Models of Development," *International Journal of Drug Policy* 20, no. 5 (2009): 424–30; Miles Kenney-Lazar, "Plantation Rubber, Land Grabbing and Social-property Transformation in Southern Laos,"

Journal of Peasant Studies 39, nos. 3–4 (2012): 1017–37; Janet C. Sturgeon, "Cross-Border Rubber Cultivation between China and Laos: Regionalization by Akha and Tai Rubber Farmers," *Singapore Journal of Tropical Geography* 34, no. 1 (2013): 70–85.

83 Chamberlain, *Participatory Poverty Assessment II.*

84 Tira Foran, Timothy Wong, and Shawn Kelley, "Mekong Hydropower Development: A Review of Governance and Sustainability Challenges," Mekong Program on Water Environment and Resilience, 2010, 10.

85 Richard M. Friend and David J. H. Blake, "Negotiating Trade-offs in Water Resources Development in the Mekong Basin: Implications for Fisheries and Fishery-based Livelihoods," *Water Policy* 11, Suppl. 1 (2009): 13–30.

86 Jonathan Cornford, *Occasional Paper 1: Globalisation and Change in Southern Laos*, Occasional Paper Series (Bangkok: Focus on the Global South, 2006); Michael Goldman, *Imperial Nature: The World Bank and Struggles for Social Justice in the Age of Globalization* (New Haven, CT: Yale University Press, 2005).

87 See Baird, "Turning Land into Capital"; Simon Creak, "Laos in 2013: International Controversies, Economic Concerns and the Post-socialist Rhetoric of Rule," in *Southeast Asian Affairs 2014*, ed. Daljit Singh (Singapore: Institute of Southeast Asian Studies, 2014), 149–71; Sims, "The Asian Development Bank and the Production of Poverty"; and, for comparison, Ian G. Baird, "The Global Land Grab Meta-narrative, Asian Money Laundering and Elite Capture: Reconsidering the Cambodian Context," *Geopolitics* 19, no. 2 (2014): 431–53.

88 Somsak Pongkhao, "Laos Losing Out to Land Concessions," *Vientiane Times*, 27 April 2011, 2.

89 Lyttleton and Nyíri, "Dams, Casinos and Concessions"; Sims, "The Asian Development Bank and the Production of Poverty."

90 Sengdara Douangmyxay, Deputy Head of the Department of Housing, Vientiane, personal communication, 3 February 2012.

91 Mohan, "Beyond the Enclave"; Power, "Angola 2025."

92 Hall, Hirsch, and Li, *Powers of Exclusion*, 196; Lyttleton and Nyíri, "Dams, Casinos and Concessions," 12–13.

93 Saskia Sassan, *Expulsions: Brutality and Complexity in the Global Economy* (USA: Belknap Press, 2014), loc. 37 and 39 of 4834, Kindle.

94 "Table of Country Scores," *Freedom in the World 2018: Democracy in Crisis* (New York: Freedom House, 16 January 2018), https://freedomhouse.org/report/freedom-world-2018-table-country-scores; Reporters Without Borders, "2017 World Press Freedom Index," https://rsf.org/en/ranking_table.

95 Bertelsmann Stiftung, "BTI [Bertelsmann Transformation Index] 2016: Laos Country Report," Bertelsmann Stiftung, Gütersloh, Germany, 2016, https://www.bti-project.org/fileadmin/files/BTI/Downloads/Reports/2016/pdf/BTI_2016_Laos.pdf.

96 Worldwide Movement for Human Rights, "Three Government Critics Jailed for up to 20 Years," International Federation for Human Rights (FIDH), Paris, 16 May 2015, https://www.fidh.org/en/region/asia/laos/three-government-critics-jailed-for-up-to-20-years.

97 Nirmal Ghosh, "Report Reveals Plunder of Lao Forests," *Straits Times*, 25 October 2015, http://www.straitstimes.com/asia/se-asia/report-reveals-plunder-of-lao-forests.

98 Prasanth Parameswaran, "China Gifts Military Equipment to Laos," *The Diplomat*, 14 April 2017, https://thediplomat.com/2017/04/china-gifts-military-equipment-to-laos/.

99 Alastair Greig, David Hulme, and Mark Turner, *Challenging Global Inequality: Development Theory and Practice in the 21st Century* (Basingstroke, UK: Palgrave Macmillan, 2007), 27.

CHAPTER 12

Distance and Dominance
CHINA, AMERICA, AND SOUTHEAST ASIA'S NORTHERN TIER

John D. Ciorciari, *University of Michigan, United States*

Over the past quarter century, China's engagement in mainland Southeast Asia has expanded dramatically. Analysts now routinely refer to the prospect or existence of a Chinese "sphere of influence" in the subregion.[1] References abound to the gravitational pull on mainland Association of Southeast Asian Nations (ASEAN) members to fall into China's "orbit."[2] China's growing economic footprint and concomitant political sway have caused concern in all five states along ASEAN's "northern tier" — Myanmar, Thailand, Laos, Cambodia, and Vietnam — given their historical experiences of Chinese intrusion. Submission to a Chinese sphere of influence is anathema to their stated foreign policy aims, all of which emphasize independence. Yet each has accommodated Chinese influence to a degree that makes Chinese primacy, or even hegemony, more likely in their neighborhood. China's power and proximity are not the only reasons. As this chapter will emphasize, their decisions to accept heightened Chinese influence have also reflected their "vulnerable distance" from other nodes of power — above all the United States.

China's rise in mainland Southeast Asia has been neither uniform nor unidirectional. At times, each of the northern-tier states has sought to reduce or repel Chinese influence to decrease its vulnerability to territorial loss, communist subversion, or economic subjugation, among other threats. These states have variously endeavored to hedge against China, diversify their foreign relations, and draw Beijing into constraining regional institutions. To be effective, each of these strategies requires help from powerful partners. America's geographic remoteness and political distance, whether manifest in enmity or wavering friendship, has undermined America's appeal as a hedging partner and stunted the northern-tier states' ability to diversify and integrate into the ASEAN-centered institutional matrix. When relations with the United States have chilled, all five states have turned to China for support and accepted the resultant risks.

The "vulnerable distance" of the northern-tier states is not fixed by latitudes and longitudes. It reflects how policymakers interpret geographic constraints, set strategic priorities, and navigate ideational differences. Mainland ASEAN members' vulnerability to Chinese influence is partly a product of their own policy choices, which frequently have privileged near-term domestic regime stability at the longer-term expense of relative international isolation. Decisions by the US government and others to sanction and ostracize them have also contributed — moves often satisfying domestic audiences at a significant cost to US strategic influence in Southeast Asia.

This chapter begins by elaborating on the causes and effects of political distance between the United States and China's mainland ASEAN neighbors. It describes how that distance arose historically in US relations with mainland Southeast Asia and gave the Mekong states incentives to lean on China, particularly in the midst and wake of domestic crises. It then discusses how President Barack Obama's "rebalance" sought to reverse those trends with limited success, as legacy issues and contemporary fallouts imposed continued political distance. It concludes with policy implications, stressing that the greatest near-term threat to the autonomy of ASEAN's northern tier may arise less from a spike in Chinese assertiveness than from isolationism in the United States. In this context, the "America First" presidency of Donald Trump merely illustrates and exacerbates a condition that it did not create: Southeast Asia's "vulnerable distance" from the United States.

Proximity, Distance, and Vulnerability

Smaller states along a great power's periphery face obvious vulnerability to the nearby colossus.[3] A great power has more or less permanent interest in projecting influence in its neighborhood, and adjacency facilitates its ability to do so — whether via the flow of ideas, commerce, or infantry columns. As Steve Chan notes, geographic and cultural proximity is a "double-edged sword"[4] that can foster communication, trust, and mutual interest or generate enmity and fear by facilitating great-power intrusion. Often, adjacency has both effects simultaneously, the former tending to attract allegiance and the latter to compel it. Importantly, proximity gives the large power the plausible future capacity to pry away territory, cut lopsided trade deals, or exert political control even when its current capabilities are limited and its intentions appear benign. Thus, even when China has been weak or suffered diplomatic setbacks, mainland Southeast Asia often has been depicted as part of its "natural sphere of influence."[5]

While proximity to a great power does impose structural constraints on smaller neighbors, their strategic dispositions cannot be deduced deterministically from their relative capabilities or positions on a map. Their susceptibility, receptiveness, or resistance to a great power's influence reflect a variety of material and ideational factors. Power disparities are clearly a factor. Stephen Walt argues that smaller neighbors are apt to resist a great power when they can and accommodate it when they must.[6] When they harbor deep-seated fears and have powerful friends, even small or weak states sometimes dare to balance assertively against nearby giants, such as Cuba and Nicaragua vis-à-vis the United States during the Cold War and Georgia vis-à-vis Russia more recently.[7] More often, as both Walt and Robert Ross argue, smaller states lack the confidence or capacity to balance against a great power in its own backyard, which is a dangerous game. They accommodate it to varying degrees, largely for lack of other options.[8]

Ideational factors also contribute. Ideology and civilizational identity are oft-cited factors conditioning neighborly responses. David Kang contends that Asian traditions of hierarchy and cultural deference have inclined some of China's neighbors to accept higher degrees of influence from Beijing than the states arrayed around other great powers.[9] Martin Stuart-Fox emphasizes the role of varied historical experiences in mainland Southeast Asian responses to the rise of China.[10] These present alternative, and often complementary, explanations for the observable rarity of outright balancing in ASEAN's northern tier and the virtual absence of such behavior since the end of the Cold War.

The vulnerability arising from proximity nevertheless gives smaller neighbors ample reason to guard their autonomy. When balancing is an unattractive option, they seldom lie prostrate and submit to subjugation. Instead, they adopt other counter-dominance strategies. These include entering into limited countervailing security alignments, diversifying diplomatic ties, hedging via cooperation with both the nearby great power and its rivals, and using regional rules and interdependence to shape the large neighbor's behavior. These strategies, well-studied in the literature on Southeast Asian responses to the rise of China, are much more common along ASEAN's northern tier than outright balancing or unfettered accommodation. Such approaches, in combination, can help even a weak state achieve considerable autonomy, leverage, and protection. Each one depends on capable partners, and for mainland ASEAN members facing China, each hinges significantly on US support.

This is perhaps most evident for states seeking limited security alignments to guard against Chinese overreach, as Vietnam recently has done. Limited alignments offer a potential layer of protection without the risks of tight defense pacts, but they only provide effective insurance when backed by a heavy counterweight — a role the United States alone has the military muscle to play.[11] The broader range of strategies that constitute "hedging," which include efforts to cultivate a "middle position"[12] between China and the United States and offset risks by investing in cooperation with both powers,[13] similarly rely on an American counterweight.

The United States also plays an important gatekeeper role when China's neighbors seek to diversify or engage in multilateral diplomacy. To varying degrees, all Southeast Asian governments seek to diversify and spread their foreign policy risk across numerous relationships. They also seek to "bind" and "enmesh" China and other external powers in webs of shared norms and interests.[14] With the exception of Thailand, the mainland states have had relatively short, rocky relations with ASEAN and other key Asia-Pacific powers such as India, Australia, and Japan, leaving them fewer options. The United States has sometimes helped the northern-tier states forge diplomatic and economic connections. In other instances, US pressure on friends and allies to shun a disfavored government has reduced the flow of international aid and obstructed access to prospective bilateral partners and regional forums. In short, when relations with Washington are distant or hostile, China's neighbors often have an unappetizing menu of counter-dominance options and little choice but to court and accommodate Beijing.

Geography does impose distance on US relations in mainland Southeast Asia. Transporting goods is more costly, dispatching troops is more difficult, and high-level political visits consume more time. While adjacency gives Beijing an evergreen interest in mainland Southeast Asia, security and environmental challenges in the Mekong area only tend to impact US national interests visibly when linked to broader regional or global threats, such as communist expansion or violent Islamic extremism. The resulting ebb and flow of US engagement has left little confidence in US staying power and renders abandonment a perennial concern of US security partners. Adding to the challenge is the widespread belief that after the Vietnam War, the United States cannot commit credibly to deploy large-scale ground forces to continental Southeast Asia. China thus holds a strategic trump card of sorts — by contrast to the Korean Peninsula or maritime Southeast Asia, where US naval primacy makes spatial distances easier to bridge.[15]

However, there is little evidence that the shadow of the People's Liberation Army is the prime driver of mainland Southeast Asian accommodation of Beijing. Since China sought to "teach Vietnam a lesson" for the invasion of Cambodia in 1979 (and emerged instead with a bloody nose from its pupil), the prospect of major land-based conflict has been relatively remote. China has seldom relied on coercive pressure, and when it has been most assertive or intrusive, its neighbors have tilted away. Beijing's bulldozing behavior in the South China Sea has alienated Vietnam, and its heavy hand in Myanmar has prompted its friends in Naypidaw to take a step back. China has gained influence primarily through consensual means as the "Mekong five" reach northward for assistance, welcome aid and investment, and confer clout on Beijing in the process.[16]

Northern-tier leaders have turned to China most readily when other avenues for aid have been obstructed. Washington, while hardly the sole sponsor of sanctions against these states, has almost always led the charge. Sanctions and other forms of international ostracism have driven up the vulnerability of mainland Southeast Asian countries — or at least their governments — and their need for protection against external predation, economic loss, and other domestic threats to regime stability. Ostracism boosts the appeal of a mighty neighbor with the means to help remedy the problem, while the vulnerable weaker party loses leverage to resist advances that it disfavors. The northern-tier states' vulnerability to Chinese influence thus reflects their geographic and political distance from Washington, not just their nearness to Beijing.

US distance has been partly a matter of American choice. US foreign policy has been the product of a multilevel game in which regional issues are sandwiched between domestic political pressures and global strategic imperatives. The worldwide nature of US interests and commitments means that senior officials' attention is almost always tugged toward crisis flashpoints, which alongside major-power relations leaves little residual room on their agenda. When mainland Southeast Asia is not itself the flashpoint or a prime locus of great-power jockeying, senior officials turn their eyes elsewhere, and relatively small domestic coalitions can exert an outsized impact on US policy. In particular, a dearth of high-level executive focus leaves more scope for interest groups and their allies on Capitol Hill to impact policy, often through the relatively blunt measures available to a legislature through the power of the purse strings. In the case of mainland Southeast Asia, expatriate organizations and human rights groups have had a strong impact on US policy, tending to disfavor engagement and promote sanctions that have magnified US political distance and encouraged the northern-tier states to turn to Beijing for succor.

Of course, China's neighbors do not simply respond to exogenous shocks in their foreign relations. Their own policy choices affect the course of their relations with the United States and other partners as well. Their foreign policies have been driven more by concerns rooted in their domestic and local environments than by efforts to effectuate change at the systemic level — a phenomenon common among small or weak states and throughout the Global South.[17] As Amitav Acharya contends, Southeast Asian foreign policies have long expressed, in particular, "the fundamental importance of regime security."[18] When facing local challengers, mainland Southeast Asian leaders generally have worried first and foremost about consolidating power and guarding their flanks domestically and have fretted less about the foreign policy consequences. In many cases, their responses have been repressive, with foreseeably adverse effects on their relations with Washington given applicable US law and policy pronouncements. Leaders along the northern tier often have backed themselves into vulnerable international positions for largely domestic reasons. The 1997 putsch by Cambodian prime minister Hun Sen against his royalist rival is one example; the Myanmar junta's brutality against Buddhist monks a decade later amid the Saffron Revolution is another.

Distance in US relations with mainland Southeast Asian capitals and added exposure to Chinese influence thus stem from more than gravitational pushes and pulls. They reflect agency. Although most of the action in mainland Southeast Asia has occurred in the form of modest shifts and realignments, rather than dramatic ruptures or rapprochements, there have been important punctuation marks. The following sections illustrate how distance to Washington inclined the northern-tier states to turn to Beijing at key junctures and continues to affect their foreign policy orientations.

The Legacy of US Political Distance

Since the Vietnam War, US relations with mainland Southeast Asia have been marked by long periods of drift, punctuated by crises that have widened the political distance between Washington and the region. Inconsistent US strategic commitment to the mainland and repressive governance by resident Southeast Asian regimes share responsibility for this tendency to varying degrees across the five northern-tier capitals. Alongside this secular trend, crisis-driven fissures have opened doors for China to engage robustly even with neighbors whom it menaced during the Cold War.

America's strategic drift began well before its withdrawal from Vietnam. Tremors of concern ran through Bangkok and other ASEAN capitals as the 1969 enunciation of the Nixon Doctrine and ensuing Sino-American rapprochement foreshadowed a diminishing US commitment to mainland Southeast Asia. As the Vietnam War drew to a close, Thai leaders had to recalibrate. The danger of abandonment was obvious as the last choppers flew off the rooftop of the US embassy in Saigon. The opposite danger of entrapment reared its head when US marines defied Thai leaders and used U-Tapao air base to rescue the SS *Mayaguez* from Khmer Rouge forces that had punched America provocatively in the nose. In July 1975, the government of Kukrit Pramoj restored ties to Beijing despite years of mutual hostility and Chinese support for the Communist Party of Thailand. That inaugurated a hedging arrangement designed to reduce reliance on the United States in the face of possible Vietnamese expansion.

The Vietnam saga left legacies in US domestic politics that have long constrained foreign policy. The "Vietnam Syndrome," fed by public exhaustion and distrust, essentially ruled out US re-engagement on the mainland even as evidence of Khmer Rouge atrocities mounted. It also fed Congressional resistance to providing reconstruction aid to Vietnam, which Hanoi demanded when the Carter administration sought to normalize relations and lift sanctions in 1977. Consequently, the mainland state with the most salient history of resisting Chinese domination, Vietnam, remained distant from the United States, relying instead on its alliance with the Soviet Union for protection as its relations with China entered a tailspin and descended into the brief Sino-Vietnamese War of 1979.

The Vietnam War created American constituencies with lasting interests in mainland Southeast Asia and profound opposition to engaging with the communist regimes of Indochina. Among these groups were veterans and their families; large émigré populations including Vietnamese, Hmong, Montagnards, and Khmers who had fought beside Americans; and some journalists, scholars, and human rights advocates who continued to focus on Indochina after covering the war. Even today, moves to mend fences with Vietnam, Cambodia, and Laos remain highly suspect in relevant US domestic political circles. The same is true for Burma — renamed Myanmar in 1989 — as refugees and rights advocates have long featured prominently in policy discussions, often as champions of stiff sanctions.

Waxing political distance between the United States and the northern-tier states was not solely a result of US withdrawal, of course. Mainland

Southeast Asian governments frequently gave Washington ample reasons to remain distant, disengage, or sanction them. This was apparent in the US response to the Vietnamese occupation of Cambodia. The Carter and Reagan administrations faced the difficult decision of how to help Thailand strengthen a Cambodian resistance that relied on odious Khmer Rouge forces to do most of the fighting. In the event, the United States dispatched arms to Thailand and helped forge a political coalition led by Prince Sihanouk to occupy Cambodia's seat at the United Nations. The United States stayed at more than arm's length from the Khmer Rouge guerrillas, however. The Thai military turned primarily to Beijing to supply them, deepening the Sino-Thai partnership.

Neighboring Burma was the object of little US attention until the dramatic events of 1988–90, when the military junta crushed the "8888 Uprising," ousted Ne Win, imposed the State Law and Order Restoration Council (SLORC), negated national election results, and placed Aung San Suu Kyi under house arrest. The wave of US-led international sanctions that ensued drove the vulnerable junta to turn to Beijing, which likewise faced international opprobrium for the Tiananmen Square Massacre. Myanmar veered from its traditional policy principles of independence and non-alignment and leaned into a close security and economic partnership with China. Chinese arms and investment helped the junta batten down the hatches domestically, but fears of overdependence soon prompted SLORC leaders to look for ways to hedge and diversify. Myanmar acceded to ASEAN in 1997 and sought rapprochement with India — modest steps that nonetheless demonstrated the junta's interest in staying out of China's corner.

US relations strengthened elsewhere on the peninsula in the early 1990s. The return of civilian rule in Bangkok in 1992 eased Thai-US tension after a military coup the preceding year brought a suspension of US aid. In Cambodia, UN-sponsored elections provided an opening for US re-engagement, and ties with Vietnam thawed with the removal of US sanctions and exchange of diplomatic missions in 1994–95. In July 1997, however, back-to-back crises magnified US distance from some mainland Southeast Asian states and drew China closer.

The first crisis took place in Cambodia. Hun Sen seized power after his partisans defeated royalist forces loyal to Prince Ranariddh in a series of bloody street clashes. Many international observers deemed his move a coup, and the US government quickly imposed sanctions. So did Europe. Western ostracism helped delay Cambodia's entry into ASEAN. China took advantage. Beijing gave Hun Sen a combined financial lifeline and show of political support in the form of a USD $10 million loan soon followed by a promise of $28 million in military equipment. The ruling Cambodian People's Party (CPP) returned the favor by closing Taiwan's local representative office and taking other steps to cut ties to Taipei.[19]

Apart from hurting Cambodia's economy, these events were a watershed in Sino-Cambodian relations. The relationship had and retains a certain structural logic. Cambodia seeks protection from its larger immediate neighbors and China seeks a counterweight to Vietnamese influence on the peninsula. Yet the friendship was far from ordained. The two states were bitter adversaries during the era of the Third Indochina War, when China backed the Khmer Rouge resistance against a Cambodian government led from 1985 onward by Hun Sen. Only after the UN-sponsored elections in 1993, as Hun Sen and his royalist rival Norodom Ranariddh jockeyed for position, did Chinese leaders foresee that Hun Sen would likely emerge on top and begin to make amends.[20] Underwriting Sino-Khmer rapprochement was the CPP's estrangement from other potential partners, including the United States.

The other pivotal event in July 1997 was the onset of the Asian Financial Crisis. In the response to the crisis, the US Treasury played a critical but criticized role. Thai officials, resenting the stringent conditions attached to International Monetary Fund (IMF) loans, saw the episode as an American betrayal. Much has been written criticizing the IMF's conditions as a dose of the wrong medicine from an economic standpoint, but they also affected strategic trust more broadly. To Thai and other Southeast Asian audiences, this was not how to treat one's friends, let alone — in the Thai case — one's ally. China again capitalized, winning goodwill in Bangkok and across the region by refusing to engage in competitive devaluation by weakening the renminbi. Beijing also stepped into the breach in Laos, helping to avert financial catastrophe there. Across the region, Southeast Asian governments rued the extent of their reliance on the United States. They began looking for other options. They launched ASEAN Plus Three and pursued regional financial cooperation ventures that included East and Southeast Asia but excluded the United States, such as the Chiang Mai Initiative in support of financial liquidity.

While US relations with Vietnam remained cool, those with Cambodia, Myanmar, and Laos were frigid. The US government had ample reason to criticize Hun Sen's abuses in Cambodia, but sanctions did not dislodge his Cambodian People's Party. Instead, predictably, they pushed Cambodia to reduce its reliance on Western trade and aid and embrace other partners, particularly China. Moreover, invective from the US Congress in the late 1990s spilled over from appropriate censure into far-fetched threats, most notably in a push by Congressman Dana Rohrabacher to try Hun Sen for war crimes rather than the leaders of the Khmer Rouge. The extended maintenance of Congressional sanctions on Cambodia and the degree of US opprobrium for the CPP reflected Cambodia's distance and, to many US lawmakers, its unimportance. The US State Department generally sought to engage, and American officials were instrumental in the creation in 2004 of a special tribunal to address Khmer Rouge atrocities. Yet Washington initially provided little funding to the court, limiting the scope for American leadership, and key figures in Congress barred direct funding to the Cambodian government more generally. China took advantage, becoming what Hun Sen described in 2006 as Cambodia's "most trustworthy friend."[21]

Laos, long an afterthought in US foreign policy, remained distant politically as well as geographically — a sparsely populated, landlocked state beyond the prime areas of contemporary US commercial and strategic interest. US-Lao relations were driven mainly by concerns related to the Vietnam War. These included the recovery of remains of Americans missing in action, the removal of vast quantities of unexploded ordinance, and the Lao government's treatment of ethnic Hmong once allied to the US war effort. Until 2004, Laos was one of only three countries denied normal trade relations with the United States, alongside Cuba and North Korea. Even then, prominent Hmong-American groups opposed trade normalization, and the US Senate passed a concurrent resolution condemning Lao violations of human rights.

With little attention from the West, Lao foreign relations were concentrated in a narrow circle involving its neighbors Vietnam, Thailand, and increasingly China. As in Cambodia, Laos's proximity to China was not always a basis for friendship. During the 1980s, the Vietnam-backed government in Vientiane spewed invective at Beijing and regarded "hegemonistic" China as a mortal threat. Since the 1990s, however, Lao leaders have been motivated to cooperate with China based on their thirst for investment and infrastructure, and their desire to wean their country from its double dependence — economically on Thailand, politically on Vietnam. China gradually became Laos's top source of investment, a major trading partner, and a political patron comparable in importance to Vietnam.

As in the case of Laos, US policy toward Myanmar was driven largely by a modest number of civil society leaders and key figures on Capitol Hill focused on human rights. Critics called Washington's approach "one-dimensional."[22] Hero worship of Aung San Suu Kyi and a (largely ineffective) regime of sanctions pleased some Western audiences attentive to politics in Myanmar but gave the junta ample reason to resist opening the country to the United States. A massacre in Depayin (2003), the repression of the Saffron Revolution (2007), and the mishandling of the response to Cyclone Nargis (2008) all backed Myanmar further into a diplomatic corner. Spurned by the West and viewed without enthusiasm by India and ASEAN, the generals turned once again to China. Beijing obliged by vetoing, in 2007, a key UN Security Council resolution that would have demanded political reforms, and by providing a steady supply of aid, trade, and investment that muted the effect of international sanctions — at least for Myanmar's ruling elite.

The distance from Washington to Bangkok also grew. In 2006 the Thai military ousted populist prime minister Thaksin Shinawatra. As it had in 1991, the United States demanded reform and suspended some military and economic aid, incurring the ire of the junta. China again won favor by furnishing the incumbent generals with a steady diet of support and voicing respect for Thailand's internal affairs. US sanctions did not prevent further political upheaval in 2007 when "yellow shirt" forces with ties to the military and the royal palace toppled another elected government. If the impact on Thai politics of cutting off American aid was unclear, the effect on US-Thai relations was not. Deep-seated Thai concerns about US abandonment were reinforced.

US policy toward Southeast Asia's mainland faced unenviable dilemmas. In each of the five states, authoritarian leaders seized or firmly retained power and used it to repress legitimate opposition. Most of them committed serious and serial violations of human rights — anathema to the stated aims of US foreign policy. These actions prompted censure, and in that respect mainland Southeast Asian leaders were themselves the authors of their distance from Washington (among other capitals), their increased need for support from Beijing, and thus their greater vulnerability to Chinese influence.

US policy contributed to these trends, sometimes unnecessarily. Any interstate relationship requires setting priorities and balancing multiple competing values and interests. Mainland Southeast Asia was a US foreign policy sideshow after 1975. Unsupported by major economic interests and lacking frequent attention from high-level officials, American policy toward the subregion grew imbalanced, often relying on blunt instruments and broad gestures that resonated well in relevant domestic circles but left fewer openings for constructive US engagement. The price of setting disfavored Southeast Asian regimes adrift became increasingly apparent after several years of war in Iraq and Afghanistan, when US officials cast their gaze again to the ASEAN region to find China building roads, gaining friends, and cultivating other means of influence.

Shifting Proximities and the US Rebalance

The Obama administration's "rebalance" toward Southeast Asia was meant to reverse the drift, to resist the gravitational forces associated with geographic remoteness. Although far from a policy of containment, the rebalance aimed to restore US influence and credibility in areas where China's clout had risen, including in ASEAN's northern members. The policy's most novel elements — its emphases on multilateral diplomacy and engagement with 20th-century adversaries — epitomized Obama's broader approach to foreign policy. He and senior US officials logged millions of air miles to boost the American diplomatic presence in Southeast Asia. US naval deployments and support for the Trans-Pacific Partnership also served to show that spatial distance could be surmounted. Yet the rebalance met significant impediments in mainland Southeast Asia, largely due to political distance emanating from historical legacies and contemporary rifts alike.

US strategic goals in the northern tier were more incremental than transformative: to reinvigorate the Thai-US alliance; build a strategic partnership with Vietnam; reach out to old foes in Cambodia, Myanmar, and Laos; elevate ASEAN's role in the area; and thicken economic ties. The United States did try to sponsor a new construct in the sense of the 1955 Baghdad Pact that had enlisted Turkey, Iraq, Iran, and Pakistan in a belt of anti-Soviet containment. The rebalance was nevertheless intended to counter Chinese influence and prevent Beijing from acquiring and exercising hegemony there or in the rest of Southeast Asia.

The rebalance did see major breakthroughs in mainland Southeast Asia, particularly in Myanmar and Vietnam. Yet it suffered significant limitations due to domestic constraints in the United States, governance problems in Southeast Asia, and cautious local responses to American overtures due to residual concerns about US credibility and staying power. Because of these legacies of political distance and related obstacles to closer bilateral relations, the effects of the rebalance on the strategic landscape of mainland Southeast Asia and China's role in the subregion were uneven, incomplete, and therefore arguably fleeting.

Tension in the Thai-US Alliance

The Thai-US alliance has long been the backbone of American engagement in mainland Southeast Asia, and Bangkok has served as the hub for many US regional operations. At the same time, Thailand was and is one of China's most important mainland partners. Bangkok's strategy of relative equili-bration between Beijing and Washington limited Thai receptiveness to the rebalance, while political upheaval and another military coup in 2014 put further stress on the alliance relationship.

Even before the coup, competition between the United States and China overlapped with conflict inside Thailand between mass-populist "reds" and elite-royalist "yellows" to the detriment of Washington's engagement. Thai critics of the rebalance — particularly "yellow"-leaning conservatives with links to the military — warned that Sino-American polarization could strain Sino-Thai relations. That contributed to Bangkok's 2011 rejection of an American request to use the U-Tapao airfield for NASA operations, a move motivated by concerns about possible military motives behind Washington's interest.[23] Some conservative Thai elites saw Obama's 2012 visit to Bangkok, the warmth he showed toward Prime Minister Yingluck Shinawatra, and his remarks about democracy as evidence that Washington favored the "red shirt" movement. To some, that was a stab in the back after decades of defense cooperation. After the coup in May 2014, the United States suspended $4.7 million of assistance, canceled a bilateral military exercise, and scaled down another — the large, multinational, Thai-based set of maneuvers known as Cobra Gold. Thailand's prime minister, General Prayut Chan-o-cha, replied to these penalties by vowing, "Thailand must stand on its own dignity."[24] He and other leaders of the junta promptly reached out to their Chinese counterparts, who stepped forward to provide new investment — a familiar dance across ASEAN's northern tier.

In a January 2015 speech at Chulalongkorn University — the first by a visiting senior US official after the coup — Assistant Secretary of State Daniel Russel said that the US-Thai relationship had been "challenged" by the coup, criticized Yingluck's removal and impeachment, and pressed the junta to end martial law and restrictions on free assembly and take steps "toward stable and participatory democracy."[25] Prime Minister Prayut said he was "upset" by the remarks and summoned the US chargé d'affaires.[26] In February, days before the 2015 Cobra Gold exercises were scheduled to begin, Chinese defense minister Chang Wanquan visited Bangkok, where he stressed that Beijing would not "interfere" in Thailand's domestic pol-itics and pledged further military aid.[27] The Thai defense ministry later considered granting China permission to refurbish the Sattahip naval base on the Gulf of Thailand. A senior Thai official described the move as a way to "rebalance" after decades of US access to U-Tapao.[28] Sino-Thai military exercises, begun in 2010, were also expanded, including joint drills on land and at sea. These moves reflected the junta's desire for a modicum of realignment, its appreciation for the steadiness of Chinese military support, and its doubts about the utility and reliability of the American security commitment.

Nevertheless, some senior Thai officials remained wary of China, recalling its support for communist insurgents during the Cold War and uneager to grant Beijing leverage to push through investment deals disadvantageous to Thailand. China's economic role in Thailand was and remains sizable, but among the mainland states, Thailand has enjoyed the most diversified economic relations with Japan, Europe, and the maritime members of ASEAN, among others. Thailand's cooperation with US forces as a non-NATO ally still dwarfs its military cooperation with China, and even two coups and two aid curtailments in an eight-year period had still not prompted a major shift. The troubles in Thai-US relations were and are more appropriately viewed as constraints on the scope for US re-engagement than as likely reasons for an outright rupture.

Vietnam's Recalibration

The feud in the South China Sea — the latest in a long history of Sino-Vietnamese conflict — made Hanoi an obvious focus of Obama's rebalance. America's relations with Vietnam had improved during the Clinton and George W. Bush administrations, and waxing Chinese assertiveness at sea gave Washington a wide opening to re-engage on the security front. In December 2009 China announced plans to develop tourism on several of the Paracel Islands claimed by Hanoi, which Beijing had taken by force in 1974. The move triggered outrage in Vietnam. In 2010 China expanded naval exercises and patrols in disputed waters. In July of that year in Hanoi, then secretary of state Hillary Clinton asserted an American "national interest" in the South China Sea. Vietnamese officials demanded that China "immediately cease and stop the recurrence of [its] violations of Vietnam's sovereignty,"[29] and the US and Vietnamese navies conducted their first joint exercises since the Vietnam War, albeit focused on the less sensitive subject of safety at sea.

Sino-Vietnamese tension worsened in 2011 when a Chinese ship rammed and cut the cables of a Vietnamese seismic-exploration vessel. The launch of an annual Vietnam-US Defense Policy Dialogue in 2010 and a visit by Defense Secretary Leon Panetta to Cam Ranh Bay in 2012 were among the key steps toward the "Comprehensive Partnership" agreed to by the two presidents, Truong Tan and Obama, in 2013. The agreement featured an American pledge of support for Vietnam's capacity to conduct coastal patrols.[30] In 2014 China stationed an oil rig in disputed waters.[31] Subsequently, as Beijing accelerated its island-building campaign in the Spratly Islands, Vietnam leaned closer to the United States. Especially important, strategically and symbolically, was the lifting of the 30-year-old US arms embargo on Vietnam — begun in 2014 and completed with Obama's visit to Hanoi in May 2016.

Some observers have advocated a robust security alignment between Vietnam and the United States, or even a formal security treaty.[32] In 2017 one analyst proposed a de facto "US-Vietnam alliance that can neutralize Chinese primacy in Southeast Asia."[33] Such an outcome has been and remains, however, an unlikely prospect. In the foreign and domestic policies of both countries, important barriers to closer cooperation have precluded an outright alliance, even without the name. First, mistrust arising from the ideological gulf between the United States and Vietnam limits each side's willingness to invest in the other. Chinese scholar Li Kaisheng had this gulf in mind when he referred to Vietnam's policy as "two-faced," that is, turning to Washington for support in the South China Sea, but keeping the Americans at arm's length on matters of political reform — a mirror image of how Hanoi engages with Beijing.[34] Even as the Obama administration lifted the arms embargo, critics in the United States flayed the White House for neglecting Vietnamese human rights abuses. On Hanoi's side, US pressure for domestic political reforms was seen as threatening Communist Party rule. Notable in Obama's May 2016 announcement of the lifting of sanctions was the caveat that "sales will need to still meet strict requirements, including those related to human rights."[35] Notwithstanding President Trump's apparent lack of interest in human rights, domestic politics on both sides virtually ensure that the conditions attached to substantial security support will require careful negotiation.

Second, Vietnamese leaders have been reluctant to bear the brunt of Chinese anger in exchange for an uncertain American commitment to their country's security. In October 2016 two US Navy vessels visited Vietnam's main naval base and deepwater port at Cam Ranh Bay — the first such occurrence since 1975 — but Hanoi has been careful to allow other countries access as well. Beijing's interest in the South China Sea is firm and long term, in contrast to the doubts of Americans about confronting China over "a bunch of rocks" on the other side of the world.[36] China also has become Vietnam's top trading partner and a major source of investment, crucial to Hanoi's development plans. That mix of need and vulnerability helps explain why Hanoi has been loath to rely too heavily on the United States.

Vietnam has sought instead to create a spiderweb of diverse ties — arms purchases from Russia, joint exploration with India, defense cooperation with Australia and Japan, and diplomatic ententes with other ASEAN claimants in the South China Sea. Hanoi has worked assiduously to "internationalize" its feud with China by engaging Washington, but also to "multilateralize" it by driving discussions into regional forums such as ASEAN and the East Asia Summit.[37] This blend of counter-dominance strategies is no panacea for a state long wary of excessive Chinese influence, but it represents Vietnam's effort to "satisfice" in the light of strong residual concerns about politically interventionist American motives on the one hand, and the risks of American inconsistency and possible abandonment on the other. As of 2017, Vietnam had not renounced its traditional "three noes": "no foreign troops on Vietnamese soil, no allying with one country to counter another, and no military alliances with foreign powers."[38]

Engagement of the "CML" Countries

The boldest aspect of the rebalance in mainland Southeast Asia was the Obama administration's effort to engage the regimes furthest from Washington politically, notably those in power in the four northern-tier states of Cambodia, Myanmar, Laos, and Vietnam. Leaving aside US relations with Vietnam, which were warming before Obama took office and strengthened considerably during his tenure, the "CML" states were all tilted clearly toward China as the rebalance began. Engaging them in some fashion was a *sine qua non* for restoring US influence along the northern tier.

The most dramatic changes occurred in US relations with Myanmar. Myanmar's generals had long looked to Beijing for support, but they had reasons to resent China's footprint. Those reasons included Chinese support for ethnic rebel groups; the influx of Chinese people, goods, and money into the area around Mandalay, "effectively Sinicizing northern Myanmar"; and worry over the effects of Chinese influence on Myanmar's prized sovereignty and independence.[39] Suspicious of the generals and wary of domestic American blowback, the Obama administration pursued ties cautiously at first, but moved more quickly and decisively after Aung San Suu Kyi's National League for Democracy (NLD) won by-elections in 2012. Steps in the process of rapprochement included the incremental reduction of US sanctions, more or less in tandem with developments including Myanmar's release of political prisoners; the junta's consent to nationwide elections; the appointment of the first US ambassador in more than two decades; and Obama's high-profile meetings with President Thein Sein and Aung San Suu Kyi.

The Obama administration regarded this punctuated process of rapprochement as a signal foreign policy achievement.[40] By 2014, however, Washington's investment in Myanmar was coming under domestic fire. Officially sanctioned brutality against the embattled Muslim Rohingya population in Rakhine State prompted charges of genocide, while tepid responses from Aung San Suu Kyi undermined her appeal. Bipartisan critics on Capitol Hill flayed the Obama administration for having embraced the junta too soon. Occasional flare-ups in other contested ethnic areas and the military's continuing hold on key ministries, businesses, and a sizable share of parliament also called into question the sustainability of Myanmar's reforms.

The NLD-led government that took office in 2016 pledged to adhere to the country's traditionally independent and non-aligned foreign policy. In theory, that suggested a possible reorientation to a position equidistant between China and the Western governments that had long supported the NLD. To be sure, irritants abounded in Sino-Myanmar relations, ranging from the cancellation of the controversial Beijing-backed Myitsone dam project to the accidental killing of several Chinese by Myanmar border forces in 2015. Yet the NLD leadership found itself doubly preoccupied — keen to help keep the army in its barracks without assuming the additional risk of bad relations with China, the first state to dispatch a high-ranking visitor to Myanmar after the new government took office. The party's relations with the United States were also not devoid of complications, including US ambassador Scot Marciel's polite but firm refusal in 2016 to accede to the government's request to stop using the term "Rohingya."[41] Myanmar's bureaucracy in 2017 was still populated with the old guard, and the legacy of mutual distrust between Washington and Nyapyidaw still constrained cooperation in defense and other domains.

In Cambodia also, the challenges of overcoming past and present sources of political distance have been apparent. The US rebalance was built on America's gradual opening to the Cambodian People's Party (CPP) during the Bush years and featured Obama's unprecedented meeting with Hun

Sen in 2012, as well as high-profile visits by then Secretary of State Hillary Clinton and her successor John Kerry. The shift from a sanctions-first policy to wary engagement did open channels for added US influence. But long-standing distrust, Hun Sen's ongoing repression of political dissent, and the strength of Sino-Cambodian ties have kept Washington–Phnom Penh relations cold.

One might have expected Cambodian leaders to welcome the rebalance as a way to address the increasing imbalance in their country's foreign relations. Over the past two decades, China has acquired clear primacy among Cambodia's external partners. While the United States remains a major market for Cambodian exports, in most other respects China's material offerings have come to dwarf US economic engagement and aid. China has dominated foreign investment in Cambodia, buttressed the CPP politically, and emerged as the country's main military patron. In exchange, Cambodia has provided easy access to resources and occasional diplomatic favors related to China's "core interests."[42] This drift into a patron-client relationship has raised many eyebrows in Cambodia, a weak country that has long struggled to avoid external predation or subjugation, and Cambodia has sought trade, investment, and other forms of cooperation from other partners. Nevertheless, its foreign policy has been and is less hedged and less diversified than almost any other Southeast Asian state. The lure of economic gain and comfort of trusted protection have enticed the CPP to stay close to Beijing, while continued impasses with the United States (and other states) have reduced the appeal of countervailing options.

US officials have struggled to achieve the right balance between engaging the CPP and censuring its bad behavior. Obama's "tense" 2012 meeting with Hun Sen, in which the president emphasized human rights, did not signal rapprochement between the two governments; it reinforced the gulf between them.[43] Cambodia's role as ASEAN chair that year, when it blocked the foreign ministers' communiqué and otherwise defended Chinese interests, demonstrated the region-wide implications of its increasing fealty to Beijing. After the 2013 Cambodian elections, when the opposition did unexpectedly well and its supporters filled the streets demanding electoral investigations and reform, the US government responded more cautiously than it had in the past. More recently, US talks with Cambodia have concentrated on trade, although human rights groups, Cambodian-Americans, and some members of Congress have continued to press the administration to focus on Hun Sen's breaches of democratic norms and human rights.

When US officials have urged observance of human rights, Hun Sen has not been shy about playing the China card. In 2009, when the US government canceled a shipment of 200 military trucks in protest of Cambodian repatriation of Uighur asylum-seekers, Beijing offered 257 replacement vehicles, which Phnom Penh gratefully accepted.[44] In 2014, when the United States suspended aid to demand an investigation into alleged fraud in Cambodia's 2013 elections, China again extended support.

Hun Sen's relative affinity for Beijing and his suspicions of Washington — long a supporter of his main domestic rival, Sam Rainsy — present formidable obstacles for the exercise of US influence in Cambodia. Decades of distrust has made CPP leaders loath to put breakable eggs in an American basket, and partly for that reason, Washington has not developed leverage sufficient to compete with Beijing for local influence and gain local traction toward Cambodian political reform. Barring an unlikely near-term change of the domestic guard in Phnom Penh, China will likely remain ascendant.

Obama's rebalance also affected Laos — one of the ASEAN states most reliant on Chinese patronage and formerly most neglected by the United States. In 2012, Hillary Clinton became the first US secretary of state to visit Vientiane since 1955. John Kerry followed in January 2016 as Laos's position as ASEAN chair thrust it into the limelight, a rare bit of prominence for the small, insular state. Kerry bore gifts. He announced a new aid package including $6 million for school meals for impoverished pupils and possibly stepped-up funding for the $19.5 million US program on unexploded ordinance.[45] Though subtly stated, the subtext of Kerry's visit was clear. After meeting with Prime Minister Thongsing Thammavong, Kerry stressed their agreement on the importance of a "unified ASEAN." He thus hinted at American fears that Laos would follow Cambodia's 2012 example and do China's bidding on matters regarding the South China Sea. A few months later, Chinese foreign minister Wang Yi confirmed his expectation that Laos (and Cambodia and Brunei) would do precisely that.[46]

By 2016, China had gained a dominant economic position in Laos and arguably had eclipsed Vietnam as Laos's most important tutor on diplomacy as well. Alongside Cambodia, Laos is one of the two Southeast Asian states that has drifted most clearly into a Chinese sphere of influence. That has not occurred without pushback. Concerns regarding sovereignty and independence have mounted in Vientiane.[47] But Lao policy alternatives are limited. To Laos, perhaps more than any other Southeast Asian state, the United States cannot offer a credible invitation to hedge against Beijing. Millions of dollars in aid cannot match billions in Chinese investment. For Laos, counter-dominance must focus instead on diversification, including through engagement with other Southeast Asian states and involvement in multilateral institutions — settings that might, if only modestly, help to cushion the small and landlocked country against Chinese demands.

Strains on ASEAN Centrality

A distinctive feature of the rebalance was the elevation of ASEAN in US Asia policy. Singaporean diplomat Tommy Koh asserted rightly that "ASEAN has never had a better friend in the White House."[48] In Obama's first term, the United States appointed a resident US ambassador to ASEAN in Jakarta, acceded to the Treaty of Amity and Cooperation in Southeast Asia, joined the East Asia Summit, and inaugurated a US-ASEAN summit that Obama would attend several times. American-ASEAN relations also benefited from Myanmar's opening, which removed a longstanding irritant to US multilateral diplomacy in Southeast Asia. Added engagement with ASEAN helped Washington answer charges of US "diplomatic absenteeism" stoked by the wars in Iraq and Afghanistan.[49] In paying attention to ASEAN, the United States helped to position it as the core cog in Asia's evolving institutional structure. Obama's team saw ASEAN's centrality as a way of advancing a "rules-based order" in the Asia-Pacific consonant with US values and useful in reducing the costs and conflicts involved in shaping the behavior of regional states, especially China.

ASEAN was and remains nonetheless subject to serious centrifugal forces. As Amitav Acharya argues, the association has become "more diverse and divided," and thus "the principle of ASEAN centrality has increasingly come under stress."[50] The most obvious instances of turbulence involving China have arisen over the South China Sea. Cases in point include China's use of its Cambodian proxy to thwart an ASEAN consensus on the matter in July 2012 in Phnom Penh; the comparably China-driven and sea-related failure of the ASEAN Defense Ministers Meeting-Plus to issue a communiqué in November 2015; and the pushback against Beijing's partly presumptuous claim that Laos, Cambodia, and Brunei had all agreed to support the Chinese position on the South China Sea in ASEAN talks in 2016.

A fault line has also begun to emerge between mainland and maritime Southeast Asia. A modest subregional architecture has existed since the establishment of the Mekong River Commission (MRC) in the mid-1990s. But competition for influence has risen in recent years, as China, the United States, and other external powers have courted the "Mekong five." The US Lower Mekong Initiative and annual Mekong-Japan summits, for instance, both launched in 2009, have concentrated on development aid and the environment, as has the MRC.

The Lancang-Mekong Cooperation (LMC) forum is China's answer. This Beijing-led body was launched in 2015 to encourage broad cooperation between China and the northern-tier states. The forum embodies China's interest in exerting stronger leadership on its southern periphery. It features leaders' meetings and a broad agenda based on three topical "pillars" strikingly similar to those that summarize ASEAN's concerns: political/security, economic, and socio-cultural. The LMC's significance also lies in its links to Beijing's Belt and Road Initiative and related China-led ventures such as the Asian Infrastructure Investment Bank. Although modest in its initial aims, the LMC has the potential to harness vast Chinese resources and promote a wide array of projects between China and participating Southeast Asian countries — a proactively bilateralist agenda that could further disunite ASEAN.

A Wobbly Economic Pillar

Last but not least, Obama's rebalance was meant to reduce the distance between the United States and Asia in economic terms — the domain in which Chinese primacy has been most readily apparent along ASEAN's northern tier. The prime vehicle for that effort was the Trans-Pacific Partnership (TPP). Singapore's prime minister Lee Hsien Loong described it as the "beef in the hamburger" of American pledges to stay engaged in Asia.[51] Domestic political developments in the United States in 2016 dispensed with the meat. In the race between presidential candidates in 2016, the Democrats' Hillary Clinton abandoned the TPP under pressure from her party's left despite having been an author of the rebalance. Her opponent, Donald Trump, excoriated the pact as anti-American and withdrew the United States from it on the first working day following his inauguration. In any event, even with the United States on board, the TPP would not have rectified the steeply skewed character of trade and investment flows across mainland Southeast Asia. Vietnam, a likely winner had the pact gone through, was the subregion's sole participating state.

Two American initiatives, Expanded Economic Engagement (E3) and ASEAN-US Connect, aimed to help ASEAN members plug into US trading grids and prepare for future TPP accession. But these efforts were scant compared with the boom in Chinese economic activity. By the end of 2016, China accounted for 24 percent of Myanmar's total (two-way) foreign trade and sizable shares in Cambodia and Laos (21 percent each), Vietnam (20 percent), and Thailand (16 percent). China was the top trading partner in all northern-tier states save Laos, where it was second to Thailand. Chinese trade with each country dwarfed US levels, which ranged from 9 to 13 percent of total trade in Thailand, Cambodia and Vietnam to negligible sums in Laos and Myanmar. [52]

China also has become a major player on the investment side. It has become the dominant investor in Laos, where it accounted for nearly 65 percent of foreign direct investment inflows in 2015 and 2016, and was the second-largest investor in Cambodia (25 percent, slightly behind the European Union) and Thailand (9 percent, behind only Japan) and a significant contributor in Vietnam (6 percent). [53] Its share of investment in Myanmar has ebbed as other investors have seized opportunities since the country's opening, but China's stock of investment there remains large. Between 2001 and 2012, China accounted for more than 40 percent of Myanmar's foreign direct investment inflows. [54] Physical proximity and linkages by land have made trade and investment the domains in which China enjoys the clearest comparative advantage. That competitive edge has helped Beijing amass influence in its near neighborhood, though not without prompting Southeast Asian desires to prop doors ajar for other entrants.

The Trump Factor and Its Implications

The Trump administration's relations with mainland Southeast Asia generally have demonstrated the dangers of the region's vulnerable distance. Trump inherited a number of delicate political relationships along ASEAN's northern tier but has invested less than his predecessor in trying to strengthen them. Trump's focus on domestic payoffs, willingness to starve the State Department, and failure to articulate a coherent Asia-Pacific strategy have curtailed US engagement with individual states and undermined American leadership in the region as a whole.

Governance problems in some mainland states, such as the Rohingya crisis in Myanmar, ongoing military rule in Thailand, and suffocation of political dissent in Cambodia presented the Trump administration with unenviable dilemmas as it took office. Preventing drift in those relationships would be challenging. The downgrading of human rights and democracy in Trump's foreign policy raised the possibility of strengthening ties by lowering governance standards. However, even traversing this problematic path would require robust engagement in pursuit of a clear strategic vision. Thai prime minister Prayut Chan-o-cha's October 2017 state visit to Washington thus conveyed a rapprochement of sorts, but one highly qualified by Trump's insistence on shrinking the bilateral trade deficit, US demands for Thai cooperation on security matters also of concern to China, and general Thai uncertainty about Trump's foreign policy direction.[55]

With Thailand's northern-tier neighbors, the Trump administration has reverted to a pattern familiar in mainland Southeast Asia — inconsistent diplomatic engagement coupled with periodic (often ineffectual) American slaps on the wrist for bad domestic behavior. Recent US criticism of Hun Sen's civil society clampdown and reluctant imposition of targeted sanctions in Myanmar have irked officials in each country but done little to address their governance failures. Both Cambodia and Laos, which has receded in US policy since its year as ASEAN chair expired, continue to gravitate toward Beijing.

Vietnam stands as a possible exception to the drift. Prime Minister Nguyen Xuan Phuc's May 2017 working visit to Washington was the first by a Southeast Asian leader during Trump's presidency. Trump lavished praise on Vietnam during his visit to Hanoi for the Asia-Pacific Economic Cooperation (APEC) forum several months later, and interest alignment in the South China Sea provides an ongoing basis for cooperation. Vietnam was also widely perceived as a prime beneficiary of the TPP, however, and Trump's continued focus on an America-first trade agenda lowers the likelihood of a mutually appealing bilateral deal. Instead, early in 2018, Vietnam and the United States locked horns in the World Trade Organization, with Washington issuing a complaint against several state-owned Vietnamese firms and Hanoi challenging US tariffs on fish fillets. As throughout the northern tier, the Trump administration's erraticism and inward-facing orientation render Vietnamese leaders loath to invest too much in the relationship.[56]

Overall, most economic, diplomatic, and strategic trends on the mainland continue to flow away from the United States and in favor of China. Some scholars and statesmen have argued that a Chinese sphere of influence would be a natural reflection of relative power and proximity — what Robert Ross has called a "geography of the peace."[57] Zbigniew Brzezinski similarly has admonished the United States to "respect China's historical and geopolitical role in maintaining stability on the Far Eastern mainland."[58] The maintenance of that "stability" would imply more than a degree of US deference and disengagement; it would also entail some forfeiture of freedom by the states on China's continental periphery. Their autonomy is better insured by a balance of external influence than by pledges of Chinese non-interference alone.

This analysis suggests a path whereby US officials could help facilitate such a balance. Doing so would require pairing strong governance critiques with engagement packages that communicate credibility and long-term partnership.[59] It would require embracing incrementalism and occasional steps backward with Thailand, Vietnam, and Myanmar, leveraging regional ties to engage Laos and Cambodia, refocusing on ASEAN centrality, and filling the void created by US withdrawal from the TPP to help mainland states maintain diverse economic portfolios. Above all, these elements would need to be woven into a coherent overarching strategy. Few of these features have been apparent during the Trump era. Without a change in the current course, geography may indeed come to resemble destiny. The prime near-term threat to the autonomy of ASEAN's northern tier therefore may come less from a surge in domineering Chinese behavior than from a distracted or uninterested United States.

Notes

1 See, for example, Catharin Dalpino, "Japan-Southeast Asia Relations: Abe Opens New Fronts," *Comparative Connections* 17, no. 1 (May 2015); Pornpimol Kanchanalak, "The Significance of Strategic Partnership with Japan," *The Nation* (Thailand), 12 February 2015; Benjamin Reilly, "Southeast Asia: In the Shadow of China," *Journal of Democracy* 24, no. 1 (2013): 160.

2 See, for example, Thitinan Pongsudhirak, "Myanmar as the Ultimate Global Pivot," *Nikkei Asian Review,* 23 November 2013; Chien-peng Chung, *Contentious Integration: Post-Cold War Japan-China Relations in the Asia-Pacific* (London: Routledge, 2016), 155; Carl Thayer, "China and Vietnam Eschew Megaphone Diplomacy," *The Diplomat,* 2 January 2015.

3 Kautilya's *mandala* theory in *The Arthasastra* thus treats a large state as the natural enemy of the immediate neighbors arrayed around it. See the translation in Patrick Olivelle, *King, Governance, and Law in Ancient India: Kautilya's Arthasastra* (Oxford: Oxford University Press, 2016), 273–76.

4 Steve Chan, *Looking for Balance: China, the United States, and Power Balancing in East Asia* (Stanford, CA: Stanford University Press, 2012), 85.

5 See, for example, C. P. Fitzgerald, *China and Southeast Asia since 1945* (Victoria: Longman, 1973), 96; Leo Suryadinata, *Overseas Chinese in Southeast Asia and China's Foreign Policy* (Singapore: ISEAS, 1978), 19; Thitinan Pongsudhirak, "Myanmar and Thailand in a Mainland Great Game," *East Asia Forum,* 14 July 2013.

6 Stephen M. Walt, *The Origins of Alliances* (Ithaca, NY: Cornell University Press, 1987), 23–24, 30–31. He points out, for example, that the Soviet Union had to defeat Finland twice within five years to bring about "Finlandization."

7 Chan, *Looking for Balance,* 84.

8 Robert S. Ross, "Balance of Power Politics and the Rise of China: Accommodation and Balancing in East Asia," *Security Studies* 15, no. 3 (2006): 392–93; Walt, *The Origins of Alliances,* 31.

9 See, for example, David C. Kang, *China Rising: Peace, Power and Order in East Asia* (New York: Columbia University Press, 2007), chs 3 and 6.

10 See Martin Stuart-Fox, "Southeast Asia and China: The Role of History and Culture in Shaping Future Relations," *Contemporary Southeast Asia* 26, no. 1 (2004): 116–39.

11 John D. Ciorciari, *The Limits of Alignment: Southeast Asia and the Great Powers since 1975* (Washington, DC: Georgetown University Press, 2010), ch. 1.

12 Evelyn Goh, *Meeting the China Challenge: The U.S. in Southeast Asian Regional Security Strategies*, Policy Studies 16 (Washington, DC: East-West Center, 2005), viii.

13 See Cheng-Chwee Kuik, "The Essence of Hedging: Malaysia and Singapore's Response to a Rising China," *Contemporary Southeast Asia* 30, no. 2 (2008): 159–85.

14 Amitav Acharya, "Will Asia's Past Be Its Future?" *International Security* 28, no. 3 (2003/04): 153; Evelyn Goh, "Great Powers and Hierarchical Order in Southeast Asia: Analyzing Regional Security Strategies," *International Security* 32, no. 2 (2007/08): 119.

15 Largely for this reason, Ross concludes that China already "dominates mainland Southeast Asia" in a strategic sense. Robert S. Ross, *Chinese Security Policy: Structure, Power and Politics* (New York: Routledge, 2009), 47.

16 See, for example, Cheng Guan Ang, "China's Influence over Vietnam in War and Peace," and Evelyn Goh and David I. Steinberg, "Myanmar's Management of China's Influence: From Mutual Benefit to Mutual Dependence," both in *Rising China's Influence in Developing Asia*, ed. Evelyn Goh (Oxford: Oxford University Press, 2016).

17 See, for example, Mohammad Ayoob, *The Third World Security Predicament: State Making, Regional Conflict, and the International System* (Boulder, CO: Lynne Rienner, 1995); William Reno, *Warlord Politics and African States* (Boulder, CO: Lynne Rienner, 1999); Robert Rothstein, *Alliances and Small Powers* (New York: Columbia University Press, 1968).

18 Amitav Acharya, *Constructing a Security Community in Southeast Asia: ASEAN and the Problem of Regional Order* (London: Routledge, 2001), 58.

19 Long Kosal, "Sino-Cambodia Relations," CICP Working Paper No. 28, Cambodian Institute for Cooperation and Peace, Phnom Penh, July 2009, 8.

20 For example, China invited Hun Sen to Beijing in 1996 and paid full freight for his visit. Ian Storey, *Southeast Asia and the Rise of China: The Search for* Security (London and New York: Routledge, 2011), 180–81.

21 "China Gives Cambodia $600m in Aid," *BBC News,* 8 April 2006.

22 See, for example, Lex Rieffel, "The Moment," in *Myanmar/Burma: Inside Challenges, Outside Interests,* ed. Alexis Rieffel (Washington, DC: Brookings Institution Press, 2010), 22–23; Ian Holliday, "Rethinking the United States's Myanmar Policy," *Asian Survey* 45, no. 4 (2005): 603–04.

23 Sasiwan Chingchit, "After Obama's Visit: The US Alliance and China," *Asia-Pacific Bulletin* 189, 4 December 2012.

24 Pavin Chachavalpongpun, "The Politics of International Sanctions: The 2014 Coup in Thailand," *Journal of International Affairs* 68, no. 1 (2014): 176.

25 Daniel R. Russel, "Remarks at the Institute of Security and International Studies," Chulalongkorn University, 26 January 2015, https://2009-2017.state.gov/p/eap/rls/rm/2015/01/236308.htm.

26 "Thai Junta Chief 'Upset' by US Criticism," *Agence France Presse,* 28 January 2015.

27 N. Wassana N. and J. Patsara, "Thailand, China Bolster Military Ties as US Relations Splinter," *Bangkok Post,* 6 February 2015.

28 Shawn W. Crispin, "Thai Coup Alienates US Giving China New Opening," *YaleGlobal,* 5 March 2015 (quoting senior defense official Panitan Wattanayagorn). A transport ministry proposal to convert U-Tapao into commercial use would further alter the strategic balance by curtailing US military use.

29 John Pomfret, "Concerned about China's Rise, Southeast Asian Nations Build Up Militaries," *Washington Post,* 9 August 2010.

30 See US Department of State, "U.S.-Vietnam Comprehensive Partnership," fact sheet, 16 December 2013.

31 Vietnamese Prime Minister Nguyen Tan Dung said China had "seriously threatened peace." C. Larano, "Vietnam Says Chinese Oil Rig Poses 'Serious Threat' to Security," *Wall Street Journal,* 21 May 2014.

32 Tuong Lai, "Vietnam's Overdue Alliance with America," *New York Times,* 11 July 2014; Josh Kurlantzick, "America's Real Pivot: Time for a Treaty Alliance with Vietnam?" *National Interest,* 14 October 2014. See also M.J. Totten, "Dispatch from Vietnam: Will the US Foster a Natural

Ally?" *World Affairs* 177, no. 4 (November/December 2014): 59–70 (arguing that "an alliance with Vietnam [is] ours for the taking").

33 Alex Vuving, "What Vietnam Can Offer America," *National Interest*, 27 May 2017, http://nationalinterest.org/feature/what-vietnam-can -offer-america-20874.

34 Li Kaisheng, "Vietnam Dancing between US Alliance and Chinese Brotherhood," *Global Times*, 10 February 2014.

35 "Remarks by President Obama and President Quang of Vietnam in Joint Press Conference," Hanoi, Vietnam, 23 May 2016, https://www .whitehouse.gov/the-press-office/2016/05/23/remarks-president-obama -and-president-quang-vietnam-joint-press.

36 David Feither, "China's Next Sea Fortress," *Wall Street Journal*, 3 August 2015, https://www.wsj.com/articles/chinas-next-sea-fortress -1438621122.

37 John D. Ciorciari and Jessica Chen Weiss, "The Sino-Vietnamese Feud in the South China Sea," *Georgetown Journal of International Affairs* 13, no. 1 (2012): 64–68.

38 Ngo Di Lan, "Vietnam's Foreign Policy after the 12th National Party Congress: Expanding Continuity," *cogitASIA*, 9 February 2016, https:// www.cogitasia.com/vietnams-foreign-policy-after-the-12th-national-party -congress-expanding-continuity/.

39 Storey, *Southeast Asia*, 145.

40 See Catherine A. Traywick and John Hudson, "Hillary's Burma Problem," *Foreign Policy*, 27 March 2014.

41 "US Defies Myanmar Government Request to Stop Using Term Rohingya," *The Guardian*, 11 May 2016.

42 See John D. Ciorciari, "A Chinese Model for Patron-Client Relations? The Sino-Cambodian Partnership," *International Relations of the Asia-Pacific* 15, no. 2 (2015): 245–78.

43 "Obama, Hun Sen in 'Tense' Talks," *Radio Free Asia*, 19 November 2012.

44 Sopheng Cheng, "China Gives 257 Military Trucks to Cambodia," *Associated Press*, 23 June 2010.

45 Pamela Dockins, "US Announces Initiatives to Aid Laos," *VOA News*, 25 January 2016, https://www.voanews.com/a/secretary-of-state-john -kerry-asia-asean-laos-north-korea/3161239.html.

46 "China Reaches Consensus with Brunei, Cambodia, Laos on South China Sea Dispute," *Xinhua*, 23 April 2016.

47 Sebastian Strangio, "China's Footprint Kicks Up Concerns in Tiny Laos," *Nikkei Asian Review*, 21 April 2016.

48 Tommy Koh, "Taking stock of US-Asean ties on eve of Sunnylands Summit," *Straits Times*, 13 February 2016, https://www.straitstimes.com /opinion/taking-stock-of-us-asean-ties-on-eve-of-sunnylands-summit.

49 See, for example, the remarks by Surin Pitsuwan, "Beginning a New Era of Diplomacy in Asia," press conference, 18 February 2009, https://2009-2017.state.gov/secretary/20092013clinton/rm/2009a/02 /119422.htm.

50 Amitav Acharya, "Security Pluralism in the Asia-Pacific: Reshaping Regional Order," *Global Asia* 11, no. 1 (2016): 13.

51 Lee Hsien Loong, "Transcript of PM's Speech at the USSFTA 10th Anniversary Reception at the US Chamber of Commerce in Washington DC on 24 June 2014," https://www.pmo.gov.sg/Newsroom/transcript -pms-speech-ussfta-10th-anniversary-reception-us-chamber-commerce -washington.

52 Data from *Key Indicators for Asia and the Pacific 2017* (Manila: Asian Development Bank, 2017), https://www.adb.org/publications/key -indicators-asia-and-pacific-2017.

53 ASEAN Secretariat and UN Conference on Trade and Development, *ASEAN Investment Report 2017* (Jakarta: ASEAN, 2017), 31, 34, 37, 40; Harry Handley, "Thailand in 2017: A Changing Investment Landscape," *ASEAN Briefing*, 17 February 2017, https://www.aseanbriefing.com/news /2017/02/17/thailand-2017-changing-investment-landscape.html.

54 UN Conference on Trade and Development, "Bilateral FDI Statistics: Myanmar," Table 1, http://unctad.org/en/Pages/DIAE/FDI%20Statistics /FDI-Statistics-Bilateral.aspx.

55 Prashanth Parameswaran, "Managing the US-Thailand Alliance in the Trump Era," *The Diplomat*, 11 October 2017.

56 Thomas Jandl, "Vietnam's Diplomatic Acrobatics in the Post-American Era," *East Asia Forum*, 14 January 2018.

57 Ross, *Chinese Security Policy*, 45.

58 Zbigniew Brzezinski, "Balancing the East, Upgrading the West: U.S. Grand Strategy in an Age of Upheaval," *Foreign Affairs* 91, no. 1 (2012): 101, https://www.foreignaffairs.com/articles/2011-12-13/balancing-east

-upgrading-west. In part, he advises the United States to avoid "any binding ties with competing powers on the Asian mainland." Zachary Keck, "The Interview: Zbigniew Brzezinski," *The Diplomat,* 10 September 2012, https://thediplomat.com/2012/09/the-interview-zbigniew-brzezinski/?allpages=yes.

59 For similar views, see Ernest Z. Bower and Murray Hiebert, "Revisiting U.S. Policy toward Post-Coup Thailand," *CSIS,* 25 June 2015; Ian Storey, "A Chance to Restart U.S.-Thai Relations," *Wall Street Journal,* 21 March 2016.

CHAPTER 13

China's 21st Century Maritime Silk Road
A ROUTE TO PAX SINICA IN SOUTHEAST ASIA?

Jörn Dosch, *University of Rostock, Germany*
Shannon Cui, *Independent Scholar, Rostock, Germany*

From its inception, China's expansive Belt and Road Initiative (BRI)[1] has been identified with the authority and future legacy of China's most powerful man — its president and the general secretary of its ruling Communist Party, Xi Jinping. It was Xi who announced the scheme's two planned components — a Silk Road Economic Belt (SREB) proclaimed in September 2013 on a state visit to Kazakhstan, and a 21st Century Maritime Silk Road (MSR) declared a month later in a speech to Indonesia's legislators. In Jakarta, Xi stressed China's desire to partner with the countries of Southeast Asia in jointly building the MSR.

The Belt and the Road, linked in the BRI, were meant to realize Xi's vision of "the great rejuvenation of the Chinese nation" known as the "China Dream." Anchored in China, chains of connectivity were pictured fanning northwestward across Eurasia and southwestward through Southeast Asia. The chains comprised roads, railroads, ports, pipelines, and related projects, notably in energy generation and transmission. With China as their hub, these spokes would form, Beijing hoped, the largest and most far-reaching grid in the world.[2]

No less important to President Xi were the plan's geopolitical and geo-economic aspects. At a Chinese Communist Party conference in November 2014, he envisioned turning "China's neighborhood areas into a community" sharing a "common destiny" with China based on "win-win cooperation and connectivity."[3] China's strategy, in Xi's phrasing, represented no less than a "new round of opening to the world," a second such opening after the Open Door Policy that Deng Xiaoping had begun in 1978 to attract foreign capital on behalf of China's modernization. According to official estimates as of 2017, BRI projects — "once completed" — were expected to involve 75 percent of global energy reserves, more than 65 percent of the world's population, and over half of global gross domestic product (GDP). "More than 100" countries and international organizations were said to "support" the BRI, although fewer — "more than 40" — had actually signed agreements to cooperate with Beijing.[4]

The two Silk Roads — the SREB and the MSR — would roughly reincarnate and reactivate two sets of ancient trade routes that once loosely linked imperial China westward toward the Atlantic Ocean. The SREB would run overland from Beijing to Urumqi (Xinjiang) and on through Central Asia, Russia, and the Middle East to Europe. The MSR, on which this chapter focuses, would begin with three westward routes. The first would run from Beijing through Kunming (Yunnan) to Myanmar's west coast and on into the Bay of Bengal. The second would link Beijing to Kunming to Singapore, turn up through the Strait of Malacca, and join the first in the Bay of Bengal. The third would extend from Beijing to coastal Guangzhou (Guangdong), continue through the South China Sea and the Strait of Malacca, and join the first two in the Bay of Bengal. That combined maritime route would continue to the Pakistani port of Gwadar, where it would meet the southwestern end of an overland SREB-offshoot railway line being planned from Kashgar (Xinjiang) through Kashmir to the Arabian Sea, before turning north through the Red Sea into the Mediterranean, finally reaching the European terminus of the SREB. An even more elaborate version of the MSR bifurcates its course in the Indian Ocean, where one offshoot goes to the west and north as just described while a second turns southward to Tanzania and Mozambique, around the Cape of Good Hope, and up through the eastern Atlantic to West Africa, where it bifurcates again, one branch to the Caribbean and one southward to Brazil and Argentina.[5]

Given these sprawling and overlapping itineraries, it is not easy to determine precisely the BRI's financial sources and sums that have been proposed, promised, or realized, or the allocation of such funds between the SREB and the MSR, or their distribution across projects within each of the two variously mapped sets of connections. At a forum celebrating the BRI held in May 2017 in Beijing, President Xi pledged funds that could bring the total commitment from all sources to a total figure in renminbi worth more than USD $150 billion at that time.[6] Most of these funding sources, such as the Silk Road Fund, are controlled by China. An exception is the China-inspired but multilateral Asian Infrastructure Investment Bank (AIIB), which began lending in 2016. As of July 2017 it had approved $2.5 billion worth of projects, most of which were being carried out under the BRI umbrella.[7] Yet these sums are minor compared with the estimate made by one China specialist, writing in 2016, that the "total funding" offered by China for the BRI "approaches US$1 trillion, on financial terms yet to be negotiated."[8] Further complicating this picture, at least in English, has been the use of "Silk Road" in BRI rhetoric in ways that could denote the entire initiative or only the MSR or the SREB.

Framing the Debate

The vast Belt and Road Initiative raises issues of regional order, national power, and their interactions, especially in Southeast Asia. The region's proximity to China has placed it at the center of an evolving debate about the implications of China's rise.[9] Were Beijing to become, for better or worse, a dominant actor in world affairs, the onset of that role would surely be manifest first in China's behavior toward its nearest neighbors, or so it is easy to believe. The implications of the MSR in Southeast Asia are worth considering in this larger if hypothetical context.

Broadly conceived, the debate about China's impact on Southeast Asia through the MSR implicates three distinct academic perspectives: structural realism, economic liberalism, and social constructivism. Each one is conducive to a different expectation. They are worth briefly mentioning here insofar as the reader may wish to keep them in mind as this chapter's evidence and argument unfold.

Realism   One could, from this standpoint, construe the MSR as a major step toward the establishment of an enduring regional order in Southeast Asia under Chinese auspices due mainly to the accumulation and exercise of Chinese power.[10] The realist case for hegemonic stability guided by Beijing relies on asymmetry: When one state is much larger than its neighbors and has far more economic, political, and military power than they do, it is likely to induce their cooperation by using that preponderance to coerce or co-opt them into deferring to the stronger state. By increasing the cost of defection and decreasing the risk of cooperation, the dominant state — the hegemon — ensures regional stability and peace. One analyst, for example, has argued with reference to Southeast Asia that China "is changing the scope of action for other international actors in a manner that produces the international outcomes it desires," including through its assertiveness in the South China Sea and by leveraging its giant economy for trade and investment with its Southeast Asian neighbors.[11] Leaving aside the threat and use of superior force, could the MSR spin a growing and deepening web of material transactions centered on China underpinning a Sinosphere based on commerce not coercion?

Liberalism   Yes, from a liberal perspective, the kinds of intensified economic exchanges between China and its neighbors that the MSR could promote should facilitate regional comity and security without inflicting hegemony. In this view, cross-border networks of trade and investment, sped and broadened by infrastructural extensions and improvements, should foster economic interdependence. That pattern should in turn shift the nature of international politics in a given region away from outright imposition or one-way co-optation toward a world of more or less co-equal "trading states," mutually engaged in material betterment and with shared stakes in a stable, liberal peace.[12]

Picture a Sino-Southeast Asian concourse of modernized "silk roads," on land, over water, by air, perhaps also in cyberspace, China willing. As mutually beneficial transnational activities multiply and become institutionalized, cooperation may supersede enmity, and the chance of military conflict may diminish. Eventually, if the process continues, a "pluralistic security community" may emerge, as envisioned by Karl Deutsch, who coined the term. War will have lost its attraction as a means of solving problems between members, who will instead settle their differences in peaceful ways.[13] That would maximally illustrate a transaction-based liberal vision of what the MSR could do.

Constructivism   This approach deals less with interactions than with norms. A constructivist view of the MSR would begin by celebrating the Association of Southeast Asian Nations (ASEAN) as a paradigmatic case of norm formation. Constructivists have used ASEAN to reverse the liberal chain of causation whereby a dense pattern of material transactions gives rise to a shared sense of community. Constructivism puts ideation and identity first. In this light, for Amitav Acharya, ASEAN is best described as "some sort of [an] *imagined* community" that is "*preceding* rather than resulting from political, strategic, and functional interactions and interdependence."[14] Common vulnerability, shared consciousness, a "we-feeling," the adherence of regional elites to the "ASEAN Way" of consensus, and the institutionalization of cooperation are, for Acharya, the main pillars of collective identity in Southeast Asia.[15] By implication, as it orchestrates the MSR, China would do well to learn from ASEAN's experience by designing the scheme to incubate a Sino-Southeast Asian community based at least as much, if not more, by moral identity through norms than by material utility through transactions.

If China's initiative does succeed in spreading and deepening multiple and voluntary strands of connectivity between China and Southeast Asia, will a Deutschian security community emerge? Such a peaceful and plural-istic outcome will presumably not arrive if China's authoritarian leaders see in the MSR's corridors and connections a skeleton of hegemony over their country's "near abroad." What if, on the other hand, extrapolating Acharya's vision, enhanced connectivity benefits and strengthens ASEAN's own collective identity as a viable alternative to a transactionally "greater China" linked to Beijing by the MSR? Would the "ASEAN Way" resist the Sinosphere? Would they co-exist? Or would China dominate Southeast Asia in a stable hegemony based on realist expectations?

These questions reach beyond Southeast Asia. Since the 1990s, ASEAN's creative regional diplomacy has inspired cooperative arrangements extend-ing well beyond Southeast Asia: the ASEAN Regional Forum (ARF), ASEAN Plus Three (APT), and the East Asia Summit (EAS), to mention a few. How will these ASEAN-acknowledging diplomatic networks compare in influence to the infrastructural ones called for in Beijing's MSR? Some might even pic-ture ASEAN using its soft-power embrace to socialize China into becoming a "responsible regional power."[16]

These questions, and the differing perspectives they imply, are stimulating in theory. As a practical matter, however, the MSR's impact on regional order must, for now, remain mainly a subject for speculation. The initiative is too recent, the evidence still too scant. Cherry-picking the data to date, some may cast the MSR in a positive light as an admirable service to its participants that is laying the basis for a peaceful, stable, and beneficial Sino–Southeast Asian version of a pluralistic security community. Citing other signs, others may view the MSR as a would-be framework for extraction, intrusion, and control — the lineaments of an emerging Pax Sinica featuring coercion, co-optation, and deference to superior Chinese power.

The history of relations between Southeast Asia and China is reviewed elsewhere in this volume. Suffice it to note here two recent antecedents in those relations that, as guides to the future of the MSR, point in contrast-ing directions. Mainly on the positive side lies the ASEAN-China Free Trade Agreement that came into effect in 2010. The resulting trade area has bene-fited ASEAN's member economies to varying degrees — Malaysia's the most, Vietnam's the least. But the agreement has, on balance, been a win-win factor in China's relations with Southeast Asia. It was also in 2010, however, that China's relations with ASEAN over the South China Sea began to sour. At an ASEAN Regional Forum meeting that year, infuriated by pushback against China's apparent claim to almost all of the South China Sea, the Chinese foreign minister stared directly at his Singaporean counterpart and made a famously realist remark: "China is a big country, and other countries are small countries, and that's just a fact."[17]

Keeping in mind such evidence of ambiguity and ambivalence in Sino-Southeast Asian relations, the rest of this chapter seeks, first, to summarize the MSR as it is being presented in Beijing; second, to focus on the Mekong subregion where interactions with China are long-standing and intense; and third, to place China's initiative in the context of parallel efforts by others and to ask whether Beijing has the ability to make the MSR succeed. A final section will revisit the three ways of framing the MSR and offer a concluding guess as to whether or not China is building the infrastructure of an eventual Pax Sinica in Southeast Asia.

Rationalizing the Road

The four officially authorized goals of the BRI are far-reaching: "to [1] promote the connectivity of Asian, European and African continents and their adjacent seas, [2] establish and strengthen partnerships among the countries along the Belt and Road, [3] set up all-dimensional, multi-tiered and composite connectivity networks, and [4] realize diversified, independent, balanced and sustainable development in these countries."[18]

In these terms, the only inhabited continents not explicitly included in the plan's scope are Australia and the Americas. The document does involve Australia by implication, however, by specifying that a southern extension of the MSR is meant to run "from China's coast through the South China Sea to the South Pacific," perhaps stopping in Darwin along the way.[19] As for South America, the inclusion of Salvador (Brazil) and Mar del Plata (Argentina) on the map of MSR distribution centers agreed to by Chinese and Thai officials in 2014[20] suggests the involvement of that continent as well. By these signs, North America alone is neither on the Belt nor on the Road. But it could be, if Canada, Mexico, or the United States were to test the sincerity of China's formal assurance that the BRI is "open to all countries."[21]

Matching this near-global spatial scope is the detailed comprehensiveness of the BRI by sector and by activity. Beyond mere physical connections through infrastructure, the initiative envisions "free trade areas," "trade and investment facilitation," "investment cooperation mechanisms," "international technology transfer centers," "maritime cooperation centers," "renminbi bonds," "closer economic ties," a "regulation coordination mechanism," "jointly running schools," "mutual assistance in law enforcement," "social security management," "cooperation on traditional medicine," "mutual political trust," "communication between political parties and parliaments," "joint research" by "think tanks," "enhanced cultural exchanges," "media cooperation," and "leverag[ing] the positive role of the Internet and new media tools to foster [a] harmonious and friendly cultural environment and public opinion."[22]

From a standpoint favorable to China, one could construe this extraordinarily broad yet granular vision as extremely generous — a willingness to offer so much. A skeptic, however, might bridle at the presumption and intrusiveness of China's intentions. "Social security management"? China itself lacks an effective social security system. Enforcement of existing law has been "very lax, and the majority of workers are still denied the social security benefits they are legally entitled to."[23] China offering to ensure that "public opinion" is "harmonious and friendly" through "media cooperation" to ensure that the internet plays a "positive role"? Such an arguably invasive promise seems ironic in view of the BRI's professed commitment to "mutual respect for each other's sovereignty" and "mutual non-interference in each other's internal affairs."[24]

Unsurprisingly, officials and analysts inside China have favored the BRI. Noteworthy are three such legitimating interpretations: One associates the initiative, and especially its MSR, with Chinese-led cooperation among Asians and for Asians. A second locates the idea as essential to a broader frame of South-South cooperation that includes Asia but involves Africa and Latin America as well. From a third, most encompassing standpoint, the BRI is a gift of public goods to all of humanity — the whole world.

Asia   The Boao Forum for Asia was founded by China, is headquartered in Beijing, and meets annually on China's Hainan Island east of Vietnam. Speaking at the forum in March 2016, Chinese prime minister Li Keqiang reiterated his government's support for groupings and gatherings based in Asia and limited mainly or wholly to Asian participation. In this context, he re-expressed Chinese support for a Regional Comprehensive Economic Partnership (RCEP) including China but not the United States. RCEP would span fourteen Asian states including all of ASEAN but only two non-Asian members — Australia and New Zealand. Although RCEP had been ASEAN's idea, it came to be seen as a Beijing-backed rival to a Trans-Pacific Partnership (TPP) that Washington was promoting at the time. The two memberships overlapped to an extent, but in contrast to RCEP, the TPP did not include China and covered only a few ASEAN states, while adding the United States and several other member countries in far-off North and South America. At the Hainan forum, Prime Minister Li also proposed setting up an Asian Financial Cooperation Association (AFCA) intended to strengthen

Asia's role in managing the global financial system so that the United States and Europe would no longer control its decisions.[25]

In January 2017, US president Donald Trump withdrew the United States from the negotiations to achieve a TPP. A centrally American alternative to RCEP ceased to exist. At a launching six months later in Beijing, Li's proposed ACFA followed the also China-sponsored Asian Infrastructure Investment Bank (AIIB) to become "the latest addition to the Belt and Road Initiative."[26]

The South   As seen by Zhang Guihong and Qiu Changqing, the BRI is an opportunity for developing countries to work together to coordinate and upgrade their strategies for economic growth.[27] This view stresses the BRI's affinity with the nature and objectives of "South-South cooperation" as defined by the United Nations Office for South-South Cooperation (UNOSSC): "a manifestation of solidarity among peoples and countries of the South that contributes to their national well-being, their national and collective self-reliance and the attainment of internationally agreed development goals." For Zhang and Qiu, the BRI is a way of implementing South-South cooperation as defined by UNOSSC: that it "must be determined by the countries of the South, guided by the principles of respect for national sovereignty, national ownership and independence, equality, non-conditionality, non-interference in domestic affairs and mutual benefit."[28] By this account of the BRI, China as a developing country is well suited to lead the initiative for the benefit of the rest of its "Southern" cohort.

The world   Looking beyond the developing South, China's foreign minister Wang Yi has described the BRI as a "public good provided by China to the world."[29] According to this most bountiful and expansive reading of China's initiative, it embraces global multipolarity, including economic globalization and cultural diversity, and is designed "to uphold the global free trade regime and the open world economy in the spirit of open regional cooperation."[30] In this win-win rhetoric, everyone can expect to gain from the public goods that the BRI will generate. In a world inspired by the BRI, consumption by one person will not diminish consumption by another. Benefits will accrue to all. Tu Yonghong has gone still farther to suggest that the beneficence of the BRI will give birth to a new mode and concept of cooperation, including a new way of organizing international finance.[31]

The BRI is a work still in progress. It is hard to characterize with confidence, given its recency and the different ways of understanding it. To what extent is it economic or strategic in nature? Is it a Chinese attempt to create a system that will parallel, rival, and prospectively even replace the existing, American-minted world order? Or does it represent a less ambitious Chinese desire to gain regional leverage in a stably multipolar world? In the context of these uncertainties, it may be helpful briefly to focus down on the MSR in Southeast Asia to see how it has unfolded in a specific place — the Greater Mekong Subregion.

The Mekong, the Road, and the "Mekong Mode"

The Mekong is Southeast Asia's longest river and the 12th largest in the world. It originates in Tibet, flows through the Chinese province of Yunnan, and continues southward across or alongside Cambodia, Laos, Myanmar, Thailand, and Vietnam — half of ASEAN's 10 member states — before spilling into the South China Sea. The five ASEAN countries and the Chinese provinces of Yunnan and Guangxi, spanning some 2.6 million square kilometers and 326 million people, constitute the Greater Mekong Subregion (GMS).[32]

Concern for regional infrastructure predates the MSR. Soon after the Cold War ended, a window of opportunity for reconciliation opened on the formerly war-torn mainland portion of Southeast Asia. Since 1992 and for more than a quarter century thereafter, the Asian Development Bank (ADB) has been helping the six participating countries cooperate in the development of the GMS by funding projects in transportation, energy, telecommunication, trade, investment, education, and the environment, among other sectors.[33] Unlike China's MSR, this GMS program to facilitate and expand the movement of goods and people across the subregion's borders is multilateral and has taken a more market-based approach to building and improving regional infrastructure.[34]

Beijing's interest in connectivity in the GMS also predates the MSR. In December 2010, China signed a preliminary agreement with Laos and Thailand to build a high-speed railway from Kunming (Yunnan) to Bangkok that could eventually extend through peninsular Malaysia to Singapore. The section that China would build through Laos would be financed through Chinese loans then worth $7 billion, a sum larger than the far smaller country's GDP.[35] In the course of further plans, negotiations, disagreements, and delays, the proposed railway from Singapore to Kunming broadened, on paper, into a larger pattern of tracks. A stem from Singapore to Bangkok would open, north of the Thai capital, into three separate lines, all ending in Kunming: one through Myanmar, another through Laos, and a third through Vietnam.

In July 2014, the authorities in Myanmar canceled the $20 billion project to build the western line through their country due to growing public resistance to Chinese influence — pushback enabled in part by an earlier relaxation of repressive rule.[36] The setback did not deter Beijing, however. In November 2016 in Mandalay, speaking to a presumably ethnic-Chinese audience at a Chinese temple, China's consul general Wang Zongying promoted the canceled project in glowing terms: High-speed trains on the line would achieve a velocity of 350 kilometers (217 miles) per hour. One could speed from far-northern Muse on the Myanmar-China border to Myanmar's southern ex-capital Yangon in a (physically impossible[37]) single hour. "We [China] want to connect Southeast Asia with a trans-Asia railroad that will go as far as Indonesia," said Wang, presuming a railroad bridge across the Singapore Strait. The local chair of the China-Myanmar Friendship Association added that the railroad would create jobs and develop Myanmar's economy.[38]

Since 2015, China has also been pushing a proposed railway linking Kunming to Kolkata via Mandalay that would require the support of the three countries en route — Myanmar, Bangladesh, and India. Given Myanmar's concerns and India's opposition, one can understand an Indian observer's opinion in mid-2017 that the project "remained consigned to oblivion" — however too assured that view may someday turn out to have been.[39]

China's enthusiasm for regional infrastructure is both economic and strategic in character. The proposed linkages would convey Chinese goods to foreign markets; bring needed resources into China; and speed the development of relatively poor Yunnan. Already since 2015, pipelines have been funneling oil and gas from the Bay of Bengal through Myanmar clear to Kunming. That connectivity amounts to an insurance policy against the possible closure of the Malacca Strait — a chokepoint through which pass annually an estimated 82 percent of China's imported oil, 72 percent of its coal imports, and 30 percent of its maritime intake of natural gas.[40] Myanmar-to-Yunnan connections by rail would open that southwestern "back door" for trade and transport even wider for Beijing's compensatory use should a hostile power ever block China from using the South China Sea.

Mixed economic and strategic motivations are also evident in a "Mekong mode" of discourse often favored in Chinese accounts of their country's plans for infrastructure in Southeast Asia's northern tier. This "mode" (or model) embodies China's above-mentioned portrayal of the MSR as a means of delivering "public goods" for the "public good" of the region's people.

Lu Guangsheng and Zhang Li are at Yunnan University, where presumably support for the MSR is strong, given the opportunities for Yunnan Province that the scheme affords. They have described the Mekong River as "a transboundary water public good."[41] According to this view, widely shared in China, such public goods "are typically," and by implication appropriately, "dominated by countries *within* the region, with the aim of providing infrastructure, security, financial support, training, education, and dispute settlement mechanisms to the region's countries, organizations, social communities, and individuals."[42]

The "Mekong mode" has also been cited as a way to improve the safety of shipping on the river. In October 2011, two Chinese cargo ships were attacked on a section of the Mekong in the Golden Triangle area overlapping Burma and Thailand. All 13 crew members were killed. The massacre prompted an agreement by the adjacent countries — China, Laos, Myanmar, and Thailand — jointly to patrol the waterway. Lei Jun later gave credit for this result to the "Mekong mode," by which he meant recourse to local but not necessarily co-equal collaboration. In his understanding of the model, "public goods, namely security cooperation mechanisms, are *dominated* by China and *supported* by other Mekong countries."[43]

This "Mekong mode" is of interest beyond the GMS insofar as it implies a more general self-definition of Chinese leadership in Asia. Lei argues that the sources of regional public goods are usually and mainly provided by one powerful hegemonic state (e.g., the United States in NAFTA); by a pair of regional powers (e.g., Germany and France in the European Union); or by several such powers (e.g., China, South Korea, Japan, and ASEAN in East Asia). In contrast, for Lei, the "Mekong mode" is a new and different approach to the regional provision of public goods. The overall framework is still one of multilateral cooperation. But China sets the tone and plays the dominant role. The smaller states in the region (e.g., in the GMS) are meant to collaborate with China and support its initiatives (presumably including the MSR). Chinese officials categorically reject "hegemony" as a description of Chinese intent. Instead, in the Mekong model, hegemony is dressed as a benevolent kind of dominance where preeminence justifies control. The geopolitical context — great-power rivalry — implicitly vindicates the approach. That Beijing should have announced its MSR in the wake of the unveiling of Washington's "pivot" toward Asia was not coincidental.

Increasingly since 2012, China's leaders have described their country as a "great power" having "great-power relations" with other major states. If those relatively symmetrical relations require "mutual respect" for each other's interests, however, implicitly different rules would appear to apply to China's relations with "small countries."[44] The Mekong model renders those "great-to-small-power" rules less implicit by emphasizing Chinese prominence to the point of predominance. That adaptation of "great-power relations" could be taken as replacing the need for "mutual respect" between equals with a one-way obligation of the smaller actor to respect the interests of the larger one, but not the other way around. A raised American profile in Southeast Asia was a further reason for China to raise its priority on ensuring the deference of its neighbors. Notwithstanding the shift in American rhetoric under President Trump, from pivoting toward Asia to putting "America first," Sino-American rivalry still helps to warrant, in Beijing, the strategic purpose of the MSR.

This power-sensitive interpretation of China's infrastructural designs in Southeast Asia relies on realist reasoning of the kind cited earlier in this chapter. An economic-liberalist outlook on the MSR would, in contrast, feature evidence of material cooperation in the provision of public goods and the evolution of peaceful interdependence. As for constructivist arguments, one can hope that China can be socialized somehow into adopting ASEAN's norms and adapting MSR-driven connectivity to the promotion not only of transactions but of equitably distributed burdens and benefits in conditions of cross-border comity as well. Relevant to the likelihood of that optimistic outcome is a constructivist question briefly considered next: Rather than being a candidate for socialization into ASEAN's norms, is the MSR more plausibly regarded as a huge and strenuous effort by Beijing to revive China's heralded past and reconstitute *as guiding norms* the center-periphery inequalities that the Middle Kingdom once enjoyed?

Tributaries of imperial China can be found in, or are relevant for, the genealogies of most of the sovereign states in present-day Southeast Asia. Tributaries are necessarily inferior in the eyes of the emperor who receives their tribute. It would be wrong — anachronistic — to assume that the superiority of imperial China during its heyday was necessarily rejected by the Southeast Asian polities that paid tribute to it. From time to time in some parts of Southeast Asia, the northern imperium was indeed seen as a more advanced power, a source of enlightenment more than a cause for resentment. Centuries later, the stellar record of economic growth that China managed to achieve after Mao did contribute to a revival of that opinion.

That said, historically based admiration should not be overdrawn. Official Chinese discourse on the BRI including the MSR often showcases the 15th-century Ming dynasty admiral Zheng He. The oversea voyages undertaken by him and his ships through maritime Southeast Asia clear to the east coast of Africa have been resurrected and recast by Beijing as generously peaceful—a virtual blueprint for a benignly guided MSR. Nevertheless, and quite apart from the scholarly case against this reconstruction of what may well have been a more muscular set of expeditions,[45] few in Southeast Asia are persuaded by China's justification of its modern maritime leadership as historically grown and naturalized by ancient relations and voyages. Nor is that mythology made more attractive to Beijing's neighbors by its recourse to Sinophile history and archeology to warrant its claims to sovereignty in the South China Sea—a topic considered elsewhere in this book.

If a constructivist understanding of China's imperial legacy reworked in "soft power" terms is an insufficient basis for legitimating Beijing's infrastructural leadership in Southeast Asia, how well can China's economic prowess serve that purpose?

Other Roads, Other Problems

China's promotion of the MSR plays up the economic and downplays the political. By stressing the benefits of win-win cooperation through infrastructure for development, Beijing hopes to distract and soften local pushback against intransigent Chinese unilateralism in the South China Sea, and against the sometimes-onerous Chinese conditions for cooperation on MSR projects. On the latter score, for example, controversies have arisen as to whether projects employ Chinese versus local workers, generate energy solely for Chinese use, entail land-use terms that disadvantage those who lose their homes, or unduly damage the environment.

When Beijing negotiates MSR projects, its leverage depends in part on the extent to which it is seen as an unstoppable economic force destined to determine Southeast Asia's economic future. That impression was strengthened in 2010 when China surpassed Germany as the top exporting country and replaced Japan as the second-largest economy.[46] Xi Jinping announced the MSR in 2013. In 2014 China edged out the United States to become the world's biggest economy in purchasing power parity terms according to the International Monetary Fund.[47] China's economic leadership of Asia has come into question, however, especially since 2015. In that year the Chinese economy grew more slowly than it had in a quarter century, albeit at a still remarkable 6.9 percent.[48] François Godement was right to say that China did not face "a deep-rooted economic crisis," but rather "a crisis of [disappointed] expectations on the part of Chinese and international observers alike."[49] Perception, including expectations, is exactly the issue at stake. Does Beijing still have sufficient current and probable future clout to be accepted as Asia's premier economic mover?

In Southeast Asia, through the ASEAN-China Free Trade Agreement (ACFTA), Beijing has provided a suitable framework for its neighbors to translate their disparate economic development strategies into a tangible regional drive. ACFTA is a major reason why the ASEAN states have been receptive to the opportunities afforded by China's growing economic power. Yet Southeast Asians have also regretted its downsides, such as trade imbalances, especially when cheap Chinese imports have disadvantaged local competition. Another concern in the region has been ACFTA's potential to induce overdependence on China's economy and therefore on Chinese initiatives as well, including the MSR.

That worry has been lessened, however, as the ASEAN states have capitalized on ACFTA-stimulated economic growth to diversify their options by developing stronger ties with other economic partners. The results include a range of FTAs, negotiated collectively by ASEAN or individually by its member states, with Japan, India, South Korea, and Australia. Even Laos, subordinated to China by poverty, proximity, and size, has leveraged its links to Chinese interests to obtain benefits from other international actors, including World Bank funds for large (and controversial) hydropower projects.[50] In Laos, for instance, Chinese investors seeking contracts face Asian competitors from Vietnam and Thailand. Also in Laos, South Korean investors have been active in education and have rivaled their Chinese counterparts in energy and mining.[51]

In 2016 PricewaterhouseCoopers predicted that the BRI could receive as much as $1 trillion in financing from China's government over the ensuing 10 years. If that figure is met, and depending on how much of it is spent in ASEAN member states, China's Maritime Silk Road may turn out to be, by far, the largest externally financed infrastructural effort ever attempted in Southeast Asia. Its projects, however, will not be the only such undertakings in the region. The Japan-led ADB and the World Bank have supported a number of major initiatives for infrastructure in Southeast Asia, and likely will continue to do so.[52]

In addition, economic growth in Southeast Asia has enlarged the indigenous pool of capital available to invest in regional linkages generally — and specifically to implement an indigenous scheme now known as the Master Plan on ASEAN Connectivity (MPAC) 2025.[53] First announced at an ASEAN summit in October 2010, well before the MSR's inception, the plan was in part an effort to "claw back" the poorer northern members of ASEAN from the risk of future subordination by China in a Sinified GMS operating in "Mekong mode" — deferring to Beijing.[54]

In 2011 the ASEAN states and the ADB agreed to establish an ASEAN Infrastructure Fund (AIF) to assist in the financing of MPAC 2025. Headquartered in Kuala Lumpur, the fund began operating in 2013 with an initial capital base of $485 million. Two-thirds of that sum had been raised from Southeast Asian sources, notably in Malaysia and Indonesia; the rest came from the ADB. Although the amounts that China promises to invest in the MSR dwarf the AIF's capital base, a number of the projects that the ASEAN fund has supported have already been implemented. By comparison, the MSR has been slowed by its sheer scope and complexity, by the asymmetry on which it relies, and by the suspicions that its political connotations have engendered among China's would-be local hosts in Southeast Asia.

Complexity also marks and limits China's own political economy in ways that may curtail Beijing's ability to move the MSR from vision to reality. As Alice Ba has noted, the "fragmented authoritarian" system that prevails inside China impedes policy coordination and implementation. Providing foreign assistance can involve as many as 40 different government departments. Chinese financial institutions are underdeveloped. Priorities that serve domestic economic and other priorities and interests inside China further limit the extents to which Beijing is willing to loosen state controls on capital accounts and rates of exchange.[55]

The eventual success of the MSR will depend on China's ability to recognize and remove impediments to the scheme's fruition — and on both the willingness and the ability of Southeast Asian leaders to avoid trading autonomy for aid.

Conclusion

The Maritime Silk Road points toward a strategic vision of the future that has captured imaginations in China and Southeast Asia alike. Officially, in Beijing, three priorities animate the vast Belt and Road Initiative to which the MSR belongs. They are strategic, tactical, and grand. The strategic priority is to realize Xi Jinping's "Chinese dream of the great rejuvenation of the Chinese nation"[56] — China's future as a prospering and consequential power. The tactical priority is to promote and defend China's specific economic and security interests on behalf of that hoped-for future. The grand and potentially global priority is to foster interdependence among countries within and beyond Asia based on win-win scenarios led by Beijing.

In these contexts, the MSR is meant to undergird a stable supply of energy into China, to enable the flourishing of Chinese trade with and investment in Southeast Asia, and productively to interconnect southwestern China with Eurasia through Southeast Asia. The MSR is also intended to establish China's legitimacy and leverage as a growing maritime power, thereby off-setting Southeast Asian and American objections to Chinese dominance in the South China Sea. In complementary fashion, the "Mekong mode" depicts Chinese primacy in the Greater Mekong Subregion as naturally given in a Sino-Southeast Asian "community of destiny" that is not a contingent grouping, but rather a "necessary condition" of peace and prosperity.[57]

If the Maritime Silk Road causes Southeast Asia to prosper, as advertised, on a major scale and in "win-win" terms, China will have gone a long way toward enlarging and legitimating its leadership in and of the region. If the MSR fails in major ways, or imposes "win-lose" terms that dispropor-tionally benefit Beijing, China may have to decide whether to suspend its regional ambition, soften it to allay fears of hegemony, or harden it with intimidation. The first outcome has been made more likely by the growing acceptance of a prominent economic role for China in Southeast Asia quite apart from the MSR. That role has not, however, been institutionalized as a norm that would privilege China as a true friend of the region. The ASEAN Way is not a Chinese way. ASEAN's multilateralist MPAC and China's bilat-eralist MSR embody the difference. As for the MSR's promise of economic interdependence between China and Southeast Asia, that prospect need not gestate a pluralistic security community along liberal lines. Already notably illiberal trends in both places, if prolonged, could undermine the potential for connectivity to incubate accountability.

That leaves intact a realist expectation that the ASEAN states — with some exceptions, for different reasons, and to varying degrees — will continue to cooperate with all major outsiders, China included, while trying to avoid overreliance on any one of them, China also included. Beijing will need to make the Maritime Silk Road magnetically attractive to local leaders for them to stop hedging their bets. Travelers on China's 21st Century Maritime Silk Road will still have a long way to go before they reach, if ever, an uncon-tested Pax Sinica in Southeast Asia.

Notes

1 Originally called "One Belt One Road," the plan was renamed the "Belt and Road Initiative" in 2015 for reasons discussed in Wade Shepard's "Beijing to the World: Don't Call the Belt and Road Initiative OBOR," *Forbes*, 1 August 2017, https://www.forbes.com/sites/wadeshepard/2017/08/01/beijing-to-the-world-please-stop-saying-obor/#255a254417d4.

2 Ren Junhua, "Different Communist Party of China: Great Rejuvenation of Chinese Nation," CCTV.com English, 7 April 2016, http://english.cctv.com/2016/07/04/ARTI7oF0CzL3wh67VdnCCK4t160704.shtml; Shaheli Das, "The Awakening of Xi's Chinese Dream," East Asia Forum, 7 April 2016, www.eastasiaforum.org/2016/04/07/the-awakening-of-xis-chinese-dream. See 新玉言, 李克 [Xin Yuyan and Li Ke], 《崛起大战略："一带一路"战略全剖析》 [The rise of a great strategy: a full analysis of the "One Belt One Road" strategy] (Beijing: Taihai Publishing House, 2015); 向洪, 李向前 [Xiang Hong and Li Xiangqian], 《新丝路, 新梦想 "一带一路"战略知识读本》 [New Silk Road, new dream: a knowledge reader for the "One Belt One Road" strategy] (Beijing: Red Flag Publishing House, 2015).

3 Michael D. Swaine, "Xi Jinping's Address to the Central Conference on Work Relating to Foreign Affairs: Assessing and Advancing Major Power Diplomacy with Chinese Characteristics," *China Leadership Monitor*, no. 46 (2014), 6, http://www.hoover.org/sites/default/files/clm46ms.pdf.

4 "Belt and Road Forum: A Historic Test," *China Daily*, 7 May 2017, http://www.chinadaily.com.cn/newsrepublic/2017-05/07/content_29240215.htm. The burgeoning literature on the BRI includes, e.g., Christopher K. Johnson, *President Xi Jinping's "Belt and Road" Initiative* (Washington, DC: Center for Strategic and International Studies, March 2016), https://csis-prod.s3.amazonaws.com/s3fs-public/publication/160328_Johnson_PresidentXiJinping_Web.pdf; and Antoine Bondaz et al., "'One Belt, One Road': China's Great Leap Outward," China Analysis [London], European Council on Foreign Relations, June 2015, http://www.ecfr.eu/page/-/China_analysis_belt_road.pdf.

5 Compare, for example, the map of the MSR in James Kynge, "Finance Will Create New Alliances across Asia," *Financial Times*, 4 May 2017, 5, with the more expansive and bifurcated one that stops short of Europe but links a dozen coastal "Strategic Maritime Distribution Centers" along its far-reaching paths in Brian Eyler, "China's Maritime Silk Road is All

about Africa," *East by Southeast*, 14 November 2014, http://www.east
bysoutheast.com/chinas-maritime-silk-road-africa/.

6 Promises of sums in renminbi equivalent to USD "$124 billion" and "at
least $113 billion in extra funding" announced at the 2017 forum were
reported, respectively, in Brenda Goh and Yawen Chen, "China Pledges
$124 Billion for New Silk Road as Champion of Globalization," Reuters,
13 May 2017, http://www.reuters.com/article/us-china-silkroad-africa
-idUSKBN18A02I; and in Zheping Huang, "Your Guide to Understanding
OBOR, China's New Silk Road Plan," *Quartz*, 15 May 2017, https://
qz.com/983460/obor-an-extremely-simple-guide-to-understanding-chinas
-one-belt-one-road-forum-for-its-new-silk-road/. The "extra funding" in
Quartz likely takes into account China's initial promise of $40 billion for
the Silk Road Fund upon its inauguration in 2015.

7 Remy Stuart-Haentjens, "China and the AIIB on the Belt and
Road: Power sans Control," *Global Risk Insights*, 6 July 2017, http://
globalriskinsights.com/2017/07/china-aiib-belt-road-power-sans-control/.
China's 28 percent voting share in the AIIB more than triples second-
place India's 8 percent — a proportional disparity unmatched in any other
multilateral development bank; Martin A. Weiss, "Asian Infrastructure
Investment Bank (AIIB)," Congressional Research Service, 3 February
2017, https://fas.org/sgp/crs/row/R44754.pdf.

8 Lowell Dittmer, "China, Southeast Asia, and the United States,"
*Contemporary Chinese Political Economy and Strategic Relations: An
International Journal* 2, no. 1 (2016): 130.

9 See, for example, Chong Guan Kwa and Mingjiang Li, eds., *China-
ASEAN Sub-regional Cooperation: Progress, Problems, and Prospect*
(Singapore: World Scientific, 2011); Emile Kok-Kheng Yeoh, ed., *Regional
Political Economy of China Ascendant: Pivotal Issues and Critical
Perspectives* (Kuala Lumpur: Institute of China Studies, University of
Malaya, 2009); Ian Storey, *Southeast Asia and the Rise of China: The
Search for Security* (London and New York: Routledge, 2011); Bronson
Percival, *The Dragon Looks South: China and Southeast Asia in the New
Century* (Westport, CT and London: Praeger Security International,
2007); Joshua Kurlantzick, *Charm Offensive: How China's Soft Power Is
Transforming the World* (New Haven: Yale University Press, 2007).

10 An especially hard-edged version of realism pictures Southeast Asia
as a field for eventual war between China and the United States. That
scenario is ignored in these pages. China's MSR is too unlikely a catalyst
for Sino-American combat, and the context here is China's relations with

Southeast Asia, not its rivalry with the United States. Writings on the latter topic include, e.g., Shuaihua Wallace Cheng, "China's New Silk Road: Implications for the US," *YaleGlobal Online*, 28 May 2015, https://yaleglobal.yale.edu/content/chinas-new-silk-road-implications-us.

11 Naila Maier-Knapp, "The Non-traditional Security Concept and the EU-ASEAN Relationship against the Backdrop of China's Rise," *Pacific Review* 29, no. 3 (2016): 412.

12 Richard Rosecrance, *The Rise of the Trading State: Commerce and Conquest in the Modern World* (New York: Basic Books, 1986).

13 The locus classicus of this argument is Karl W. Deutsch et al., *Political Community and the North Atlantic Area: International Organization in the Light of Historical Experience* (Princeton, NJ: Princeton University Press, 1957).

14 Quoted by Dominique Schirmer, "Communities and Security in Pacific Asia," in *Asian Security Reassessed,* eds. Stephen Hoadley and Jürgen Rüland (Singapore: ISEAS, 2006), 327–28. Italics added.

15 Amitav Acharya, *Constructing a Security Community in Southeast Asia: ASEAN and the Problem of Regional Order*, 3rd ed. (Abingdon, Oxon: Routledge, 2014).

16 Nicholas Khoo, "Is Realism Dead? Academic Myths and Asia's International Politics," *Orbis* 58, no. 2 (2014): 182–97. See also Hiro Katsumata, "What Explains ASEAN's Leadership in East Asian Community Building?" *Pacific Affairs* 87, no. 2 (2014): 247–64; and, in contrast, Catherine Jones, "Great Powers, ASEAN, and Security: Reason for Optimism?," *Pacific Review* 28, no. 2 (2015): 259–80.

17 Joshua Kurlantzick, "The Belligerents," *New Republic*, 26 January 2011, https://newrepublic.com/article/82211/china-foreign-policy.

18 "Background" in "Vision and Actions on Jointly Building Silk Road Economic Belt and 21st-Century Maritime Silk Road," National Development and Reform Commission, 28 March 2015, http://en.ndrc.gov.cn/newsrelease/201503/t20150330_669367.html. The document was "issued by the National Development and Reform Commission, Ministry of Foreign Affairs, and Ministry of Commerce of the People's Republic of China, with State Council authorization."

19 "Framework" in "Vision and Actions." Oceania is explicitly listed as a BRI zone by Qiu Changqing, "'One Belt, One Road' Fuels South-South Cooperation," *Chinese Social Sciences Today*, 17 September 2015, http://www.csstoday.com/Item/2558.aspx.

20 Eyler, "China's Maritime Silk Road."

21 "Principles" in "Vision and Actions," where it is also stated that the BRI "covers, but is not limited to, the area of the ancient Silk Road."

22 "Vision and Actions," passim.

23 "China's Social Security System," *China Labour Bulletin*, August 2012, updated March 2019, http://www.clb.org.hk/content/china%E2%80%99s-social-security-system.

24 "Principles," in "Vision and Actions."

25 Robert Sutter and Chin-hao Huang, "China-Southeast Asia Relations: South China Sea, More Tensions and Challenges," *Comparative Connections* 18, no. 1 (May 2016): 62.

26 "China-led Asian Financial Cooperation Association Launches," *Central Banking*, 25 July 2017, https://www.centralbanking.com/central-banks/financial-market-infrastructure/3275151/china-led-asian-financial-cooperation-association-launches. Notwithstanding its Asian focus and Chinese chair, AFCA's participants were not limited to Asians. Financial organizations from around the world were reported to have signed up to join the new association. This AFCA should not be confused with the already existing Asia [no "n"] Financial Cooperation Association comprising Chinese banks.

27 Zhang Guihong and Qiu Changqing, "The Construction of One Belt One Road and South-South Cooperation," in *One Belt One Road and International Cooperation* (Shanghai: Shanghai People's Publishing House, 2015), 3–15, in Chinese. In English, see Qiu, "'One Belt, One Road.'"

28 United Nations Office for South-South Cooperation (UNOSSC), "About South-South and Triangular Cooperation," 2017, https://www.unsouthsouth.org/about/about-sstc/.

29 Foreign Ministry of the People's Republic of China, "'One Belt One Road' Is a Public Good Provided by China to the World," 23 March 2015, http://www.fmprc.gov.cn/mfa_chn//ziliao_611306/zt_611380/dnzt_611382/ydyl_667839/zyxw_667918/t1247712.shtml, original in Chinese. See also, in Chinese, Yang Haiyan, "The Provision Dilemma and Cooperation Possibilities of Regional Public Goods," in *One Belt One Road and International Cooperation* (Shanghai: Shanghai People's Publishing House, 2015).

30 "授权发布:推动共建丝绸之路经济带和21世纪海上丝绸之路的愿景与行动" [Vision and proposed actions outlined in jointly building the Silk

Road Economic Belt and the 21st-century Maritime Silk Road], Xinhua, 28 March 2015, http://news.xinhuanet.com/world/2015-03/28/c_111479 3986.htm.

31 涂永红 [Tu Yonghong], "中国在'一带一路'建设中提供的全球公共物品 [The global public goods of OBOR],《光明日报》, 22 June 2015, http://epaper.gmw.cn/gmrb/html/2015-06/22/nw.D110000gmrb_20150622 _3-05.htm.

32 Asian Development Bank, "Greater Mekong Subregion," 2017, https:// www.adb.org/countries/gms/main. The Guangxi Autonomous Region, as it is officially known, is the only one of the GMS's seven constituent jurisdictional units that the Mekong does not touch.

33 Japan and the United States have the largest voting shares in the ADB — 13 percent each — followed by China at 6 percent. That 7 percent gap is roughly a third as large as the 20-point interval between the largest (Chinese) and next-largest (Indian) voting shares in the AIIB, respectively 28 and 8 percent. Cf. "Members, Capital Stock, and Voting Power (as of 31 December 2016)," https://www.adb.org/sites/default/files/institutional -document/237881/oi-appendix1.pdf; and Weiss, "Asian Infrastructure Investment Bank."

34 For an assessment of the GMS Program and the associated Mekong River Commission (MRC) during their early years, including their conflict-preventing aspects, see Susanne Schmeier, "Regional Cooperation Efforts in the Mekong River Basin: Mitigating River-related Security Threats and Promoting Regional Development," *Austrian Journal of South-East Asian Studies* 2, no. 2 (2009): 28–52, http://www.ssoar.info /ssoar/bitstream/handle/document/36281/ssoar-aseas-2009-2-schmeier -Regional_cooperation_efforts_in_the.pdf?sequence=1.

35 "Plans for High Speed Railway to Thailand and Laos," *RailPersonnel*, 8 December 2010, http://www.railpersonnel.com/railnews/railnews 101210txt.htm; Simon Montlake, "China Pushes Rail Links into Southeast Asia: Is Laos Aboard?," *The Christian Science Monitor*, 14 June 2011, https://www.csmonitor.com/World/Asia-Pacific/2011/0614 /China-pushes-rail-links-into-southeast-Asia-Is-Laos-aboard.

36 Adam Pasick, "China's Cancelled Burma Railway Is Its Latest Derailment in Southeast Asia," Quartz, 25 July 2014, https://qz.com /240436/chinas-cancelled-burma-railway-is-its-latest-derailment-in -southeast-asia/.

37 The distance by road from Muse to Yangon is over 1,000 kilometers. To cover that distance in an hour, the train would have to travel at roughly three times the claimed speed of 350 km/hour. Even a straight route between the two is over 800 kilometers.

38 Khin Su Wai, "China Eyes High Speed Railway as Part of One Belt, One Road Strategy," *Myanmar Times*, 5 December 2016, http://www .mmtimes.com/index.php/national-news/24040-china-eyes-high-speed -railway-as-part-of-one-belt-one-road-strategy.html.

39 Raghu Dayal, "China's One Belt, One Road Gamble," Hindu Business Line (Chennai), 20 May 2017, http://www.thehindubusinessline .com/opinion/china-building-a-complex-web-of-rail-road-networks -crisscrossing-asia/article9693579.ece.

40 Anthony Kuhn, "Full Steam Ahead for China's Rail Links Abroad?," NPR, 14 June 2011, http://www.npr.org/2011/06/14/137111321/full -steam-ahead-for-chinas-rail-links-abroad; Christopher Len, "China's 21st Century Maritime Silk Road Initiative, Energy Security and SLOC Access," *Maritime Affairs: Journal of the National Maritime Foundation of India* 11, no. 1 (2015): 1–18, https://doi-org.stanford.idm.oclc.org /10.1080/09733159.2015.1025535; Jeremy Bender and Armin Rosen, "This Pentagon Map Shows What's Really Driving China's Military and Diplomatic Strategy," *Business Insider*, 13 May 2015, http://www .businessinsider.com/this-map-shows-chinas-global-energy-ties-2015-5.

41 卢光盛, 张励 [Lu Guangsheng and Zhang Li], "论 '一带一路' 框架下澜沧江-湄公河 '跨界水公共产品' 的供给" [On the supply of "transboundary water public goods" in the Minjiang River-Mekong River under the framework of the "Belt and Road Initiative"], in《一带一路与国际合作》["One Belt One Road" and international cooperation] (Shanghai: Shanghai People's Publishing House, 2015), 144.

42 Lu and Zhang, "Transboundary Water Public Goods," 137. Italics added.

43 雷珺 [Lei Jun], "区域性公共产品视角下的湄公河流域联合执法安全合作机制" [Mekong Basin joint patrol security cooperation mechanism under regional public goods] in《国际公共产品 变革中的中国与世界》[International public goods], ed. 王逸舟 [Wang Yizhou], (Beijing: Peking University Press, 2015), 142–59. Italics added.

44 Dittmer, "China, Southeast Asia, and the United States," 132.

45 Zachary Reddick, "The Zhenge He Voyages Reconsidered: A Means of Imperial Power Projection," *Quarterly Journal of Chinese Studies* 3,

no. 1 (October 2014), https://www.questia.com/library/journal/1P3-3527 185101/the-zheng-he-voyages-reconsidered-a-means-of-imperial.

46 Alice D. Ba, "Is China Leading? China, Southeast Asia and East Asian Integration," *Political Science* 66, no. 2 (2014): 149.

47 Ben Carter, "Is China's Economy Really the Largest in the World?," *BBC News*, 16 December 2014, http://www.bbc.com/news/magazine -30483762. In 2017, in exchange-rate terms, the United States was still larger, but China continued to gain.

48 Mark Magnier, "China's Economic Growth in 2015 Is Slowest in 25 Years," *Wall Street Journal*, 19 January 2016, https://www.wsj.com/arti cles/china-economic-growth-slows-to-6-9-on-year-in-2015-1453169398.

49 François Godement, *China's Economic Downturn: The Facts behind the Myth* (London: European Council on Foreign Relations, ECFR, 2015), 1.

50 Evelyn Goh, "The Modes of China's Influence: Cases from Southeast Asia," *Asian Survey* 54, no. 5 (2014): 837.

51 Ba, "Is China Leading?," 157

52 Asian Development Bank, *Meeting Asia's Infrastructure Needs* (Manila: ADB, 2017), passim, https://www.adb.org/sites/default/files /publication/227496/special-report-infrastructure.pdf.

53 The initiative is described in detail in *Master Plan on ASEAN Connectivity* (Jakarta: ASEAN Secretariat, August 2016).

54 Geoff Wade, "ASEAN Divides," in *Regional Outlook: Southeast Asia 2011–2012*, eds. Michael J. Montesano and Lee Poh Onn (Singapore: Institute of Southeast Asian Studies, 2011), 21.

55 Ba, "Is China Leading?," 158.

56 Xi Jinping, *The Chinese Dream of the Great Rejuvenation of the Chinese Nation* (Beijing: Foreign Languages Press, 2014).

57 Wei Ling, "A Community of Common Destiny," *China Daily*, 9 October 2013, http://www.chinadaily.com.cn/opinion/2013-10/09/content _17016269_2.htm.

CHAPTER 14

China's Myanmar, Myanmar's China
MYTHS, ILLUSIONS, INTERACTIONS

David I. Steinberg, *Georgetown University, United States*

A chapter whose review of Myanmar-China relations features myths and illusions is aptly begun with excerpts from a poem, "For Friends in Burma," written in 1956 by China's then vice premier Chen Yi:[1]

I live by the river's head. You live by its tail. Limitlessly, we love each other. We drink the same river's water. I drink from the upper flows. You drink from below. Endlessly the river flows. . . . We are neighbors. Our friendship lasts. . . . [T]he waters flow forever. Our lands are connected. At the mountain's foot, beside the same river, anti-imperialism begets freedom. We are peacefully united. We are *paukphaw* [siblings]. Our languages are connected. We are united and help each other. Peace is powerful. . . .

Chen Yi was a close associate of China's then leader, Chairman Mao Zedong. The classical-style poem — its harmoniously naturalist metaphors, its appeal to abstract solidarity, and the touch of agitprop in its invocation of shared anti-imperialism — summarized an illusion: that Chinese-Burmese relations were everlastingly tranquil, steeped in brotherly amity as permanent as the two countries' physical adjacency and the mountain-river, upstream-downstream complementarities evoked in Chen Yi's lines. (A comparably idealized representation is maintained to this day at the Sino-Myanmar friendship monument in Mangshi, Yunnan Province, not far from the Myanmar border.) Bilateral antagonisms have existed and still do. Controversial efforts by China to generate hydroelectric power for its own use by damming the Irrawaddy and Salween rivers, for instance, have belied the riverine goodwill projected by Chen Yi. Water access and usage have been major irritants in the bilateral relationship.

Myths and illusions are often linked, but they are not coterminous. Myths acquire the patina of history; they are generally positioned in the past. Illusions are more likely to be contemporary. That said, both imply degrees of unreality and both may shape policy. Scholarship attempts to impose intellectual rigor on myths and illusions alike, but the task is complex. Particular instances may contain important kernels of reality. Changes in evidence and interpretation over time may induce shifts in perception and consensus. Relevant too are the personal predilections that a given analyst may have. In one scholar's blunt judgment, "Writers recreate reality to fit their moral dispositions."[2]

This chapter does two things: First, it recounts and interprets key junctures in the record of China-Myanmar relations since the birth of the People's Republic of China (PRC) in 1949 and its recognition by Burma that same year. Second, retrospectively in that context, it notes the roles of myths and illusions, not only bilaterally between China and Myanmar but also with reference to the views and policies of the United States. Sometimes those outlooks and actions harmed or delayed the development of Burma (and later of Myanmar) more than they yielded the ostensibly constructive results that advocates anticipated. Variously at play in these fields of opinion and decision were: the legitimacy of Burmese governments; national unity along Burma's northern reaches; issues of regional security and international relations; Sino-US relations regarding Myanmar; and the future of Sino-Burmese relations. Although the treatment herein is mainly historical, the risk of credulity in myths and illusions is not. Old ones continue to evolve even as new ones arise.

Unequal "Siblings," a "Fifth Column," and "Party-to-Party" Relations

It is important not to analyze myths and illusions from a smugly superior point of view, as if the analyst alone were immune to self-deception. The Chinese and the Burmese who have shaped their countries' interactions, not to mention the scholars who have studied them, have not been blind to the gaps between wishes and fears on the one hand and realities on the other. The effective use of myths and illusions does not require the user to believe in them. No smugness is intended in the following account and its passing references to four concerns and their manifestations in Sino-Burmese relations: *paukphaw* equality, "fifth-column" conspiracy, "party-to-party" solidarity, and northern-border disputation.

Chen Yi was hardly the last to invoke the sibling illusion—*paukphaw*. On 8 June 2016 in Yangon, Chinese and Burmese officials celebrated the two countries' first China-Myanmar Paukphaw Friendship Day and inaugurated a China-Myanmar Paukphaw Friendship Foundation for economic and cultural cooperation.[3] In August Myanmar state counsellor Aung San Suu Kyi met with Chinese president Xi Jinping in Beijing. They "spoke highly of China-Myanmar 'Paukphaw' friendship," according to the joint statement issued on that occasion.[4]

With rather more cant than candor, the term *paukphaw* was first used by the Burmese side to connote fraternal equality between the two neighbors. On the Chinese side, however, the preferred analogy would have been to China as the elder brother, superior in age, to whom the younger Burmese sibling should defer. In conversation with the author in Kunming early in this century, for instance, a Chinese official extrapolated his country's imperial past into the future by describing Myanmar as "our tributary forever." As for the Burmese, they spoke and speak of paukphaw wishfully, but also warily, aware as they were and are of China's vast advantage in size and power. Not without reason did Burma's first prime minister, U Nu, refer to his country as a tender plant hemmed in by cactuses—not only China in the north, but bristly neighbors such as India and Thailand to the west and east as well.[5] Or, in the more colorful phrasing of an old Burmese adage, "When China spits, we swim."[6]

Burma gained independence in 1948. A year later, under Prime Minister U Nu, it became the first non-communist state to recognize the People's Republic of China (PRC). That move was prompted more by strategic fear than paukphaw affinity, however. China's civil war was spilling over into Burma. Burmese leaders recalled the local repercussions of intra-Chinese strife following the replacement of the Ming dynasty by the Qing dynasty in the 17th century. The Sino-Burmese border had never been officially approved by any Chinese regime—neither the PRC, the Kuomintang (KMT), nor the Qing or the Ming. U Nu thought that diplomatic ties with the PRC might help to alleviate the threat of intrusions into northern Burma by Chinese communist forces hoping to defeat the Chinese nationalist troops who had retreated there. Beijing, he feared, might use the presence of KMT troops in northern Burma as an excuse to lop off a slice of his country. Not until 1960 was a border agreement reached with the PRC.

In this context, the large and relatively well-off ethnic-Chinese minority in Burma operated dozens of Chinese-language schools; many offered courses in communist ideology. For half a century, China had upheld an amplified version of *jus sanguinis* whereby all ethnic Chinese, wherever they might have been born or reside, were citizens of China and owed allegiance to it. These conditions helped to popularize among Burmese (and American) officials the specter of a "fifth column" committed to Chinese and communist expansion. Premised in part on the need to stop the "Sino-Soviet bloc" from metastasizing, American foreign aid to East Asia included quasi-private efforts to introduce anti-communist texts into Chinese-language school curricula in Southeast Asia.[7] Burma was then a democratic socialist state, generally moderate but decidedly anti-communist. The government in Rangoon deplored Chinese support for the Burma Communist Party, later justified by the Chinese on the grounds that "party-to-party" relations were different from state-to-state ones. The northern border between the two states was also in dispute. No Chinese regime — neither the Qing dynasty nor the Chinese-nationalist KMT nor the PRC — had ever formally agreed to the 1914 MacMahon Line marking Britain's imperial expansion from Afghanistan to Thailand. Significant portions of northern Burma fell inside China on official KMT and PRC maps alike. The above four concerns were eventually mitigated, but the process took decades to unfold.

In the 1950s the two prime ministers — China's Zhou Enlai and Burma's U Nu — enjoyed close relations, illustrated by Zhou's nine visits to Burma. It was Zhou who effectively revoked *jus sanguinis* by saying that ethnic Chinese in Burma should obey Burmese laws and customs. The border issue was resolved in 1960 with another Burmese victory: China recognized the traditional frontier and Burma returned only three Kachin villages to China that the British had appropriated. Beijing wished to show the world that it had no territorial ambitions. Rangoon, wishing to prevent China from acting unilaterally, joined Beijing in successful military campaigns against the KMT in northern Burma. No longer a serious threat, the KMT remained only as an annoyance, although it continued to profit from opium production. Meanwhile Burma-US relations suffered from the clandestine but obvious American support for the KMT. That intervention was based on an American illusion that these remnant nationalist forces left over from China's civil war — never more than 15,000 troops — could somehow prompt a popular uprising inside China against communist rule. Adding to Rangoon's mistrust of Washington was the latter's refusal to allow the UN to take up the issue.

Compared with the KMT, the Communist Party of Burma (CPB) posed a more intractable challenge. Burma's communists had been in revolt since independence in 1948. Support was evident early on, but later the CPB retreated north. In its own version of Mao's Long March, the party moved from central Burma to the Chinese border, recruiting minority peoples into its ranks along the way. A coup in 1962 brought an anti-communist military regime into power. Following anti-Chinese riots five years later, Beijing vigorously backed the CPB. Chinese territory became a haven for some of the party's leaders. China broadcast pro-communist messages into Burma from a radio station in Yunnan Province. These efforts did not bear fruit, however, and by 1989 the party had dissolved due to internal strife, including ethnic factionalism. The heritage of the CPB and China's efforts on its behalf is nevertheless still evident in the Burmese jurisdictions adjacent to China, notably in the Wa Special Region where Mandarin is used for official business and in the schools, and commercial transactions are made in China's currency, the renminbi.

Maoism, Visibility, and Pushback

The 1962 coup would not be Burma's last. Another broke out in 1988 following the collapse of the ruling Burma Socialist Programme Party (BSPP) in the wake of massive demonstrations against military rule. In the period between the two coups, Sino-Burmese relations reached their nadir in 1967. It was then that Mao's Great Proletarian Cultural Revolution spilled over into Burma.

Beijing tried to popularize Mao and Maoism in Burma, but soon ran into trouble. When, for example, badges bearing his likeness were distributed to pupils in Chinese-language schools, Rangoon prohibited their being worn. Riots broke out. Chinese shops were looted. A mob occupied the Chinese embassy. Ambassadors were withdrawn. Burmese authorities did little to stop the riots; more than 30 people were killed.[8]

The resident ethnic-Chinese population in Burma felt betrayed by Beijing. In their view, by not protecting them, China had belied its status as a strong country that could not be pushed around. As for Burma's leader, General Ne Win, many observers felt he had allowed the rioting to flare up against the Chinese population, hoping to shift domestic opinion toward nationalism and away from attention to the failure of his economic policies. Before World War II, Burma had been the largest rice exporter in the world. Now it could not even feed itself. Economic conditions were dire.

The men who led the PRC following its formation in 1949 doubted that any developing country could be truly neutral or authentically socialist. Notwithstanding any claims to the contrary, it must favor the imperialists. Accordingly, in its official, classified communications, Beijing expressed skepticism when the 1962 coup in Burma brought to power the self-named "socialist" BSPP, founded and chaired by Ne Win, who headed the state as well.[9] China's leaders deemed the junta state-capitalist, not socialist, and its party and leader hardly communist in character. Since Burma was officially "socialist," however, Beijing did not express these judgments in public. In 1963, following his coup, Ne Win, in a fit of nationalist anger, repressed the country's immigrant communities. The victims were mainly those of South Asian descent, but ethnic Chinese suffered as well. Accused of exploiting the Burman majority, some 100,000 Sino-Burmese fled or were expelled. While New Delhi complained, Beijing kept silent.

Chinese influence in Myanmar grew in the wake of the 1988 coup, as Western governments responded to the crushing of revolt and the seizure of power by withdrawing support. The United States successfully pressured Japan to stop its development aid, which had amounted to about half of the total economic assistance Myanmar had been receiving from all foreign sources.[10] But Tokyo did not apply sanctions while continuing instead to provide extensive debt relief and humanitarian help. As the 1990s progressed, the PRC's presence in Myanmar became more and more evident. China became, for example, the largest foreign investor in the country's economy.

As Beijing's visibility grew, so did local concerns regarding Chinese behavior and motivation. China's multiple involvements in building infrastructure and extracting resources, often using Chinese rather than Burmese labor, appeared mainly to benefit the PRC. To clear space for such projects, Burmese farmers were removed from their lands with little or no compensation. Chinese-language schools and Chinese shops sporting signs in Chinese characters proliferated. As time went by, in addition to worrying government officials, these trends offended public opinion as well. In 2011–15, as Myanmar began to experiment with political and economic reforms, the more relaxed atmosphere allowed anti-Chinese sentiments to circulate more freely in the media and in literature.[11] Such views have been fed by Myanmar's trade deficit with China, larger in 2016 than with any other country save Singapore.[12] Since then the scale and visibility of China's presence have continued to grow. In addition to the Chinese projects in construction and extraction, Myanmar has borne an influx of illegal migrants from its northern neighbor. Whatever the exact number of ethnic Chinese in Myanmar—estimates range from 1.7 to 2.3 million[13]—China's ethno-economic presence has fueled feelings of insecurity and vulnerability and a concomitant increase in ethnic nationalism among the Burman majority.

China's imposing presence did not make the Burmese feel subservient; it made them apprehensive. At the same time, on the Chinese side, it was associated with yet another illusion — Chinese overconfidence. Contributing to that attitude were Burma's history as a tributary state; China's pride in its own premodern prominence, in its current rise, and in the ostensible superiority of Chinese culture; along with a corresponding disdain for seemingly inferior Southeast Asian cultures.

In formal terms, Myanmar's military junta transitioned to partly civilian rule on 30 March 2011. In May, President Thein Sein, a retired general, flattered China by making Beijing his first foreign destination and by using the occasion to agree to a bilateral Comprehensive Strategic Cooperative Partnership with the PRC.[14] But the illusion that, domestic reforms notwithstanding, Myanmar would defer to its superior neighbor led China to overplay its hand. Beijing expected Myanmar's *tatmadaw* (armed forces), which relied on Chinese equipment and training, to retain influence sufficient to ensure the new government's compliance with Chinese desires. China's shock was thus profound when, in September 2012, without notifying Beijing, Thein Sein suspended Chinese construction of the Myitsone Dam in Kachin State for the rest of his 2011–16 presidential term. This was Myanmar's largest hydroelectric project, estimated in value between USD \$3.6 and \$8 billion for a series of dams along the Irrawaddy River — the lifeline of the country. The river held great symbolic value for the Kachin people. They opposed the project. Objections spread to the general population. China blamed the United States, noting that several Burmese environmental NGOs had criticized the dam and Myanmar's foreign minister had visited Washington just prior to the announcement of the project. Beijing soon appointment a new Chinese ambassador to Myanmar. A second high-level post was also created, ostensibly to cover Asia broadly but in fact to focus on Myanmar and deal with the unexpected blow that the project's suspension had delivered to China's position. The decision to halt the project instanced the cost of illusion. The suspension kept Chinese officials busy trying to undo the damage that their wishful self-assurance had made so unexpected. At the same time, the government in Naypyitaw enjoyed an uptick in nationalist legitimacy, indicating a change that Beijing would have to reckon with in future.[15]

Legitimacy's Role in Myanmar-China Relations

The legitimacy of any regime necessarily varies over time. Legitimation is always a contingent process, never a permanent result. Five of the many possible ingredients of legitimation will be reviewed briefly here — dynasty, democracy, identity, sovereignty, and vulnerability — with particular reference to China's impact on the process historically in Burma-now-Myanmar, including the role of myth as it illustrates Burmese vulnerability to China and services a distinctively Burmese identity.

Regime legitimacy in newly postcolonial states often benefits from the aura and euphoria associated with a leader of the struggle for independence from foreign rule. As time passes, attempts may be made to re-embody that role and the associated glow in one of the leader's relatives by blood or marriage. Southeast Asian examples include the presidencies of Cory and Benigno Aquino in the Philippines and of Megawati Sukarnoputri in Indonesia — and the upward arc of Aung San Suu Kyi in Myanmar. Suu Kyi's nationalist father, Aung San, founded the Burmese Independence Army in 1941 and led a revolt against Japanese occupation in 1945. In 1947 Aung San managed to negotiate a British promise of independence and a national-unity agreement with non-Burman minorities before his assassination later that same year. Having led Myanmar's National League for Democracy (NLD) since 2011, his daughter Suu Kyi was installed in 2016 as her country's state counsellor, minister of the president's office, and minister of foreign affairs. In Myanmar as elsewhere, however, dynastic solutions to the problem of legitimacy may fail to reincarnate the founding father's prestige, especially as the temptations and compromises of incumbency erode the moral purity of the heir. As for democratic legitimation, Suu Kyi's increasingly authoritarian behavior could undercut that aspect of her image as an icon of the struggle for human rights under the fully military former regime.

More relevant to Myanmar-China relations than dynastic or democratic paths to legitimacy are the strengths and vicissitudes of national identity, sovereignty, and vulnerability.

Defending Myanmar's national identity is a cardinal tenet of the *tatmadaw*. But it is hard to defend what one has never had. Burma-now-Myanmar is a state, but it is not a nation, for it lacks an inclusive character-in-common with an ethos to match.[16] Nevertheless, the idea that any foreign actor deserves to dominate the country is an anathema. One might call this a commitment to sovereignty without a consensus on identity. Perhaps in part due to the absence of a shared "we-ness" that could foster national confidence that their country's sovereignty will endure, Burmese tend to harbor strong feelings of vulnerability to mistreatment — socioeconomic, cultural, and political — at the hands of foreigners, Chinese hands included. Even the appearance, let alone the reality, of foreign domination plays a major role in Myanmar-China relations. For example, if in the future,

Myanmar were for some reason thought by its people to have traded an intrusively Chinese patron for a no less presumptuous American one, the same dynamic could damage the appeal of both dyads alike.

A regime that fails to protect the country from outsiders who are seen as exploiting or plotting to exploit its vulnerability will lose popular respect. It is not coincidental that the 2008 constitution's Article 59(f) withholds the offices of president and vice president not only from any foreigner, but from any Burmese whose near relatives by kin or marriage include a foreigner. In addition to using that provision to block the dynastic solution by citing Suu Kyi's marriage to a British citizen, the tatmadaw also used it to deny a vice-presidential nomination to one of its own generals whose daughter had married a foreigner.

If foreign predation is anathema to the Burmese, so is cowardice in the face of it. Scholars have debated where the well-known chronicle *Tayoke Pye Min* falls on a spectrum from myth to truth,[17] but either way the story remains a fixture in Burmese history and folklore. King Narathihapate was the last ruler of Pagan. When the Mongol emperor Kublai Khan proposed to assimilate Pagan into China, as the story goes, Narathihapate did more than refuse. He executed the emissaries who brought the request. In retaliation, the "Chinese" emperor — Burmese viewed Mongols as Chinese — sent an army to seize Pagan. Narathihapate lost his will to resist, turned tail, and fled south to the Irrawaddy Delta. For that he was called "the King Who Ran from the Chinese" — *Tayoke Pye Min* in Burmese. In 1287, after Narathihapate died, poisoned by his own son, Mongol troops occupied Pagan.[18] The story, still invoked in Myanmar today, shows how large China looms in how Burmese, or ethnic-majority Burmans at any rate, understand the legitimacy of those who rule them.

Before the 1967 riots against China's Maoist intrusion, relatively good relations with Beijing were maintained successively by U Nu's civilian-democratic government and General Ne Win's military-socialist regime. The largely positive tone of those interactions tended to benefit the domestic reputations of both Burmese administrations, partly as reassurance to leftist but non-communist elements that Burma's leaders would favor a balanced (neutralist) position in foreign affairs.[19] Following the 1949 formation of the PRC, Beijing was inclined to doubt that any non-communist regime could be politically legitimate, and thereby to consign Burma to the "imperialist camp." But Beijing found that improved relations with Burma served China's interest by assuaging international fears of aggressive behavior by the newborn PRC. It was in this context, in 1960, that Ne Win negotiated a border settlement with China highly favorable to Burma.

Facilitating that success was his reminder to the Chinese that they were likely to get a worse deal if they waited to negotiate with elected civilians following his military-run 1958-to-1960 "caretaker" government's soon-expiring time in power. Even before China's willingness to settle the Sino-Burmese border, Burmese concerns about the northern behemoth had been assuaged by U Nu's close relationship with Zhou Enlai and their joint advocacy of coexistence, including Burma's prominence at the 1955 Bandung Conference that both men attended.

Knowing the important role played by Buddhism in Burmese notions of legitimacy, Beijing also put religious mythology to diplomatic use. Many Buddhists revere ostensible relics from the cremated body of the Buddha. As a sign of friendship in 1955–56, Beijing sent such relics to Burma on temporary loan for local circulation and veneration. Chinese "tooth diplomacy" in Myanmar would recur in 1994, 1996–97, and 2011.[20]

More conventionally and narrowly, Chinese military aid doubtless bolstered the regime loyalty of the officers in Myanmar's juntas — the State Law and Order Restoration Council (SLORC, 1988–97) and the State Peace and Development Council (SPDC, 1997–2011). Two-thirds of all Burmese military training overseas in this period took place in China.[21] Beijing supported the junta in other ways as well, for example, by vetoing an American denunciation of the SPDC in the UN Security Council in 2007.[22]

Global attention has been drawn to the negative views of Burmese Buddhists toward the small Muslim Rohingya minority. Long resident in Myanmar, the Rohingya were indigenous to the Indian subcontinent, including what is now Bangladesh. In Myanmar's Burman Buddhist majority, ethno-religious prejudice is widespread. There were riots against Muslims in the 1930s, and restrictions against religious minorities, including Muslims, were adopted as recently as 2015. In the tatmadaw, for example, there are no Muslim officers with the rank of colonel or higher. The government in Naypyitaw calls the Rohingya "Bengali" as if they weren't Burmese at all. Myanmar-China ties are not affected because Beijing benefits from being able to ignore ethno-religious repression in Myanmar — silence that Washington cannot afford in the light of American concern for human rights.

Myanmar's National Unity and China

A major Western illusion about Burma/Myanmar has resulted from viewing the country through the normative lens of liberal democracy. The most critical issue facing the state since independence has not been democracy, however it is defined — a "discipline-flourishing" regime as the tatmadaw would have it, or an idealized version based on Western experience that circulates in the international community. The issue is *equity*: how to create and sustain, in some authentically Burmese sense, a viable distribution of political power and economic resources between and among the diverse ethnic groups that make up the country. Even before independence was granted, foreign and local actors debated whether to replace British colonial rule with a single "Union of Burma" or a set of autonomous or even sovereign states. To this day, the matter has not been resolved to the satisfaction of diverse relevant actors, some of whom have championed independence, autonomy, or some sort of federal structure. The process of ethnic reconciliation is ongoing, but it will remain arduous and prolonged.

The curved shape of a horseshoe describes the geography of the mountainous regions on the western, northern, and eastern frontiers of Myanmar. Inhabiting them are a seeming myriad of ethnic minority cultures of varying degrees of political and military organization.[23] The horseshoe surrounds the central river valleys that are home to the ethnically Burman (Bamah) majority — about two-thirds of the country's peoples. As a matter of territorial integrity, no area is more important than the enduring, contentiously disputed northern border with a potentially expanding China.

Yet the primary goal of the tatmadaw since independence has not been projected outward — to defend the country from incursion by its overweening neighbor. The military has turned inward to preserve national unity under its own rule — to deter the ethnic minorities from secession while keeping the communists among them out of power. Beginning in 1963, General Ne Win, then head of state and ruling-party chair, expressly rejected any form of federalism as a first step toward secession. This remained the military's mantra until about 2014 when some sort of federal structure — imprecise, undefined — became publicly acceptable to the Thein Sein regime. Those details have still not been clarified, let alone negotiated. Competing groups, divergent elements inside the tatmadaw arguably among them, retain deeply felt alternative views on the subject. Nowhere is the territorial issue more acute than on the Sino-Burmese frontier, where large and well-armed ethnic rebellions persist and remain deeply involved, economically if not politically, with their ethnic cousins on the Chinese side of the border. These complex activities include both legal trade and rent-seeking. They are lucrative, often obscure, and important not only to local officialdom but to the central authorities in both countries.[24] Although solving these problems could significantly boost Myanmar's economic and political development, that prospect is resisted by those who profit from the combination of uncertainty, ambiguity, and contested control.

More than three dozen ethnic rebellions, small and large, have plagued the central government at various times since independence. Despite the many ceasefires that have been negotiated for varying periods of time since 1989, more than half a dozen active insurgencies still existed in 2018, and a way to achieve peace, also called "reconciliation," remained an elusive hope. Thein Sein's government had wanted to proclaim a truly national ceasefire, but its announcement in October 2015 did not include eight entities that were still actively in revolt.

Some form of federalism was promised at an inter-ethnic conference held in Panglong, Shan State, on 12 February 1947 — still celebrated as Union Day. The meeting was led by Aung San Suu Kyi's father, Aung San. Not all of Burma's minorities attended. But, as already noted above, five months later he was dead — assassinated — and the promise was never kept.

Another inter-ethnic "Panglong" conference met in Naypyitaw on 31 August 2016 to address the unfinished agenda from the earlier gathering nearly seven decades before.[25] Led by Myanmar's foreign minister, the meeting ran four days but made little progress. The conference is scheduled to reconvene every six months for a number of years. Even if a national ceasefire can be arranged, that would be just the first step toward a comprehensive solution. Total dissident ethnic armed forces are still some 50,000 to 100,000 strong. Because most of those fighters operate close to or along the porous Chinese border, they cannot be defeated by the tatmadaw alone.

Another illusion can be seen in the neat inter-ethnic symmetry implied by Myanmar's third and current constitution, adopted in 2008, which envisions seven "regions" (provinces) basically for the Burman majority and an equal number of "states" (provinces) mainly for the ethnic minorities. This seemingly equitable allocation ignores the actual imbalances in power and access to resources. It also ignores the complexity and diversity of the minorities' natures and locations. Notably distinctive, for example, are the four special zones along the Chinese border. Among these, the Wa area is large and unconquerable by the Burmese; the Kokang area is small but lies on a vital communications link with China; the Shan inhabit the largest minority land area; and the Kachin occupy Myanmar's northern reaches.

Consider the Wa. They occupy a long, impenetrable region on the frontier with China. Ethno-linguistically, they differ greatly from most of their neighbors. They are a formidable advocate for autonomy in a separate state inside Myanmar. Their armed forces are extensive — some 20,000–30,000 men armed with fairly sophisticated weaponry, some of it said to be supplied by the Chinese. Opium is grown and methamphetamine is produced on a major scale in their area where the Wa live.

The area's infrastructure connects with China and involves the Wa in Chinese patterns of influence. Some 400,000 Wa live in China's Yunnan Province. The Wa region has become, in effect, a socioeconomic adjunct of southwestern China. That said, there is no evidence of Wa irredentism on either side of the frontier. Ambiguous interactions allow local entities to pursue their interests with a degree of freedom that could be destroyed by too sharp an opposition to, or too close an association with, the authorities in either Myanmar or China.

Kokang is in many respects the opposite of the Wa region. Kokang is small, was ceded to Burma by the Chinese in 1897, and the population comprises ethnic Chinese who are Burmese citizens and have their own small army. In 2009, the Chinese, concerned that an illicit arms factory in the Kokang area could provide arms to the Tibetans and the Uighurs, told the Burmese to eliminate it. Major clashes broke out between the Kokang army and the *tatmadaw*. Some 37,000 refugees from the fighting fled into Yunnan, a situation the Chinese found intolerable. Dissatisfied with the efforts of Yunnan officials to deal with the problem, Beijing took a more direct role in managing it, which included involving the People's Liberation Army more actively in frontier affairs.

When Kokang violence broke out again in 2015, possibly due to rivalries among local leaders, Naypyitaw declared a state of emergency in the region. As of this writing, the conflicts remain unresolved. North of Kokang district, in the mainly Christian Kachin zone, a ceasefire was breached in 2011 and deteriorated into active fighting that continues, off and on, between government troops and the Kachin Independence Army. The area is rich in jade, timber, gold, and potential sources of hydroelectric power. In private discussions with actors on the Burmese side, up and down the Sino-Myanmar border, Chinese officials have conveyed Beijing's desire to keep the Americans from playing any role in these conflicts.

The Burmese government has continuously reiterated the myth, supposedly begun by Aung San, that the country's ethnic groups traditionally lived together in harmony through times of prosperity and adversity — "weal and woe" — only to see that amity destroyed by the British policy of dividing, the better to rule. Applying their model for India, the British did indeed divide Burma, separating the heartland Burman areas from the frontier peoples, the more easily and economically to govern. But the responsibility for the ongoing lack of ethnic cohesion and the resulting persistence of ethnic strife is by no means theirs alone.

China, India, and Japan

An emphasis on domestic ethnic conflict is especially appropriate in relation to yet another illusion, regularly encountered in the literature on international relations: that smaller states such as Myanmar either "bandwagon" with larger states, "balance" against them, or "hedge" between them. The implication is that the smaller state is reacting to its environment. On the contrary, Myanmar's behavior in the international arena is based as much on its *internal* needs as on its external interests.[26]

Myanmar's 2008 constitution, authored by the military, does call for the country to practice an "independent, active, and non-aligned foreign policy aimed at world peace and friendly relations with nations." But beneath that anodyne formula lies the tatmadaw's commitment to its version of national unity and its aversion to attempts by foreigners to take advantage of ethnic differences within the country. Nor has Aung San Suu Kyi, since becoming foreign minister, succumbed to foreign pressure to criticize the brutal treatment of the Muslim Rohingya at the hands of Buddhist Burmans in Rakhine State. Little public (authorized) discussion of Myanmar's foreign policy has taken place inside the country, and the topic has not been debated in any of the country's parliaments since Ne Win's coup in 1962.

Among Myanmar's major Asian neighbors, China has an especially strategic view of the country with which it shares by far the longest land border between itself and a Southeast Asian state. One can argue, accordingly, that Beijing sees Myanmar as its most important link to the world beyond Southeast Asia, especially in meeting China's economic needs. Myanmar figures prominently in Chinese plans for overseas investment to extract minerals and generate hydroelectric energy, for example. These plans are vital for Yunnan, as that province is among China's poorest and its trade with Myanmar is critical to its development. In 2014, Yunnan's trade with the 10 members of ASEAN totaled $14.3 billion — 49 percent of it with Myanmar.[27]

Strategically, Myanmar is China's link to the Indian Ocean. This is most evident at Kyaukpyu, one of the ports accessible to China as part of its "string of pearls" — a sequence of ports from Hong Kong to Djibouti and beyond, meant to protect Chinese shipping but potentially playing political and even military roles as well. Facilitating Beijing's reach, crude oil and gas pipelines run from Kyaukpyu overland into China, respectively terminating in Yunnan's capital, Kunming, and in eastern Guangxi Province. The lines help protect China from the loss of access to imported energy that hostile control of the Malacca Straits could entail. Kyaukpyu is also the site of a major Chinese-sponsored industrial zone. For these reasons alone, Myanmar's ties to China are clearly in the latter's strategic interest.

China's relationship with Myanmar has been of some concern inside Southeast Asia. Singapore, among other ASEAN members, wanted to lessen Chinese influence in Myanmar by having Myanmar join the association, which it finally did in July 1997 over strong US objections. Some speculate that the military intelligence chief, General Khin Nyunt, also hoping to reduce China's footprint, may have convinced the leadership to join. Whoever was responsible, the affiliation did little to diminish Beijing's role in a country of such strategic importance to China.[28] Nor has Beijing since softened its neuralgia toward any initiative to weaken its influence in Myanmar, including President Obama's "pivot" — later "rebalancing" — to Asia and the related effort to improve US-Myanmar relations.

If Beijing saw the Americans as trying to surround and contain China inside East Asia, New Delhi felt the Chinese were attempting to cordon off India inside "its" region, South Asia. Three decades ago, that fear impacted Sino-Burmese relations. In 1988, with China next door claiming the northern portion of Arunachal Pradesh, with Pakistan a Chinese ally, and with Burma under Chinese influence, India turned against its Southeast Asian neighbor. Under Rajiv Gandhi, New Delhi vigorously criticized the junta.

By 1993, New Delhi had recognized that its frown diplomacy had failed, as Chinese influence in Myanmar had increased, so India tried cooperative diplomacy instead. It had two goals in mind. The first was to rival and thereby mitigate Chinese influence by increasing its own political and economic engagements with Myanmar. The second was to prevent northeastern India — bordering Myanmar but almost wholly cut off from the rest of India by Bangladesh — from cultivating Burmese support for secession. Nearly a dozen rebellions against New Delhi having already taken place in that region, India's leaders hoped to reduce if not preclude the prospect of ethnically based Burmese helping the northeastern rebels' secessionist cause. A number of ethnic groups, notably the Chin and the Naga, straddle the India-Myanmar border.

As for Japan, it has long had strategic interests in Burma, even before World War II. Its attraction to the country reflected a mix of motives, including a practical desire for economic linkages and a diplomatic interest in helping less-developed countries by providing economic aid. Japan's outreach occurred, of course, against the background of its wartime predation in Southeast Asia. Notable in that context was the remarkably empathic character of Kon Ichikawa's 1956 anti-war film *The Burmese Harp*. In it, at war's end, a Japanese soldier decides to remain in Burma as a surrogate Burmese Buddhist priest in order to bury the Japanese dead.

In more recent and secular terms, Japan's interests in Myanmar have been heightened by a felt need to counter Chinese influence there. In different ways and to differing degrees, Washington, New Delhi, and Tokyo all share that concern.

Conditional Interdependence

Just as it would be wrong to deny or dismiss the misreadings of Sino-Burmese relations recounted in this chapter, it would be wrong to impute hallucination to all parties concerned. Myanmar's leaders remain acutely and rightly conscious of China's influence and power. In the words of one perceptive observer, Myanmar's relations with China have been characterized by "defiance and deference" alike. That said, Naypyitaw understands "that China has a sphere of interest, if not influence, and that China's legitimate strategic interests should not be undermined."[29] Myanmar's rulers know that excessive acquiescence to what China wants will undercut the domestic legitimacy of their regime.

Also nuanced is the role played by China in Myanmar's ethnic conflicts. Although the unrest cannot be blamed wholly on China, China's interactions with the armed ethnic groups in northern Myanmar have complicated the chances of resolving the conflicts. China is not the master key to unlocking a solution, but it can obstruct the peace process if it so wishes. China by this reading may be a necessary but insufficient condition of success in putting the northern strife to rest.[30]

It is likely that any Burmese administration will try, more or less delicately, to balance its relations with China. Myanmar's leader since 2016, Aung San Suu Kyi, was brought up in India, China's rival, when her mother was Burmese ambassador there. Suu Kyi did make a discreetly polite visit to China in 2015, and she returned in August 2016 to reassert the paukphaw (sibling) illusion. Insofar as Burma's/Myanmar's policies toward China have for decades relied heavily on Burmese military assessments, Suu Kyi's new role as foreign minister may enable her to test her own civilian views. But the tatmadaw is unlikely to tolerate any shift that would jeopardize Myanmar's delicate relations with China.

Myanmar needs China to help settle ethnic unrest in the north and to stop illegally exploiting Burmese resources, such as timber, jade, and gold. China, in return, needs Myanmar to accommodate Chinese-run projects to generate hydropower; to extract minerals; to lay and operate pipelines; and to achieve and retain coastal access to the Indian Ocean through the Bay of Bengal. Official Chinese investments are in infrastructure, which cannot be relocated as could a garment factory. The immobility of these investments limits Beijing's ability to reject or ignore Burmese conditions regarding their terms and impact. At the same time, Naypyitaw knows that such conditions cannot be too onerous for China. A delicate interdependence therefore prevails between the two states despite the enormous disparities in size and power between them. Conditional interdependence is real; outright subservience is not.

Consider the Letpadaung copper mine in central Myanmar. A Canadian firm first involved in the project withdrew to avoid the stigma of working with a repressive military regime. Lacking such qualms, Wanbao, a Chinese mining company linked to a large Chinese arms manufacturer, bought out the Canadians in a joint venture with the tatmadaw. When local anger over land compensation and environmental damage turned violent, the case was investigated by a Burmese parliamentary commission headed by Suu Kyi herself. The legislators did make recommendations. However, noting the delicacy of Myanmar-China relations, they kept the mine open and the contract intact — to the fury of many in the local community.[31] Nor are such tensions alleviated by the prominence of ethnic Chinese businesspeople in the administration of Thai, Singaporean, and Malaysian investments in Myanmar, not to mention those from Taiwan.

Beyond Illusions?

Misreading Myanmar is not the monopoly of any one observer, foreign or domestic. The Burmese juntas thought they could keep their country free from foreign influence through media control and self-isolation. Modern technology defied them. China's leaders thought they could exercise commanding influence over their small neighbor. They could not. They thought the Americans were trying to recruit Myanmar into containing China, while in fact the United States was more interested in democratizing Myanmar than in deputizing it. American policymakers thought they could change the regime by leveling and enforcing sanctions against it. Their policy likely delayed the very reforms they sought. Some of the ethnic minorities meanwhile re-imagined themselves as more able to forge their own futures through autonomous action than they really were. Beijing and Washington alike overestimate the importance of China's rise in shaping Myanmar's behavior.

The concept of leverage is a key ingredient in these illusions. Archimedes is said to have remarked that with a long-enough lever and a place to stand, he could move the world — as if that were not a fantasy but proof. To Beijing, military and economic assistance were leverage enough to turn Myanmar into a pliant state. To the United States, sanctions were leverage for regime change and respect for human rights. To Aung San Suu Kyi, the remaining American sanctions — euphemistically known as "restrictions" — were leverage insofar as they reminded the military to cooperate with her government to get them removed. All of these imputations of leverage are dubious inferences from questionable evidence.

Consider state counselor Suu Kyi's would-be long-enough lever — sanctions. Except for those related to matters such as drug trafficking and trade with North Korea, they were canceled by the Obama administration in September 2016 on the grounds that "Burma" (Myanmar) no longer threatened American policy goals. Suu Kyi is said to have wanted some to remain in force as "leverage" against remilitarization. She had failed to realize that, for the Obama administration, the restrictions had become liabilities — complex obstacles to the opening of Myanmar's economy to the flows of investment and assistance that Washington now desired.

In 2018 the US Treasury Department did impose sanctions on two Burmese units and four Burmese commanders for "ethnic cleansing" against the Rohingya and "serious human rights abuses" against other ethnic minorities.[32] At least in the near-to-medium term, however, a liberal democracy in Myanmar will remain a mirage. However attractive that vision may be among Westerners and educated Burmese, wishful thinking will not bring it about. Better to trade this illusion for a less unrealistic scenario that could engender a kind of pluralism, attuned to Burmese conditions, that would allow for greater reconciliation, more accountable administration, and more participatory institutions. The possible precursors of such pluralism already exist in legislative formats at provincial and local levels. Ironically, however, their operation has been severely constrained by the very provisions of the 2008 constitution that authorized their existence.

Occasionally, for convenience, this chapter has referred to China and Myanmar as if they were unitary actors. Seen from outside, they are. Seen from inside, they are not. The domestic agents and contexts that influence Chinese foreign policy as a singular noun are plural in various degrees and respects. On the Chinese side of the hyphen in China-Myanmar relations lie the sometimes differing and conflicting interests pursued in Beijing as the national capital, in the Yunnan-provincial capital, Kunming, and along Yunnan's long border with Myanmar. Yunnan and Myanmar alike encompass multiple ethnic cultures that have grown their own local myths and priorities, which often diverge from the outlooks encountered at provincial or national levels of rule.

The same holds for America. US policy is not the purview of the Department of State alone, nor even of the executive branch. Congress has been active on Myanmar, often consequentially so. Disputes over policy toward Myanmar have implicated bureaus inside State and between State and other agencies — the National Security Council, Treasury, Commerce, the US Trade Representative, not to mention the intelligence community. Add to this mix the assessments and recommendations, however inaccurate, that circulate in the media. In Myanmar, as limitations on speech freedom have diminished, Burmese political parties, ethnic associations, religious groups, and others in civil society have conveyed alternative views of their country, of China, and of Myanmar-China relations. As for Myanmar's military, that singular noun also warrants unpacking. It is safe to surmise that the tatmadaw, notwithstanding its opacity, is also not a top-to-bottom monolith of unanimous agreement, reflexive support, and singular intent.

No one is immune to misconceptions. But officials and analysts alike should be aware of the risk of unfounded belief and the prevalence of influential myths and illusions about Myanmar that are circulated inside the country and among outside actors. Maintaining such an awareness is not easy. Misjudgments often rest on a substratum of reality that may be obscured by wishfulness or fatalism, by political expedience or ahistorical naïveté. It is nonetheless vital and urgent to distinguish the shadows on the wall from the light outside — as Plato so presciently warned us in his allegory of the cave.

Notes

1 In this chapter, without political intent, the term "Burma" is used when referring to the country before 1989; "Myanmar" references the country since then; and "Burmese" is used for both periods either as an adjective or as a noun meaning a citizen of the country or its official language. In July 1989 the military government changed the name of the state from Burma to Myanmar (an older written form). Officially since 2011 the state has called itself the Republic of the Union of Myanmar. Today most governments and the United Nations use Myanmar. Burma is still used, however, by American and British officials, based on the preference expressed by Aung San Suu Kyi when she led the opposition to military rule. In April 2016, as state counsellor, she told foreign diplomats it did not matter whether they called her country Burma or Myanmar. Yet Washington and London still use Burma, while the Burmese military continues to prefer Myanmar. Chen Yi's poem appears in full in David I. Steinberg and Hongwei Fan, *Modern China-Myanmar Relations: Dilemmas of Mutual Dependence* (Copenhagen: NIAS Press, 2012), 41.

2 John Badgley, review of *Myth and History in the Historiography of Early Burma,* by Michael Aung-Thwin, *Journal of Southeast Asian Studies* 30, no. 2 (1999): 364.

3 "China-Myanmar Paukphaw Friendship Foundation Set Up in Yangon," Xinhua, 9 June 2016, http://news.xinhuanet.com/english/2016 -06/09/c_135423248.htm.

4 "Joint Press Release between the People's Republic of China and the Republic of the Union of Myanmar," Ministry of Foreign Affairs, Beijing, 20 August 2016, http://www.fmprc.gov.cn/mfa_eng/zxxx_662805/t1390889 .shtml.

5 Hugh Tinker, *The Union of Burma: A Study of the First Years of Independence* (Oxford, UK: Oxford University Press, 1957), 337.

6 Renaud Egreteau and Larry Jagan, *Soldiers and Diplomacy in Burma: Understanding the Foreign Relations of the Burmese Praetorian State* (Singapore: NUS Press, 2013), 289.

7 The Chinese were quite heterogeneous. See Jayde Roberts, *Mapping Chinese Rangoon: Place and Nation among the Sino-Burmese* (Seattle: University of Washington Press, 2016).

8 See Steinberg and Fan, *Modern Myanmar-China Relations*, ch. 4; and Fan Hongwei, "The 1967 Anti-Chinese Riots in Burma and Sino-Burmese

Relations," *Journal of Southeast Asian Studies* 434, no. 2 (June 2012): 234–56.

9 Steinberg and Fan, *Modern China-Myanmar Relations*, 81.

10 David I. Steinberg, "Japanese Aid to Burma: Assistance in the *Terenagashi* Manner?," in *Managing Japan's Foreign Aid: Power and Policy in a New Era,* eds. Bruce Koppel and Robert Orr (Boulder, CO: Westview Press, 1993).

11 See Min Zin, "Burmese Attitude toward Chinese: Portrayal of the Chinese in Contemporary Cultural and Media Works," *Journal of Current Southeast Asian Affairs* 31, no. 1 (2012): 115–31; and Maung Aung Myoe, "Myanmar's China Policy since 2011: Determinants and Directions," *Journal of Current Southeast Asian Affairs* 34, no. 2 (2015): 21–54.

12 The value of Myanmar's total legal trade with China — USD$10.1 billion in 2016 — exceeds that of Myanmar's trade with any other country; World Bank Group, "Myanmar Exports, Imports and Trade Balance by Country 2016," World Bank Group, https://wits.worldbank.org/CountryProfile/en/Country/MMR/Year/2016/TradeFlow/EXPIMP/Partner/by-country. The value of Myanmar's extensive illegal overland trade with China is unknown.

13 The 1.7 million figure corresponds to data in *The World Factbook,* compiled by the Central Intelligence Agency, accessed on 12 March 2018, https://www.cia.gov/library/publications/the-world-factbook/geos/bm.html. The Chinese Embassy in Myanmar has put the figure much higher — 2.3 million — as noted in Li Chenyang's unpublished paper, "Effects of the Conflict between the Ceasefire Groups and the Myanmar Military Government in Northern Myanmar on China since 2009." An even higher estimate — more than 2.5 million — can be inferred from Zhuang Guoto, "A New Estimate of the Ethnic Chinese Population of Southeast Asia," *Journal of Xiamen University,* 3 (2009): 66–67.

14 For the text, see Steinberg and Fan, *Modern China-Myanmar Relations*, appendix 5.

15 Yun Sun, "China's Strategic Misjudgement in Myanmar," *Journal of Current Southeast Asian Affairs* 31, no. 1 (2012): 73–96.

16 For more, see David I Steinberg, "The Problem of Democracy in the Republic of the Union of Myanmar: Neither Nation-State nor State-Nation?," in *Southeast Asian Affairs 2012,* eds. Daljit Singh and

Pushpa Thambipillai (Singapore: Institute of Southeast Asian Studies, 2012), 220–37.

17 Compare Michael A. Aung-Thwin, *Myth and History in the Historiography of Early Burma: Paradigms, Primary Sources, and Prejudices* (Athens: Ohio University Press, 1998), with Maung Htin Aung, *A History of Burma* (New York: Columbia University Press, 1967), 70.

18 Aung Zaw, "Restless Rulers," *The Irrawaddy* 14, no. 10 (October 2016), http://www2.irrawaddy.com/print_article.php?art_id=6426.

19 In the mid-1950s, the legal, pro-communist leftist political party had secured about one-third of the popular vote.

20 "Chinese Buddha Sacred Tooth Relic Tour Concludes in Myanmar," Xinhua, 24 December 2011, http://news.xinhuanet.com/english/china /2011-12/24/c_131325256.htm.

21 Maung Aung Myoe, *Building the Tatmadaw: Myanmar Armed Forces since 1948* (Singapore: Institute of Southeast Asian Studies, 2009), 139.

22 Actions by the United States and to a lesser degree the European Union were meant to deligitimate military rule. They included recognizing the validity of the 1990 elections that had been swept by the NLD and endorsing democracy's embodiment in the person of its leader and 1991 Nobel laureate, Aung San Suu Kyi. David I. Steinberg, "Aung San Suu Kyi and U.S. Policy toward Burma/Myanmar," *Journal of Current Southeast Asian Affairs* 29, no. 3 (September 2010), http:// journals.sub.uni-hamburg.de/giga/jsaa/article/view/292.

23 The government claims there are 135 "races" in the state, but that figure derives from a colonial-era calculation of languages and dialects. Clarity is further impeded by the Burmese use of the term *lu-myo*, which can mean not only race, but ethnicity or nationality as well.

24 In Yunnan, there are approximately 150,000 Kachin (Jingpaw), 400,000 Wa, 1.3 million Shan, and other groups as well. *Yunnan Province Yearbook, 2013.*

25 See Matthew Walton, "Ethnicity, Conflict, and History in Burma: The Myths of Panglong," *Asian Survey* 48, no. 6 (November/December 2008): 889–910.

26 On hedging, see Antonio Fiori and Andrea Passeri, "Hedging in Search of a New Age of Non-alignment: Myanmar between China and the USA," *Pacific Review* 28, no. 5 (2015): 679–702.

27 Billy Wong, "Belt and Road: Trade and Border Cooperation between Yunnan and Myanmar," *Hong Kong Means Business*, 10 May 2016, http://hkmb.hktdc.com/en/1X0A61GH/hktdc-research/Belt-and-Road -Trade-and-Border-Cooperation-between-Yunnan-and-Myanmar.

28 Some believe that General Khin Nyunt (Secretary One and head of military intelligence) convinced the leadership to join, hoping to mitigate Chinese influence.

29 Maung Aung Myoe, "The Logic of Myanmar's China Policy," *Asian Journal of Comparative Politics* 1, no. 3 (2016): 287.

30 For more, see Yun Sun, *China and Myanmar's Peace Process*, Special Report, U.S. Institute of Peace, March 2017, https://www.usip.org/public ations/2017/03/china-and-myanmars-peace-process.

31 Chan Mya Htwe and Khin Su Wai, "Protesters Decry Restart to Letpadaung Copper Mine as Police Phalanx Builds," *Myanmar Times*, 6 May 2016, http://www.mmtimes.com/index.php/national-news/20160 -protesters-decry-restart-to-letpadaung-copper-mine-as-police-phalanx -builds.html.

32 Edward Wong, "U.S. Imposes Sanctions on Myanmar Military over Rohingya Atrocities," *New York Times*, 17 August 2018, https://www .nytimes.com/2018/08/17/us/politics/myanmar-sanctions-rohingya.html.

Index

Indochina
French and Soviet influence, 46
Indochina Wars, 49, 272–73, 305, 307
Indonesia
"all directions" foreign policy, 230
and the ASEAN-China Free Trade
Agreement, 77–78
and the Asian Financial Crisis, 66
as Belt and Road Initiative portal, 233
Chinese incursions into EEZ, 134
Chinese influence, 102–3, 235
and confidence in US leadership,
103–5, 104t
disinterest in ASEAN, 234
"dynamic equilibrium" concept,
229–30
and the East Timor independence
struggles, 224–25, 226
economic challenges, 69, 78, 223–24,
228–29
emphasis on self-reliance, autonomy,
226
fear of Chinese invasion, 222–23, 235
foreign direct investment, 76, 233
"free and active" policy, 224–25
global maritime fulcrum concept,
232–34
lack of response to Chinese
ascendance in the region, xxv
Malacca Strait Security Initiative, 227
military autonomy and power, 8,
221–23, 225–28
Muslim majority, 222
North Natuna Sea incursions, 146,
224, 233–35
overseas/ethnic Chinese in, 184–85
Sea Policy Action Plan, 232
Soviet influence, 49
unilateralism, 233
and the "zone of neutrality," 226
interdependence
and conditional interdependence,
368–69
sensitivity interdependence (SI), 200
types of, 200

vulnerability interdependence (VI),
69–70, 198–99, 200, 332
"win-win" trope, xxvi, 32n10, 47, 118,
154, 157, 204, 344
International Court of Justice (ICJ), 138,
147, 166n43
Irrawaddy River hydropower project,
Myanmar, 353, 359
"island," definition of, 143

J
James Shoal dispute, 123
Japan
accelerated globalization, 52
aid to Laos, 276
and confidence in US vs. Chinese
leadership, 103, 104t
control of the Diaoyu/Senkaku
Islands, 251
denial of permanent seat in the UN,
250
development model, 99–101, 100t
escalating conflicts with China, 56
foreign direct investment, 74–75, 75t
relations with Myanmar, 358, 367–68
role in Sino-ASEAN relations, xxi
Joint Declaration on Cooperation in the
Field of Non-Traditional Security
Issues, 115–16

K
the Kachin zone (Myanmar/China), 359,
364–65, 374n24
Kang, David, 301
Kausikan, Bilahari, 25
Keliat, Makmur, 78
Keohane, Robert O., 200, 214
Kerry, John, 315, 317
Khin Nyunt, 367, 375
Kith Meng, 258–59
Koh, Tommy, 318
Koh Kong Province (Cambodia), removal
of villagers from, 260
the Kokang region (Myanmar), 364–65
Kol, Preap, 255

Xi Jinping (*continued*)
  efforts to enhance China's
    international influence, 89–90
  foreign policy, 90
  frequent meeting with Jokowi, 233
  geo-political, geo-economic vision, 329
  Maritime Silk Road (MSR) proposal,
    121–22
  power within China, 90
  proto-structural strategy, 27
  structure-changing agency of, 27
  "united front" organizations, 175
  on win-win economic cooperation
    with Cambodia, 247
Xu Bu, 184–85

Y

Yang Jiechi, 6, 41, 145
Yeay Phu, 255, 257–58
Yingluck Shinawatra, 311
Yudhoyono, Susilo Bambang (SBY),
  221–24, 229–30, 235, 238n12
Yunnan Province, China. *See also*
  Myanmar (Burma)
  and Chinese infrastructure projects in
    Southeast Asia, 338

and cross-border cooperation, 119
development plans for, 366
as a future transportation nexus, 120
and the Greater Mekong Subregion
  (GMS), 119–20
and the "Mekong mode," 339
as model for development in Laos,
  275–76, 292n28
Yunnan Natural Rubber Industrial
  Company, 281

Z

Zainuddin Yahya, Datuk, 182
Zhang Guihong, 336
Zhang Li, 258, 339
Zhang Min, 202
Zhang Shaoqin, 179
Zhang Zhaozhong, 140
Zhejiang Chamber of Commerce in
  Myanmar (ZCCM), 179
Zheng Bijian, 129n9
Zheng He, 147, 340–41
Zhou Enlai, 171–73, 356
Zhu Rongji, 66–67, 76, 117